Bill,
Best wi
old friend.

Carl

An Introduction to Religion and Religious Themes in Rock Music

4-24-26

An Introduction to Religion and Religious Themes in Rock Music

Carl Olson

With a Foreword by
Helene Russell

The Edwin Mellen Press
Lewiston•Queenston•Lampeter

Library of Congress Cataloging-in-Publication Data

Olson, Carl.
An introduction to religion and religious themes in rock music /
Carl Olson ; with a foreword by Helene Russell.
p. cm.
Includes bibliographical references and index.
ISBN-13: 978-0-7734-3923-8 (hardcover)
ISBN-10: 0-7734-3923-4 (hardcover)
1. Rock music--Religious aspects. I. Title.
ML3921.8.R63 047 2011
781.66'159--dc23
2011032386

hors série.

A CIP catalog record for this book is available from the British Library.

The Edwin Mellen Press
Box 450
Lewiston, New York
USA 14092-0450

The Edwin Mellen Press
Box 67
Queenston, Ontario
CANADA L0S 1L0

The Edwin Mellen Press, Ltd.
Lampeter, Ceredigion, Wales
UNITED KINGDOM SA48 8LT

Printed in the United States of America

DEDICATION

This book is dedicated to my cousin Diane, who introduced me to rock music a long time ago, to all the frosh students in my rock seminars over the years in Gatorland, and for those students who served faithfully as student freshmen advisors such as Holly Olson, Albert Polanac, Jon Bell, Iona Dickinson, Jason Cashing, Michael Roth, Katie Richter, Ashley Pike, Eric Tineo, Lauren Moore, Jessica Swigonski, and Scott Keefer.

TABLE OF CONTENTS

FOREWORD

An *Introduction to Religion and Religious Themes in Rock Music* is a fresh approach to engaging persons in the study of religious and theological themes. This book had its originating creative moments as a seminar for first year students at a small liberal arts school in which Professor Carl Olson teaches. Let me let you in on a secret rivalry between the faculty members of the religion and philosophy department. It all started when one of the new hires offered a first year seminar that not only filled, but also had a waiting list well over 100. Well, with that, the game was afoot. A little friendly competition can inspire heightened creativity on all sides. Professor Olson along with other teachers focused our creative juices on ways to engage first year students in thinking critically with depth and understanding on the serious topics of religion and philosophy. Sin and Cinema, Hollywood Heroes and Christ Figures, Religious Themes in Rock and Roll Music—these are just a few of the titles of first year seminars. The course that inspired this book is a great course. I wish I could have taken it, and now with this book, we can all benefit from Olson's creativity and insights.

With this book, we concede; Olson wins best course.

It overcomes one of the main problems college professors often have with new students—they would rather listen to their iPod than a lecture, watch a video than read a book. Olson makes use of their love of popular music, rock and roll music to be exact, in order to both inspire interest and to explain difficult concepts. He helps the students get interested in a topic that many ignore as irrelevant to their life and culture. The explicit connections he makes between the themes in the lyrics and the concerns of religious literature and ritual engage students and readers in exploring these questions more thoroughly.

It is the work of pedagogical genius—he engages young people to think by making them feel. And in feeling, students and readers can better identify with the religious sensibilities and intensity of concern and passion. He uses the media of music and emotion to engage a subject matter that is predominately about emotions and experiences, ethereal truths and values. His approach is also helpful for encouraging critical reflection upon embedded belief systems and assumed theological tenets by providing external examples and parallels of religious questions in songs. This book is interesting and helpful for both newcomers and scholars in the study of religion.

This creative and intriguing book addresses many themes that tug at our heart and soul—questions about the meaning of our lives and loves, losses and hopes. Religion and rock and roll music both offer answers to these profound questions about why and how we cope with these problems of life and love.

What indeed doth Cleveland have to do with Jerusalem? Carl Olson shows us by using multiple, engaging and lyrical examples from rock and roll songs followed by simple, clear and instructive discussions of corresponding religious practices, rituals and theology.

Olson's work flies in the face of a popular opinion that rock and roll is antithetical to religious and theological sensibilities. Olson's myriad of examples from the lyrics provides detail after detail of his clear thesis: religious themes abound in rock and roll music.

Music and religion have a long and powerful, even if rocky at times, association with each other. For example the Christian tradition, including reformers and Roman Catholic popes, has extolled the religious value of music over the centuries. Theologians from Augustine to Wesley have noted its ability to rouse the emotions and sooth our sufferings. It is praised as a divine gift, and a delight of and for the spirit. Used in worship to accompany the psalms and other liturgy, it stirs the soul profoundly, uniquely readying our human hearts for a deep and clear resonance with God's own will and with God's presence encountered in prayer, praise and gratitude. Music even takes on a sacramental quality for some religious communities. And while most theologians focus on the function that music serves in liturgy and in prayer, the sheer aesthetic value and the emotional effects of music add to the meaning and impact of the lyrics and poetry in various venues. Music is indeed a powerful tool for bonding people together and for motivating these groups of persons toward a common goal. Music inspires us to action, empowers our emotional commitment, and also it can comfort and calm us.

This intensely moving quality of music is one reason that some Christian churches are suspicious of the impact of music upon the morals of youth and society in general. They warn against secular music, especially "Rock and Roll," crying that rock is the devil's music and insist that listening and dancing to it will lead one down a sinful path. This fear of secular music is shared amongst various forms of religion. One Muslim leader Seyyed Hossein Nasr, proclaims that “All music which is lascivious, which may arouse the lower passions, has been banned.”[1]

The power of music to move the human heart and soul and body are only part of the reason for the warnings. Rock song lyrics are often associated with sex, drugs, self-mutilation, aggression and violence. Contrarily religion, especially the mainline and Evangelical Christianity, is associated with love of neighbor, ethical behavior and peaceful community. These two associations would seem to be at odds.

Yet religious groups and leaders and rock and roll stars have much more in common than it would appear at first glance. Both religion and rock and roll are used to distract people from the doldrums of work and the sufferings of life. Both are interested in capturing the hearts and minds of persons, young and old. Both use music, movement and charisma to do so. Both address themes that are existentially meaningful. Both use ritual and emotion to entice folks toward action and offer paths towards meaning.

It is these similarities and other resonances that Carl Olson highlights in his book, which opens our minds, invites our curiosity and gives us a glimpse into the intriguing parallels and connections between religion and rock and roll.

While we have discussed that traditional religions have noted with exuberance the heavenly benefits of accompanying music in

[1] Seyyed Hossein Nasr, “Islam and Music: The Legal and Spiritual Dimensions,” in Lawrence E. Sullivan, ed., *Enchanting Powers: Music in the World’s Religions* (Cambridge: Harvard University Press, 1993), p. 227.

worship services and experience, this book does not focus so much on the explicitly religious questions and answers found in albums of many rock stars, such as Johnny Cash's gospel songs, or Christian rock. But rather it holds up those themes that are found in rock and roll lyrics that are not intentionally engaging in western Christian God talk. As such it circumvents some of the natural resistances that many have to religious themes in popular music. Olson focuses on the religious qualities of music and lyrics that are explicitly not associated with liturgy or prayer in any type of religious service or in conjunction with any type of religious community. And it is this conclusion that is unexpected. The critiques against rock and roll focus on the power that the music affords the negativity of the lyrics and the suggestiveness of the music and words. Yet, Olson's point here is that the lyrics are expressing religious questions and spiritually deep responses to life's most profound concerns.

I would like to draw the reader's attention to three particularly intriguing features of this book. The first is the actual content of the material. Olson gives a rich analysis of religion and theories of how and why humans are religious. He includes a vast array of examples from major religions of the world, which makes this book helpful for exploring common themes in world religions as well as those highlighted in Christianity and Judaism. Even in the chapter on Jesus, Olson points out other paths of understanding and reaching salvation, such as spiritual rebirth and reincarnation. Many of the popular rock and roll artists have explored non-Christian religious practices and use their experiences as inspiration for their songs. Some even integrate the themes of Hinduism with the religious sensibilities of their upbringing. For example Stevie Wonder's song "Come Back as a Flower" explicitly names the Eastern notion of reincarnation while joining the Western emphasis on the work of "dispensing love." Olson, a well-respected scholar of Hinduism and other Eastern religions, makes use of his depth of knowledge in world religions to make the explicit numerous links between religion and rock and roll.

Olson's study also addresses religion in its grand plurality and multiplicity by using examples, themes, theologies and practices from many of the world religions. His decision to highlight primary themes from Christianity is also particularly helpful because it adds a self-critical dimension to this work.

The second insight to which I want to draw your attention is the way he makes the connections between the themes of religion and rock and roll. Olson has an intriguing approach: he highlights the spiritual themes and existential questions in the lyrics of the rock songs first and then uses his vast knowledge of religious theories and practices in the world's religions secondarily to analyze and point out deeper developments of these themes in the literature of religious studies

He uses rock and roll to hook the students into using their own inquiring concern for meaning and transformation. Students are curious about the meaning of lyrics and are hungry for ways to respond to the suffering and joy of love, death and birth. This is true for seekers of all levels and ages. Once our love for rock and roll music opens us to our wonder and we begin to search for meaning to explain life and desire, then Olson swoops in with his vast expertise on world religion and primary theorists in religious studies to engage our questions more deeply. For example, once the reader recognizes the common experiences of the cycles of life, birth, death, rebirth and renewal, etc. in songs like "In the Living Years," Olson points out that this notion is similar to one further developed by Eliade's theory of the myth of eternal return. He engages the students in the existentially meaningfulness of the nature of religion, and the way that religion functions in the inquiring, questing and wonder filled nature of religiously natured humans.

The reader will especially find Olson's chapter on Self, Other and God a particularly insightful treatment of the ways that rock and roll music address the ways that others are treated, misunderstood, blamed, shunned, desired, and idolized. Classic theorists Buber and Kierkegaard are explained here in a refreshing way. Olson engages the reader first in the experiences of encountering others and existential crises so intensely exemplified in rock music and then he unpacks the religious insights of these complex and often thick religious thinkers. He also includes an important section on dealing with death. These themes are quite clearly in line with themes addressed in most of the world's religions and particularly in the western Christian tradition.

This technique leads to the third feature of this work that is its most intriguing. This feature concerns the pedagogical implications and suggestions for this work. While this feature is indirect and is something we need to read between the lines to discover, it is delightful. As you enjoy these analogies and connections between rock and roll, and religion, imagine it as a way of teaching and learning that engages both interest and clarity about religion. It is not only engaging to students and curious folks of all ages, but also clarifying and instructive.

He uses music and songs to illuminate concepts and ideas that are often difficult to explain with direct prose. Religion often addresses the inexplicable, the mysterious, that which defines our understanding. It is best encountered, not explained in direct dry language. Olson engages students and readers in what is already known and felt. And then he moves to the theories and concepts of religious studies.

Further, this method is not only helpful, but also, it is disarming. Some approaches to religion can bring with it unwanted baggage—embedded assumptions and values judgments about a set of beliefs. Yet this approach aids in unpacking these assumptions without the usual biases and resistances to critical study of one's own religious worldviews. By using the similarities between the questions that theologians and religious thinkers have pondered as well as the resonances between the problems of suffering and death that we all must face, he makes the parallels heuristically to help explain the intricacies of religion. Religion and rock and roll music are two particularly significant ways that people respond to these concerns and hopes.

This book is a case study in creative pedagogy. It is an example of the pedagogical process of incorporating popular culture into the teaching of religious concepts.

Rock and roll songs are an aspect of popular culture that is one that most college students are familiar with and thus serves as a good foundation for addressing otherwise unfamiliar religious thoughts and concepts. This is a particularly helpful tool for students to use to approach concepts that for many are unfamiliar and sometimes alien. It is a fruitful avenue to introduce religious ideas and feelings and sensibilities.

This is an unusual book in its theme as well as its media and format. In this book you will find many interesting examples and details to illuminate the connections between the themes in Rock and Roll songs and religious and theological motifs. Olson makes use of these clear connections in important and helpful ways. Read it for fun, to enhance your study of religion, to inspire your understanding and sense of meaning and wonder. Read with your iPod next to you, blaring away your favorite rock and roll songs and you will be amazed at how profound the lyrics have always been.

Whichever way you choose to read it, enjoy this creative and clever approach to taking the medicine of the study of religion with a spoon full of sugar—a "lovin' spoonful" of rock and roll will help the learning go down.

Helene Russell
Christian Theological Seminary

PREFACE

The introduction to religion class has been a challenge for many Religious Studies instructors over the years, who have devised thematic based courses, used comparative textual approaches, covered various world religions, or offered mini-theology types of courses in an effort to initiate novice students into the subject matter. During the frosh year especially, students are not well prepared for the discipline of Religious Studies, and they often enroll in these introductory courses with naïve, uninformed, and, or false expectations about the nature of the subject. As a pedagogical experiment, I started to use rock lyrics as a way of introducing students to themes and issues in religion by utilizing a popular form of entertainment with which students are very familiar. This pedagogical approach proved to be a successful way to engage students in dialogue and to introduce them to sophisticated topics.

It has proven useful to often play tunes in class and then to discuss the messages embodied in the lyrics. Thus the instructor gets to become a DJ during class along with being a discussion leader. Due to the difficulty of understanding the lyrics being sung by an artist, it helps to distribute copies of the lyrics, which can be collected from internet sites, before playing the number for the class. Of course, I could also simply share the lyrics with the class without playing the tune, but when students hear the actual song being performed this proves to be a more effective way of grasping the lyrics in my opinion, based on my own classroom experience.

Since I play in class what can be called “oldies” or “classical rock,” I always allow students to give presentations related to course themes on their favorite artists. This exercise gives students a more personal stake in the success of the course. It also enables me to learn something new, and it gives students an opportunity to apply a theme or issue covered in the course to the lyrics of a more contemporary composer/performing artist.

Just as many students assume that they know something about religion, they also think that they know plenty about rock music. The reality is quite different, and students are not the know-it-all experts on popular culture that they think. Based on considerable personal experience gathered in the classroom, students are often very ignorant about the history of rock music and the political and social context of its early history. In order to overcome this problem, I use a video on the history of rock music produced by PBS in Boston and the BBC called Rock and Roll, consisting of five volumes of video with each one 120 minutes in length. These particular videos provide the cultural context of the 1950s, 1960s, and later, including footage of many influential artists performing and interviews with some of the pioneers of the music. It is common for students to become absorbed by the narrative and the images on the screen. I never get tired of watching their faces when young teenage girls scream for Elvis or the Beatles on the video footage.

By using rock lyrics and recordings to teach about religious issues and themes, an instructor reaches beginning students within their present context. By following this approach, an instructor is able to take a student from the familiar (e.g., rock music) to issues that may be strange. Hopefully, this gets them to rethink the familiar and to grasp it in a new light and enable them to bring a more insightful and critical perspective to the material. Although it might take some time with the shier students, a discussion of rock lyrics enhances participation in classroom discussions. It is not long before everyone feels comfortable and gets involved in the discussions. This scenario leads to less passive students, enhanced class dynamics, and exchange of ideas.

By using the so-called Devil's music to teach about religious issues and ideas, there is an irony embodied in the very structure of the course. Despite what critics claim about rock music being the Devil's music, there are many religious themes and messages in rock lyrics, if one takes the time to listen to them carefully. As will be demonstrated in the initial chapter, conservative elements of the Christian community on both the Protestant and Roman Catholic sides, as well as some liberal and moderate social and political people in the United States have claimed since the inception of rock and roll music, that it is decadent, godless, immoral obscene, offensive, lewd, sinful, a threat to Western civilization, a Communist plot, contributes to drug abuse, juvenile delinquency, violence, and Satanic. In short, rock is the Devil's music. Even though many sincere religious leaders have warned others against the evils of such music, have advocated rejection of such decadence, and sponsored record burnings, rock music has been misrepresented and misunderstood by such ardent critics. It is the contention of this work that the critics have not taken the time or effort to listen to the lyrics of rock songs. If they did take the time to listen to the lyrics, they would discover that rock music embodies many religious messages and themes. It is the intention of this book to elicit these different religious themes.

Whatever its cultural and aesthetic merits, rock music has been a force in American popular culture for nearly six decades among young people and many adults. Critics have been waiting for its imminent demise for some time without success. In fact, rock music not only embodies religious messages; it also manifests elements of a religious cult. The loyal followers of the Grateful Dead, for instance, resemble members of a religious cult who follow a life-style similar to that of pilgrims by following their band from one concert venue to another and partaking of a Eucharist celebration consisting of various kinds of drugs. Another significant cult is that revolving around Elvis Presley. Members of this religious cult can make a pilgrimage to Graceland in Tennessee to view the tomb and relics of the dead leader. The alleged sightings of Elvis are akin to appearances of the Virgin Mary in Roman Catholicism. This type of phenomenon is connected to failures by many members to accept that he is dead. It is also odd that performers like Jimi Hendrix, who actually immigrated to England to gain stardom during his life, and Janis Joplin give the impression of being more popular after their deaths. These types of phenomena need to be explored further in order to discern their implications for American religiosity and culture, which will be attempted in the final chapter of this study.

In order to provide some orientation to readers, it seems wise to assert as lucidly as possible what this book is not about. This study is not a new contribution to the theory of popular culture or the place of rock music in popular culture in a theoretical sense. I propose to approach my material as a historian of religions, or more precisely in this case as a historian of ideas, which implies that my approach will be informed and grounded in the history of religions and religious ideas, symbols, metaphors, and phenomena in a comparative spirit. My goal will be to discern what the various religious themes in rock lyrics mean and what they reflect about religious notions in American popular culture. This study will be confined to what I call classical rock music in contrast to what is called heavy metal or rap for the most part. This exclusion of certain types of material makes my task a bit more manageable. And it does not intend to suggest that religious themes are absent in these other types. It is my contention that classical rock music expresses a series of messages, and part of its message is religious or reflects religious themes in sharp contrast to what its critics claim. This will involve referring to various religious figures to draw parallels and to elucidate the meanings and implications of the lyrics being studied. These parallels will be made with biblical material, classical Christian authors, and mainly Jewish and Christian thinkers active during the period of the birth and development of rock music. Thus this study will be mostly concerned with religious ideas and features of human existence with religious implications. And here

I have been informed by the focus of many contemporary religious thinkers, and I have followed their lead on these issues. This book will not be concerned with the personal lives of performers, the record business and how it operates, modes of production, or modes of consumption. I will also not engage in so-called critical theory that is common in popular culture studies with its Marxist bias and agenda. This study is more concerned with religious ideas.

ACKNOWLEDGEMENTS

This book is not due to the efforts of one person because many people made contributions along the way to its completion. I need to thank Peggy, the saint in my life, for all her help at home and during my stay in England by taking care of Casey and for searching for items that I forgot to take with me. I want to thank my colleagues Glenn for his suggestions about Randy Newman and my former colleague Helene for her suggestions regarding U2, and to wish her all the best in her future adventures in higher education. My students at Allegheny College have been a huge help. I also want to thank those fans who took the time to place lyrics on the internet. You are my heroes by providing a rich resource for a scholarly hack like me. Sincere thanks and love go to my daughters Holly and Kelly and my son-in-law Marlon for sharing their record collections with an old rocker and broadening his horizons. Additionally, gratitude goes to former President Richard Cook and former Dean La Lloyd Michaels for giving me the Teacher-Scholar Professorship of the Humanities that gave me the free time to bring this project to a conclusion. Thanks also to the current college leadership Dean Linda DeMerritt, who could rock if her feet would allow her, and our new President Jim Mullen, who has set a positive tone that is encouraging for the future. Computer folks at Allegheny College were a huge help like David Anderson, Jim Fadden, Chris Sherman, and Phil Reinhart for services large and small. I also want to thank the staff and administration at Clare Hall of Cambridge University for granting me a visiting fellowship that provided me a quiet atmosphere in which to conclude my work. Graduate student extraordinary Chad Pecknold of the University of Cambridge gave me some helpful tips about works of theology and numerous pleasant conversations. The efforts in the library by Allegheny College student assistants Erin Barr and Tibor Sybolski, the wrong-way man himself, must not go unrecognized and appreciated. I would be neglectful if I forgot to thank Dr. Julius Lipner, a man with a heart as big as he is and a wonderful sense of humor for a serious and first-rate scholar, for being my sponsor and contact person at Clare Hall, and I appreciate your giving me your imprimatur for the work, even though this is not the usual scholarly work conducted at Clare Hall. Special thanks go to Roger Price, Clare Hall's computer wizard, for helping me get started in the lovely medieval town. Finally, I want to extend my best wishes to all the scholars from all over the globe that I encountered at Clare Hall, for Richard Eden's gracious gift of his history of the postgraduate college, the gals at the Thursday noon meeting of the women's group, the Religious Studies Department at the University of Lancaster for inviting me to speak on rock music, and the graduate and undergraduate students with whom I had the pleasure to speak inside and outside of the classroom. Moreover, I want to thank my late and dear colleague Jim Sherdian, Mr. Opps himself, for his continuing encouragement with respect to this book, his friendship for more than 20 years, his sagacious advice, the shared laughter, and wonderful conversations about philosophy and religion. You are a part of this book and my life as you were part of the lives of so many students over the years. None of us can ever repay you except to keep your memory alive in our hearts and minds and to drink a martini occasionally in your memory.

Finally, I want to acknowledge that there is a certain poetic justice that this book is composed by a teacher from Allegheny College because I venture to guess that it is one of the few universities or colleges with its own faculty rock band. Thanks must be extended to the members of the faculty rock band Credit/No Credit (Josh and Lisbet Searle-White, Jennifer Hellwarth, Jim Reedy, and Ron Mumme) for keeping the campus rocking and to my follow members of the "Hot Stuff All Stars" (David Miller, Eric Pallant, Ben Slote, Tom Erdos, Ben Hellwarth, and Ron Cole) for their dancing spirit, cheerful willingness to be humiliated in public, and ability to unite everyone with humor. Finally, I want to acknowledge the editorial help and skill of my dear colleague Glenn Holland, an individual of many talents among which is the ability to make one laugh.

Chapter 1
Introduction

In the rock musical *Grease*, depicting the early period of the music featuring so-called do-wop songs, Frankie Valli sings the title song that embodies various religious themes. Although the musical is about a love story between a good girl—a cheerleader type—and a so-called greaser, who assumes the demeanor of a bad guy with greasy, ample, and duck-tailed shaped hair, black leather jacket, tight pants, and lack of interest in his high school subjects, it reflects a dichotomy in many high schools of the period between the greasers (also called hoods) and the more behaviorally sedate, non-threatening, short-haired male students (so-called straights or jocks). In addition to the leading female character being converted to the side of the rebellious, non-conforming greasers, the musical contains many religious themes connected with personal identity, meaning, light symbolism, love, belief, illusion, and reality. Overall, the title of the musical is a metaphor for how a certain group of teenagers live their lives and represents the religious aspect of rock music.

In the lyrics to the title song "Grease," the resolution of life's problems is directly associated with becoming aware of the light, evoking the image of Jesus as the light of the world (John 1:4). Another message refers to believing in oneself and becoming who we truly are by realizing our potential, whereas an additional theme equates love with reality. Grease, a metaphor for teenage life, is both eternal—a time, place, and motion—and it is an internal subjective feeling. Grease is revolutionary and a rejection of ordinary life that offers the hope of salvation in its lyrics that involves beginning to believe as soon as possible before it is too late. The hope of salvation offered by the lyrics is grounded in the word "grease" itself that is repeated continuously by the lyrics. The word is an orally heard, meaningful message.

The repetitive utterance of "grease" as the word holds a remarkable resemblance to the Gospel of John, also called the Fourth Gospel, with its emphasis on the Word (*logos*). In his prologue (1:1), John states that the Word is identified with the beginning and God. It is, according to the Fourth Gospel, the Word identified with Jesus, that saves humans. Within the Greek culture of John's historical period, the *logos* is a rational principle for the Stoics that orders the universe, it designates a power that allows humans to know themselves and God in Hermetic literature, and it refers to the creative Word of God among Greek-speaking Jews. The term "grease" from the Broadway and motion picture musical harkens back to the Gospel of John, and reinterprets the "word" for the teenage generation of the 1950s. In short, *Grease* represents Word or the Gospel—good news—of rock music.

As these comments about *Grease* imply, this is a book about religion as it is elicited from rock lyrics—ironically the so-called Devil's music. Therefore, this introduction to the subject of religion uses the degenerate Devil's music to teach about the nature of religion and the types of issues that concern it. Based on my past teaching experience, it seems safe to assume that most people know, or have a vague idea, about the nature of religion, but they have difficulty defining it just like scholars of the subject who get paid to teach it to undergraduate college students. Many of these learned scholars of religion have resolved that religion is a human construct of the scholar's research and reflections in his/her office. If scholars collectively—those who care about precision and clarity—constructed it, why can't they define it? Many definitions have been created, but none of them has been universally, or nearly so, accepted by a large majority in the field because of inherent flaws or a lack of cross-cultural validity.

Since scholars of religion cannot agree on a definition of the subject, why not adopt a more indirect and ironical approach to understanding the nature of religion for those just commencing their study of the subject? Why not introduce interested students to the nature of religion and the kinds of issues that are associated with it by approaching it from the perspective of the demonic figure personified in the West as the Devil? Therefore, what this introduction to the study of religion proposes is the following: To use the so-called Devil's music—rock 'n' roll lyrics—to raise issues germane to the subject of religion. This approach does not attempt to define religion, but it does demonstrate themes and issues that are important to the subject. In short, this is a strange, or at least not a previously attempted, introduction to religion by being more indirect. This more circuitous route to the study of religion through a medium of popular culture possesses a built-in advantage of teaching more about an aspect of a popular medium that people take for granted and do not think about very deeply.

This introduction to religion via rock lyrics begins with an examination of the human situation and how it is shaped by such elements as loneliness, boredom, angst, fear, evil, sin, temptation, guilt, and hopelessness. After considering the relational nature of religion with a discussion of the self, other, and God, the book moves to consider supernatural beings (gods, goddesses, and the Devil), the depiction of Jesus Christ within the context of two musicals and a simulated Anti-Christ figure, before turning to issues of time, death, responses to death (anxiety, grief, and courage) and the relationship between memory, love, and death. Then the discussion moves to consider issues concerning the end of time with eschatology (doctrine of last things) and its connection to apocalyptic speculation before moving to prophetic themes in rock music. This book concludes with a review of various religious phenomena—cults, revival meetings, pilgrimage, ritual, and rites of passage—manifested by the performative nature of rock music and attempts to discern in what sense rock represents a religion itself.

If a teacher plays a game of word association with students by asking them to write down on a piece of paper ten terms or ideas that come to their minds when they think of rock music, invariably the vast majority of student lists will include sex and drugs. This is exactly the problem from the perspective of the critics of rock lyrics. Since pre-martial sex and illicit drugs are by definition immoral, their promotion or encouragement is necessarily evil in the minds of many people. In fact, rock 'n' roll is the music of the Devil from the perspective of conservative religious critics, with rock lyrics exemplifying the work of demonic forces in American culture. From the viewpoint of its religious critics, rock lyrics are satanic, immoral, unethical, unrighteous, contrary to wholesome family values, and anti-religious. It is also just simply bad music from an artistic and aesthetic viewpoint, according to its critics.

It is not the case that my new undergraduate students are right and conservative critics totally wrong. Before the arrival of evangelical Christian groups and their discovery that rock music could be used to spread the message of Jesus as they interpret the good news, conservative religious critics of rock 'n' roll music never really took the time to listen to the religious message in many rock songs. In fact, this could also be affirmed of more liberal leaning people. This book is a small step in the direction of focusing on the religious message of rock lyrics without resorting to using blatantly Christian groups, which means that I want to concentrate instead on mainstream or traditional rock groups. By excluding specifically Christian rock artists and focusing on more widely recognized rock acts, we will find that there is no single message because there are many voices heard among rock composers. Just as there is a wide diversity among rock artists, there is also a broad array of religious messages, and some of these messages are outside of the mainstream Judeo-Christian tradition and convey a more eastern religious perspective. There are probably many within the still prevalent Judeo-Christian tradition that would lament this kind of development. However, the eastern perspective of some rock composers is a reflection on the proliferation of foreign religions in the West. It does not take a genius to conclude that as the influence of such cultures grow in strength in America due to increasing immigration of peoples from eastern countries into the West that we will witness more examples of eastern influence upon rock lyrics. In other words, as America becomes more religiously pluralistic, this will also become true of rock lyrics. Examples of this trend are some of the lyrics composed by James Taylor for his album *Hourglass* and Madonna's album *Ray of Light.*

Before we survey eastern and western religious themes in rock music, it is necessary to set some boundaries in order to allow me to convincingly prove my contention that rock lyrics embody a variety of religious themes and to keep the discussion within manageable margins. Thus I have decided to exclude what is called rap or heavy-metal music. I have, however, included material from the 1950s through the 1990s to make my case. I will concentrate for the most part on lyrics that reflect what might be called "classical rock." By the terms "classical rock," I refer to lyrics with a message shaped by 1950's artists, such as the many terrific black groups and individual black artists like Little Richard, Fats Domino, and Chuck Berry. Mention should also be made of figures like Elvis, Buddy Holly, Bob Dylan, and the Beatles. The spirit of this so-called "classical rock," a designation also used by many radio stations around America, is captured well by the hit record entitled "Old Time Rock and Roll" by Bob Seger and the Silver Bullet Band, which can also serve as the theme song of this book. I will also exclude with some minor exceptions so-called Christian rock groups because they have a specific purpose of witnessing to the Gospel and saving souls. If I were to use Christian rock groups it would make my task easier, but I am more interested in traditional rock artists because these are the figures that conservative religious voices have criticized over the decades, although many religiously conservative people continue to be suspicious of Christian rock bands in spite of the overt Christian message. Besides, Christian rock groups are already aware that the music can be utilized to convey a religious message.

I will refrain also from identifying a "golden age" of rock music because each decade of its existence contains both great and awful songs. Of course, such a distinction is dependent upon personal taste. It is even true that some of these awful songs become hits for a variety of reasons that I do not want to examine because it would divert me from my primary focus. Moreover, it is common for people to identify the golden age of rock music with their own teenage years. Research for this book has impressed upon me how few songs become genuine hits out of all the songs that are composed and recorded within a given year. But I will not confine myself simply to songs that have become hits. If songs have a religious message, this is what makes them a hit for my purposes. Of course, many of the songs mentioned and discussed in this book will be familiar to many fans. I also make no pretensions about being totally exhaustive with my treatment of rock lyrics and its religious themes. In the subsequent chapters, I will cite numerous examples of a given religious theme as it appears in a particular song without claiming that I have mentioned each and every song in which a particular theme appears. In other words, this book does not aspire to become an encyclopedia of rock lyrics and religion.

Before we can survey the many religious themes in rock lyrics, it seems wise to investigate more closely what critics find objectionable in rock music because such criticism is part of the history of the music and represents a reaction to it by segments of American culture. Then, it is necessary to review its social and historical context in America to discern the kinds of issues that attracted the attention, creative imagination, and shaped the lyrics of rock composers. After enumerating some of the major characteristics of rock music, we finally examine theoretical issues related to rock music, popular culture, and religion in this chapter.

The Historical Venom of Rock Critics

Almost from its inception, the critics of rock music and its artists have called it obscene, vulgar, offensive, lewd, immoral, and many other negative things. These types of criticism have motivated well-meaning people and organizations to ban the music or destroy records in protest. A fundamental motivation for these kinds of reactions is protecting impressionable youth from what are perceived to be obscene materials and their morally corrupting potential. But this is only part of the story.[1]

As far back as the late 1950s, the hit record entitled "Wake Up Little Susie" by the Everly Brothers was banned in Boston because the lyrics contained references to a young couple on a date who fall asleep in the boy's car and miss the curfew set by their parents. The lyrics suggested to the Boston critics that young couples were engaged in possible pre-martial sex, a serious moral transgression at that time in American history. Boston was not the only city to launch an anti-rock campaign. In 1958, the Catholic Youth Center in Minneapolis attacked records that lowered the moral standards of youngsters. Again, Boston was not to be out-done by another city because the Boston Catholic Youth Organization canvassed record shops in their area to demand that disk jockeys refrain from playing sexually explicit or suggestive lyrics. A grass roots organization called the Parents' Music Resource Center in Washington, D.C. spoke out about sexually explicit and pornographic lyrics. Fundamentalist religious groups in San Antonio, Texas expressed vehement objections to what the group interpreted as obscene lyrics, satanic connections, and immoral rock concerts. The United States Congress got into the act of censorship after the release of "Louie, Louie" in 1962. Since the lyrics were indecipherable, congressional speculation concluded that the lyrics must be obscene! After an investigation, a congressional committee declared that the record was indecipherable at any speed. During the 1970s, the Nixon administration conducted a campaign against lyrics that advocated drug use. Moreover, organizations around the country were not only concerned with lyrics, but they also attempted to ban dances like the Twist due to its alleged vulgarity and offensiveness.

The print media was also involved in the chorus of criticism. In 1954, *Billboard* magazine condemned songs with sexual double entendres, whereas *Variety* published a three-part series about obscene lyrics. A writer for the *Catholic Sun* criticized Elvis Presley for being lewd, sexually suggestive, obscene, and symbolic of defiance. Not to be outdone, other critics labeled Bob Dylan filthy-minded. Articles appeared periodically announcing the imminent demise of rock music which, in hindsight, from the early twenty-first century, represented wishful thinking by the critics of the music. In fact, there was a mock funeral in 1959 sponsored by radio station WLEV in Erie, Pennsylvania that culminated with the dumping of records into Lake Erie. Even a publication devoted to rock music carried a story about the obscene nature of a concert involving Jim Morrison of the Doors at a performance in Miami, Florida in 1969 when the lead singer allegedly exposed his penis during a concert, and simulated masturbation and oral sex. The title of the article summarizes the composer's moral position "Morrison's Penis Is Indecent." In June 26, 1975, the *Christian Science Monitor* ran an essay by Lynde McCormick that claimed that the Rolling Stones "promote debauchery." In 1976, the Reverend Jesse Jackson, head of Operation PUSH (People United to Save Humanity) campaigned to remove sexual lyrics from the radio that Jackson connected to illegitimate births and abortions in major America cities.

Besides claiming that rock was music for morons composed by cretins, other critics focused their criticism on religious issues, such as Monsignor Gonzi, Roman Catholic Archbishop of Malta, who connected rock music to corruption of human souls. The Reverend W. G. McPherson, a minister in Toronto, Canada, distinguished Christian music from rock music, claiming that the former moved people by the spirit of God and the latter appealed to baser human emotions like the heathen music of African tribes. Grounded in their religious convictions about the evils of rock music, two brothers named Steve and Jim Peters, who were ordained ministers of the Jesus People Fellowship in St. Paul, Minnesota, organized a bonfire and album-smashing event in 1981. Members of the Maranatha Christian fellowship located in Gainesville, Florida, toured various college campuses, in 1983 with a seminar called "Is Rock and Roll a Highway to Hell?" with the fundamental purpose of exposing the satanic messages of the rock lyrics.

During the mid-1980s, Tipper Gore, wife of the Democratic senator from Tennessee and later candidate for President of the United States in 2000 Al Gore, discovered some lyrics that appeared to allude to masturbation in the song entitled "Darling Nikki" by Prince on his album *Purple Rain*. Upset by what she thought that she had discovered, Tipper Gore founded the Parents' Music Resource Center in order to lobby Congress to place warning stickers on albums with offensive content. Joining forces with Susan Baker, wife of Secretary of State James A. Baker III, these forceful women exerted enough pressure to get Senate hearings held on the issue of morally and ethically offensive lyrics. But it was not always the lyrics that upset some people.

In the following decade in America, Senator Bob Dole, who became an eventual Presidential candidate, was not to be up-staged by influential women. He led a campaign in the United State Senate against the conglomerate Time-Warner, focusing his attack on the conglomerate for promoting rap artists, such as Snoop Doggy Dogg who had been contractually signed to a subsidiary of the corporation. Dole claimed that such rap artists promoted harmful and hateful attitudes toward authority and women, promoted negative behavior, and were an affront to the American people and its values. Eventually, Dole's public pressure proved successful because the conglomerate broke its links with its subsidiary. Apparently, the negative publicity was not worth the business profits to be gained by their continued legal association with the subsidiary.

Sometimes rock artists said provocative things that offended the religious sensibilities of others. In 1966, Maureen Cleave interviewed John Lennon of the Beatles for *London Evening Standard.* Lennon was quoted as saying that Christianity would disappear, and that the Beatles were more popular than Jesus at that point in history. Conservative Christians were offended and reacted strongly against Lennon and the Beatles by calling for boycotts of their concerts and destruction of their records, pictures, and memorabilia. Lennon caused further controversy in 1969 with his record entitled "The Ballard of John and Yoko," a song in which Lennon compared himself to Christ and complaints about being crucified, which caused the BBC in London and many American radio stations to consider Lennon's lyrics blasphemous.

Other rock artists were provocative by their actions, such as Peter Townshend of the Who smashing his guitar to pieces during concerts, or Jimi Hendrix dousing his guitar with lighter fluid and setting it ablaze before smashing it. Members of Led Zeppelin engaged in gratuitous violence when a member destroyed paintings at a Danish art gallery, destroyed their dressing room on a Canadian tour, and manhandled a government official recording the volume level at a concert and destroyed his equipment because the band wrongfully thought that he was trying to record the concert for profit.[2] Such violent public outbursts as well as suggestive lyrics prompted critics to blame rock music for motivating young people to commit suicide, and some rock concerts led to riots around the country. Violence and rock music were most dramatically associated in the sick mind of mass murderer Charles Manson, who thought that the Beatles song "Helter Skelter" represented a hidden message for him and his so-called "Family" to begin killing people.

Some critics gave their comments a racist perspective. The group called the North Alabama White Citizens Council picketed a concert by Bill Haley and the Comets in May of 1956 in Birmingham carrying signs that referred to "jungle music," degradation, sin, and Communism. In the 1960s, the Grand Dragon of the Ku Klux Klan in South Carolina burned Beatle albums on crosses. In Cleveland, Alan Freed, Jewish father of rock music, was called a "nigger lover" and harassed for mixing the races at non-segregated dances. The Jimi Hendrix song "How Would You Feel" was not given any airplay in 1965 because the lyrics discussed how blacks were mistreated in America. Overall, racially-motivated critics perceived rock music as a product of African heritage that represented something heathen and barbaric.

Similar types of critics viewed rock music as a threat to western civilization. The editors of *Music Journal*, for instance, depicted rock as a threat to civilization because of its direct link with juvenile delinquency. The Reverend David Noebel, a member of the fundamentalist Christian Crusade, connected the rock music of the Beatles with a Communist plot to undermine the character of American youth and to ultimately weaken America in its struggle against nefarious Communism. Church groups in Clark County, Washington also connected rock music to Communism, and began a letter-writing campaign. This campaign also portrayed it as the invention of the devil and contrary to the teachings of Jesus Christ.[3] The Communist hysteria and its alleged association with rock music are best grasped within the context of a continuing fear mongering about the imminent threat of Communism to the American way of life. The specter of Senator Joseph McCarthy and his Committee on Un-American Activities cast a long, ominous shadow over the country during the 1950s and through the 1970s, even though McCarthy was censured and discredited by others.

Besides associating rock music with Communism, critics often made the connection of rock music to the devil. The Catholic Church and right-wing Christian fundamentalist groups viewed rock music as leading youth astray on a path of sinful, sexual transgression, and drugs.[4] Mick Jagger of the Rolling Stones was not only accused of practicing black magic, but he was also depicted as Satan. English clergy claimed that rock music was evil and represented a revival of devil dancing that threatened to turn youngsters into devil worshipers. Even as late as 1980, talk show host Mike Harrison of KMET-FM in Los Angeles referred to opponents of rock and their assertion that it was the devil's music. The rock group AC/DC aroused suspicions when critics claimed that the band's name represented "Anti-Christ, Devil's Child," whereas Punk rockers have been called the Devil's children. And a heavy metal group like Kiss has been accused of leading youngsters to Satan after they intentionally appropriated satanic elements into their act on stage. A young musician named Bob Larson published a book in 1967 entitled *Rock and Roll: The Devil's Diversion*, a further example of the association of the music with satanic forces. Critics also saw something satanic in the rock musicals about the life of Jesus, *Jesus Christ Superstar* and *Godspell*. Even an early rock star from a very conservative religious background, such as Jerry Lee Lewis, thought that his hit recording of "Great Balls of Fire" was a product of the devil and that by singing it he would be committing a sin. But Lewis sang the song anyway, and he sinned eventually with an underage female cousin, sending his career into a downward spiral.

In the small rural town in which I live there has been a debate about the use and place, if any, of rock music within the context of Christian worship. A Sunday edition of the local newspaper, *The Meadville Tribune* (August 19, 2001), invited local readers to respond to its "Sound-Off" column without having to sign their names to their opinions. The question was the following: "Do you believe contemporary Christian music is an appropriate and successful way to attract people to worship? Or is it mere entertainment that diminishes the seriousness of faith?" These questions were followed by many responses. A couple of respondents complained that rock music did not necessarily induce youngsters to attend church, but it did drive older church-goers from the church. Moreover, it was the older generation that sustained the church with their support, whereas youngsters tend to eventually leave town. Presumably, the respondents appeared to be implying the church leadership should not be catering to the tastes of young people, but that they should adhere to the needs of the older generation who form the continuing basis of support of the church. A couple of other respondents thought that Christian rock music belonged in a concert venue and not in a church, while other respondents could not understand how rock music could be made into Christian music when it is basically satanic. On the same page, a local Baptist pastor composed a letter to the editor containing citations from Christian scripture to make his case that Christian rock music confuses the distinction between the world and church, flesh and the spirit. From the perspective of this Baptist pastor, there should be no compromise between these realms, and there should always be a complete separation between the sacred and the profane. The possibility that rock lyrics might be able to carry a religious message appears to be impossible from the perspective of this pastor and many like-minded Christians.

In retrospect, critics perceived rock music as an evil threat to western culture, awful music on aesthetic grounds, a corrupting influence on youngsters that could lead them into drugs, juvenile delinquency and violence, hazardous to one's health, mind numbing, a Communist plot, anti-religious, and a satanic force of considerable danger. Retrospectively, it is also possible to see a correlation between the increasingly vocal, strident, and venomous criticism and the growing popularity of rock music among young people. In fact, the critics were so strident that they failed to stop and listen to the lyrics of many songs that carried religious themes until Christian rock artists began to realize its potential to communicate with younger audiences.

The postmodern a/theologian Mark C. Taylor thinks that religion is a slippery subject that is continuously slipping from one's grasp, which makes it difficult to know where to look for it. If the critics of rock music only perceive something negative and devoid of genuine religion, I tend to agree with Taylor when he remarks that religion is "most interesting when it is least obvious."[5] Nonetheless, the critics of rock music form part of the historical and social context of the music, although the negative response is not the complete story.

Social and Historical Context of Rock Music

Because any cultural movement must be grasped within its social and historical context in order to be comprehended, the lyrics of rock composers are no exception to the importance of social and historical context. During its initial three decades, rock 'n' roll music developed during a period of great turmoil and change in American society. With its roots in jazz, black spiritual or gospel music, country and western, and the blues, rock music was not readily embraced because of racist attitudes and social stereotypes associated with its sources in black culture and performers. Only a few late night radio stations played this unnamed evolving music in the early 1950s. White disc jockeys play-ed records of independent record companies because rhythm and blues was characterized as black music. What respectable white person would listen to such music? Rhythm and blues music spread from places in southern America, such as New Orleans and Memphis, northward to Chicago with the migration of black workers to this area in search of employment opportunities. From Chicago, rhythm and blues spread eastward to New York City and westward to Los Angeles. The first performer to gain acceptance from both white and black listeners was the non-threatening Fats Domino, who combined rhythm and blues with country and western music. He opened the door for the more flamboyant and energetic Little Richard, whose personal roots were grounded in fundamentalist Christianity of the rural southern part of America and gospel music. In contrast to the more sedate Fats Domino, Little Richard's high-pitched screams (which continued to be copied by subsequent artists) evoked the sound of something primitive, un-civilized, and bestial, and his invented nonsensical terminology ("awopbopalooban") is reminiscent of the religious practice of speaking in tongues that dates back to the early Christian movement (1 Cor. 14) when the Holy Spirit inspired people to speak in unknown languages.

During the 1950s, rock music spread via the radio and influential disc jockeys. This was also an era in which there was a dramatic shift to television as a popular mode of entertainment that was accompanied by fears about the demise of radio and the motion picture industries by many within those media. The advent of television motivated radio executives to redesign and reorient their media toward a younger audience. This reorientation toward youthful musical tastes was accompanied by technological developments with transistor radios, inexpensive portable radios that were ideal for the beach or outdoors, and, probably most importantly, the improved car radio that became part of the youth practice of cruising with friends and listening to the latest hits.

These types of development helped rock music to attract more listeners during the period of the Korean War, a conflict justified in part as a fight to stop the cancerous spread of godless Communism. The infancy of rock music also occurred during the Communist witch-hunts of Senator Joseph McCarthy and his attempt to expose subversive elements in government and the entertainment industry. By this time, the Cold War between the United States and the Soviet Union had taken hold in the geo-political sphere, reaching a crucial point with the Cuban missile crisis in the early 1960s during the Kennedy presidency. In addition, long festering social problems reached a climax with the beginning of the civil rights movement and feminist advocacy for social and economic fairness.

Attempts by blacks to achieve social integration of educational institutions, public parks, public transportation, restrooms, and eating establishments were met with white resistance. Pressure by civil rights groups using methods of social disobedience, public demonstrations, and legal means forced the federal government to exert its legal powers of enforcement and protection. In addition to creating economic opportunities for blacks and introducing black styles and values into the mainstream American culture, rock music is given credit for promoting racial integration. Of course, more conservative social forces also criticized it for bringing the races together, whereas African Americans viewed it as a promoter of racial harmony and as having socio-economic advantages for talented black entertainers. Nonetheless, some middle class and upwardly mobile African Americans were concerned about the unfavorable image of black culture created by rock music.

In addition to the social flux caused by the civil right's movement, the Vietnam War alienated many young people from their government. Through the medium of television, this war was brought into the homes of Americans each evening, and it gave people another cause around which to rally in addition to the civil rights movement. The deaths of President John F. Kennedy, presidential candidate and Senator Robert Kennedy, and civil rights leader Martin Luther King, Jr. contributed to the socio-political malaise of the 1960s, and the Watergate scandal of the 1970s that led to the fall of Richard Nixon from office added to the distrust of government and its leaders. Moreover, race riots in urban settings like Newark, Detroit, Watts, and other cities were symptomatic of the period.

During the initial three decades of rock music development, many of the more probing and thoughtful lyrics were shaped by the socio-political situation in the country and by Existential philosophy and theology. New Age religious movements and experiments were also influential, representing an amorphous collectivity of thought and practice. In fact, the New Age movement was difficult to locate due to its unstable boundaries, goals and practitioners. The New Age movement was a diffuse, boundary-collapsing collectivity of seekers practiceing alternative forms of spirituality. With its apocalyptic roots and millennialarian expectations for a future earthly paradise, New Age spirituality envisioned humanity on the eve of a new and major cultural shift that would have a utopian result.[6] For some people, the New Age was symbolized by the flower children, who embraced the nascent environmental movement and ecological consciousness. The poetry and literature of Beat artists with their stream of consciousness style of writing and emphasis on Eastern spirituality, by figures such as Jack Kerouac and Alan Ginsberg, also added to the cultural mixture of ideas for rock lyrics. Due to the dominance of male performers during the early decades of rock music and a strain of misogynist attitudes expressed in the lyrics, the influence of feminist thought was not a major factor in the shaping of the lyrics with some exceptions.

Another source of influence during this time was the evolving drug culture among the young and the emphasis on the experience of alternate states of consciousness. Timothy Leary, former Harvard University professor, was the most vocal promoter of the "psychedelic revolution." For Leary, the drug LSD was the sacred Eucharist of a new age that was dawning. Author Ken Kesey was another advocate for what he called "Acid Tests" in which LSD was distributed to participants. The basic presupposition of this revolution was the conviction that a person could change the world if he/she could change his/her mode of consciousness.

This scenario led to so-called "psychedelic rock," which was intended to expand a person's conscious experience when combined with drugs. Such music was characterized by improvisation by such early groups as the Grateful Dead and Country Joe and the Fish. At live concerts, it was not unusual for bands to play a single song for over an hour as it improvised. Locations like Golden Gate Park and especially the intersection of Haight-Ashbury in San Francisco became synonymous with the drug culture; members of the Grateful Dead lived in a single house in this area with Janis Joplin and members of her band living nearby. This emphasis on drugs was advocated by rock lyrics, or at least condoned by composers. In fact, the members of the Grateful Dead composed music while in drug-induced states to enhance the drug-induced states of listeners. "Psychedelic rock" promoted a backlash from mainstream American society that resulted, for example, with a ban on the song "Eight Miles High" by the Byrds from the radio.

Within this unfolding scenario, technology should not be neglected because it played its part to spread rock music. Beginning with the radio, moving to the record player, and evolving to the high-fidelity set before the advent of the CD player, rock music got its message to the masses. Finally, it reached an even greater audience with television and stations devoted to just rock music like MTV. Concert venues grew from night-clubs in the 1950s to auditoriums. Eventually, demand could only be met by resorting to the use of sports stadiums in order to accommodate the many fans. Listening to rock music on the latest technological device and attending concerts was made possible by a period of economic affluence and the growing power of labor unions. With more disposable income, youngsters were able to give economic impetus to a fledging record industry and its performers with their buying power.

The social and political flux and turmoil of the early decades of rock music alienated many young people from the prevailing American culture. These adolescents created an alternative culture in which rock music conveyed the message and inspired aspects of the counter-culture.[7] Even with its counter-cultural roots, rock music represented a paradoxical entity in the sense that it represented the counter-culture as it merged into the fabric of mainstream American culture for contemporary teens and those that grew to maturity listening to it. With its distrust of authority and suspicion of leaders, the counter-culture called many things into question, such as education, work, measures of success, the consumer lifestyle, science, technology, economic growth, material progress, male-female relations, urbanism, and sexuality. Paradoxically, over time rock music became more a mainstream part of American culture. Even so it tends to retain its counter-cultural credentials with such developments as heavy metal, punk rock, and rap music.

During the same period of history that young people were becoming alienated from the mainstream American culture because of the uncertainties caused by social and political turmoil, rock music was ironically being institutionalized into the prevailing culture, at least at the popular level. An excellent example of this development was the initial publication of *Rolling Stone* in November 1967. This enduring and popular magazine contained stories and interviews with artists, concert and record reviews, and industry news. The appearance of the magazine implied that rock music had arrived, would be here to stay, and had to be taken seriously as a form of artistic expression.

As rock music continued to develop, there were some people who viewed it as a unifying force in American culture. Eventually, it was certainly a unifier of American youth, but the predictions for the music's potential to unify America were extremely optimistic. An historian of the music indicates the conflicting effects of the music within American culture:

> Although rock 'n' roll was a commodity, produced and distributed by a profit-making industry, and therefore subject to co-optation by the dominant culture, it continued to resist and unsettle "mainstream" values. For African Americans, rock 'n' roll was a mixed blessing. At times a force for integration and racial respect, rock 'n' roll was also an act of theft that in supplanting rhythm and blues deprived blacks of appropriate acknowledgment, rhetorical and financial, of their contributions to American culture. Rock 'n' roll deepened the divide between the generations, helped teenagers differentiate themselves from others, transformed popular culture in the United States, and rattled the reticent by pushing sexuality into the public arena. Anything but a "great unifying force," rock 'n' roll kept many Americans in the 1950s off balance, on guard, and uncertain about their families and the future of their country.[8]

Characteristics of Rock 'N' Roll

Let us play a game of word association with the terms rock 'n' roll music. What kinds of things come to mind when one uses this designation? Sex and drugs have already been mentioned at the beginning of this chapter. In fact, the origin of the term rock 'n' roll reflected 1950s black slang for sexual encounters that was used to label the unnamed music at the time by disc jockey Alan Freed. There are many other notions that come to mind: dancing; fun; girls; boys; life style; cars; surfing; love; hedonism; narcissism; school; teenage years. All of these activities, notions, and ideas appear in rock lyrics, and it is not uncommon for these things to be interrelated. In fact, many of these themes have appeared in rock lyrics for decades and will continue for the foreseeable future. Prior to rock music, sex possessed religious significance as a symbol, metaphor, and act with profound meaning in both East and West.

With their groupies, celebrated drug abuse, and death from the use of illicit drugs, the life style and actual lyrics of rock artists create an image of sex and drugs in the minds of its critics and fans; a hedonistic life style that is often celebrated in song. In Eric Clapton's song "Cocaine," for instance, the drug is depicted as a female who is truthful, and you are invited to take her out, if you want a disruptive experience. The cast of the musical *Hair* takes a comic look at the topic of drugs with the number "Hashish." The Grateful Dead sing and lament about sweet Jane, who lives on reds, vitamins, and cocaine. Although the group vehemently denies any connection to drugs with their song "White Rabbit," the fans of the Jefferson Airplane were convinced that references to the mind moving after eating some kind of mushroom and the injunction to the listener to remember the message of the door mouse to "Feed your head" were explicit references advocating drug use. During the period of 1966 to 1967, the Scottish artist Donovan Leitch appointed himself the chief priest of the hippie drug culture with hit songs like "Mellow Yellow,"

"Sunshine Superman," and "Sunny Goode Street." After the fading of hippie flower power in the San Francisco area, Donovan transformed himself into the leader of transcendental meditative rock.[9] The use of mind-altering substances are nothing new because the use of drugs dates back at least to ancient Indian Vedic religious culture (c. 1500 B.C.E.) with is cult of soma, and the religious use of peyote among Native American Indians.

Drugs are only part of a projected hedonist life lived by rock stars. Sometimes, the hedonist life style is expressed as a general license for pleasure in such songs as "Born to Be Wild" and "Magic Carpet Ride" by Steppenwolf, "Somebody to Love" by Jefferson Airplane, and the "Lido Shuffle" by Boz Scaggs. Any frustration of one's quest for pleasure is apt to be lamented, as in the lyrics of "(I Can't Get No) Satisfaction" by the Rolling Stones. According to the lyrics of "Pleasure, Little Treasure" by Depeche Mode from their album *Music for the Masses*, people are looking for a leader and some meaning to life. The subject says that he knows a reason to live: Pleasure. In the song "Dance Naked" by John Mellencamp from an album of the same titled, the subject asks a girl to dance naked so that he can view and enjoy her body, although he promises not to tell anyone or touch her. Pleasure can include sadomasochism with such suggestive examples as "Hurt So Good" by John Mellencamp and "Steel Bars" by Michael Bolton. This voyeuristic or sadomasochistic kind of hedonism, or any other search for pleasure, can be connected to the prevalence of narcissism within rock musical culture.

The figure of Narcissus can be traced to the *Metamorphoses* by the Greek poet Ovid, who depicts his figure as a prideful and self-absorbed person isolated in his own beauty and unable to reciprocate the affection that both males and females have for him. By rejecting those who love him, Narcissus is finally punished by the goddess Artemis who causes him to fall in love with his image reflected in the water of a virgin spring. Therefore, Narcissus destroys himself by loving himself to death.

In 1914, Sigmund Freud composed an incomplete theory of narcissism in which he argued that during a child's psychosexual development there was a primary narcissism that focused a child's libidinal attention upon his/her own body in order to secure a love object. The primary narcissism was later abandoned when the ego developed from self-love to human objects due to social criticism. Freud thought that narcissism was never overcome or outgrown, but it was rather re-channeled.

The Marxist philosopher Herbert Marcuse views narcissism as a potentially positive and liberating force in history with the ability to reconcile *Eros* (desire) and *Thanatos* (death), an undefeatable force. Within the context of Jacques Lacan's postmodern, psychoanalytic theory, one type of narcissism makes possible the organization of reality, and a second kind enables one to relate to others. Lacan's theory emphasizes otherness, difference, and the dissymmetrical character of narcissism, whereas the theory of Hans Kohut stresses conditions that can lead to self-destructive impulses.

Approaching the problem of narcissism more as a philosopher, Christopher Lasch offers a critique of American culture and the role of narcissism within it. Lasch sees people as dependent on the state, business corporations, and other types of bureaucracies. He observes the following:

> Narcissism represents the psychological dimension of this dependence. Notwithstanding his occasional illusions of omnipotence, the narcissist depends on others to validate his self-esteem. He cannot live without an admiring audience. His apparent freedom from ties and institutional constraints does not free him to stand alone or to glory in his individuality. On the contrary, it contributes to his insecurity, which he can overcome only by seeing his 'grandiose self' reflected in the attentions of others, or by attaching himself to those who radiate celebrity, power, and charisma. For the narcissist, the world is a mirror, whereas the rugged individualist saw it as an empty wilderness to be shaped to his own design.[10]

Even though his book often lacks contextualization and tends to make sweeping general claims, Lasch's comments at least approximate the truth with regards to some rock stars.

An early example of narcissism in rock music is the hit number "Johnny B. Goode" from 1957 by Chuck Berry, which intended to suggest an autobiographical narrative about a poor country boy who is poorly educated. He can, however, play a guitar with great skill, and his mother predicts future musical success. In a similar vain, the song "Creeque Alley" is the story of each member of The Mamas and the Papas and how they formed a rock group. By strutting around a concert stage singing "Jumping Jack Flash," there was no better example of a narcissistic figure in his more youthful days than Mick Jagger, lead singer of the Rolling Stones! At one point in his career, he even married himself in a narcissistic sense by means of his nuptial union with a woman named Bianca, who bore a striking resemblance to him. On stage, Jagger is literally "Jumping Jack Flash," a rock messianic figure with a spike sticking through his head. Other examples like "Travelin' Band" by Creedence Clearwater Revival, "I'm Just a Singer" by Moody Blues, "Roll on Down the Highway" and "Takin Care of Business" by Bachman Turner Overdrive indicate the importance of self-absorption, whereas Carly Simon takes a critical look at the narcissistic attitude best with her hit tune "You're So Vain." This does not mean that all rock artists advocate drugs, a hedonistic life style, or are narcissistic. These features are, however, tendencies that have manifested themselves over a period of time.

There are also less destructive forms of activity celebrated by rock composers, such as driving a car and surfing. The duo Jan and Dean recorded songs about cars and surfing that found the hit musical charts. But no single person, duo, or group was as successful as the Beach Boys with such hit recordings as "409," "Surfin Safari," "Surfin U.S.A," and "Surfer Girl." These young men pitched a life style that became associated with southern California, its beaches, sun, sun-tanned bodies, and bikini clad young girls. Surfing and driving a car are often experienced as liberating by young people.

In contrast to these superfluous activities, liberation and rebellion are related themes of rock music. The soundtrack for the 1955 film *Blackboard Jungle*, which was based on a best-selling book of the same title about urban gangs and juvenile delinquency, included Bill Haley and the Comets' song "Rock Around the Clock." The film depicts students in a schoolyard surrounded by a high, chain link fence that forms a symbolic jail, while the music blaring in the background is an invitation to rebel, break out of their jail, and become liberated. Rebellion and liberation themes are often aimed at parents, teachers, social codes, and social institutions. Although other films would portray the tension between generations and conclude with reconciliation, the *Blackboard Jungle* indicated a more endemic generational gap and tension within American culture.

The theme of a younger generation rebelling against an older generation without hesitation is evident in the tune "School Days" by Chuck Berry and the later number "Volunteers" by the Jefferson Airplane. Berry's song celebrates the liberating power of music beginning with a celebration ("Hail") and a message of liberation ("Deliver me from the days of old"). The song hints at oppression and deliverance in conjunction with a religious message involving the unity of body and soul. If we take into consideration the French existential philosopher Jean-Paul Sartre's distinction between the rebel and the revolutionary, it is possible to distinguish the rebel, who secretly conspires with the established order that he reacts against, with the revolutionary, who finds satisfaction by merging with the social collective. The rebel's goal is not to create a better society or political system; he/she just wants to break the rules that a person finds confining.[11]

If there has been a single obsession of rock musical composers, it has been women, who have been the primary subject for countless songs. To randomly select a single year to illustrate the predominance of women in rock lyrics, there were four major hit recordings featureing women during the year 1957. There was, for example, "Party Doll" by Buddy Knox, "Little Darlin" by The Diamonds, "Peggy Sue" by Buddy Holly, and "Diana" by Paul Anka. The Beach Boys recorded at least three hit records focusing on women: "Help Me Rhonda;" "California Girls;" and "Barbara Ann," a trend that continued with many other groups and individual artists. Some women are often depicted as wicked or evil, or they are juxtaposed with each other, such as Bob Dylan's song "Desolation Row" in which two women are important, namely Cinderella and Ophelia. The former is a prostitute in Dylan's lyrics, who confronts Romeo, an idealistic lover, whereas Ophelia is the opposite of Cinderella because she is a professional virgin. By sacrificing love and affection for her career, this iron-vested woman is already an old maid at age twenty-two. By donning armor for her body and mind, Ophelia protects herself against love and sexuality. But Dylan's creative lyrics are not necessarily the standard fare for rock music when it comes to songs about women.

The proliferation of songs about women can partly be attributed to the dominance of male performers throughout rock history, although females have become successful in greater numbers in more recent decades. Moreover, these women are objects of male lust. Due to the ever present threat of censorship, the lust embodied within rock music needed to be expressed in double entendre lyrics. Since gender is a socially constructed category unlike biologically grounded sexuality, some have argued that there is no intrinsic relationship between rock music and the sexuality of the artist.[12] A female critic views this from a somewhat different perspective: "Rock music is not male in any fixed or essential way but actually made as male through social practice and ideology, part of a continual process through which a variety of masculine roles and categories are defined, contested and transformed."[13]

Nonetheless, in some rock lyrics men need a dancing partner and vice versa. Of course, dance is often a metaphor for sexual dalliance. Within the context of rock music, Mike Jagger of the Rolling Stones, who is quoted as saying "What I'm doing is a sexual thing; it makes the direct and intimate connection between dance and sex explicit. I dance, and all dancing is a replacement for sex."[14] In the final chapter of this book, we will examine the truth of this statement with evidence from indigenous cultures.

With its emphasis on women, many rock lyrics express sexist attitudes as many feminist critics have already observed. By focusing on just one group, it is possible to demonstrate evidence of sexist attitudes. The imagined woman in the lyrics to the Rolling Stones song "Under My Thumb" does what she is told. The Rolling Stones, who adopted their name from a Muddy Waters blues number, depict a woman who is the worst thing in the world with their song "Stupid Girl." With the lyrics to "Yesterday's Papers," the Rolling Stones equate women with old newspapers, whereas their song "Brown Sugar" equates the conquest of black women with female slaves who were exploited by their masters. Ironically, males and females dance to such tunes, a case in which rhythm appears to trump lyrics.

If rock music is necessarily for dancing, the artists and fans of rock music have been very inventive creating new kinds and styles of dance, such as the Watusi, Fruge, Jerk, Twist, Disco, Break Dancing, and many others. The Beach Boys summarize its importance with their number "Dance, Dance, Dance." The Mamas and the Papas recording of "Dancing in the Street" makes it a public event, whereas the Pointer Sisters make it relevant to the current scientific age with "Neutron Dance." An artist like Chubby Checker made a career break-through with a single dance and song like "The Twist" in the early 1960s. During the height of the twist craze, it was common to find Chubby Checker on the television giving lessons to ordinary housewives. There was even a small revival of this dance when the Beatles released their own rendition of "Twist and Shout" recorded originally by the Eisely Brothers in 1962. As exemplified by the motion picture *Animal House*, where would any respectable college fraternity Toga Party be without the Kingsmen's version of "Louie, Louie" and its unintelligible lyrics? As observed earlier, this song was criticized because its lyrics were indecipherable, which implied to the critics that the lyrics must be dirty. Most of the major hits of a group like KC and the Sunshine Band are primarily designed for dance like the trio of "Get Down Tonight," "(Shake, Shake, Shake) Shake Your Booty," and "That's the Way (I Like It)" with simple and repetitive lyrics but with a beat that encourages you to dance.

The often wild, sexual, and uninhibited style of dancing characteristic of rock 'n' roll history was always bothersome to its critics, who saw human nature reduced to its most primitive and animalistic form and urges. From the conservative critics' perspective, dancing, or jumping around a floor, as they perceived it, evoked images of primitive tribal dances. The tribal members were rebelling against civilization shaped by the sober message of the Judeo-Christian tradition of restraint and propriety. In short, it represented a struggle between the forces of order against the powers of chaos. In a certain sense, the conservative critics were right, even though this correctness neglected the slow dance that was also associated with rock. Countless young people danced slowly to the numerous hits of the Platters, Pat Boone, the Everly Brothers, and such tunes as "Earth Angel" by the Penguins. Moreover, when we dance we use our bodies to celebrate something, and we at the same time celebrate our bodies. The Protestant thinker Harvey Cox states, "A people who dance before their gods are generally freer and less repressed than a people who cannot."[15] Two features are possible by means of dance: social solidarity or personal liberation, which can often overlap with each other.[16] Furthermore, it is also impossible to dance without being sensual.

Not only is rock music something to which one can dance with abandon, it is enjoyable and fun. The Beach Boys capture this aspect of rock music with their song "Fun, Fun, Fun," a number that manifests the influence of the guitar work of Chuck Berry. Likewise, Kool and the Gang ask us to celebrate and have a good time with their hit tune "Celebration." Sly and the Family Stone echo the same spirit with their hit "Fun." In her song entitled "Holiday," Madonna invites her listeners to forget about bad times and concentrate on the positive in order for us to bond and relieve the pressure of ordinary life. Since many rock composers ask us to celebrate life with them, numerous rock songs affirm life and the world.

The fun aspect of rock music appeals to teenagers, although it is no longer exclusively a teenage phenomenon because many older men and women growing up listening to rock music have remained loyal listeners. This loyalty and nostalgia for lost youth are reasons for the proliferation of radio stations playing simply classical rock, oldies, or a mixture of oldies and more contemporary selections. Issues important to teenagers has always been part of rock lyrics. Chuck Berry was among the first to learn this lesson with successful results with such hits as "School Days," and its reference to a typical school day, the bother-some guy behind you in class who will not leave you alone, and the mean looking teacher resonated with many young people. Steely Dan echoes the earlier success by Berry with "My Old School," and the Coasters were also attuned to their audience with some of their hits. With her tight dresses and lipstick, Chuck Berry connects again with his teen listeners with such hits as "Sweet Little Sixteen" in 1957 and "Sweet Little Rock and Roller" the following year. Berry captures some of the spirit of teen life with "No Particular Place to Go," whose lyrics relate teens just driving around with nothing specifically to accomplish, parking with a date, and being unable to unloosen one's seat belt as sexual arousal increases in intensity.

An important part of teenage life style is appearance and the choice associated with hairstyle. The long slicked back hair of the 1950s influenced by a performer like Elvis Presley manifested rebellion and raw sexuality in the minds of many. In the musical *Hair*, long hair is symbolic of rebellion, freedom, sexuality, anti-war, anti-political, and anti-establishment attitudes. During this period of time, many family arguments were precipitated by the long hair of its males as more conservative and reserved parents sought to exert their authority over their teenage sons. For young men, long hair was an erotic symbol suggesting a liberated libido, whereas parents and elders tended to unconsciously view it as a form of dirt, a form of bodily waste. The anthropologist Mary Douglas defines dirt as matter out of place,[17] an observation that tends to emphasize the rebellious nature of long hair. Long teenage hair was thus unclean, unkempt, and unseemly from the perspective of the older generation. In the meantime, teenagers continued to listen to more rebellious types of messages on the radio or their hi-fi sets. The family friction caused by hair length is captured in the musical *Hair* when the singer of the lyrics to the song "Hair" compares his long hair to that of Jesus, and he asks why his mother cannot love him like the mother of Jesus did her son.

Just as Jesus was asked to define himself during his lifetime, rock artists possessed an image of the music they were creating and what kinds of implications it suggested for American culture, although today rock 'n' roll has become truly global. This fact became lucid for me as I examined the stacks of a bookstore in Madras, India in 1997. As I looked over the books with a security guard vigilantly peering over my shoulder and following me around the store because I apparently looked suspicious to him, I was amused to hear American rock music over the store loudspeaker blaring forth for its customers. The nearly global reach of rock music was also evident when the Rolling Stones performed a concert in China in 2006. In a sense, rock has nearly conquered the earth, although in many foreign countries it is criticized for being decadent and a perfect example of the immorality of American culture. This simply proves the point that Chuck Berry was trying to make in 1956 with his hit song "Roll Over Beethoven." Berry was well aware that rock 'n' roll was revolutionary. The news that he wanted us to tell the classical composer Tschaikovsky was that other forms of music must move over or get out of the way to make room for this new musical revolution. Rock represents the kind of musical revolution that will make Beethoven role over in his grave.

The theme of revolution is also evident in the Rolling Stones 1968 song entitled "Street Fighting Man," which suggests that rock is different from any prior type of music. In the lyrics to "Radio Head" by the rock group Talking-Heads from their album *True Stories*, the subject imagines that his girlfriend's mind is a radio, and he possesses a receiver in his own head where he is able to pick up sounds. What he hears is the sound of a new world. The song "Rockaria" by the Electric Light Orchestra, for instance, stresses the distinction between rock and opera with the former type of music representing a revolution in an economic and business sense because it revolutionized the mode of production of popular music, and it challenged the various kinds of hierarchies in place that defined the business.[18] The revolutionary aspect of rock music extends to its salvific nature.

Rock 'n' roll is a form of music with not merely soul, but also the ability to save you, from the perspective of some performers. This salvific feature of rock is captured by the Beach Boys with their rendition of "Rock and Roll Music" which comes to the rescue. If artists such as Aretha Franklin serve as the unofficial "Queen of Soul," this type of designation suggests that rock music itself represents a religious force. In their hit song "Old Time Rock and Roll," Bob Seger and the Silver Bullet Band claim that old time rock and roll not only possesses soul, but it also holds the power to soothe your troubled soul because it allows you to reminisce about days long gone bye. In a similar vain, Paul Simon sings that rock can purify one's soul in his number "Take Me to the Mardi Gras" in his album *There Goes Rhyming Simon*, whereas the Irish band U2 sings about trying to save one's soul and searching for God to fill the hole in one's life in their song "Mofo" from their album *Pop*. In other words, it is rock music that fills the hole in one's life and provides salvation. From the perspective of Meat Loaf and his song "I'd Do Anything for Love, But I Won't Do That" from his album *Bat Out of Hell II: Back Into Hell*, there is a God of rock 'n' roll to whom he prays. Therefore, rock 'n' roll is not devoid of God or religiosity from the perspective of some of its performers and composers.

If a place such as Asbury Park, New Jersey serves as a microcosm for the wider conflicted, sinister, and dark world for Bruce Springsteen, his music helps listeners make sense of such a microcosmic world and our insecure and tangled lives within such a morass. An admirer of his lyrics thinks that his career manifests a religious vocation that he calls "a ministry of healing."[19] Similar in spirit to the Apostle Paul (1 Cor. 13:13), Springsteen believes in love, faith, and hope, and they remain when everything else is gone, according to the lyrics of "Badlands" from the album *Darkness on the Edge of Town*. Moreover, the artist would agree with Paul that love is the greatest of these virtues based on the whole of his lyrical works.

There is precedence for these kinds of attitudes about the salvific power of music in the Christian tradition, even though the thinkers probably could not have imagined anything like rock music. The Roman philosopher and statesman Boethius (c. 489-c.524) composed, for instance, a work entitled *On Music* of which only the last part has survived. Boethius, a martyr for the faith and canonized saint, differentiated music into three kinds: music of the spheres (*musica mundane*), music reflecting the harmony of soul and body (*musica humana*), and music of human voices or instruments (*musica intrumentorum*). Augustine (354-430), a bishop in North Africa, also composed a book on music entitled *On Music* in which he referred to the music of the soul in addition to cosmic and divine harmonies. This interest in music was continued by Hildegard of Bingen (1098-1179), representing the only medieval woman sanctioned by the pope to compose theological works and to preach publicly to clergy and laity, who composed a musical anthology called *Symphony of the Harmony of the Celestial Revelations* between 1150 and 1160. In her theology of music, she equated Adam's fall with that of music that she imagined as a vehicle of grace that corrects the fall. It was the Devil's reaction to Adam's singing that motivated him to corrupt the first man. Not only was the Devil out of harmony with God, but the universe is inherently anti-musical. But this sinful condition could be overcome by singing, which reflected a celestial harmony and recalled the Incarnation of Christ. From Hildegard's perspective, when we make music, an incarnate act of praise, we unite body and spirit, reconcile the individual with the cosmos, and restore internal and external harmony. These Christian thinkers share a common conviction with some rock composers about the connection between the human soul, harmony, and music.

From its earliest period, rock artists were aware of the sensual nature of the music. The gyrating hips of Elvis accompanied his singing "All Shock Up," and it manifested a dangerous sensuality to critics. Elvis was the first genuine Dionysian figure of rock music, and like the Greek deity Dionysius he sent women into a mad frenzy. For a brief time, Jerry Lee Lewis was able to capture the sensuality of rock in a way similar to Elvis with such hits as "Whole Lot of Shakin Going On" and "Great Balls of Fire," but he did not have the staying power of the person they were to call the King of rock 'n' roll. The American Dionysius named Elvis was challenged, but he was never truly dethroned by a single male figure during his lifetime, even though the Beatles eclipsed him for a time. But Elvis became even bigger after his death, and he still reigns supreme as the embodiment of rock 'n' roll sensuality. Other single male performers and groups have emphasized the sensual nature of rock music. Johnny Rivers performance of "Seventh Son" depicts a person with religious like gifts, possessing the ability to raise the dead and make girls speak in tongues. Jimi Hendrix's song "Voodoo Child" celebrates phallic power, whereas female performers like Madonna, Britney Spears, and other female stars manifest feminine sensuality. In contrast to these trends, the group Nirvana and the grunge sound is called "the sound of castration blues," a confession of impotency, being neutered, and spayed.[20]

In contrast to having castration blues, traditional rock music performed by males tends to emphatically stress phallic power for its adoring female audience. This kind of emphasis is evident in tight pants, leather pants, bare chest, or the guitar itself. On stage, the guitar often functions as a phallic symbol that is typically held straight up like an erection, waved around like a flag symbolic of the male artist's masculinity, or suggestively played between a performer's legs. Although no one would accuse Jimi Hendrix of being sexually subtle, he not only played, for instance, his guitar between his legs, but he also often simulated sexual intercourse with it. The guitar player is celebrated by Bread in their hit song "The Guitar Man," who has the ability to make an audience love, cry and get high. In addition, there is a mysterious quality that motivates him and keeps him playing. While performing on stage or for a camera, the tendency among contemporary female artists is to stress their sexuality with ample breast cleavage and belly exposure, a provocative style of dress that causes high school administrators to forbid copying such attire during school time.

Many rock artists are aware of the power of rock lyrics to function as a conveyer of social and political criticism, a power that is especially evident in the musical *Hair*. Issues like racism were encountered with such songs as "Colored Spade" and "I'm Black." A call for peace and freedom was made by numbers like "Ain't Got No," "I Believe in Love," and "Three-Five-Zero-Zero." Before the musical *Hair* gained popularity with audiences, Bob Dylan was protesting and warning others with songs like "The Times Are a-Changin" and "Blowin' In the Wind." Composers like John Lennon, with numbers such as "Give Peace a Chance" and "Power to the People," carried the legacy of social and political criticism forward. Many other artists followed the lead of these figures by composing lyrics critical of social injustice and political expediency. The prophetic role of rock composers will be examined at greater length in a later chapter.

The social and political consequences of rock music extended beyond what artists were protesting because it embodied certain concrete features that involved important consequences. Socially, a figure like Elvis Presley not merely sounded black, but he also encouraged race mixing. Moreover, he suggested that black and white social differences could co-exist.[21] Early rock performances were interracial events that helped to allow underlying social forces to find expression and to resolve their various antagonisms (or, perhaps, reinforce these antagonisms).[22] From a political perspective, when persons listened, danced, or performed rock music, the individual or group was engaged in a political act without necessarily intending to be political.[23] During its formative period, rock music was very controversial, and any association with it embodied a kind of political message from one generation to the next.

Connected to its socio-political consequences, its sensuality, its association with the drug culture, its narcissism, rebellious characteristics, its obsession with the opposite sex, and the importance of dance to it, rock music tends to be excessive and liminal. The drug and alcohol abuse among many rock stars, the female groupies that follow male performers, the trashing of hotel suites, or the loss of huge sums of money by wasteful spending, personality flaws, or for some other reason are all examples of the excessive lifestyle of rock performers. Moreover, rock music is always pushing boundaries and encouraging chaos with heavy metal bands, punk rockers, and rap artists being some of the more recent attempts to push the boundaries. If liminality means to be betwixt and between positions assigned by law, custom, convention, or ceremony,[24] it involves having an ambiguous nature without status or rank. This is most dramatically expressed by the bisexuality or androgyny of such rock stars as Michael Jackson, David Bowie, Mick Jagger, Boy George, Marilyn Manson, or Prince.

From the perspective of a critical theorist like Adorno, rock music is standardized because it extends from general features to more specific ones,[25] and it also promotes passive listening in the sense that meets a need for a stimulant and escape for people exhausted by work within the capitalist system where it is dull. Moreover, it functions as a socially cohesive factor to psychically adjust people to certain types of obedient and emotional kinds of mass behavior.[26] From another perspective, the postmodern cultural critic Fredric Jameson describes rock music as copies for which there exist no original texts. He continues to argue that rock music's popularity is not really dependent upon innovation or imagination; it tends towards a sense of what is familiar, which is conducive to immediate audience appropriation.[27] Jameson critically implies that rock music is boringly repetitive.

From the perspective of the Danish Christian thinker Søren Kierkegaard (1813-55), repetition is not necessarily negative because it is an immensely rich theme in religion that pervades our entire lives. It possesses innumerable forms like, for instance, the mass production of consumer goods, repeatable scientific experiments, the transformation of value into something like money, or the quest for universal norms that we can share in common. Kierkegaard, a knight of faith from his perspective, thinks that repetition possesses an intrinsic relation with the new.[28] He uses the narrative of Job from the Hebrew Bible to illustrate his point that Job loses everything, but at the end of the story he receives everything back double the amount that he originally lost.[29] This means that Job's dire situation at the beginning of the narrative is resolved by an abundant repetition, a gift or blessing from God. The repetition, which is always transcendent, is paradoxical in the sense that it was completed, but it still continues into the future. According to Kierkegaard, eternity is a true repetition.[30]

Rock Music, Popular Culture, and Religion

Rock music is a product of popular culture, an observation that presents problems right away because the nature of "popular culture" is not self-evident to everyone. It is usually differentiated from folk or high culture. The differentiation between pop culture and folk culture is sometimes difficult to make lucidly, according to some scholars.[31] Other scholars challenge the distinction between high culture and popular culture. If we examine high culture, the notion of a canon of classic literature, art, and music is unstable because an estimation of what are the best changes according to the historical and socio-economic context in which a judgment is made by a critic.[32] Therefore, if the judgment about what constitutes high culture is dependent upon the historical context of a critic, the contents of high culture are not universal and timeless like some kind of divine archetype. It is thus possible to view the notion of high culture as a human construct.[33] By drawing a sharp distinction between high culture and popular culture, we run the risk of not seeing the complexity of a culture for the majority of the people. As Raymond Williams argues in an essay on the working class, their culture possesses its own integrity, and includes many people who enjoy classical music and poetry in addition to popular forms of culture.[34]

In addition to problems with distinctions between high culture and popular culture, the term "culture" is not without its own problems. The notion of "culture" is historically a fairly recent development that possesses a connection with Western national identities and the presumption of political hegemony of the West. Some scholars have called for a fundamental re-evaluation, re-examination, and re-configuration of the prevailing logic of culture that tends to reinforce who and what we are.[35] Another scholar questions the very notion of the wholeness of culture that is immediately understandable or easily demonstrable.[36] This scholar concludes that the notion of culture is "less a conceptual tool than a bundle of arguments, moral persuasions, in brief, an icon of a certain epistemological position we are persuaded to assume."[37] The problem with this type of skeptical position is that the author tends to see modernity as a monolithic and imperious something. The scholar also misses the fact that we are thrown into a culture, or whatever one decides to call it, within which we discover ourselves, our language, our customs, and our religion. And sometimes this culture in which we find ourselves competes with other cultures or overlaps with them. A third scholar views culture as not something that is simply ascribed or inherited by birth, but it rather emerges from "processes in which people are slowly educated by those around them to make judgments the group considers appropriate about a great host of things, and to make meta-judgments about the relative value of their own and other's judgment."[38] Besides proceeding to stress the importance of recognition, he goes on to make a distinction between capital-C Culture and lower case-c culture. The former tries to exercise hegemony upon the latter, and the latter attempts to resist being suppressed, contained and devalued.[39]

Popular culture is this lower case-c that reflects the tastes of ordinary, non-elite people. It is a product of what one might call mass culture in the sense that it is a product produced for mass consumption. If "mass" culture is the commercially produced cultural system offered to the whole population, popular culture can be distinguished from "mass culture" by focusing on what people do with the items mass produced in their lives. What people do with the mass produced items might have little relation to the intention of the commercial producers.[40] Moreover, the products produced by this mass culture are mediated by print and electronic sources for the purposes of economic profit. Since these materials are massed produced, manufacturers of these items advertise their availability and desirability to a large audience by print and electronic media, which does not suggest that these massed produced items are without some merit and have intellectual depth. The consumption of mass produced products enable consumers to express their personal and social identities, and consumption patterns also express their vision of the good life.[41] As we have already begun to show by reviewing some religious concerns of rock composers, the religious messages of popular culture embodied in rock lyrics reflect a popular religiosity that also influences the collective social body in subtle ways, helping to further develop popular culture.

Within the context of a predominant culture, popular culture embodies the potential to become a genuine form of cultural resistance. According to Hall, popular culture acts as an opposing dialectical force to the dominant culture, even as the influential attempt to shape and control mass culture. In a paradoxical way, members of popular culture concede cultural control to some extent, but they also resist such control and cultural influence by the social elite.[42] If a type of socio-cultural struggle is characteristic of it, maybe what is needed is a more open definition of popular culture that enables us to think about it in terms of environment, practices, and resources of everyday life. Lynch offers this type of approach in order to be prepared to study anything of significance in a particular society.[43]

Popular culture is something in a constant state of flux, which suggests that it "is devoid of fixed forms and fixed meanings."[44] Within the arena of popular culture, it is possible to witness the struggle with dominant values and alien notions. Popular culture tends to be in tension with the high culture in which there is no final word or resolution. Many years ago, the Protestant theologian Reinhold Niebuhr noticed the irony with which Christianization and commercialization have regularly co-existed and interacted in American culture, claiming that the two have frequently blended with little sense of contradiction or need for distinction.[45] In contrast to Niebuhr, another scholar views the relationship between rock music and religion as a more ambivalent relationship.[46] In fact, this scholar argues against the position that rock 'n' roll is not a religion. He argues that by using the model of the potlatch it is possible to refocuses the definition of religion and to view it as a repertoire of cultural practices and performances, of human relations and exchanges, in which people conduct symbolic negotiations over material objects and material negotiations over sacred symbols.[47] Thus, why cannot rock 'n' roll be considered a religion? Even though there is considerable disagreement over the term "religion" and what it signifies, it is possible to find the presence of religion in American popular culture. Concluding that religion functions within contemporary society, some scholars have studied film in popular culture for its religious dimension.[48] Another scholar calls attention to the musical ministry of evangelical Christianity with its overt Christian lyrics, although he argues that the intended evangelical outreach to young audiences became a structured, commercialized music geared to a particular religious subculture.[49] This book will be, however, an attempt to build on awareness about the presence of religious themes in popular culture and specifically rock music.

Three Goals

I would be remiss if I did not respond to a pair of scholarly collaborators who contend that rock gives rise to a religion without beliefs.[50] Rather than respond to this assertion at the present moment, I want to let the chapters of the book as a whole refute such a claim that rock is a religion without beliefs. The initial goal of this book is to show that these religious beliefs might not be theologically sophisticated, but they are present, if one refers to various religious thinkers and texts to draw parallels to make one's case. By following this scenario, the second goal of this book will be achieved by enabling students to learn something about religious ideas, issues, and phenomena by way of rock lyrics. Although he does not use the texts of popular music, Lynch advocates using popular culture as a medium for theological reflection because it is a "means of exploring essential questions about our existence in ways that connect with the symbols, concepts, and concerns of contemporary culture."[51]

These initial two goals of this study are accomplished by examining the texts of rock music, or more precisely its lyrics. When listening to or reading rock lyrics a person learns to inhabit the world or horizon of the text, which enables one to enter its tradition of practice of which the text is an index. By entering imaginatively the world of the text, a person inhabits the subjectivity or subjectivities that it articulates. When a person inhabits a text, this event can also be grasped as an embodiment of the text by its reader or listener. It is possible that the intentionality of the text might exceed the author's intention. An initial reading is getting to know what Peter Ochs calls the "plain sense" of the text, which refers to the meaning of a text "within the rhetorical context of some body of received literature."[52] In order for me to enter into the text, it must be part of a tradition of which I am a part.

As we proceed from one chapter to another, I offer a dialogical reading that assumes being socially and historically situated outside of the text. When one remains outside of the text, while simultaneously entering into it, the interpreter arrives at an understanding of the text. With respect to rock texts (that is, lyrics), there are different communities of readers or listeners for whom different readings will resonate. Therefore, different readers will manifest different levels of textual engagement and often for different purposes. In the following chapters, I will offer my interpretations of rock lyrics without claiming that they are definitive in any sense. I will not extensively quote rock lyrics because the holders of the copyrights charge exorbitant fees to reproduce the lyrics within a book. For those who want to check the lyrics against the interpretation offered by me, the Internet is a good source for the lyrics.

Rock lyrics and their religious messages are tied to a tradition of previous religious thinking that goes back to the Bible, which is later developed by leading thinkers of the ancient, medieval, Reformation, and modern periods. The contributions of such thinkers form the cultural tradition that is eventually inherited by rock composers and others by virtue of their living within a particular cultural milieu. The theological concerns of these thinkers have filtered down and permeate the culture to different degrees through the educational system, religious affiliations, family members, friends, and religious leaders, such as priests and pastors. Thus, before a rock composer attempts to compose any lyrics, his/her religious sensibilities and understanding have been shaped by the religious tradition within which he/she has lived and interacted with others. In subsequent chapters, I will draw connections between rock lyrics and various religious thinkers. This process legitimizes the creations of rock composers by showing that the issues mentioned are also of concern to professional religious thinkers, and it serves as a way to further examine an issue beyond what can be expected in a short song. The theologians chosen meet three general criteria: my familiarity with their work, their grasp of an issue mentioned by a rock composer, and their influence during the historical time period of rock musical compositions, although some exceptions are made with older figures. A nineteenth century figure, such as Kierkegaard, is rediscovered, for instance, in the twentieth century, and he exerts a profound influence during the period of rock compositions beginning in the 1960s. Kierkegaard, more recent religious thinkers, and rock composers are concerned with certain existential issues that will become evident as we proceed, which reflects the influence of Existential thought in the aftermath of two world wars during this time period.

If my initial goal is to discern what the various religious themes in rock lyrics mean to some degree and what they reflect about religious notions in American popular culture, this study will be confined to what others and I call classical rock music in contrast to what is called heavy metal or rap for the most part. Within the designation "classical rock music," I do not find it useful to further refine this classification into artists that could be classified as folk rock singers, rhythm and blues singers, or pop singers. If I refined "classical rock music" into sub-classifications, I would fall into a hair-splitting exercise that could only result in more disagreement. For the narrow purposes of this book, it is my contention that classical rock music expresses a series of messages, and part of its message is religious or reflects religious themes in sharp contrast to what its critics traditionally claimed before its use by Christian artists. This study will be mostly concerned with religious ideas; it will not delve into the personal lives of performers, the record business and how it operates, modes of production, or modes of consumption.

My approach is also intended to respond to the claim by early critics that rock music is the Devil's music. These critics have failed to take the time to listen to the lyrics of many recordings that embody religious themes and messages. And these religious themes and messages have been present in the music from its inception because rock music is rooted in the blues and gospel music, representing the sounds and voices of the folk of American culture.[53]

The variety of religious examples provided by the artists previously cited tends to emphasize the importance of religious themes mentioned by rock composers. In the chapters that follow, we will attempt to examine other themes in a more systematic and through manner. We will examine the following major religious themes in rock 'n' roll lyrics: the human situation with its own themes of loneliness, boredom, angst, fear, despair, captivity, evil, sin, temptation, guilt, hopelessness, impermanence, and responses to the human situation; self, other, and God; faith and love; supernatural beings; Jesus as superstar and clown figure; time and death; eschatological themes; and prophetic notions. Finally, we will examine religious phenomena associated with major historical religions that are manifested by activity associated with rock music. My third and final goal of this study is to examine whether or not it makes any sense to refer to rock music as a religion, which is discussed in the final chapter of the book. This final chapter will complement the texts by viewing popular culture as a way of life for particular people in specific contexts. This will afford us an opportunity to look at wider structures, relationships, patterns and meanings of everyday life as connected with rock music.

I have included some British, Canadian, and Australian groups and individual performers in my examples. Although this book concentrates on rock music in America, it is my contention that many of these artists have become Americanized to various degrees because they have been influenced by music with deep American roots. And these performers have toured and lived in America for extended periods of time. Some foreign artists have even assumed permanent residency in America. Moreover, through their music they have contributed to shaping American popular culture.

Endnotes

---

[1] Many of the examples have been taken from Linda Martin and Kerry Seagrave, *Anti-rock: The Opposition to Rock 'n' Roll* (Hamden, CT: Archon Books, 1988).

[2] Paul Friedlander, *Rock & Roll: A Social History* 2nd Edition (Boulder, CO: Westview Press, 2006), p. 234.

[3] "Ever Feel They Don't Dig Us?" *Rolling Stone* No. 58 (April 2, 1970), p. 8.

[4] Martin and Seagrave, p. 112.

[5] Mark C. Taylor, *About Religion: Economies of Faith in Virtual Culture* (Chicago: University of Chicago Press, 1999), p. 1.

[6] Steven J. Sutcliffe, "The Dynamics of Alternative Spirituality: Seekers, Networks, and 'New Age,'" in *The Oxford Handbook of New Religious Movements*, ed. James R. Lewis (Oxford: Oxford University Press, 2004): 466-498.

[7] Theodore Roszak, *The Making of a Counter Culture: Reflections on the Technocratic Society and Its Youthful Opposition* (Berkeley: University of California Press, 1968; reprint 1995), p. xxxiv.

[8] Glenn C. Altschuler, *All Shook Up: How Rock 'N' Roll Changed America* (Oxford: Oxford University Press, 2003), p. 34.

[9] David Pichaske, *The Poetry of Rock: The Golden Years* (Peroria, IL: The Ellis Press, 1981), p. 31.

[10] Christopher Lasch, *The Culture of Narcissism: American Life in an Age of Diminishing Expectations* (New York: W. W. Norton Company, Inc., 1978), p. 10.

[11] Simon Reynolds and Joy Press, *The Sex Revolt: Gender, Rebellion, and Rock 'N' Roll* (Cambridge: Harvard University Press, 1996), p. 3.

[12] Simon Frith and A. McRobbie, "Rock and Society," in *On Record: Rock, Pop and the Written Word*, ed. Simon Frith and A. Goodwin (New York: Pantheon, 1990), pp. 371-389.

[13] Sara Cohen, "Popular Music, Gender and Sexuality," in The *Cambridge Companion to Pop and Rock*, ed. Simon Frith, Will Straw and John Street (Cambridge: Cambridge University Press, 2001), p. 231.

[14] "Pop's Bad Boys," *Newsweek* 66:92 (November 29, 1965), p. 54.

[15] Harvey Cox, *The Feast of Fools: A Theological Essay on Festivity and Fantasy* (Cambridge: Harvard University Press, 1969), p. 48.

[16] Will Straw, "Dance Music," in *The Cambridge Companion to Pop and Rock*, eds. Simon Frith, Will Straw and John Street (Cambridge:

Cambridge University Press, 2001), p. 159.

[17] Mary Douglas, *Purity and Danger: An Analysis of Concepts of Pollution and Taboo* (New York: Praeger Publishers, 1966).

[18] Trent Hill, "The Enemy Within: Censorship in Rock Music in the 1950s," in *Present Tense: Rock & Roll and Culture*, ed. Anthony DeCurtis (Durham: Duke University Press, 1992), p. 62.

[19] Jeffrey B. Symynkywicz, *The Gospel According to Bruce Springsteen: Rock and Redemption, from Asbury Park to Magic* (Louisville: West minster John Knox Press, 2008), p. xii.

[20] Reynolds and Press p. 97.

[21] David Marsh, *Elvis* (New York: Thunder's Mouth Press, 1982; reprint 1992).

[22] Hill, pp. 45-46.

[23] Philip H. Ennis, The Seventh Stream: The Emergence of Rocknroll in American Popular Music (Hanover, N.H: Wesleyan University Press, 1992), p. 19.

[24] Victor Turner, *The Ritual Process: Structure and Anti-Structure* (Chicago: Aldine Publishing Company, 1969), p. 95.

[25] Theodor W. Adorno, "On Popular Music," in *Cultural Theory and Popular Culture: A Reader*, ed. John Storey (Englewood Cliffs, N. J: Prentice Hall, 1997), pp. 202-203.

[26] Ibid., pp. 211-212.

[27] Fredric Jameson, "Reification and Utopia in Mass Culture," *Social Text*, Vol. 1 (1979): 25.

[28] Søren Kierkegaard, *Repetition: An Essay in Experimental Psychology* (New York: Harper & Row Publishers, 1964), p. 33.

[29] Ibid., p. 117.

[30] Ibid., pp. 90, 126.

[31] See Wade Clark Roof, "Blood in the Barecue? Food and Faith in the American South," in *God in the Details: American Religion in Popular Culture*, edited by E. Mazur and Karen McCarthy (New York: Routledge, 2001), pp. 199-122.

[32] See I. Levine, *The Opening of the American Mind: Canons, Culture and History* (Boston: Beacon Press, 1996), pp. 91-93.

[33] D. DiMaggio, "Cultural Entrepeneurship in Nineteenth-Century Bos-ton: The Creation of an Organizational Base for High Culture in Am-erica," in *Cultural Theory and Popular Culture: A Reader*, edited by J. Storey (Harlow: Prentice-Hall, 1998).

[34] Raymond Williams, "Culture is Ordinary," in *The Raymond Williams Reader*, edited by J. Higgins (Oxford: Blackwell, 2001), pp. 10-24.

[35] See Raymond Williams, *Culture and Society 1780-1950* (New York:

Columbia University Press, 1983).

[36] Tomoko Masuzawa, "Culture," in *Critical Terms for Religious Studies*, ed. Mark C. Taylor (Chicago: University of Chicago Press, 1998), p. 78.

[37] Ibid., p. 90.

[38] Bruce Lincoln, "Culture," in *Guide to the Study of Religion*, ed. Willi Braun and Russell McCutcheon (London: Cassell, 2000), p. 410.

[39] Ibid., p. 413.

[40] See John Fiske, *Understanding Popular Culture* (London: Unwin Hyman, 1989).

[41] See M. Fetherstone, *Consumer Culture and Postmodernism* (London: Sage, 1991); C. Campbell, *The Romantic Ethic and the Spirit of Modern Consumerism* (Oxford: Blackwell 1987); J. Pavitt, *Brand New* (London: V & A, 2000); D. Lyon, *Jesus in Disneyland: Religion in Postmodern Times* (Cambridge: Polity, 2000); C. Bartholomew and T. Moritz edited *Christ and Consumerism: Critical Reflections on the Spirit of our Age* (Carlisle: Paternoster Press, 2000).

[42] See Stuart Hall, "Notes on Deconstructing the 'Popular'" in *People's History and Socialist Theory*, edited by R. Samuel (London: RKP, 1981), pp. 227-240.

[43] Gordon Lynch, *Understanding Theology and Popular Culture* (Oxford: Blackwell, 2005), p. 17.

[44] George Lipsitz, *Time Passage: Collective Memory and American Popular Culture* (Minneapolis: University of Minnesota Press, 1990), p. 14.

[45] Reinhold Niebuhr, *Pious and Secular America* (New York: Scribner's Sons, 1958), pp.. 1-13.

[46] David Chidester, "The Church of Baseball, the Fetish of Coca-Cola, and the Potlatch of Rock 'n' Roll: Theoretical Models for the Study of Religion in American Popular Culture," *Journal of the American Academy of Religion*, Vol. LIX, 4 (1996): 753.

[47] Ibid., p. 756.

[48] J. Lyden, *Film as Religion: Myths, Morals and Rituals* (New York: New York University Press, 2003), p. 108.

[49] See William Romanowski, "Evangelicals and Popular Music: The Contemporary Christian Music Industry," in *Religion and Popular Culture in America*, edited by B. Fordes and J. Mahan (Berkeley: University of California Press, 2000), pp. 105-124.

[50] David Shenk and Steve Silberman, *Skelton Key: A Dictionary for Deadheads* (New York: Doubleday, 1994), p. ix.

[51] Lynch, p. 41.

[52] Peter Ochs, *Pierce, Pragmatism, and the Logic of Scripture* (Cambridge:

Cambridge University Press, 1998), p. 6.

[53] See the following books by Jon Michael Spencer, *Sacred Symphony: The Chanted Sermon of the Black Preacher* (New York: Greenwood Press, 1987); *Protest and Praise: Sacred Music of Black Religion* (Minneapolis: Fortress Press, 1990); *Theological Music: Introduction to Theomusicology* (New York: Greenwood Press, 1991); *Theomusicology* (Durham: N. C: Duke University Press, 1994).

Chapter 2
The Human Situation

In his influential poem *The Waste Land*, T. S. Eliot depicts the world in which twentieth-century people live as a barren place devoid of real hope. Eliot presents the reader with bleak and broken images in his poem, such as "dead tree," "dry stone," "fear in a handful of dust," and "dead sound." We find the dark spirit of Eliot's ground breaking poem in the lyrics of many rock compositions with respect to the world in general and the human situation in particular, which suggests a situation of human powerlessness.

Characterizations of the World

From the 1920s, phenomenological philosophers, such as Edmund Husserl and his student Martin Heidegger, have made it clear that humans find themselves within a world. Being in the world is a fundamental given of human existence and a situation in which human beings find themselves. Building upon the facticity of being-in-the-world and shaped by the horrors of military conflict and Jewish extermination during World War II, existential philosophers, such as Jean-Paul Sartre and Karl Jaspers, defined more specific aspects of the human situation within the world. The philosophical reflections of these thinkers and others filtered down to popular culture and rock lyrics, which is additionally rooted in feelings associated with the blues, reflecting the social experiences of black people and poor white folks. The world in which we find ourselves is not merely acknowledged as a given fact of human existence by rock composers; they also frequently characterize it negatively. Other lyrics refer specifically to the human situation and reveal that it is characterized by such existential issues as loneliness, boredom, *angst*, fear, despair, and feelings of captivity. Rock composers have also examined religious issues like evil, sin, temptation, guilt, hopelessness, and impermanence. These kinds of existential situations and feelings motivate people to feel powerless, or more accurately to express their impotence. Besides examining such issues, rock composers have also reviewed the human response to such problems.

The rock group Earth, Wind, and Fire express a profound problem with the world in their song "That's the Way of the World." According to their lyrics, the way of the world transforms originally good people into something more negative. For people so transformed and desirous of regaining their lost goodness, the group provides a response that includes looking inside your heart and soul and finding peace of mind. Even if the world is a cold and unfriendly place, it is important to remain young at heart and not become concerned about getting old.

Another rock group, Pink Floyd, sing "Dogs" on their album *Animals* that presents a world that is a house full of suffering. Human beings are like dogs trained and told what to do, such as cheating and lying in order to succeed. We also grow old, sad, and die alone. Another group called Tears for Fears in their song "Mad World" offers a slightly different emphasis on the nature of the world. The world is mad because people run around in circles with no particular place to go. Their faces are expressionless and look tired, along with being nameless and unknown. Others look through you and not at you. In contrast to this mad world, there is a private world of dreams that is more satisfying. In their song "Can't Get There from Here" from their album *Eponymous*, R.E.M. offers a more nightmare-like depiction of the world which they describe as analogous to a monster that threatens to swallow you. If you do not believe that human existence is precarious, "Radio Song" from their album *Out of Time* states that by listening to the radio you can learn that the world is falling apart. To R.E.M. it is ironic that we have become captives of the radio.

On their album *Remain in Light*, the Talking Heads refer to finding oneself in several strange and unexpected situations in their song "Once in a Lifetime." Discovering oneself in strange situations motivates one to ask naturally either of the following questions: How did I get here? And what have I done? In their album *Little Creatures* and the song "Road to Nowhere," one becomes aware that one is proceeding on a road to an unspecified location, and one becomes aware also that one does not know where one has been in the past. Thus the past is unknown, but the future is certain in the sense that one is traveling on a road to paradise, a no-place, and others are invited to join.

The negative views of the world expressed by rock groups can also be discovered in individual performers. Cat Stevens in his composition entitled "Wild World" is in the process of separating from his girlfriend, and the singer warns her about the dangers that she will encounter in the world. Since it is a "wild world," she must be tough and not expect to get by on her charm. An even more stark depiction of the world is summarized by "Desolation Row" by Bob Dylan, which tells the tale of a person lost in the chaos of the world that is full of grotesque features on dead and empty streets. The subject of the lyrics experiences the nothingness of his life and acknowledges his irrelevance. In a song with a mythic quality that is set in a medieval castle, Dylan sings about two disinherited social characters, a joker and a thief, in his song "All Along the Watch Tower." Both characters agree that life is a cruel joke, although Dylan thinks that there are many that do not share this conclusion.

In his album *Oh Mercy* released in 1989, Bob Dylan sings that whatever you can imagine is broken in the world in the tune "Everything is Broken," and in the same album another perspective is offered in his song "Political World." Since we live in a political world, this means that it is a time of crime, wisdom is captive and misguided, mercilessness reigns, courage is lost, life is short and brutish, loneliness prevails, civil strife is common, and we are unaware of God's identity. This strongly suggests that there is evidence that traditional religious beliefs have become devoid of meaning, which is the position of the sociologist of religion Peter Berger, who published a book entitled *A Rumor of Angels* in 1970, just as the death of God movement in theology was waning. Berger and Dylan share a common perspective about religion.

In his album *New Morning*, Dylan composes a song called "Three Angels" that is very instructive about the world and the place of religion within it. In this song, three decorative angels playing horns are constructed as a Christmas display and are left standing long after the holiday season. People, animals, and vehicles pass the outdated display. None pay attention to the three angels or the tune that they play on their musical instruments because busy people are preoccupied with everyday life and ignore signs of something holy and its message. The three angels represent rumors of the holy within the world and its unresponsive, uncaring, and unaware inhabitants. Dylan's lyrics express the main position of Berger that supernatural elements have become obscured and traditional religious language now expresses this-world referents instead of otherworldly ones. Among other things, Berger traces this development to secularization, a pluralism that undermines certainty, and the relativity of knowledge that renders us incapable of conceiving either angels, demons or other signals of transcendence that have become non-reputable rumors.[1] If transcendence has been reduced to rumors, it behooves us to explore these rumors, which is also the very point being made by Dylan.

In response to Dylan, Natalie Merchant asks in her song "Carnival" from her album *Tigerlily* whether or not she is right to be oblivious to all that is happening around her. Has she been blind, lost, wrong, hypnotized, and mesmerized by what she has seen? She thinks the world is like a carnival in the sense that it is a visual spectacle that can be grasped as a "mad house asylum." If the world in which human beings live is wild, mad, and devoid of the sacred, the condition of the world does not suggest that the human situation will be easy.

If one asks about how one got into the world, the answer given by the Doors is that one has been thrown into the world, according to their song "Riders on the Storm." This position suggests that there is no rhyme or reason for one being in the world. Within the world is where one finds oneself "like a dog without a bone." There is, therefore, no way to explain it, but we must simply accept it as a fact of human existence. The Door's song possesses echoes of Gnosticism, which presented a serious challenge to the early Christian community, in the sense that the cosmos is demonized because it is an eroded image of the real world in which humans are trapped in matter.[2]

According to the Danish thinker Kierkegaard and some rock lyrics, the most effective form of communication is indirect, which is designed to drive a person away from language by using negative hints and modes like irony and humor. By using such means as irony and humor, this forces a person from language and toward a confrontation and personal appropriation of the other. This position suggests that the art of communication is about taking away or luring something away.[3]

Instead of irony, binary opposites characterize life for the rock group U2 in their song "Some Days Are Better than Others" from their album *Zooropa*. There may come a day when you hear an internal voice that transports you to another place. In their song "Acrobat" from their album *Achtung Baby*, U2 sings that there is no rhyme or reason to anything because everything is out of joint, but there is no way to know who is to blame. They would join a movement, if there were one that they could trust. Thus it is important not to believe what you see or hear. By closing off your senses, you can feel the enemy within oneself. In contrast to the binary opposites characteristic of U2's compositions, Harry Chapin in his song "Circle" imagines life as a circle by using examples from nature and the cycle of the seasons, which gives rise to a feeling of *deja vu* and a sense that some time in the future people will be reunited with loved ones. If there is a suggestion of rebirth in Chapin's lyrics, there is an even stronger eastern cultural emphasis in the lyrics of "The Grand Illusion" by the rock group Styx. If you think that your personal life is confusing, you can take comfort because life itself is a grand illusion, although all human beings are the same. In contrast to these rock artists, Bob Dylan emphasizes the various absurdities of human existence in his early composition "Subterranean Homesick Blues" from his album *Bringing It All Back Home*, whereas INXS equates the world with hell and claims that everyone carries the devil inside of themselves in their song "Devil Inside" from their 1987 album *Kick*.

A different kind of lament is expressed by the rock group Queen in their song "Machines (Or Back to Humans)" from their album *The Works* about the age of machines and their replacing human beings. Machines have certain advantages over human beings because they do not become mentally distressed, are not bound by time, are not emotional, and lack any concept of "love or defeat." But machines do not have souls like humans. This impersonal emphasis is also expressed by October Project in their lyrics entitled "After the Fall" from their album *Falling Farther In*. The lyrics depict a city formed by a sea of faces, where doors are always locked, eyes never encounter other eyes, and a voice that calls a frightened subject to remember that the more that a person runs away from problems the greater the chance of recalling them. This city of impersonal faces is a fallen place without God and salvific grace, which is a microcosm of the greater macrocosm. Other rock artists have taken a more narrative approach to discussing the human situation.

Jon Bon Jovi discusses a young couple having a difficult time surviving because of a union strike by longshoremen and lack of income in his song "Livin' on a Prayer." The young wife brings home her pay out of love, and she and her husband have faith that they will make it because they have each other. In another of his songs "Someday I'll Be Saturday Night," a young man named Jim is not as fortunate because he must sleep in his car. Bon Jovi's subject, Jim, thinks that his life is a bargain basement; he contemplates suicide, and wishes that he possessed another person's face and soul. There is a ray of hope as Jim tells himself that he will get back on his feet someday. Elton John tells the story of a juvenile delinquent from the lower working class of England whose father is a drunkard, his mother is detached, and his greasy-haired sister "looks cute in her braces and boots" in his number called "Saturday Nights Alright for Fighting." The young delinquent is tired of life's aggravation and social discipline. He wants to get drunk on a Saturday night, meet a woman, dance, and maybe get involved in a good fight. The lyrics emphatically suggests the shallowness of his existence.

In another narrative song, Bruce Springsteen tells the tale of the dying steel industry in "Youngstown" from his album *The Ghost of Tom Joad*. This factory made cannon balls that helped the northern army win the Civil War. His father worked in these very same mills as he does now, but the subject laments that those who worked in the mills have been forgotten in a dying industry, and he feels that he is sinking in the city of Youngstown. He makes a bitter response to his situation that includes wanting no part of heaven and praying that the Devil takes him when he dies to "the fiery furnaces of hell." Springsteen seems to suggest that his subject would be more comfortable and at home in hell than he is currently in the dying city of Youngstown. Like Springsteen's laid-off steel worker, an old man named James Dean Monroe finds life difficult in Sheryl Crow's tune "Hard to Make a Stand." In order to make some money, he sells things, but all he receives is fear. He writes a note that states "If I'm not here, then your're not here." This serves as a way for him to prove his existence to himself. Monroe asked to be called "Miscreation, I'm a walking celebration." Even though a friend of his got shot down in cold-blood, he and others still argue over who God is. Within the context of these awful times of fear, death, suspicion, and little ambition, we need a revelation.

Within the Confines of Loneliness

A common theme used to express the human situation in many rock 'n' roll lyrics is the personal experience of loneliness, an experience that touches virtually everyone at some point during their life. The Everly Brothers give expression to feelings of loneliness and emptiness with the loss of love and happiness in their 1950's hit "Bye Bye Love." The subject of Paul Anka's song "Lonely Boy" is lonely without anything to do, and he thinks that having someone to love will alleviate his loneliness.

The Beatles confront the problem of loneliness in a couple of their songs. They sing about, for instance, a sad and lonely "Eleanor Rigby," who dies and no one comes to her funeral. The priest Father McKenzie, who writes a sermon for a service that no one will attend, amuses himself with mundane tasks. With a certain poetic justice, the lonely priest performs a funeral service for a lonely woman. The end result is that "No-one was saved." The title song of the album title, "Sergeant Pepper's Lonely Hearts Club Band" invites all lonely people to join their organization. The lyrics suggest very strongly that loneliness is so pervasive that there are sufficient numbers to create a club for those suffering from the malaise. The lyrics are also indicative of a desire to be comprehended and a need for fellowship. After he left the Beatles, Paul McCartney composed a song about a female office worker who leads a lonely and boring life that is reflected in her daily repetitious routine that includes bathing, grooming, dressing, working, and drinking coffee in order to stay awake in his song "Another Day."

These kinds of lyrics presuppose that meaning in life is found in our interrelationship with others. The theme of loneliness is associated with a fear that life is devoid of meaning. The feminist process theologian Majorie Hewitt Suchocki describes the condition of the lonely person profoundly in the following way: "The lonely self exists in an echo chamber, crying against the prison of its own solitariness for a relation that can set it free."[4] According to Suchocki, a person can be in relation to others, but he/she can still feel lonely due to a devaluation of relations and a feeling of isolation. Suchocki argues that loneliness renders all finite relations superficial by leveling them. The lyrics examined suggest from Suchocki's perspective that we wish we possessed meaningful relationships, but we find these wished for relations, or those that we do have, are empty, valueless, transient, and devoid of meaning.

Like other composers, Billy Joel relates the significance of loneliness in narrative form. In one of his most famous compositions entitled "Piano Man," Joel paints a sorry portrait of various people patronizing a bar on a Saturday night to listen to his music to forget about life and their personal existential condition for a brief time. Although the bar patrons are very different from each other, they all share loneliness in common. The bar is a place of escape for the patrons, and the piano man is a healer because his music is the healing potion. The piano man is asked by the bar patrons to sing in order to help them forget about their situation and overcome their loneliness for a few moments. Joel also writes about loneliness in his song "Captain Jack," which tells the story of a 21-year old man whose world is dead. Although he exists, he does not truly live. For this young man, there is not much to do and no place to go. In order to cope with the boredom, loneliness, and pain, the young man seeks refuge in drugs. In neither of these songs does Joel provide a religious answer to loneliness. He rather depicts his subjects as seeking refuge and escape in alcohol and drugs, which are very contemporary ways to respond to one's situation. Either path is self-destructive, which is the point that Joel is attempting to make for his listeners.

The situation depicted by Joel's song "Piano Man" resonates with Paul Tillich's theological reflections because the German theologian portrays finite human beings as caught between possible loneliness that can be associated with either being an individual or participating in a group.[5] Humans oscillate anxiously between these two poles for Tillich. The one pole represents existential loneliness and self-seclusion, whereas the other pole represents a feeling of belonging and its association with surrendering oneself to the impersonal group. These two poles are represented in the bar in which lonely patrons have come for a respite from their loneliness and risk being lost in the loneliness of a group of strangers.

Some artists not only compose songs about loneliness, but they also offer some kind of response to this feeling. Because his loved one is lonely, for example, the male lover asks to be let into her nightmare where he can function as her personal angel in a song by Duran Duran "Lonely in Your Nightmare" from their album *Rio*. In their tune "Mixed Emotions," Mick Jagger of the Rolling Stones is talking to a woman and telling her that she is not the only person to feel lonely and experience mixed emotions. His message is hedonistic: "Life is a party." It is important to love life until death and enjoy its pleasures to the utmost. Like the Rolling Stones, the rock group Queen sings in "Long Away" from their album *Day at the Races* that there is a sad and lonely person for every star in the sky, which is true even if one believes in heaven. With all the loneliness present, there still does not appear to be anyone who cares, even if we take into consideration all the prayers that have been uttered. From a very different perspective, Sheryl Crow sings about a woman in "Oh Marie" who is constantly in the company of men, but is still lonely. She turns to alcohol and drug abuse to relieve her problem because she is looking for some true love that she cannot find. Love, failure, and loneliness are intertwined in the "Midnight Train to Georgia" by Gladys Knight and The Pips as a failed artist, who strived to become a superstar returns to his social roots. Unlike these artists, Majorie Hewitt Suchocki thinks that loneliness can become a point for gaining an awareness of one's relation to God, which represents a profoundly different response to loneliness than being let into someone's nightmare, choosing hedonism, finding that no one cares, turning to an escape mechanism such as drugs, or going home in response to failure.

Suchocki's position is reflected in the tune "Wake Up Dead Man" by U2 from their album *Pop*. Confessing to be alone in a messed up world, the subject begins by asking Jesus to help him by teaching him about eternity. Then he asks Jesus to put in a good word for him with his heavenly Father, who created the world in seven days. The song continues with an interruption of a confusing rhythm, the sound of a saxophone, a hum of a radio, sound of rotating blades, and the sound of street traffic. This is the world interrupting and making it difficult to hear the message of Jesus. The subject asks Jesus if he is in fact near or has he become preoccupied. Presumably, the subject did not receive a reply to his original questions, and he is becoming impatient. But from Suckocki's perspective, the subject of the song is moving in the right direction by turning to God.

Loneliness possesses pejorative connotations because it suggests that a person feels alone and abandoned, but the lonely person can exercise some power, if his/her actions are appropriately aligned with actions of other agents. It is possible to witness these motifs in the thematic album *The Wall* by Pink Floyd. Serving as a metaphorical separation between the audience and artists, the wall follows the narrative of a young man named Pink Floyd who constructs a barrier to isolate himself from others and the world because of anger and resentment triggered by several unfortunate events from his past. Unfortunately for the subject, the self-constructed wall is not a solution, because it rather transforms the subject into someone out of touch with reality and suffering hallucinations. When he gradually returns to reality, his loneliness convinces him to tear down the wall that he created between himself and others.

Boredom, *Angst*, Fear, and Despair

With arguably the finest capturing of the spirit and significance of boredom in rock lyrics, Otis Redding in his song "(Sittin' On) the Dock of the Bay" tells the story of a man wasting time from morning until night sitting on a dock watching the tides roll in and out. Since the lone man cannot do what others want, his life is not going to change. The lonely and bored individual despairs that he has nothing to live for any longer. Again, we witness a reflection of Suchocki's point that loneliness is associated with feelings of futility, emptiness, and meaninglessness.

The theme of emptiness is insightfully portrayed by a man in a bar around mid-day who announces to those in the place that he just wants to have some fun before he dies, and the female patron wonders to herself if he has ever had any fun in his life in lyrics of "All I Wanna Do" by Sheryl Crow from her award winning album *Tuesday Night Music Club*. Those drinking beer in the bar can see people in a big car wash where people are washing their automobiles during their lunch hour. Afterwards, they will drive their shinny, clean cars back to their jobs. But not the two characters at the bar. She confesses to enjoying a "good beer buzz early in the morning," while her companion enjoys peeling the labels from his beer bottles. While this is occurring, the bartender is reading the want ads in the newspaper. Crow's insightful composition contrasts people idly wasting time in a bar and those outside busy during a Tuesday workday. The people outside are too active to be bored, whereas the bar patrons are consumed by their boredom. Crow's lyrics are a good example of music confronting boredom, even though it does not necessarily successfully conquer it.

The *angst* in The Eagles song "Take the Devil" is personified as the devil who resides in one's mind. In the soul of the subject there is a restlessness that induces him to escape from his present situation. He is trapped because there is no place to go. He asks God if he will guide him wherever he wanders. A different kind of wandering and *angst* are expressed in the song "Even Flow" by Pearl Jam from their album *Ten*, which tells the story of a homeless person who lives on the streets. His thoughts flow through his head "like butterflies," and he prays to something that has never responded to him, while looking forward to a time when he can start life all over again.

Long before these rock artists incorporated the notion of anxiety into their lyrics, the nineteenth-century Danish religious thinker Søren Kierkegaard examined it in considerable depth. Kierkegaard shows that anxiety lacks a specific object. In fact, Kierkegaard tells us that its object is nothingness.[6] Just as nothingness gives rise to a person's anxiety, a person is declared guilty. Because anxiety is always ahead of itself, it is able to anticipate consequences.[7] And if the escape from anxiety presupposes repentance, this escape can only be accomplished by oneself by means of faith in God.

Refining and developing further the insights by Kierkegaard on anxiety, Paul Tillich identified three types of anxiety: anxiety of fate and death; anxiety of guilt and condemnation; and anxiety of emptiness and meaninglessness. Since death is an absolute threat and fate is a relative threat, Tillich argues that the first type of anxiety is the most basic, universal and inescapable, and increases with individualization. Spiritual anxiety is related to emptiness, a relative threat, and meaninglessness, an absolute threat of nonbeing that reflects a loss of ultimate concern.[8] Emptiness develops out of a situation in which one's beliefs and actions lose their meaning and are transformed into matters of indifference. With the anxiety of meaninglessness and loss of ultimate concern, there is nothing to give meaning to life, which leads to a loss of creativity, boredom, and an all-pervading doubt that encloses one's spiritual life. The final type of anxiety for Tillich threatens one's moral self-affirmation. Since the self is responsible for his/her being, the self judges itself and discovers itself lacking, which in turn produces anxiety of guilt. Everything that one attempts to accomplish is permeated by ambiguity, an awareness of which leads to a feeling of guilt. This type of anxiety can lead to a feeling of being condemned and to despair over having lost one's destiny.[9] In contrast to Tillich, Reinhold Niebuhr, another Christian theologian, views anxiety as an internal precondition of sin, which is inevitable due to the paradoxical human situation of freedom and finiteness. This does not mean that Niebuhr equates anxiety and sin because the former is not the actuality of sin but merely its precondition.[10]

Another important aspect of the human situation for many is fear. In a scenario that is enacted in numerous households, a son leaves home in the song "No Son of Mine" by Genesis from their album *We Can't Dance*. When the son later returns home his father rejects him because the father thinks that his son abandoned his parents. The lyrics express very powerfully feelings of fear, sanity, regret, peace of mind, anguish, and rejection. Waiting for another opportunity, Sarah McLachlan composes "Angel" from her album *Surfacing*. She admits that she needs to be released from her feelings of fear and find peace of mind. She even imagines finding solace in the arms of an angel. The topic of fear is also evident in "We Don't Need Another Hero" by Tina Turner, who sings about being children of the last generation looking for something upon which to depend instead of the fear under which one is now living. Turner's expression of fear evokes feelings of despair because nothing remains. Likewise, Bruce Springsteen sings about trying to survive in "Devils and Dust" from an album of the same title and how fear can transform your heart from being filled with God to something black because its divine presence is replaced with devils and dust.

John Mellencamp's song "Too Much to Think About" from his album *Dance Naked* contains a vivid expression of despair. The subject of the song is confused because of the multitude of his personal problems and the many things for him to ponder. He despairs of ever being able to make up his mind, discern the reason for his existence, and discover the truth. Common wisdom says that he just needs to open his heart, but the subject disagrees with such a simplistic solution because his experience is something different from the encountered complex situations to be solved by pat answers.

The song "Age" by Jim Croce provides a description of life hitting bottom. The subject of the song admits that he has been living on a carousel. He is now without money and friends, and he has lost his ideals and soul. In the Radiohead's "The Bends," the subject wants to know the identity of his real friends. Do they have the bends? Singing from a context of despair, waiting for something to happen in a tavern, and wishing for happiness, the subject is in despair of ever finding freedom from despair and happiness because he is cursed by the "bends," a metaphor for the pain of despair and feelings such as fear of death.

Confusion, being disillusioned, and pain cause despair for Steve Winwood in his song "Stranger to Himself." The despair of the subject transforms him into a stranger to himself, whose depths of despair are expressed as being suspended from a rope while he is inside a bucket located in a hole. By scratching at his soul, his hands have become torn and bloodied. This stark and dramatic expression of despair is shared by the thought of Kierkegaard on the subject that he claims is universal and what he calls the "sickness unto death," which is not death or earthly suffering. Despair is the sickness unto death in the sense that death is the end of all things, and to be sick unto death is to be unable to die, which happens when death becomes one's hope in the sense of dying eternally and yet not dying.[11] When one is in a condition of despair it is common to regard oneself as a victim of external circumstances. By recognizing that the problem is internal as suggested by Winwood's lyrics, one's predicament is only intensified for Kierkegaard, a predicament he traces to one's estrangement from God. Besides unconscious despair, conscious despair assumes two forms: (1) unwillingness to be oneself that becomes enslavement to outward circumstances; (2) willingness to be oneself that manifests an attempt by a person to overcome his/her finiteness and necessity over his/her own power by sheer exertion of will. A danger with this second form is that it can become atheistic in practice because one proposes to create oneself, and Kierkegaard considers one irresponsible without a judge over him/her.

In contrast to the Danish religious thinker, rock lyrics sometimes express a combination of boredom, *angst*, fear, and despair more vaguely as pressure. A good example of this trend is "Pressure" by Billy Joel, a song that reflects modern life and the constant pressure that one encounters daily. Pressure is something to which we all have to respond. Faith and naive, optimistic advice will not enable you to cope with pressure. Joel's message is that you have to rely on yourself and your inner strength. In another song "Close to the Borderline" from the album *Glass Houses*, Joel examines pressure from another perspective. The subject of the song demonstrates strained, annoying, and contentious relations with people on the street, neighbors, and friends. These troubled relationships cause him grief and drive him to the edge of life. Moreover, medical and financial pressures complicate his life even further, driving him to the edge of his endurance and existence.

The pressures of modern life as expressed by Joel's lyrics do not fit exactly the notion of despair in the thought of Tillich because his three types of anxiety contribute to despair, which is for him the ultimate boundary-line situation. Because despair suggests a situation without hope in which one feels that nonbeing is victorious, Tillich argues that the person in despair wants to get rid of it but he/she cannot.[12] Feeling overwhelmed or under pressure does not necessarily suggest the sense of hopelessness necessary to qualify for despair in Tillich's thought.

Being in Captivity

Similar to theological thinkers, there are rock composers who view the human situation as a condition of captivity. Two of the best examples of being captive are offered by Bob Dylan in his song "Stuck Inside of Mobile with the Memphis Blues Again" from his album

Blonde on Blonde, a self-portrait album according to one writer,[13] and the classic number "Hotel California" by The Eagles. Dylan writes about a subject trapped in a specific place from which there is no escape. While he is caught there, strange and absurd events unfold. A famous person like Shakespeare, for instance, is talking to a French woman in an alley. The subject would like to send a message, but someone stole the post office. He encounters a railroad worker who smokes his eyelids and punches his cigarette. His Grandpa built a fire on the main street of town before he died. He encounters a minister with "twenty pounds of headlines stapled to his chest," a senator giving away free tickets to the wedding of his son, honky-tonk Ruthie, and a rain-man with strange cures. All the while, he keeps wondering how he can escape.

Driving along a desert highway at night in the song by The Eagles, the driver grows tired and decides to stop for some rest. He sees a woman in the doorway of the hotel and hears the mission bell. He reflects to himself "This could be heaven or this could be hell." A mysterious woman lights a candle to show the tired traveler the way. He hears voices welcoming him to the hotel and emphasizing its loveliness and roominess. The mysterious woman has many male friends with whom she dances. The subject calls the captain for some wine, who replies that such a thing hasn't been available since 1969. During the middle of the night, strange voices call. Within the subject's room, there are mirrors on the ceiling and pink champagne on ice. A woman admits that everyone there is a prisoner of their own design. There is a strange feast in the master's chambers where they are unable to kill an unspecified beast with their sharp knives. The subject of the song tries to escape from his strange hotel, but the night watchman tells him to relax because in this hotel a person can check in at anytime, but one can never leave the premises. Is this real life or is it a nightmare? The lyrics remind one of the play "No Exit" by the French existential philosopher Jean-Paul Sartre, in which three people are confined to a room from which they cannot escape. In part, Sartre's point is that human relationships are a living hell.

Instead of the strange hotel of The Eagles number, Elton John sings about a subject living on a street from which he would like to find an exit in "On Dark Street" from his album *The One*. The subject is unemployed and living on the street. Since his wife is leaving him, he is losing his family. Furthermore, he nearly loses his pride. Rather than a lovely island of his dreams, he receives a bucket of sand. A different type of situation confronts the girl in Melissa Etheridge's song "All American Girl" from her *Yes I Am* album. The all American girl is a waitress who gives up her baby because she could not care for it. Her job is getting more difficult to cope with, and she cannot understand why she cannot break out of her situation. She would like to escape, but she cannot. On top of her depressing life and its pressures, a friend tells her that her lover is HIV positive.

Religious Problems

Besides the fundamental existential troubles contained in rock lyrics, rock artists have also included some more specifically religious problems, although religious problems are not as widespread in rock lyrics. By more specifically religious problems, I am referring to such problems as evil, sin, temptation, guilt, hopelessness, and even impermanence.

Stevie Wonder in his song "Evil" from his album *Music to My Mind* asks a series of questions directed to evil itself. Wonder wants to know, for instance, why evil captures many hearts, destroys minds, infuses our thoughts with hatred, steals love, blinds people, causes family disruptions, and destroys much of the world. If evil is contrary to the way life should be, Wonder's lyrics suggest the relational nature of evil in a way not unsimilar to Jewish theologian Martin Buber's thought.

Buber defines evil as rebellion against God. With no relation to God, an absence of direction, and an inability to make decisions, the subject drifts into feelings of guilt. Evil is also connected to wrong decisions that are grounded in a lack of knowledge about relationship and the presence of the Thou. These evil and wrong decisions represent an existential lie against being in which one sees oneself as a self-creator, a primal form of guilt for remaining within oneself. At this level for Buber, evil becomes especially sinister because it becomes obsessive and demonic. Buber views this as asserting oneself against God, which leads to a form of enslavement. The key moment for Buber occurs with turning toward the other, a break or mid-point in human life that occurs in the immediacy of the reality between the whole self and God.[14] Buber does not personify evil as is done by some songwriters.

The Devil plays a major role as the personification of evil in the ironically entitled song "The Garden of Allah" by Don Henley, who is also a member of The Eagles. During a dark and degenerate time of Western culture, the narrator of the tale is at a hotel where a stranger, appearing in a cloud of smoke at the midnight hour, visits him. The stranger, who it becomes clear is the Devil, announces to the narrator that his mission is to convey a message. But initially the stranger complains about the heat at the seaside resort—a Garden of Allah—because it humorously reminds him too much of home, and it makes his seersucker suit all wet. The Devil also complains that times were simpler when one could make a clear distinction between good and evil, but now the fundamental ethical and moral distinctions are not so clear-cut. The Devil tells the narrator how he was once favored, associated with deities, and had connections to power in the highest realm.

The Garden of Allah is a paradise on earth where the wealthy and sexually depraved play. Within this garden paradise, the fires of war are fanned. The Devil gives his postmodern message: The world is devoid of facts and truth. Since facts are just data to be manipulated, the Devil can get you any desired result. Since there is no wrong, there is no right, without shame there is no solution, and without remorse there is no retribution. This situation gives birth to human beings without souls. Due to this depressing situation, the Devil is disappointed and leaves because there is nothing more for him to accomplish. The Garden of Allah, a paradise by the seaside, is a living, earthly hell with rotten fruit and degenerate human beings. What the Devil finds ironically is a postmodern hell on earth.

Although personifications of the Devil or references about evil appear in some rock lyrics, it is unusual to find lyrics that refer to sin. There are, however, many songs that seem to promote sin. An excellent example of the exception is “They Won’t Go When I Go” by George Michael. He sings about a destination that will be enjoyed by his soul when it sees the kingdom, presumably the kingdom of God. The sinful will not have the same experience because they are not saved and will never see the light. The shame and hopeless condition of the habitual sinner that these lyrics highlight are echoed by the writings of the Swiss reformer John Calvin.

From Calvin’s perspective, the primordial sin of human beings is revolt against God in terms of unbelief and disobedience.[15] This entails that humans are estranged from God and willingly choose sin. Due to the crooked human will, they are saturated with evil, making humans an abyss of all kinds of corruption and depravity.[16] Calvin claims that human beings sin directly against God and fail in their duty to their fellow human beings.

Based on their song “Tension” from their album *Hope Chest*, 10,000 Maniacs raise an interesting question for a religious thinker such as Calvin: Who renders forgiveness for sins that were never committed? This is a non-issue for a thinker like Calvin because human beings are by nature sinful and their actions are tainted by sin. Although it is possible to find much agreement between Calvin’s thoughts on sin and Reinhold Niebuhr, the latter stresses that original sin is not inherited, but it is rather the existential source of actual sin, which is involved in every action of fallen human beings. Niebuhr agrees with Calvin that every person is a sinner because people rebel against God and refuse to admit their creatureliness. Unlike Calvin, Niebuhr stresses that people sin within the context of their freedom and self-determination by making incorrect use of their freedom.[17] Sin is not necessary because of human nature; for Niebuhr: "Sin is natural for man in the sense that it is universal but not in the sense that it is necessary."[18] From another perspective, Karl Barth stresses that sin is permanent, pervasive, and not a condition that we can remedy ourselves.[19]

In the album *Music for the Masses* by Depeche Mode, the song "To Have and To Hold" refers to sin. The singer acknowledges a need to be cleansed of his sins and to seek forgiveness. Beneath his sinful nature, there is an internal goodness to which someone must bear witness. The subject wants to be released from dirt, disease, and decay (all metaphors for sin). The philosopher of religion Paul Ricoeur's work *Symbolism of Evil* makes a similar point by connecting sin to defilement, a symbolic stain that marks the transgressor as a violator of a personal bond and covenant with God.[20]

The lead singer for the rock group the Divinyls in their song "Bless My Soul (It's Rock n Roll)" asks for a prayer book because she needs to be forgiven for sins. She feels that she is not in control because she is being driven by a passion. And yet, she strangely admits to being inspired by the Devil and succumbing to temptation. She tells her listeners that she will show them that one has got to set their emotions free. How this instruction will control anyone's sins is unclear. Another contradictory message concerning sin is given by the Stone Temple Pilots in their song "Sin" from the album *Core* in which holy water, a metaphor for organized religion, obscures one's thinking. The lead singer says sin blinds a person. Then he relates that sin gives him strength in a puzzling and apparently contradictory message. Rather than contradictory messages, the Dave Mathews Band relates sin with humor with interesting results in their song "What Would You Say" from their album *Under the Table and Dreaming* by connecting original sin with the fall of Jack and Jill. Humor possesses a way to cut through the thick theology of the doctrine of original sin.

The 10,000 Maniacs in their song "Jubilee" from their album *Blind Man's Zoo* also tackle the problem of sin. In this song, a person named Tyler Glen works in a church and steals coins from the poor box. He puts up a poster reading "Jesus Lives in Me," mocking the message of the preacher. The world is an impure place for him, and he equates it with Sodom, which will eventually be destroyed. This handicapped, simple-minded man is the feared, mad disciple of God. While students enjoy the Jubilee by drinking, dancing, not observing racial barriers, and engaging in sexual foreplay, Tyler sneaks through the tall grass with rags soaked in gasoline and watches from a bell tower as the flames climb higher. The lyrics about this disturbed youth contain a new rendering of the Gospel of Matthew (17.15): "Lord have mercy on my son for he is a lunatick, and sore vexed; for oftimes he falleth into the fire and oftimes into the water." The actual text of Matthew refers to epileptic seizures and not to mental illness. In the

10,000 Maniacs version of Mathew, the son comes to spread evil, a false message, and represents the Anti-Christ.

In the Rolling Stones' number "Saint of Me," composers Mick Jagger and Keith Richards refer to former sinners like the apostle Paul and St. Augustine who turned away from sin and became saints. They challenge listeners to ask themselves whether or not they could endure torture and pain and still maintain their faith. The singer admits to being a sinner and wanting to save his soul, but he is convinced that there is no way that anyone can transform him into a saint because he is certain that he is no martyr like John the Baptist. Then he thinks that he spied an angel cry for a sinner, suggesting shedding tears of purification, reconciliation, and ultimately redemption.

Although it is possible to find a few references to sin in rock lyrics that do not advocate it in a hedonist way, it is also difficult to find any references to the fallen nature of humans. George Harrison provides one example with his song "Awaiting on You All," where it is possible to become aware of one's fallen nature without a church, temple, rosary beads, or books. Within the context of his reflections about the world, Reinhold Niebuhr connects the fall into history and the fallen nature of creation as characterized by sin, which is the catastrophic transition to historical existence and more specifically rebellion against God. Niebuhr does not mean that the fall is a historical event; it is rather the perennial condition of human existence. A person's fallen nature is a perversion of the original rightness. All aspects of existence are affected by an all-comprehensive depravity, although depravity is not complete because the image of God is not totally destroyed; it is only defaced, because it is possible to find signs of original rightness in fallen human beings with respect to their responsibility, conscience and capacity for self-transcendence.

If references to sin and fallenness are unusual, the same can be stated about temptation, although there are numerous references to succumbing to it. In his album *Mr. Happy Go Lucky*, John Mellencamp sings "Life Is Hard," and he gives as examples temptation, the brevity of life, loneliness, and the frightening fact that nothing lasts forever. The tune "Hi-De-Ho" written by Laura Nyro and later performed by Blood, Sweat and Tears refers to a person being tempted by the devil with worldly things, but the subject refuses to sign away his soul, and knows that he must strive for transcendence, expressed by the lyrics "Gotta get me a piece of the sky." The lyrics of Mellencamp and Blood, Sweat and Tears reflect Protestant theologian Reinhold Niebuhr's claim that temptation is connected to the human situation of finiteness and freedom along with sin.[21]

The album entitled *Ten Summoner's Tales* by Sting contains the song "Saint Augustine in Hell," which is a lucid reference to the life of the fifth-century saint told in his autobiographical work *The Confessions*, a classic narrative of Christian piety. In the story composed by Sting, the subject spies a beautiful woman with a friend, and he desires her. Thus his flesh is very eager, but his spirit is not strong enough to guide him away from temptation. He takes some comfort in thinking that hell is populated by failed saints, religious leaders, and other accomplished people. He recalls a famous statement of Saint Augustine, the Bishop of Hippo in North Africa during the fifth century, when he asks God to make him chaste, but God does not have to hurry. Even if God does not respond swiftly, the subject can always repent before he dies. The subject of the lyrics wants redemption, but he does not want it before he is able to yield to temptation and indulge his sexual desires. Sting's figure of Augustine agrees with Niebuhr's contention that the source of temptation resides in human inclination. This can take the form of denying one's contingent nature by delving into pride or self-love, or one can attempt to escape one's freedom by indulging in sensuality, resulting in the destruction of harmony within the self.[22]

Besides the few references to topics like sin and temptation in rock lyrics in comparison to other topics, it is also difficult to find many references to guilt. On their album *Violato*, Depeche Mode sings a song called "Halo." Guilt is depicted as part of the pain of life and a form of bondage that is similar to wearing a reverse halo. Kierkegaard agrees that guilt is a form of bondage, but he also wants to affirm that we are guilty by nature. Guilt, which presupposes responsibility and stands in sharp contrast to freedom, is never something external, but it is rather becoming conscious of the inability to meet the absolute demand and suggests a deep plunge into existence. It forms the most concrete expression of existence because the self is unqualifiedly at the center of the problem.[23]

In comparison to sin, temptation, and guilt, there are numerous references to hopelessness in rock lyrics. For example, Jon Bon Jovi's song "Dyin' Ain't Much of a Livin'" is about an outlaw haunted by ghosts from his past. He wonders whether or not it is too late to ask for forgiveness for the immoral and unethical things that he did in the past. If you consider the title of the song, the outlaw feels basically hopeless, which he confirms when he states that he hopes for someone to pray for him when he dies. A simple prayer is his only hope in a generally hopeless mode of existence. Sometimes things seem so bad and hopeless that you cannot even cry anymore because you have become numb, as depicted in Sheryl Crow's song "Can't Cry Anymore" from her album *Tuesday Night Music Club*. Crow sings about a broken love relationship, bad luck that never seems to end, a brother on heroin, and a broken heart. The hopelessness in the subject's situation is nicely summarized by a claim that it "Could be worse/ Could've missed my calling." This seems to suggest that she is called to be someone who suffers hopelessness. Bruce Springsteen offers a different kind of scenario in his very popular number "Born in the U. S. A." from the album of the same title. Springsteen relates a tale about a young man who feels abused by society in part because he is sent to fight in Viet Nam after some trouble with the law. His brother is killed in the war, he loses his job at the local refinery, and does not receive any help from the Veterans Administration. Although he was born in a wealthy country, he is now lost, destitute, and hopeless.

There are examples in rock lyrics where hopelessness is placed within a religious context. A good example of this is the song "Blessed" by Simon and Garfunkel from their album *Sounds of Silence*. They use biblical language to express the pain and hopelessness of being abandoned by God. Rather than the hope originally expressed in St. Paul's Letter to Romans (8:24), the message of Simon and Garfunkel is more akin to a divine curse. From a much different perspective, the rock group Live evokes the notion of a baptismal process in their song "Pain Lies on the Riverside" from their album *Mental Jewelry*. If pain, suffering, and hopelessness lie on the shore, the answer to this situation is total immersion in the waters of healing. This total immersion of body and soul in the baptismal waters of new life enable one to cope by enabling one to swim again, to renew one's life, and to be reborn.

In addition to religious problems like evil, sin, temptation, guilt, and hopelessness, another theme with religious connotations that can be discovered in rock lyrics is impermanence, which tends to have a more Buddhist resonance than a Judeo-Christian-Islam association. The historical Buddha taught a philosophy of radical impermanence that characterizes everything within the world. There is absolutely nothing within the world that we can cling to that possesses any permanence. Thus, it is important to be detached from everything in the world from the perspective of the Buddha.

Although the radical implications of the philosophical/religious position of the Buddha are foreign to the vast majority of rock lyrics, we can find numerous examples of an emphasis on impermanence. The rock group Tears for Fears sing "Nothing ever lasts forever" in their tune "Everybody Wants to Rule the World" from their album *Songs from the Big Chair*. The Beatles song "Love You Too" and Simon and Garfunkel's tune "Leaves that Are Green" stress the swift passing of time. The impermanence and brevity of time are also expressed by The Police in their song "No Time This Time" from their album *Regatta de blanc*. The encounter between two former schoolmates sets the stage to express the quick passing of time in the song "Glory Days" by Bruce Springsteen, which stresses the impermanent nature of happy days that rapidly past and only live in our faded memories.

Responses to the Human Situation

The most common responses to the human situation are not to take refuge in Jesus or the Buddha in rock lyrics but to turn to drugs or alcohol. The Rolling Stones song "Mother's Little Helper" is a good example of a person relying on some kind of pill to get her through the day because her life is boring and getting older is difficult. She finds tranquility in her life by dulling her mind. The aging woman of the Stones number is not all that different from the infamous "Mrs. Robinson" of Simon and Garfunkel from their album *Bookends* and made famous by the character in the movie *The Graduate*. Mrs. Robinson possesses a serious addiction that she hides from her family, but Paul Simon, composer of the lyrics, includes a powerful religious message within the context of the subject's problems. With all her faults, Jesus still loves her, and there is always room in heaven for the pious. Thus it is not too late for Mrs. Robinson to turn around her life. Furthermore, Mrs. Robinson's personal problems occur at a time when there are no heroes in America. The last true hero was the baseball star Joe DiMaggio, and he left the scene some time ago, and a lonely nation mourns its loss.

The turn to drugs or alcohol is also evident in "Little Sister" sung and composed by Jewel from her album *Pieces of You*. She sings about a little sister who suffers an addiction which turns her into a zombie devoid of a soul. Jewel's response is that we should feed our souls and not our addictions. Elton John sings of a man growing older and uglier with a serious problem of alcoholism in "Social Disease," from his album *Goodbye Yellow Brick Road*. The aging man's addiction is so severe that he clothes himself in rags, does not bathe, and dreams of vineyards. Although trying to live his life without his loved one is a very difficult burden, the subject in "Tryin' To Live My Life Without You" sung by Bob Seger and the Silver Bullet Band admits to womanizing, alcoholism, and smoking numerous packs of cigarettes a day.

Responding to the human situation by proposing to begin anew is evident in Tracy Chapman's number "New Beginning" from an album of the same title. The basic premise of the lyrics is that the earth is broken and unfixable, and it is time to start all over to overcome fighting, pain, suffering, and lack of understanding. We must create new symbols, signs, and a new language in order to redefine the world. Elton John offers a much different solution in his song "Goodbye Yellow Brick Road" from an album of the same name. In this tune a farm boy sets out to find his fortune by following the yellow brick road to the Emerald City, but the city is not what he imagined, and he becomes disillusioned by what he discovers and returns home to farm life. Both Chapman and John suggest that the answer to the human situation is partially social. The importance of the social dimension is evident with Neil Diamond and his composition "Surviving the Life." Since life is both good and bad, he thinks that humans need soul in order to survive. But this response is not as simple as it appears because you need to join the human family, which is the social collective that supplies soul.

Besides a social response to the problems associated with the human situation, another typical response is greater understanding. Jackson Browne makes this clear in his song "Doctor My Eyes." His eyes have seen unspecified bad things, but he decides that he wants to understand the evil and good that he has witnessed. He wants to know if he was unwise to keep his eyes open for so long, hoping that it is not too late to grasp what he has seen. According to The Police, there are no political, legal, or revolutionary answers to the problems of the world because "We are spirits in the material world" in their song "Spirits in the Material World" from their album *Ghost in the Machine.* They advocate searching for answers and coming to understand how it is possible for spirits to survive in a material world.

In contrast to Browne and The Police, Bob Dylan emphasizes the importance of faith in "I Dreamed I Saw St. Augustine" from his album *John Wesley Harding*. He dreams that he sees St. Augustine miserable and searching for lost souls carrying a blanket and wearing a golden coat. St. Augustine calls for those lost to arise and hear his melancholy address. The saint proceeds to emphasize that there is no martyr living at the present moment. The dream includes participating in the death of St. Augustine, who represents a witness in the dream to the fact that no one is willing to die for his/her faith unlike the saint because this total kind of commitment takes courage. The theme of faith is also evident in "Don't Stop Believin'" by Journey in a never-ending drama in which there are winners and losers in life. The lyrics depict a lonely girl from a small town and a boy from the city of Detroit running away from their homes. They become strangers on the streets like so many others looking for a thrill and emotional outlet. The situation of the young runaways is contrasted with other lonely people who try to alleviate their loneliness with a chance encounter with someone of the opposite sex in a nightclub. The overall message of the song is have courage, faith, and do not give up. For Paul Tillich, courage is an element of faith that is related to its risky nature. By willing to stand in the uncertainty of faith and in spite of the threat of nonbeing, faith embodies courage, which is its dynamic character.[24]

Other responses to the human situation are somewhat reminiscent of the response of the Protestant Swiss reformer John Calvin. The British rock group Queen represents a good example of this trend in their song "Made In Heaven" from their album *Made In Heaven*. The good and the bad things that happen to people are due to the influence of heaven. There is a strong sense of predestination in these lyrics because of the assertion that it is all intended by heaven. But this position does not suggest Calvin's doctrine of election and his teaching about double predestination.

According to Calvin, predestination is God's decree willed for each individual. Predestination to life is known as election, whereas predestination to death is reprobation. It is only through God's grace given to undeserving human beings through Christ that election can become a reality. This divine election is particular in the sense that it is only given to some, even though God's proclamation of the Word is directed to everyone.[25] It is necessary to understand that reprobation is a necessary correlate of election for Calvin. God does not leave the damned to their personal devices. By passing over them, God has condemned them to death, which is the negative aspect of his doctrine that Calvin calls a dreadful decree.[26] Nonetheless, Calvin views this doctrine as completely just because human beings are odious to God due to their sins. And since everyone predestined to death are already subject to death, there is no injustice done to them.

Steve Winwood offers another response to the human situation that evokes the spirit of Chinese Daoism in his number "Take It as It Comes" from his album *Back in the High Life*. Since human beings live precariously with the prospect of death occurring at any time, Winwood's basic message is to take whatever happens to you as it comes. By taking each day as it comes and doing what others demand of you without resisting them, you will survive. This attitude is very similar to the ancient Daoist philosophy of survival in the sense of flowing with the changes of the Dao and acting in such a way as not to strive or resist, but rather to bend with ever-changing events in a totally natural and spontaneous way much like a subtle tree bends in a strong wind.

In contrast to the Daoist type of response offered by Winwood, Bob Dylan offers a more Buddhist response in his song "A Hard Rain's A-Gonna Fall" from his album *The Freewheelin's Bob Dylan*. Each part of the song begins with different questions: Where have you been; what did you see; what did you hear; who did you meet; and finally what will you do after all your experiences? He did not go to any happy places because he visited twelve misty mountains, six crooked highways, seven sad forests, a dozen dead oceans, and a graveyard. He sees many strange things, and he hears a warning and numerous strange sounds. And there is something seriously wrong with each person that he meets. In response to the question about what he will do next after all the trouble and ominous things that he sees, hears, and people that he meets, he replies that he will return to the world and get involved by thinking, speaking, and breathing the problems of the world. And he will reflect what he thinks, speaks, and breathes from the top of a mountain so that every soul can bear witness. Like the *bodhisattva* (enlightened being) of Mahāyāna Buddhism, he goes to the brink of enlightenment, and he returns to the world in order to assist others to become aware and achieve the ultimate goal of release from the suffering in the world. The *bodhisattva* is an unselfish being who is more concerned with the salvation of others than he/she is of saving himself/herself because a *bodhisattva* is motivated by his/her compassion for the suffering of others.

The response to the human situation can also have a more negative religious result. In his song "It's Alright Ma (I'm Only Bleeding)" from his album *Bringing It All Back Home*, Bob Dylan concludes that there is nothing really sacred in life. The subject of another song confesses to "Losing My Religion" in the lyrics of the rock band R. E. M. But the subject is confused because he does not know if he should be saying such an outrageous thing. The video of this song mixes religious figures from East and West. In a dream sequence, a winged figure that resembles Jesus with a wound in the side of his chest is helped by others attempting to repair his wings. The video ends with a cross superimposed over a set of wings. The subject of R. E. M.'s song can learn something by turning to the thought of Dietrich Bonhoeffer, a Protestant pastor executed by the Nazis during World War II. From his prison cell before his death, Bonhoeffer writes, "We are proceeding towards a time of no religion at all: men as they are now simply cannot be religious any more. Even those who honestly describe themselves as 'religious' do not in the least act up to it, and so when they say 'religious' they evidently mean something quite different."[27]

In contrast to R. E. M.'s song, The Moody Blues' song "Lost in a Lost World" from their album *Seventh Sojourn* depicts a subject who feels adrift in a lost world. He feels surrounded by death, illusion, ignorance, war, racism, selfishness, and pain. Within the context of this bleak situation, people are searching for answers to all the misery. Finally, the message is hopeful because love can come to those suffering if they turn to prayer, although these lyrics are not ultimately as hopeful as Dietrich Bonhoeffer's observation as he sat in a Nazi prison during World War II. Bonhoeffer smuggled out of prison the following sentence within a letter: "God is the 'beyond' in the midst of our life."[28]

Even with all the problems associated with the human condition examined in this chapter, the various types of responses to the human situation reflected in rock lyrics suggest that the individual possesses the ability to respond and resist. As illustrated in the life of Bonhoeffer, every exercise of power gives rise to resistance. Because power does not necessarily represent a system of domination, resistance is not external to power, suggesting that it does not possess an inside or an outside. Within the network of power, resistance is present everywhere and represents mobile and transitory points within the network of power that create cleavages and ruptures in a society from Fouault's genealogical perspective.[29]

Concluding Remarks

To feel lost in the world, to feel alienated, to experience loneliness, *angst*, fear, and despair, and to be subject to evil, sin, temptation, guilt, hopelessness, and impermanence represents limit experiences. The German existential philosopher Karl Jaspers refers to such experiences as limit-situations by which he means that a human being discovers oneself at an ultimate boundary or horizon of one's existence.[30] These limit situations can be painful learning experiences because they enable one to become aware of the outer boundaries of one's experience and the limits of one's existence. In other words, these kinds of situations disclose the very limits of one's being. And within these various types of limit situations, one discovers oneself radically contingent, although this does not mean that one is powerless from Michel Foucault's post-structuralist viewpoint.

Many of the lyrics examined in this chapter embody an attempt to transcend these various limit-situations. Self-transcendence refers to the struggle to transcend or overcome our individual, social, and worldly limitations. The struggle for self-transcendence is an attempt to exercise power. The rock lyrics that we examined are indicative of an almost universal attempt at self-transcendence by ordinary people, even if their music makes them famous within the confines of popular culture. Of course, fame can be viewed as a kind of paradoxical transcendence in the sense that the rock artist transcends ordinary people, but the artist's fame is still connected to his/her finite nature. If responses to the human situation and its limits include drugs and alcohol, these kinds of decisions lead often to self-destruction and a succumbing to one's situation. The types of lyrics examined in this chapter also enable us to see that rock composers were directly or indirectly influenced by existential philosophy and theology, and they were concerned with important issues related to human existence. Therefore, not all rock lyrics are about frivolous stuff. Some of it deals with serious issues that confront all human beings, although important issues might not be covered in great depth or with nuanced philosophical or religious sophistication. Just as there are limit-situations in life, there are limits to rock poetry.

Endnotes

---

[1] Peter L. Berger, *A Rumor of Angels: Modern Society and the Rediscovery of the Supernatural* (Garden City, N. Y: Doubleday & Company, Inc., 1970), p. 95.

[2] Giovanni Filoramo, *A History of Gnosticism*, trans. Anthony Alcock (Oxford: Basil Blackwell, 1990), pp. 22, 57.

[3] Søren Kierkegaard, *Concluding Unscientific Postscript to Philosophical Fragments*, ed. and trans. Howard V. Hong and Edna H. Hong (Princeton: Princeton University Press, 1992), p. 72.

[4] Majorie Hewitt Suchocki, *God Christ Church: A Practical Guide to Process Theology*, Revised Edition (New York: Crossroad Publishing Company, 1989), p. 50.

[5] Paul Tillich, *Systematic Theology* Vol. I (Chicago: University of Chicago Press, 1951), p. 199.

[6] Søren Kierkegaard, *Concept of Anxiety* (Princeton: Princeton University Press, 1980), p. 77.

[7] Ibid., p. 115.

[8] Paul Tillich, *Courage To Be* (New Haven, CT: Yale University Press, 1952), p. 115.

[9] Ibid., pp. 52-53.

[10] Reinhold Niebuhr, *The Nature and Destiny of Man: A Christian Interpretation*, 2 vols. (New York: Scribner's Sons, 1955), I:183.

[11] Søren Kierkegaard, *Sickness Unto Death: A Christian Psychological Exposition for Upbuilding and Awakening*, ed. and trans. Howard V. Hong and Edna H. Hong (Princeton: Princeton University Press, 1980), p. 13.

[12] Tillich, *The Courage to Be*, p. 55.

[13] Michael Coyle and Debra Rae Cohen, "Blonde on Blonde (1966)" in *The Companion to Bob Dylan*, ed. by Kevin J. H. Dettmar (Cambridge: Cambridge University Press, 2009), p. 148.

[14] Martin Buber, *I-Thou*, trans. Ronald Gregor Smith (New York: Scribner, 1958), p.

[15] John Calvin, *Institutes of the Christian Religion*, 2 vols., trans. John Allen (Philadelphia: Fortress Press, 1965), 2.1.4.

[16] Ibid., 2.3.1.

[17] Reinhold Niebuhr, *The Nature and Destiny of Man*, I: 116-117.

[18] Ibid., p. 242.

[19] Karl Barth, *Church Dogmatics* II/1, trans. G. T. Thompson et. al.

(Edinburgh: T. & T. Clark, 1949), p. 130.

[20] Paul Ricoeur, *The Symbolism of Evil*, trans. Emerson Buchanan (New York: Harper & Row, 1967), p. 52.

[21] Niebuhr, *Nature and Destiny of Man*, I: 251.

[22] Ibid., 185.

[23] Kierkegaard,

[24] Paul Tillich, *Dynamics of Faith* (New York: Harper & Row, Publishers, 1957), pp. 16-17.

[25] Calvin, 3.22.10.

[26] Ibid., 3.23.7.

[27] Dietrich Bonhoeffer, *Letters and Papers from Prison*, trans. Reginald H. Fuller (New York: Macmillan Company, 1962), p. 162.

[28] Ibid., p. 166.

[29] Michel Foucault, *History of Sexuality. Volume I: An Introduction*, Translated by Robert Hurley. New York: Vintage/Random House, 1980, pp. 95-96.

[30] Karl Jaspers, *The Perennial Scope of Philosophy* (New York: Philosophical Library, 1949), pp. 85-87.

Chapter 3
Self, Other, and God

During the 1950s when rock music evolved into a specific identifiable entity, J. D. Salinger's novel *The Catcher in the Rye* (published in 1951) became very popular. The main character of this novel was a young man named Holden Caulfield, who was struggling to find his personal identity within a social context of materialism, conformity, and hypocrisy. Salinger depicted adolescent idealism and defiance as natural and corrective measures for the social world of adults. The fact that Holden was depicted as aimless made him an even more authentic figure to youthful readers.

Holden Caulfield's search for his self found an echo in the lyrics of rock composers. Within the context of an impersonal world, the self needs to assert itself by crying out that it exists. It is more than a matter of asserting that the self exists because the search for a personal identity is often made more difficult when people hide behind masks that they wear in public. Thus it is possible to become a stranger to oneself and to others, an existential problem that can turn one into an impersonal number. The search for the self involves discerning between an authentic and inauthentic self by means of the decisions and choices that we make during our existence. The search can also entail becoming isolated, rejecting the other, deceiving ourselves with lies, objectifying the other, and exploiting relationships.

During the early development of rock music, the philosophy of the Jewish thinker Martin Buber was being taught and read by many people. Buber defined real existence as a life of encounter and dialogue with the other and God in his classic work *I and Thou*. For Buber, genuine selfhood represented a triadic relationship among the self, God and the other. Using Buber as our guide, this chapter will explore rock lyrics for various issues related to the search for self-identity like that pursued by Salinger's character and other youth of the time.

The rock group Three Dog Night recorded some songs, for instance, with important implications for this chapter. Their song entitled "One" relates partially to the topic of loneliness from the previous chapter and its overall discussion of the human situation. The number "one," according to the lyrics, is a lonely number, but this can also be true of the number "two." Loneliness and its often concomitant feeling of rejection are among the saddest occurrences that anyone can experience. The Jewish philosopher and religious thinker Martin Buber agrees with the sentiments expressed in the lyrics of "One" because genuine human existence is characterized by relationship and not isolation. Borrowing a song from the musical hit show *Hair*, Three Dog Night ask in "Easy to Be Hard" how people can be so heartless, cruel, and mean to others. The lyrics try to grasp the reasons people act indifferently towards others and how they can ignore their friends and social injustice all around them. The lyrics to "One" and "Easy to Be Hard" share the conviction that giving a negative response is easy. The latter song also reflects concerns of Buber's thought on the importance of interpersonal relationships, the nature of the self, the other, and God. In this chapter we will see that the rock lyrics of various artists demonstrate concerns for these same issues, although they are not fully developed by the artists. Nonetheless, the composers of rock poetry often offer insightful looks into the dynamics of the self and human relationships.

The Cry of the Self

Within the context of an impersonal world, the human self is motivated sometimes to utter a primal cry for recognition. Within the context of feeling lost and lonely in his song "I Am . . . I Said," Neil Diamond cries out "I am" to no one in particular. The implied question is whether or not anyone really cares. The subject in the lyrics to "Family Man" by Fleetwood Mac from their album *Tango in the Night* possesses a certainty about his identity because he concludes that he is a family man. Such lyrics tend to suggest that the self needs to assert its facticity and identity in spite of the nature of the world and the complex human situation in which the self finds itself. The subject of the song "Look At Me" by John Lennon from his album *Plastic Ono Band* is much less certain about his identity and what he is suppose to do in life. To cry "I am" suggests that one exists in spite of the tragedies associated with life and the prevalence of the threat of death at any moment.

It is possible to understand the cry of the self as a symbolic will to power, which is an act of self-affirmation that manifests a person's desire just for such a condition. By executing an act of self-affirmation, resistance by the other to oneself is overcome. This implies that one cannot be affirmed by the other, whose resistance is also a will to power, until one is able to execute an act of self-affirmation. The will to self-affirmation is also connected to knowing one's location within the world.

In his work *Repetition*, Kierkegaard writes a letter to his silent confidant, and he begins by asking, "Where am I?" He confesses that he is at the end of his rope because "I am nauseated by life; it is insipid—without salt and meaning."[1] Again, he raises the question of his whereabouts, and he confesses, "I stick my finger into the world —it has no smell."[2] From one perspective, to raise this kind of question and respond pessimistically or positively means to be located within the world.

In contrast to Kierkegaard, many rock lyrics want to affirm that one not only exists, but that one also possesses a personal identity. Jim Croce expresses the importance of personal identity with his song "I Got a Name" from the album of the same title. Much like pine trees, a road, a bird, or a toad, a person possesses a name. A name is your personal identity and differentiates you from others. There are also numerous lyrics that express a struggle to discover one's true identity.

Lamenting his wasted youth, the subject of the song "Everything Louder Than Everything Else" by Meat Loaf from his album *Bat Out of Hell II: Back Into Hell* reflects later in life about his true identity, and asks the reason for his existence and the meaning of life between a pause to forget about the questions and drink a beer. The pause to forget and drink seems to suggest the difficulty of both raising the questions and finding answers. These lyrics also cause one to wonder about the genuine nature of the question and the seriousness of the person raising the question. In comparison, the question about identity is raised in a more interpersonal way by Pink Floyd in "Childhood's End" from their album *Obscured By Clouds*. The lyrics suggest that when we become adults we begin to ask questions in order to discover our own identity and the identity of others. The lyrics also suggest that childhood is a time of self-absorption in comparison to a more adult attitude in which one attempts to discover one's own identity, the nature of the other, and how one relates to other beings.

It is difficult to discover our identity because we often wear masks behind which we hide when we assume a role in public. The public persona behind which people often hide is the theme of some rock lyrics. Bruce Springsteen writes a song about a man who asks himself if his girlfriend is being herself or just putting on a disguise or public persona in the lyrics to "Brilliant Disguise" from his album *Tunnel of Love*. In spite of a prediction by a gypsy that they would have a wonderful marriage, their relationship disintegrates, and he finds himself admitting that he is nothing more than a lonesome pilgrim. Then, he asks himself if he is not also wearing a disguise. After the termination of their relationship, he becomes convinced of his love and laments, "God have mercy on the man/Who doubts what he's sure of." Along similar lines, Jim Croce perceives humans hiding behind costumes forgetting to feel and be genuine, but he refuses to play a role that is untrue to himself in his song "I Am Who I Am." The disguise motif is evident in Elton John's tune "Man," where a man is depicted standing at a crossroads wearing a mask. This man is a hoax and many other things that are difficult to comprehend, although he is working on what it means to live. He stumbles along embracing his own beliefs and adorns his own defeat. According to "The Stranger" by Billy Joel, we possess a non-social face that we hide from others, and only reveal to ourselves when we are alone. There are many different faces of the stranger that we have a penchant to put on ourselves. Although the stranger is not necessarily evil or wrong, we hide this secret face from those that we love, which leads to surprises in our relationships with others.

When one discerns one's identity there is no guarantee that he/ she will be pleased with it. Bob Seger and the Silver Bullet Band strenuously object to being a number in their song "Feel Like a Number." The subject's boss does not know his name; he is simply another statistic, and he feels like a stranger. But he insists vehemently that he is not a number: He is in fact a man, and wants to shout out his personal identity. In the Counting Crows' album *August and Everything After Self*, the song "Mr. Jones" relates the story of this character and the singer who want to be something other than who they are. In fact, both of them want to be stars, but do not have a clue why or how to accomplish it, imagining that love could have something to do with it. From a different perspective, a person can wonder what one might have become. The Dave Matthews Band raises a series of questions in their number "Dancing Nancies" from *Under the Table and Dreaming*. The subject could have been a parking lot attendant, a millionaire, a person lost in Paris, a little brother, or anyone other than himself. Although he is tired of life and contemplates the possibility of suicide, he resolves to be who he is.

Instead of wondering whether she could be like the subject of the Dave Matthews Band's song, Sarah McLachlan asks to be transformed into a witness in her song "Witness" from *Surfacing*, wanting to be free of doubt and to emerge from the darkness. She asks some perplexing and odd questions about whether being in heaven is like being on earth and the possibility of our changing while we wait. These questions reveal a process of soul searching. When we find our souls will mercy be revealed or will we be blinded by it? McLachlan's lyrics reflect a time of waiting and searching for the self.

Mike and the Mechanics suggest that the self is imperfect in their song "Nobody's Perfect" from their album *The Living Years*. They lament that being an angel is difficult when there is a demonic being within each of us, and we are surrounded by imperfection. Speaking to the alleged angel, he says it must be hard being an angel when no one is perfect. The Psalms (50:2) equate God with the perfection of beauty. It is a standard assumption in the Judeo-Christian-Islamic tradition that only God represents perfection. Nonetheless, it is perfectly permissible for a Christian to pray for perfection (2Cor. 13:9) or to exhort others to strive towards perfection (Heb. 6:1). It is love, however, that binds everything together in perfect harmony (Col. 3:14). A number called "Devil Inside" by the INXS from their album *Kick* creates a picture of internal imperfection because each of us contains a devil within us. Since human nature is evil, there is no necessity for a place like hell because we are living in hell already on earth.

Moving beyond the notion of simply being imperfect, Ethan Hawke's rendition of "I'm Nuthin" for the movie *Reality Bites* tells the story of a subject whose parents abuse drugs and who feels basically worthless. With his dreadful home situation and the death of the American dream, he reflects that he was nothing before his birth, and he is nothing now, a feeling of abject nothingness confirmed by others for him.

Along similar lines of thought is "A Horse with No Name" written by Dewey Bunnell of the band America. The setting of the song is a journey through a desert where the subject becomes aware of himself, and there is no one else to cause him any pain. After nine days, he releases his nameless horse because he has reached the ocean. These lyrics suggest a journey of awareness from not knowing one's identity, in which the horse with no name is a metaphor for the human rider and his lack of identity. Once the rider discovers his true identity, he releases the nameless horse because he has discovered who he is. In the desert, the rider dies to his former nameless self, and he is reborn upon reaching the sea, a metaphor for life, renewal, rebirth, and rediscovery.

Another complex set of lyrics is offered by the Eagles in "Learn to Be Still" from their album *Hell Freezes Over.* The song begins by mentioning a person with "voices ringing in your head." This person has been unable to find simple satisfaction or any kind of happiness. The lyrics change from a singular person to the plural "we" in order to make the point that we are blind followers who are unable to function in solitude. Therefore we wander around aimlessly looking for answers, "and wind up following the wrong gods home." But due to public demand another "messiah" arrives to fill the need for another religious leader until that messianic new-comer meets with a violent end. The many contradictory messages cause confusion. But we do not have to lament the contradictory, chaotic nature of the world, or our own inner turmoil because the answer to our problem lies within us. We need to "learn to be still" and listen to the message from within ourselves. Over the course of religious history, mystics of many of the major religious traditions have also given this kind of spiritual advice.

The Other and the Life of Dialogue

Buber stresses treating the other like a Thou. To encounter another person as a Thou for Buber leads to an important consequence because it involves no longer treating the other as an object among other objects. The Thou cannot be sought; it rather meets one through grace and steps into a direct relationship with you. Both parties to the encounter respond to the meeting with their whole beings. By means of the relational encounter, one becomes a whole being: "As I become I, I say Thou."[3] This encounter is a matter of being chosen as well as choosing. Thus the I-Thou relationship is mutual, direct, present, intense, and ineffable. It is a relation of reciprocity involving meeting or encounter.

A good example of this type of an encounter is provided by Hootie and the Blowfish's recording "Hold My Hand" from their album *Cracked Rear View*. The subject of the song encounters a woman in despair, and he literally offers her a helping hand and promises to take her to a better place. Even though we all experience pain and sorrow during our lives, Bill Withers tells the listener "Lean On Me" and swallow your pride about asking for assistance. During one's life, everyone needs a person to lean on at some point to help carry on and face the problems of life. Wither's song conveys a message of reciprocity between parties. Along the same lines, there is "Bridge Over Troubled Water" by Simon and Garfunkel, who sing about being a good friend, who is defined as someone who will comfort you, relieve pain, and generally help one physically, emotionally and mentally. If the troubled water represents the various kinds of problems that we experience during life, a good friend will serve as a bridge for you. The sentiments of Paul Simon are echoed by the Beatles's song "Help." When the subject of the lyrics was young he was independent and did not need anyone's help, but growing older has brought a lack of certainty and self-assurance. As an older adult, he admits that the other can help when one is feeling insecure and suffering from despair. Finally, Led Zeppelin's song "Friends" mirrors the thought of Buber by stressing that without a friend one is incomplete, although Buber would add that true selfhood is gained by a triadic relationship between the self, other, and God. Although apparently without including God, Marvin Gaye stresses the interpersonal nature of a living relationship in his hit song "How Sweet It Is (To Be Loved By You)." Gaye's message evokes notions of shelter, understanding, and thankfulness. In fact, the other treats him better than he treats himself. Therefore, the other can also be part of a positive change in a person's life.

Born under an auspicious astrological sign, with the albatross and whales for brothers, gazing at the moon, sailing on the sea upon cool bright waters, and all alone, the subject of the Little River Band's song "Cool Change" is someone who laments that his life is so prearranged that he feels trapped in his existence and his apparent idyllic freedom. But his friends have inspired him to change his life, and he looks forward eagerly to a change. In short, his friends have inspired him to find the one thing missing in his life, which is only possible in a dialogical relationship in which people take responsibility for each other.

There are other rock lyrics that emphasize the togetherness and unity among people. Lionel Richie sings in "Sela," from his album *Dancing on the Ceiling*, about the importance of unity and helping each other, a unity of self and other that will be our salvation. "(Lay Down) Candles in the Rain" by Melanie describes the togetherness of young people to the extent of creating a feeling of *communitas* (community). Melanie sings that they are so tightly bound together that they bleed inside of each other's wounds, catch the same diseases, sing the same songs of peace, and raise their candles high in unison. They could together stand dry against the driving rain, although they came together for different reasons. Acknowledging that these reasons do not matter, what is really important is the mutual experience of *communitas*, an unstructured, undifferentiated community that is opposed to structure and normally emerges during a liminal period of existence. *Communitas*, a being with an other, evolves where there is a lack of social structure, and it possesses the potential to break through structure.[4] Melanie's song attempts to capture the spirit and magic quality of spontaneous *communitas*, an impermanent relationship among individuals that is beyond structure.

If the notion of *communitas* tends to stress commonality among individuals, the significance of difference is explored by Jewel in her song "Pieces of You" from the album of the same title. The song uses various paradigms of an ugly girl, a pretty girl, a homosexual, and a Jew to make the case that each of these people is just like you. All examples of difference hide what we have in common with these people. Jewel is trying to get us to see our relationship to these people of difference in I-Thou terms and recognize that they are parts of ourselves. The stress upon difference leads unfortunately to a feud between Americans and Vietnamese refugees in the song "China Grove" by the Doobie Brothers, and emphasizes how much difficulty some people have with accepting others with different appearances and cultural practices.

In comparison to the lyrics in Jewel's song and that by the Doobie Brothers, Steve Winwood stresses unity even further in "The Finer Things" when he refers to how his soul becomes lost in his loved one. Another kind of unity is stressed by the Atlanta Rhythm Section with their song "So Into You" that is contrary to the spirit of Buber's thought because the subject is so united to the other that it dominates his/her being and thinking. Although there is a strong mystical strain in Buber's thought, he does not go as far as the lyrics of Winwood because he wants to emphasis relationship and not necessarily unity in his writings. For Buber, relation is always primary, foundational, and original. Relationship is also characterized by exclusiveness for Buber in the sense that we can only address a single Thou at a time; moreover, relationship possesses immediacy and reciprocity.

Within the context of a fantasy that many people have about encountering a former lover many years after the relationship ends, a man meets a former girl friend in a grocery store on Christmas Eve in "Same Old Lang Syne" by Dan Fogelberg. After the man introduces himself to his surprised, former girl friend, they begin a dialogical encounter that is strained at times and drags along at other times. Unable to find a bar in which to talk, they purchase a six-pack of beer, and they drink a toast to innocence, which represents an acknowledgement of their former youth. As the difficult dialogue unfolds, both of them try to get behind the emptiness of the encounter, but neither of them really possesses the ability to accomplish this. They also drink a toast to time, a period long past and presumably irretrievable. Finally, they run out of things to say, and the song ends with an instrumental echo of "Old Lang Syne," which in this context is a salute to a human relationship from the past, long gone, and devoid of any vitality in the present moment. The dialogue between the former lovers is difficult and dies because they have little in common any more except their shared past and common humanity.

A similar type of dialogical encounter occurs between a taxi driver and his former lover in "Taxi" by Harry Chapin. The driver picks up a final fare in San Francisco on a rainy night. After the usual chatter between a driver and his passenger, the driver thinks he recognizes her face. After some time, the woman glances at the name of the driver on the taxi license, and she smiles in recognition. After sharing hellos and simple pleasantries, the lyrics recount their romantic liaisons in the back of a car and youthful aspirations. Since what they shared is long gone, they did not find much to discuss, and he just dropped her off at her house. After a false promise to meet again, the taxi driver accepts her large tip, and he reflects upon the past and present. He realizes that they both attained their ambitions because she became an actress and acts convincingly at being happily married to a wealthy man, while he became a pilot because he flies high in his taxi when he is stoned on unspecified drugs. We might ask why these dialogical encounters described by Folgelberg and Chapin failed from Buber's perspective?

Buber contends that a lack of response by either party can stop a dialogue, whereas a genuine dialogue takes place when each participant is aware of the being of the other. This involves turning to the other with the intention of establishing a mutual relationship. The life of genuine dialogue takes place between two people, and the meaning of dialogue is located in their interchange. If there is no exchange or sharing, the dialogue dies. This means to be able to see or experience the other side or the perspective of the other in a living mutual relation and realizing the other in the actuality of his/her being.[5] This involves turning toward the other with the wholeness of one's being by assuming responsibility to hear and respond to the other from the depth of one's being, whereas lying is something that will destroy dialogue. Peter Frampton's song appropriately entitled "Lying" points to this type of inauthentic dialogue in which the person who is the object of the lie rightly feels cheated. In contrast, the performances of James Brown represent a continuing dialogue with his audience, a process that continues with him improving his material based on prior responses to his live performances.[6]

A dialogue between the ego and the alter ego occurs in the song "New Religion" by Duran Duran from their album *Rio*. The ego is wandering down a path that takes it to an unknown place. Faces appear and warn the ego about the place and its dangers. Since the alter ego cannot provide a reason for the ego not to proceed, it continues on its way because it is eager to learn. The dialogue focuses on the problem of evil that follows the ego. The alter ego confesses that it gets along with evil, and it tells the ego that it must make a choice between good and evil and stop searching for certain truth because such a seeker is just a fool. But the ego thinks that it has discovered a new religion that is undefined, but it involves free speech. Is this newly discovered religion a dialogical encounter? Unfortunately, no clear answer is provided by the lyrics.

A dialogue about the nature of good and evil takes place between two female friends in the lyrics of "Closer to Fine" by the Indigo Girls. Hoping to find some insight into the distinction between good and evil, a friend helps another to take life less seriously. This relieves her emotional and intellectual burden to some degree, and it provides her with some insight: "Well darkness has a hunger that is insatiable/And lightness has a call that's hard to hear." The seeker confesses to looking all over for answers and being directed in a "crooked line." She even went to the Bible for answers, researched religious revival, and anticipated the second coming. The seeker discovered that there is more than a single answer to the questions about good and evil. The Indigo Girls are arguing for a plurality because there are no simple answers to our questions and problems. It appears safe to conclude that this dialogue is successful, but this is not always the case.

Simon and Garfunkel sing, for example, about a couple engaging in a meaningless dialogue, which reflects their lost relationship and how they have evolved into strangers to each other in "The Dangling Conversation" from their album *Parsley, Sage, Rosemary and Thyme.* Each person is lost to the other in a "dangling" dialogue at the margins of their lives, whereas Buber states that genuine dialogue is an encounter that brings people together. An inauthentic dialogue divides dialogical participants. Another divisive dialogue is evident in Madonna's song "Oh Father" from her album *Something to Remember.* She claims that her father never loved her, and confesses that she has sinned. By rejecting her father, she finally feels positive about herself. Here dialogue is used to divide people, which is an inauthentic mode of dialogue from Buber's point of view.

The Authentic and Inauthentic Self

In some rock lyrics, the self assumes a spiritual nature. Within the context of some people having lost their humanity, others falling by the wayside, and others merely surviving, Billy Joel concludes that life is difficult in his "All About Soul" from his album *River of Dreams*. In order to survive it is not simply enough to be tough because a survivor needs something more. The answer to this problem is soul, which is defined as "faith and a deeper devotion." Joel's notion of soul possesses the power of love and healing; it is joy within sorrow. Kierkegaard agrees with Joel to a certain extent, although the former would insist that the soul is one factor of human nature with the body and spirit representing the third and unifying factor. Kierkegaard argues that the spirit is the human self and represents a relationship that is related to itself, although it is not the relationship itself. The self is rather an aspect of a relationship by which the relationship is related to itself. This means that the self is a relationship because a person is a synthesis of infinite and finite, eternal and temporal, and freedom and necessity. As long as a person remains only a synthesis between two such antitheses, one is not yet a genuine self, which needs a third element to place the two opposites into a relationship. For Kierkegaard, the self is a derived relationship because it is always related to something else and does not establish itself by itself,[7] a position that is also suggested by Joel's lyrics.

In the lyrics to their song "Spirits in the Material World" from their album *Ghost in the Machine*, the Police sing about humans as spirits in a world of matter. The lyrics suggest that humans are trapped in this world, and there are no solutions to its problems. Paul Tillich disagrees with the lyrics because he thinks that it is possible to use his method of correlation in order to utilize philosophical analysis to raise various existential questions that can be answered by Christian theology. Thus, if one analyzes the human situation, it is possible to find answers in the Christian message. The ontological question about human finitude is, for instance, answered by God or Being-itself, which Tillich equates with love. Even though God transcends the basic ontological structure of finite being, the self and world are rooted in God as Being-itself.[8]

Whoever the self is, wherever the self is located, whatever the self eats, or whatever the name of the self, every self must serve either the Devil or God, according to Bob Dylan's lyrics in "Gotta Serve Some-body" from his album *Slow Train Coming*. The lyrics suggest that the self must make a choice: It is a matter of either/or. Dylan implies that the self defines itself by its decisions, which locates Dylan in agreement with Kierkegaard at this point because the existential religious thinker emphasizes the importance of decision in his works.

For Kierkegaard, one gains ethical selfhood through the subject's free decision, a willing of despair as he refers to it.[9] By means of one's free will, the self becomes a concrete existing individual. What is important for Kierkegaard is not what is chosen, but rather the reality of the act of choice itself. By the act of choosing, the self defines itself, accepts responsibility for its choices, and functions as a free agent. The ethical stage of life is characterized by an infinite requirement that results with the bankruptcy of the individual, although it can deepen one's awareness of moral conflict and prepare one for salvation, even if it cannot furnish salvation by itself. Kierkegaard also argues that it is difficult to become an authentic Christian and thoughtless of one to remain a nominal Christian. Since it is originally difficult to become a Christian, Kierkegaard wants to recapture the spirit of that difficulty by transforming one from being a nominal Christian into becoming a real possibility. In order to become a Christian in reality, a person must make a decision and this involves a leap, which Kierkegaard calls the "category of decision."[10]

An authentic self must decide to do at least two things, according to the rock group Sly and the Family Stone in their songs "Stand" and "Everybody is a Star." In the lyrics to the former song, we learn that the self must take a stand for that which one knows is right. Even if you decide to take a stand, you will still continue to be the same self, but you will be demonstrating your ability to bear your cross. Those around you will attempt to dominate you, but you must recognize that you are free just so long as your mind remains liberated. Sly admonishes others to stand for the truth in the first number, whereas the decision to be made is acceptance in the second song. We must accept and love others for what they are and not for what we think that they should be. Since everyone wants to shine like a star, give them a chance by accepting them as you find them without superimposing your own biases and prejudices upon them.

The role of choice plays contradictory parts in two songs by Jackson Browne. In the first, "It Is One" from his album *Looking East*, the subject is caught in a world and birth that he did not choose, and yet it is intimated that one must choose because "life is a battlefield between right and wrong." Moreover, we are torn between these two choices. In the second "The Pretender" from his album *The*

Fuse, Browne sounds exactly like Kierkegaard when he sings, "You are what you choose to be." For Kierkegaard, in the act of choosing a person creates and defines one's authentic self.

According to Martin Buber, authentic selfhood is achieved in relationship with others. We find this evident in the lyrics of "Everyday People" by Sly and the Family Stone and a song with the same title by The Rembrandts. We find Sly's beliefs about prejudice embodied in the lyrics, which focus on a lack of tolerance. His message is for the self and other to live together in a kind of mutual tolerance because behind our differences there is an underlying unity among us, although Sly emphasizes the differences between people. The common bond must ultimately be love. A different emphasis is discerned by The Rembrandts, whose everyday people are standing and uniting to fight for a revolution to make the world better for their children. This scenario is further depicted as a period of change with freedom bells ringing. Both songs stress the common communal nature of the effort to accomplish anything worthwhile. The emphasis on communal unity strikes a common bond with the work of Buber, although it does not resonate with Kierkegaard. Buber argues that a genuine community represents having a relation with a center that he identifies with God and one another,[11]whereas Kierkegaard is suspicious of the kind of impersonal social group that he calls the crowd because the single one can become lost within it, and it destroys the relationship between the self and God. As the power of the crowd grows for Kierkegaard, the individual becomes inessential or accidental. Thus the other becomes an obstacle on the way to God for Kierkegaard, while Buber thinks that the other is the way to God and not an obstacle.

Similar to Kierkegaard and Buber and their requirements for genuine selfhood, rock fans demand authenticity of their stars, which often means someone who not only performs but also composes his/ her own material. A rock critic insightfully observes, "If the rock musician's 'self' is not involved in originating that text she or he performs, rock believes that self is more likely to be corrupted or alienated (and that, in turn, the listener's sense of self may be diminished)."[12] Therefore, we find a situation in which performers sing about authenticity, they seek it, and fans look for it in the lyrics and performances of artists.

From the perspective of Buber, there are also inauthentic ways to strive for full selfhood based on other rock lyrics. An excellent example of inauthentic selfhood is offered by the song "I Am a Rock" by Simon and Garfunkel from their album *Sounds of Silence*. In this song a man imagines that he is like a rock or an island unto himself. This lonely man builds walls around himself to keep other people away because friendship brings pain, which suggests that his life is devoid of love and laughter, but his room is like a womb where he is safe taking comfort with his only companions: his books and poetry. For Buber, such a person is living an inauthentic mode of existence because such a lone person tries not to encounter another person and certainly does not enter into dialogue with anyone.

Another example of an inauthentic mode of selfhood is evident in the lyrics of "Shining Star" by the rock group Earth, Wind and Fire.

The group sings that the self is a shining star regardless of its socio-economic status. Since we are metaphorically off-spring of the sun, we must realize that we must stand alone. Thus, we must depend on ourselves to be what we can truly become. The lyrics do not mention the other in this process of self-realization and does not refer to God or some higher power, although the sun could be interpreted to function in this way as the father of all. Just as an individual star can form a constellation in union with other stars, human selves can form communities of mutually supporting others.

An ambivalent and strained relationship between the self and others is expressed by Melissa Etheridge in "Talking to My Angel" from her album *Yes I Am*. The relationship is characterized by a lack of tolerance and acceptance by the others, but the self is isolated and lonely because it is severed from the community. Even though this is an inauthentic mode of selfhood from Buber's perspective, the refusal by the self not to be engulfed by the crowd is closer to an authentic selfhood espoused by Kierkegaard. If the angel in the lyrics, who speaks to the singer and confirms her choice, is a representative of God, Etheridge's song shares some features with Kierkegaard with its emphasis on the dangers of the crowd, although Buber perceives the crowd differently than Kierkegaard and his emphasis on the single one.

Rejection of the other is an inauthentic way of being for Buber. A good example of rejection is represented by the lyrics of "Get Off of My Cloud" by the Rolling Stones. The subject imagines that he is living on a cloud by himself, and he wants no company. He gets angry with anyone who disturbs the solitary nature of his domain. For him, two is a crowd, although Buber thinks that this is an inauthentic mode of existence because real living involves meeting other people.

If genuine selfhood is achieved in a dialogical encounter for Buber, the non-communicative person is living an inauthentic mode of existence. We have already called attention to such individuals. The person who lies would also fall into an inauthentic mode of selfhood from Buber's perspective. The song "Better Man" by Pearl Jam from their album *Vitalogy* relates the tale of a female lover who lies by telling her partner that she is in love with him.

Another mode of encountering the other in an inauthentic way is to turn the other into an object to be used by the self. A cowboy and woman meet on a Saturday afternoon in a crude saloon in the lyrics of "Cowboy Romance" by Natalie Merchant from her album *Tigerlily*. The cowboy uses the women sexually and moves on when he grows sober. In the song "All I Wanna Do Is Make Love to You" by the rock group Heart from their album *Brigade*, a woman gives a male stranger a ride in her car on a rainy night. Without asking him for his name, she sexually propositions him. Finding a hotel, they make love all night. But before he awakes in the morning, she leaves a note that states "I am the flower you are the seed." Her note warns him not to attempt to find her, but to be content with living in her memory. Of course, she also may have used him as a sperm bank in order to get pregnant, which suggests that she rejects him after she meets her needs for sexual gratification or motherhood. A similar scenario unfolds in the very popular lyrics of "Night Moves" by Bob Seger and

The Silver Bullet Band. Although they are not truly in love, two young people use each other to satisfy their sexual drives. They are restless and bored, and they are more interested in making the front pages of the fictitious drive-in-movie newspaper. The male subject truthfully admits that he used her and she used him, and that neither one of them really cared because they were getting what they wanted out of the mutually exploitive relationship. As autumn arrives, the male subject remembers his relationship in a melancholy way.

In a similar type of song, John Mellencamp sings about "Jack and Diane" in his album *American Fool*. Jack is a teenager with an attitude, who aspires to imitate the rebel, movie star James Dean. The two teenagers use each other for mutual sexual gratification much like the subjects of Seger's song. Jack does not want to become an adult because he would rather remain an irresponsible teenager, having casual sex with his girlfriend in the rear seat of his car. Jack does not want to lose the thrill of living. And he challenges conservative Christians: "Let the Bible belt come and save my soul." With Jack's rebellious attitude, there is no way that anyone will be able to save him. Jack and Diane's relationship is just as inauthentic from Buber's perspective as the subjects of Seger's tune because the participants turn each other into objects and mutually exploit each other.

Along similar lines to those of the lyrics of Mellencamp and Seger, Meat Loaf combines sexual exploitation with dialogue in a humorous way in "Paradise By the Dashboard Light" from his album *Bat Out of Hell*. The young man in the song parks his car by a deserted lake with his date. He and his date grow sexually aroused, and he anticipates a moment of paradise in the front seat of his car when they copulate. The lyrics of the song are disrupted by a baseball radio broadcast given by Phil Rizzuto, a hall of fame New York Yankee shortstop and former broadcaster. Rizzuto describes a series of events in a game that humorously culminates with a suicide squeeze play that function as a parallel the sexual scenario taking place in the front seat of a car between two teenagers. The young girl calls a stop to the sexual advances of her partner because she demands to know that he will love her eternally. And she wants this confession of enduring love at that very moment before their amorous encounter goes any further. The young man wants to give her an answer in the morning, but she persists in her demands of fidelity. As the music reaches a higher pitch to express the desperation of the young man's dilemma, he becomes crazed and swears his unending love for his date to God and on his mother's grave as he surrenders to his hormones. After swearing that he would love her until the end of time, and presumably fulfilling his desires, he does not want to break his promise or vow. Therefore, he begins to pray for the quick arrival of the end of time because he cannot endure another minute with her. Again, this is a case of turning the other into an object for one's own use and satisfaction. From Buber's perspective, this represents and I-It relationship in which one person turns the other person into an object, which is not characterized by genuine personhood, and is thus not an I-Thou type of relationship.

It is also possible to witness the I-It relationship in Tina Turner's song "Private Dancer" in which the female dancer performs for money, treats all the gazing men impersonally, and they turn her into an object of their lust. Buber's notion of the I-It relationship lacks mutuality and is entirely subjective. It is typical of subject-object relationships, and it uses some form of utilization, domination or control. Within the context of this type of inauthentic relationship, one is not really a person because one is objectified and turned into a thing. Moreover, such a relationship is fragmented and does not represent a unity.

Although numerous rock lyrics depict impersonal and exploitive relationships, Nicholas Lash, a Protestant theologian influenced by Buber's thought, thinks that being in relation makes all the difference in the world. He writes, "It may even change the world (and, in that sense, come to make particular differences) because people in relation, in acknowledged mutual dependence, may find that they are newly enabled to cope, with fresh energy and clear-sightedness, with all the particular problems that engage their attention and responsibility."[13]

As relational beings, we are sometimes encouraged to sing with others. The apostle Paul enjoins the members of the Christian community (Ephesians 5:18-21) to sing with all their hearts to God. Being a singing self is an obvious realization of an identity. Commenting on the passages from Ephesians, the Protestant theologian David Ford writes, "Singing is seen as a desirable form of face to face address between members of the community and between singers and God."[14] It is not uncommon for the rock performer to face his/her audience and to invite them to join him/her in song. In a sense the singer and audience are addressing each other in song, and the members of the audience are addressing each other in song. In an ideal situation, Ford writes, "Singing together embodies joint responsibility in which each singer waits on the others, is attentive with the intention of serving the common harmony."[15]

Dialogue and the Eternal Thou

It is difficult to find the primary subjects in the lyrics of rock 'n' roll music carrying on a dialogue with God, although there are references to God and other supernatural beings in the lyrics that will become more evident in a later chapter on the topic. In "Have Thine Own Way Lord," John Fogerty depicts God as the potter and the devotee as the clay to be molded. The devotee asks God to mold him according to His Will. Within the context of the dialogue between the eternal Thou and the human self, the I asks God to examine and test him as well as to touch and heal him. In the final stanza of the song, the self asks for help in order to pray. In other words, the self asks for assistance to improve the dialogue between the self and the eternal Thou.

According to the lyrics of Neil Diamond's song entitled "Be," if the Hebrew Bible defines God as "I am who I am," (Gen 3:14) a person can look to the sky and find God, or a person may find God on some shore. In fact, the sky, earth, and human beings are all sacred. In addition, singing, dancing, and rejoicing are all forms of communication, although singing appears to be the primary mode of dialogue with the eternal Thou. The uttered song seeks that which is silent and forms the foundation for utterance. We should all rejoice because our soul, God, earth, sun, and sky are all sacred.

According to "Have a Talk with God" by Stevie Wonder from his album *Songs in the Key of Life*, there are people who become overwhelmed by their problems and want to give up on life. When your life becomes difficult you should discuss your problem with God, who lives within each of us, even though we tend to neglect God. But we are never alone because God is omnipresent, and we can thus communicate with him at any time. The composition of these lyrics by Wonder is a lucid manifestation of the importance of dialogues with the eternal Thou.

According to other rock lyrics, a dialogue with God is either one-sided or impossible. In their recording of "Nothing" from their album *Music for the Masses*, Depeche Mode mentions waiting and anticipating a message from God, but nothing happens because God is silent. The self initiates a dialogue through prayer, but there is no response from the eternal Thou. These lyrics are reminiscent of Samuel Beckett's play *Waiting for Godot* because the main characters in this play become bored endlessly waiting and contemplate suicide to alleviate their boredom.

On their album *Synchronicity*, The Police perform a song entitled "Oh My God" that expresses the loneliness of the self, but there is no response from God because God is very distant. In fact, God is so distant from humans that it is not possible for God to hear a petition for help. This is the *deus otiosus* of religion, which is a type of God found in various religious traditions in which the deity is very active during the period of creation and then disappears to some remote area to play a minor role in the ritual cult and everyday lives of the people. Human beings often forget this withdrawn deity, and its place is often taken by various divinities closer to human beings.[16] The song "All Babies" by Sinead O'Connor from her album *Universal Mother* suggests this type of scenario by presenting an image of babies leaving the universe being carried by angels or using the stars as ladders of ascent. The babies are crying because no one recalls the name of God, which suggests that this androgynous deity is remote and only tangentially active in the universe. The withdrawn God's remoteness and non-actuality are equivalent to its death, although this situation can inaugurate a new or true religion because the vacuum created by God's withdrawal is filled by other divine beings.[17]

It is often the case in the history of religions that these remote and silent gods pre-date the advent of the death of God. James Taylor examines this theme in his album *Hourglass* specifically in his song entitled "Up from Your Life." Taylor composes verses that suggest that it is not much sense praying because God is not at home, which suggests that God is not merely absent but that He is also dead. Therefore, we are on our own with no transcendent Being to rely upon, because we live on the earth, which is our reality. If there is nothing beyond this sphere of the earth, there is no God, no paradise, and no rebirth to another mode of existence. By becoming aware of our life, we will recognize the river, which represents unceasing change, flowing beneath our feet. Such awareness can help people in the midst of their sadness and the madness that surrounds them. By ceasing to dream and becoming aware of your existence, there is a suggestion from Taylor that we must rely upon our own power, endurance, and ability.

The position that God is dead is shared by the postmodern a/theologian Mark C. Taylor, who argues that humanistic atheists have murdered God and deified man. The basic problem with modern humanistic atheism is that it represents an incomplete and inadequate position. We are now in the postmodern period, which is a time between times that manifests a sense of irrevocable loss and incurable fault. Within this liminal period of time, we are located in a place that is no place. If we are now in a liminal time and space, this is a situation that calls for liminal thinking by marginal thinkers in order to make sense of the equation that God is death and not simply dead.[18] Modern western theology cannot handle the radical implications of the death of God because it involves some dangerous consequences, since the notions of God, self, history and book (revealed scripture) are interconnected and fall together. This implies that the death of God represents the disappearance of the self, the end of history, and the closure of the book. These implications suggest the end of theology and the beginning of a wandering divine discourse that Taylor calls erring, a wandering that leads one astray and toward carnival. From the viewpoint of the Catholic theologian David Tracy, theologians who advocate the death of God are struggling for human liberation that is independent of reliance upon God. Thus a wholly transcendent God must die necessarily in order for humans to become liberated.[19]

Needless to say, with the distant, silent, or dead God, there is no possibility for dialogue. For genuine dialogue to occur within the world, there must be two participants. Otherwise we have a monologue, although this does not necessarily suggest that silence is a dead-end. Simon and Garfunkel explore the depths of silence in their song "The Sounds of Silence." For its composer, Paul Simon, silence is inexhaustible and deep, can hold a vision, can contain light, can give us the silence of those "talking without speaking," and it absorbs words as prophetic utterances are expressed by the sounds of silence. There is something mysterious and holy about silence. In fact, mystics from different religious traditions consider silence to represent a profound message.

There is a point in the mystical experience when only silence suffices to indicate what is meant because the experience itself is so overwhelming for the individual that ordinary words are inadequate to convey the experience. By avoiding language and residing in and relying on silence, the mystic avoids objectifying his/her experience. By maintaining silence, the mystic expresses both the ineffability of his /her experience and expresses the mystic's contention that his/her experience cannot be communicated.

If we look back in Christian history, it is possible to find St. Augustine writing in his work *On Christian Doctrine* (1.6) that silence is an attempt to grasp the experience of the presence of God. Among the Cistercian monks later in Christian history, the insistence "on exterior silence fosters the interior quiet necessary for the coming of the Word into the soul . . ."[20] And during the early medieval period of

Christian history, the demand by monastic communities for solitude and separation from the world also necessarily entailed silence. External separation from the world and silence were associated with disconnecting oneself from sins of the flesh and tongue. Silence enabled a monk to quell worldly distractions, to be attentive to God, and to be part of the goal insofar as the spiritual experience required both rest and quiet in God.[21]

There also is a direct connection between silence and power. From Foucault's perspective, silence does not operate alone because it shifts and moves. As a non-static entity, silence functions as a basic mechanism of power that is built into the institutional structures of Christianity. Over the centuries of its existence, Christianity used silence to manipulate and control others. From within the context of Roman Catholic Christianity, the practice of confession was used to control others, whereas those that remained silent were free. This scenario suggests that the power of silence can be used to control others or set them free depending on the social context and interconnection of participants.

Concluding Remarks

Overall, the rock lyrics examined in this chapter demonstrate composers struggling with the issues of human identity, their relationship to others, and often their relationship to God. A cry for individual recognition, a search for personal identity, wearing of public masks, and soul searching are just some of the items discussed in the preceding paragraphs. The importance of interpersonal relationship, community, dialogue, decisions, rejection, objectification of the other, and forms of communication were related issues. We called attention to the fact that many of these lyrics indicate that humans are beings grappling with what it means to be a person, what are the implications for existing with others, what it means to be a social being, and what it means to have a God, or what it means not to be able to encounter God.

As human beings, we play varied roles (e.g., mother, sister, widow, employer, or fireman). We live in a culture with a shared language, common values, and accepted ideologies. We acquire learning and skills to help ourselves earn a living, support and nurture a family, and contribute to a community. We make decisions that shape our present and future lives. We make good choices and ill-considered ones. We succeed and fail. We agree and disagree. We rejoice and complain. We enter into dialogue with others or decide to remain silent and isolated. We seek and find our genuine identities, or we get lost in the process. We are instinctual gorillas and simultaneously philosophical and religious thinkers pondering meaningful questions. We are the complex wonder called humanity. And the lyrics of this chapter reflect some of the flux and complexity that shape a human being and the kinds of questions that concern humans.

We share in common our basic humanity, embodied nature, and being, but we are all different and unique in our own ways. Our differences should not, however, totally obscure what we share in common. The Christian theologian Gordon D. Kaufman expresses the commonality in the following way: "All human existence—that is, the existence of every individual woman and man, every community and society—is constituted fundamentally by this interlocked biology and history, and it is in terms of this bio-historical process that humans must today be conceived."[22] It is not necessary to accept Kaufman as the final authority on this unity within a pluralistic situation. As we have implied throughout this chapter, it is possible to view the unity within a frame-work of a life of dialogue like that expressed in the thought of Buber or another thinker.

The rock performer enables us to imagine an extension of Buber's life of dialogue to include singing, for which there is biblical precedence. The singer or singers communicate with the audience, the audience reciprocates by communicating with the performers, and the members of the audience communicate with each other. Singing to someone, singing with someone, and singing together mutually re-enforce and enhance the participants. The singing contributes to the creation of a community however brief its duration. It encourages and enables singer and audience to assert their identity by uttering the words to some song as if it were a sacred *mantra* (repeated sacred formula). It enables everyone to assert their personal identity and their being meaningfully in relationship with each other despite the fact that one paid a price for admission to the concert. The dialogical situation created by singing possesses the power for everyone to affirm themselves and others. It is in this sense that a rock concert begins to take on the aura of a religious meeting. As we will notice in the final chapter, a performer like Bruce Springsteen can turn a concert into a religious revival meeting.

Endnotes

---

[1] Søren Kierkegaard, *Repetition*, ed. and trans. Howard V. Hong and Edna H. Hong (Princeton: Princeton University Press, 1983), p. 200.

[2] Ibid.

[3] Buber, *I-Thou*, p. 25.

[4] Victor Turner, *The Ritual Process*, p. 126.

[5] Martin Buber, *Between Man and Man*, trans. Ronald Gregor Smith (New York: Macmillan, 1965), p. 20.

[6] Russell A. Potter, "Soul into Hip-hop," in *The Cambridge Companion to Pop and Rock*, ed. Simon Frith, Will Straw, and John Street (Cambridge: Cambridge University Press, 2001), p. 145.

[7] Kierkegaard, *Sickness Unto Death*, p. 13.

[8] Tillich, *Systematic Theology*, I: 271.

[9] Søren Kierkegaard, *Either/Or*, 2 vols., vol. 1 trans. by David F. Swenson and Lillian Marvin Swenson, vol. 2 trans. by Walter Lowrie (Princeton: Princeton University Press, 1944), 2: 212ff.

[10] Idem, *Concluding Unscientific Postscript*, p. 91.

[11] Buber, *I-Thou*, p. 94.

[12] Keir Keightley, "Reconsidering Rock," in *The Cambridge Companion to Pop and Rock*, eds. Simon Frith, Will Straw, and John Street (Cambridge: Cambridge University Press, 2001), p. 134.

[13] Nicholas Lash, *Easter In Ordinary: Reflections on Human Experience and the Knowledge of God* (Charlottesville, VA: University Press of Virginia, 1988), p. 230.

[14] David F. Ford, *Self and Salvation: Being Transformed* (Cambridge: Cambridge University Press, 1999), p. 110.

[15] Ibid., p. 122.

[16] Mircea Eliade, *Myth and Reality*, trans. Willard R. Trask (New York: Harper & Row, 1963), p. 98.

[17] Ibid., p. 95.

[18] Mark C. Taylor, *Erring: A Postmodern A/Theology* (Chicago: University of Chicago Press, 1984), p. 23.

[19] David Tracy, *Blessed Rage for Order: The New Pluralism in Theology* (New York: Seabury Press, 1975; reprint Chicago: University of Chicago Press, 1996), p. 31.

[20] Bernard McGinn, *The Growth of Mysticism: Gregory the Great through the 12th Century* (New York: Crossroad Publishing Company, 1994), p. 279.

[21] Ibid., p. 131.
[22] Gordon D. Kaufman, *God—Mystery—Diversity: Christian Theology in a Pluralistic World* (Minneapolis: Fortress Press, 1996), p. 77.

Chapter 4
Faith and Love

In the book Genesis of the Hebrew Bible, Yahweh informs Abraham that a son will be born to his barren wife Sarah. The miraculous son named Issac becomes a beloved child of his aged parents (21:1-2). At one point in the story, Yahweh asks Abraham to sacrifice his son as a burnt offering. Abraham's faith in God compels him to follow the command to sacrifice his beloved son, but God intervenes at the last moment to spare the life of the son and allows Abraham to substitute a lamb. This narrative captured the religious imagination of Søren Kierkegaard during the nineteenth century, and it inspired the Danish religious thinker to compose his Christian classical text *Fear and Trembling*. Kierkegaard argues that the commandment of God to Abraham to sacrifice Issac came to the old patriarch as something absolutely particular in sharp contrast to the universal injunction not to kill. Revolting against his ethical belief not to kill, Abraham follows God's ethical demand; he "does it for God's sake because God demands this proof of his faith; he does it for his own sake so that he can prove it."[1] Kierkegaard draws a connection between Abraham's faith and Christian faith in order to argue that it is representative of the latter because of its opaque and irrational character, and such a faith requires a leap of despair. The object of faith is the absurd, the paradoxical and incomprehensible, which is a technical expression for the conviction that with God all things are possible. Faith is not the only thing that is paradoxical for Kierkegaard, because love is also paradoxical: "Man lives undisturbed a self-centered life, until there awakens within him the paradox of self-love, in the form of love for another, the object of his longing."[2] Self-love also serves as the ground of all love for Kierkegaard.

Love is a subject that has received more attention from rock artists than any other topic, while the topic of faith has received much less attention. When rock composers write about love they usually refer to what the ancient Greeks meant by *eros*, an erotic and passion type of love. Although there are lyrics devoted to what the Greeks called *philia* or friendship, it is extremely rare to find lyrics that feature the highest type of love or *agape*, because this last type of love is pure, devoid of *eros*, altruistic, and selfless. This chapter will turn to a discussion of the nature of love in selected rock 'n' roll lyrics after a consideration of faith. Lyrics mentioning faith can be divided into three types: lost faith, misdirected faith, and traditional Christian faith. With respect to love, this chapter will review a variety of themes that appear in rock lyrics, like its violent nature, its ability to transform, its uncontrollable nature, its ability to restore power, its imperative and legalistic connotations, and its power.

River of Faith

Billy Joel refers to faith in two songs in his album *River of Dreams*. In his song "Shades of Grey," Joel mentions that the subject is older and wiser. A result of this mature growth and evolving wisdom is that choices are not as obvious as that between black and white. Since his choices possess no certainty for him, he is losing his faith. He sees shades of grey now that he is more mature in comparison to the certainty of his youth. During the present time, there is no one predominant point of view for which to kill and die. Since there are many points of view, the truth is not very clear and more difficult to discern. Having grown older, he relies now on his reason to make sense of things, and he asks to be saved from righteous, arrogant people. This summary of the major ideas expressed in the lyrics indicates that Joel is opposed to those who think that they know for certain the nature of truth. Joel perceives the self-righteous as immature and intellectually arrested in their development. There is a clear message to move from standing on the uncertainty of faith to relying on reason, which embodies an Enlightenment philosophical perspective. In Joel's song "Blonde Over Blue," he laments that no one prays anymore due to a lack of faith and nothing in which to believe, which means that a person must rely on good luck alone. These types of lyrics take an even stronger anti-faith position because they ignore the historical fact that during the decades of the 1980s and 90s there has been a major religious revival occurring in the United States. Nonetheless, Joel's sentiments reflect an intellectually postmodern perspective that is shared by many people.

To believe in nothing at all represents a danger from Danish thinker Kierkegaard's perspective because it enables evil to secure a foundation: "To believe nothing at all is the beginning of being evil, because it shows that one has no good in oneself, since belief is the good in a person that does not come with much knowledge, nor is it necessarily lacking because the knowledge is meager."[3] In contrast to the person who believes nothing, the person who "truly loves believes all things—and yet is never deceived."[4] Kierkegaard emphasizes the necessity for an individual to take a leap of faith, which also represents the title of a song by Bruce Springsteen on his album *Lucky Town*, who sings that it takes faith to survive in life. Springsteen imagines being Moses at the parting of the Red Sea, which he then erotically associates with a romantic encounter, before imaging himself as the son of Jesus.

In contrast to Joel's compositions, there is more of a struggle over faith in the lyrics of "I Believe" by Tears for Fears from their album *Songs from the Big Chair*. The subject of the song wants to believe, but he cannot because it is too late historically for anyone to believe due to all the suffering and pain in the world. The lyrics suggest that the subject turns to a faith in astrology because he is at least certain of his astrological sign. The duo of Tears for Fears answer Joel's assertion that there is nothing in which to have faith by asserting that there are at least the stars to believe, although they leave unanswered the role of the stars in the suffering and pain within the world. For many Christian thinkers, astrology represents an ancient form of paganism.

During the course of history, Europeans and members of other cultures have manifested obsessive concern with personal horoscopes and astrological predictions, features that can still be discovered in local and national newspapers and now on the Internet. Referring to the historical period 330-360 C.E., the historian W. H. C. Frend observes that all levels of society demonstrated a fear of demonic beings, a fascination with magic, divination, and sorcery, and they accepted astrology as a science. Frend writes, "Centuries were to elapse before the unknown, dominated by unseen and hostile powers, would yield to the sign of the cross."[5] During the fifth century of Christian history, Augustine used terms like "lying divinations," "empty and ridiculous follies," and "impious absurdities" to refer to astrologers and their craft, although he admits to being originally attracted to it.[6] The same kind of criticism is evident in one of his letters, where Augustine refers to the "absurdities of astrologers."[7] Augustine's opinion tended to dominate the attitude of the church, even though ordinary people continued to find comfort in astrology.

Instead of astrology, lost faith is the subject of "Sweet Rosalyn" by Sheryl Crow. Rosalyn does not believe in anything; she will tell you, however, that there are a multitude of things in which to believe. Since Rosalyn cannot give herself to love, the lyrics suggest that this is why she cannot believe in anything. Due to her loneliness, she takes a number off a bathroom wall and calls to talk to a priest named Father Tim, who tells her that her life is in trouble. Does this mean that Crow intends to imply that a life without faith is empty? Does faith give us a reason for living? Does it help us live a richer and more rewarding life? Is faith a cure for the problems in our life? Crow's lyrics make some suggestions about answers to these questions, but she does not provide definitive answers. We are left to ponder Rosalyn's situation and her struggle to find something in which to have faith.

An interesting example of lost faith is found in "Show me the Way" by Styx. After a lifetime of praying for the existence of a heaven, the young man is now uncertain that it even existed. He is confused and feels empty inside. Having lost his faith, he asks for help and directions to find the right path, and asks for purification and the washing away of his illusions. He falls asleep and dreams of peace but he awakens to dire news. While waiting for a sign that will take away his confusion, he asks if he should believe if he sees a light. Basically, he is asking how he can be certain when a sign is eventually revealed to him. Finally, he asks for both strength and courage to believe some day. The struggling figure in the lyrics represents everyone searching for answers to various kinds of religious questions and issues related to their faith.

From his album *Mercury Falling*, Sting attempts to provide some answers to questions raised by the lyrics of the previous number by Styx with his song "Let Your Soul Be Your Pilot." As strongly suggested by the title of the song, Sting's basic message is to let your soul be your guide when your life is going badly. When you have doubts and lack of information, when medicine fails to heal you, and when you are uncomfortable, let your soul be your guide. Sting does not give listeners any idea how this might be practically done. Again, Sting is vague in another of his compositions entitled "Secret Journey" performed by The Police on their album *Ghost in the Machine.* While on a secret journey, a man meets a holy man who gives advice to counter the pain of the world that includes seeing a light within darkness that he will be able to comprehend and making a secret journey to discover a missing love. Moreover, once you heed the wisdom of the holy man and complete the journey, you will become a holy man yourself.

From a conservative religious perspective, an example of misdirected faith is evident in Lionel Richie's song "Say You, Say Me" from his album *Dancing on the Ceiling* in which he advocates believing in oneself. From one perspective, it is important to have confidence in oneself and one's abilities, which is most likely the point that he is attempting to make. A conservative theologian might find something potentially sinister in this because there is the danger of directing one's faith toward a finite creature and deifying that person. This kind of scenario is a failure because it does not render to God what is due to God from a human being, an inferior, dependent, and helpless creature in comparison to God.

A negative view of those associated with faith is offered by Roger Waters of Pink Floyd in a solo album, *When the Wind Blows*. Waters' song called "Towers of Faith" examines the theme of people in positions of religious leadership. He asserts that those in their "towers of faith," a metaphor for detached and isolated religious leaders, are lonely and confined. By each leader claiming, for instance, the land of Israel, these blind leaders create conflicts over the land. The major loser in such conflicts is Mother Nature. During his life and ministry, Jesus criticizes such blind religious leaders (Mt. 15:14; 23:17; 23:26).

Paul Simon offers another negative view of faith in his song "Proof" from his album *The Rhythm of the Saints*. Simon equates faith with an island in the setting sun. What everyone wants, however, is proof that yields certainty. Such lyrics suggest that the reign of faith is past and people want something more substantial and certain. In his work the *Pensées* published posthumously from his notes, the French religious thinker Blaise Pascal (1623-62) offers a wager of faith in response to those who espouse attitudes like those presented by Simon's lyrics. Pascal states that we can wager for or against the existence of God. If one decides to remain indifferent, this results in choosing against God. When making this wager, one must consider where one's interests are best served. It is reasonable to wager for God because if one wins, one wins everything; and if one loses, one loses nothing. Not to wager means that one loses anyway. What is at stake for a person is small in comparison to what one might win. By risking what is certain with what is uncertain, and keeping in mind that there is nothing absolutely certain in life, to wager is to one's advantage. Consequently, if one wagers for God, faith becomes a real possibility, and one could win everything including eternal happiness. For Pascal, this is the sole certainty within a context of prevailing uncertainty.

In response to the previous rock artists and others who seek certainty, express negative attitudes towards faith, and misdirect it, Sarah McLachlan responds to them in her song "Trust" from her album *Touch*. She writes about searching, finding ignorance in the myths of other people, never questioning answers given to her in the past, losing faith, and the danger of trusting others. As an outsider to another faith, it is easy to find fault with their myths. Within our own faith, we tend not to question its religious tenets, even if they seem contrary to reason. Moreover, to put your faith in human beings is a very precarious decision connected to serious dangers. The discovery of faith must be our own personal pilgrimage and not blind adherence to a received religious tradition.

In response to some of the lyrics mentioned thus far, a Protestant theologian such as Paul Tillich unequivocally asserts, "Faith is the state of being grasped by the power of being itself."[8] Being grasped by the power of faith enables one to affirm oneself, to be assured that one is in turn affirmed by the power of being-itself, which Tillich ultimately equates with God, and to directly experience the power of being. In addition to faith representing a state of being grasped by the power of being, it is a means to courage, which is related to self-affirmation in spite of the threat of non-being.

Journey of Faith

When Jesus cures some people of aliments he responds at times that it is their faith that made them whole and well (Mt. 9:22; Mk. 5:34; 10:52). And the apostle Paul urges his listeners to walk in the path of faith (2 Cor. 5:7). Trying to walk in the path of faith is the subject of "I Still Haven't Found What I'm Looking For" by U2 from their album *The Joshua Tree*. The subject is a pilgrim traveling through fields, climbing mountains, and scaling walls, but he still cannot find that for which he is searching. He confesses to holding the hand of the Devil and speaking with angels without any hope of discovering the object of his search. He admits to faith in the "kingdom come," believes in Jesus as a liberator, and the person who carried the cross and the singer's shame, although in the New Testament it is possible to believe all things and yet not feel ashamed (Phil. 1:20; Rom. 5:4). Even though he believes the Christian message, he is still not able to find what he seeks. It is suggested by the lyrics that faith is insufficient because a subject might be searching for a certainty that cannot be given by faith. From Kierkegaard's perspective, faith can never be certain because its object is the Absolute Paradox (God-Man), and it is itself paradoxical.[9]

Besides the journey of faith depicted by U2, Paul Simon's song "Loves Me Like a Rock" from his album *There Goes Rhymin' Simon* testifies to the importance of faith. The Devil would call the name of the subject of the song when he was a boy, but the boy replied that he could not be fooled because he is religious, and his mother loves him, enabling him to experience love and faith.

The theme of a religious journey is common in other lyrics like the number "River of Dreams" by Billy Joel from the album of the same title. The subject of the song goes to sleep, waking to a deep, wide river and looking for something sacred that he lost. If he can get to the other side, he can find that for which he is looking. He keeps trying to cross to the other shore, but the river is too wide. He also dreams about a "valley of fear" and a "jungle of doubt," and he fears that something has been stolen from his soul. He possesses a vague notion about the identity of that for which he is searching. The subject confesses that he has not been a religious person all his life, and is uncertain about what occurs after death. But he acknowledges being baptized by fire and wading into the river that goes to "the promised land." The subject concludes that we begin our individual journeys in a particular stream, but we are all united eventually in the ocean. Some of the themes evoked by Joel's lyrics can be found in the Christian religious tradition. Among Christian mystics, the ocean is often a metaphor for union with God. At the feast of Pentecost, the Holy Spirit descends as tongues of fire, according to Acts, upon the grieving community and baptizes early followers of Jesus with fire, which represents the symbolic beginning of the church. In the Gospel of John (14.16), Jesus prophesizes 'the Spirit of truth" that is identified with the Holy Spirit.

A song that was so popular that two versions—an original uptempo and a slower tempo—were recorded is Jon Bon Jovi's "Keep the Faith." The song begins much like a prayer by asking forgiveness of his "Father." Although this could refer to God, it is probably the biological father of the subject. The subject wants to share a message with others based on his personal experience. He says that love is difficult to maintain when there is no object of one's love. Thus, everyone needs someone to love. Do not suffer from your anger like the subject and transform your love into hate. It is important to keep the faith with respect to this message. Bon Jovi's lyrics combine love and faith into a unity.

The unity of love and faith as expressed by Bon Jovi is evident in the theology of Karl Barth, a Swiss theologian, who argues that love and faith are inseparable because they are different aspects of a single event. Faith is one's response to God's justifying work, and love is a self-giving that represents one's response to the direction given by God.[10] Moreover, Barth insists that love can only flourish within the context of community.

Members of a community are the objectives of a minister in a song entitled "Sacred" by Depeche Mode in their album *Music for the Masses*. The subject of the song is a missionary whose duty is to walk, talk, and write about the holy. He confesses to being an ardent believer. Thus there is no room for doubt about his religiosity, and he is confident that he can convincingly sell the sacred story to others. He views his duty as spreading the word and faith. The lyrics depict the subject as a person of blind faith and missionary fervor. The type of person depicted by Depeche Mode is problematic for a theologian such as Paul Tillich because faith can never be absolutely certain. There is always an element of doubt within it. But doubt and even meaninglessness can be overcome by a faith "which creates the courage to take them into itself . . ."[11] Doubt is not the only problem associated with faith because sometimes faith can be indiscriminate.

A good example of indiscriminate faith is evident with the subject of the tune "Seeing Is Believing" by Mike and the Mechanics from their album *The Living Years*, who admits to believing in almost everything. He acknowledges believing in Jesus, the Mujahedin, Daniel Ortega, and magic. As he looks forward to the future, he is frightened about the prospects. Others may think that it is foolish to believe, but he possesses faith in love and the "power of the soul." The subject begins the song by stating that he believes in Jesus and ends with saying that he believes in love, which ties together the entire composition. It is no accident that Jesus begins the song and love ends it because Jesus is love according to 1 John (4.16).

Faith is associated with a miracle by Natalie Merchant in "Wonder" from her album *Tigerlily.* The lyrics tell about a medical miracle that doctors from near and far cannot believe or explain a child's totally unexpected and inexplicable recovery. Newspapers ask intimate questions and attempt to steal the glory of the story, but they come to agree with the doctors that the child is a wonder of God's creation. The child believes that fate was kind to her and that she will be gifted with such attributes as love, patience, and faith that will enable her to make her way in the world. Even though the lyrics do not make the specific connection between God's providence and personal faith, this association seems to be implied by the artist.

If we take into consideration that his critics have identified him with the Devil, another type of miracle is evident in a song on a solo album entitled *Goddess in the Doorway* by Mick Jagger. In the tune "Joy," Jagger teams with Bono of U2 to celebrate being saved by the grace of God. The duo depicts a subject driving across the desert and looking for the Buddha when he encounters Jesus Christ. Jesus smiles, shrugs his shoulders, lights a cigarette, and says to jump for joy. The subject confesses that his soul is lost in the earth where he had thrown it, and his hands are bleeding from digging it up. He relates that he looks upward toward heaven and discovers a light on his face, and he admits "I never . . . thought I'd find a state of grace."

A Friendly Kind of Love

According to the Gospel of John, Jesus calls for a public love within the community, and he encourages loving a friend (15:12-13). The way that Jesus proceeded to call his disciples to his ministry suggests that many of them were friends for some time (Lk. 34.38-39), and their friendship involved a shared experience. With possibly Jesus as a model, some rock artists imagine a friendship with others "that overcomes dishonesty, is a way to come to know ourselves, and know whom it is we present to God."[12] It is possible to witness this type of love and its implications in numerous rock lyrics.

With recordings like "You've Got a Friend" written by Carole King and performed by James Taylor and "Bridge Over Troubled Water" by Simon and Garfunkel, there is no shortage of songs about *philia*, love of a friend, although the overwhelming type of love encountered in rock lyrics is *eros* (erotic or passionate love). Within the context of friendship, the friends manifest equal regard for each other, even though it fluctuates over the course of the relationship depending on such things as mutual fondness, admiration, and esteem.[13]

The *philia* type of love is essential for human beings finding a way to cope with the problems of life and for general well-being. John Mellenchamp recognizes this in "Hand to Hold On To" from his album *American Fool*. You can take friendship for granted, but no matter what or who you become you will need it someday, suggesting that friendship is a universal human need. The same kind of sentiment about *philia* is expressed in the lyrics of "Reach Out I'll Be There" by the Four Tops. Joe Cocker expresses *philia* well when he sings "With a Little Help from My Friends." In Cocker's case, his friends are an anecdote to his loneliness. Moreover, friends can help you cope with the general problems of life.

There is a definite Christian influence in the lyrics to the song "He Ain't Heavy, He's My Brother" by The Hollies, which is also a motto of "Boys Town," a Catholic institution that focuses on assisting wayward boys. The road of life takes many twists and turns, and a person must be strong to navigate its dangers. The lyrics imply an ethical and moral injunction to help one's brother and sister. Since he/she is related to you by a common humanity, he/she is not a burden. The lyrics play with the symbolic contrasts between heavy and light, whereas the apostle Paul's letter to Rome in the New Testament emphasizes the necessity of mutuality (Rom 12:10) and the letter to the Hebrews encourages the continuance of mutual love (Heb 13:1).

The sentiments expressed by many of the previously mentioned artists are summarized nicely by the British rock group Queen and "Friends Will Be Friends" from their album *A Kind of Magic*. Friends provide assistance in times of crisis or need, they are trustworthy, dependable, and loyal through good and bad times.

Passionate Love

Erotic love (*eros*) is both a blessing and a curse. This is evident when it is often closely associated with loss, isolation, abandonment, guilt, anxiety, loneliness, domination, thoughts of suicide, and death, but also with feelings of well-being, happiness, joy, pleasure, being out of control, possessiveness, and helplessness. In her study of the Song of Songs, Carey Walsh captures the spirit of *eros* (desire) when she states the following:

> Desire is voluptuous, insistent, mercurial, careless, overpowering, and overwhelming. It is reckless, sincere, wild, a scavenger of sorts itself. It will not be tamed, restricted, re-taught, or civilized out of its potency. It always brings with it trepidation and thrill in the irresistible chance to feel more alive for as many moments as can be grabbed.[14]

Due to these kinds of characteristics, writers often use metaphors to convey its meaning and to capture its many nuances.

As Christian thinkers such as Kierkegaard, teach us, erotic love needs an object, which is also true of *philia*.[15] This is vividly evident in Michael Jackson's video to his song "The Way You Make Me Feel." Although the lyrics of the song are tame by rock standards, the video features Jackson and other men accosting a woman on an inner city street. Besides describing her comely appearance and his lustful urges in his lyrics, Jackson invades the woman's space and chases her while she attempts to escape from his thrusting pelvis. The video invites the audience to gaze at the object of desire and join in the chase. After joining and then being chased away from some female friends, the young lady is cornered by a group of the pursuing males. The woman is frightened by her situation because she knows that she is about to be raped by a gang of men snapping their fingers and simulating sexual intercourse with fire hydrants! These hydrants serve a double purpose because they shoot water into the air simulating male ejaculation. But her original perpetrator saves her from her ordeal as Jackson finally embraces her. Throughout this video, the woman is the object of erotic desire.

In sharp contrast to fire hydrants shooting water into the air, probably the best metaphorical way to express *eros* is by using fire. Bob Seger and the Silver Bullet Band make an excellent use of fire in "The Fire Down Below." All kinds of people have this fire in common, although the lyrics concentrate on men from all walks of life, socio-economic backgrounds, and professions. The primary proof is that different types of men patronize prostitutes driven by the fire in their loins. The Doors also use the metaphor of fire to express erotic love in their most famous and popular number "Light My Fire," which invites a lover to ignite the flame of passion. There is a definite religious connection when Jim Morrison sings about their love becoming a funeral pyre, which evoke images of the way the Hindus dispose of their dead. The Doors want to convey the message of an all-consuming love that is dangerous to those being burnt. Within the context of these kinds of lyrics from Seger and the Doors, there is an implied notion that love transforms the lovers just as fire transforms that which it consumes.

Connected to the metaphor of fire are the associated notions of heat and burning. On their album *X*, INXS refer to a subject's blood "getting hotter thinking about your hips" in their song "On My Way." Tina Turner alludes to the bodily heat generated by desire in her song

"Steamy Windows." The Pointer Sisters caution about the necessity of a lover taking his time in foreplay in their number "Slow Hand," and they refer to a kiss of fire in their tune entitled "Fire." Their song "I'm So Excited" refers to loosing control and feeling a pleasurable burning sensation. Such lyrics manifest feelings of excitement, loss of control, and enjoyment of desire. These kinds of feelings associated with erotic love are acknowledged by a Christian thinker like Kierkegaard, who refers to it as the "dizziness of infinity."[16]

An even more violent expression of *eros* is provided by John Mellencamp's song "Hurts So Good" from his album *American Fool* because his lyrics emphasize the pain of love, and a sado-masochistic theme runs throughout his song. At one point, he invites his lover to sink her teeth through his bones. In a similar vain, the Dave Matthews Band in their song "Crash" from the album of the same title refer to sado-masochistic wishes and express engaging in voyeurism because the subject of the song asks to be tied up, clawed, and crashed into. At one point, he watches a female at her window naked, and he later sings "Hike up your skirt a little more and show the world to me." On the surface of it, there is no religious message here, but it is possible to find a connection, assuming that one probes a bit deeper into the subject. Not only are human beings vulnerable to the excessiveness associated with desire, it can threaten our selfhood. As Walsh makes clear with her study of the Song of Songs, there is often a close connection between the pleasure associated with desire and "a pain that challenges the autonomy of the self."[17]

A less violent transformation is evident in the lyrics to "Love Is a Wonderful Thing" sung by Michael Bolton on his album *Time, Love and Tenderness*. Bolton sings that love is wonderful because it can make one smile during bad weather, turn the negative aspects of the world into a wonderful dream, make your heart sing, give life a sweet taste, and complete your life. Presumably, you are incomplete without love, and your life is less than whole. If love is loss, it ceases to be a wonderful experience. The songs "If" and "Lost Without Your Love" by Bread testify to the emotional pain associated with a lost love. With a brief allusion to Greek mythology in the former song, the subject confesses that his beloved gave him life, freedom, and the best years of his life. The subject suggests moving from erotic love to a more sacrificial kind of love (*agape*), if he can retrieve his beloved. In the latter recording, the lover does not find life worth living without his beloved, a common refrain.

If some people say that life with all its problems is not worth living, the Doobie Brothers sing in "Here To Love You" that they are glad to be alive. Without life we would not be able to fulfill our purpose in life because we are placed on the earth to transmit love to each other, which makes life worth living. Thus each of us possesses a sacred duty to transmit love to the best of our ability, which is the basic Christian message. Kierkegaard affirms that love is a duty and that it fulfills God's law.[18] Kierkegaard is, of course, referring ultimately to *agape* instead of *eros*. He makes this perfectly clear when he states, "The merely human view of love can never go beyond mutuality: the lover is the beloved, and the beloved is the lover. Christianity teaches that such a love has not yet found its true object—God. The love-relationship requires threeness: the lover, the beloved, the love—but the love is God."[19] In contrast to Kierkegaard's position, most rock musical composers focus on erotic love.

From a similar perspective, Reinhold Niebuhr also refers to love as a legal metaphor. Although love is not the only law of a person's life, it is the final law due to a person's finitude and freedom. Niebuhr's rationale for his assertion that love is the last law for a person is that a person is incapable of making oneself an end due to one's finite nature.[20] There is the ever-present danger that the self will destroy itself if it tries to seek itself too arduously. What Niebuhr intends to claim is that the excessive concern of the self for itself inexorably leads to a narrower and bounded self than that required by human freedom.[21]

Sometimes, love exceeds our ability and grasp, and it puts us into an uncontrollable condition. Probably the best early example from rock 'n' roll history in the 1950s is the hit tune "All Shook Up" by Elvis Presley, who uses notions like shaking hands, weak knees, confusion, rapid heart beat, tied tongue, and shaking insides to describe how love renders his body uncontrollable. The 1957 hit by Jerry Lee Lewis, "Whole Lot of Shakin' Going On," is more of an invitation to lose control of oneself and to let the *eros* flow out of you. Another good example of the tendency of love to lead to uncontrollable behavior is the song "I Can't Help Myself (Sugar Pie, Honey Bunch)" by the Four Tops. *Eros* takes control of a person, and once out of control the person literally cannot help oneself. The uncontrollable nature of love is also expressed by the Supremes in the hit song "Love Is Like an Itching in My Heart." Once love gains control of you, one cannot control it just like one cannot scratch an itch on one's heart.

If love is a secret ingredient for happiness for some composers, it is a short step to making it a law of life. Crosby, Stills, Nash, and Young sing about such a law in "Name of Love" from their album *American Dream*. The foursome's general principle is the following: Whatever you do should be done in the name of love. Can you execute acts of war in the name of love? If you apply the categorical imperative of love, the song implies that there will be no war. If love can function as a law to guide our life, it is something that we can trust and in which we can believe. Many religious thinkers would agree with this line of thought about love.

Huey Lewis and the News ask "Do You Believe in Love?" in one of their many hit songs. They also ask what is it that love begins? Do you believe it's true? It is a short step from asking a question to definitely declaring that one believes in love like Elton John in his number "Believe." John sings that cultural institutions and political leaders disappear, but love endures. Love is boundless, borderless, simple and cheap. He confesses that without love he could not believe in anything to the extent of not believing in himself or others. Thus, love possesses existential and social implications and dimensions.

Stevie Nicks composed and performed the song "Sara" that appears on the Fleetwood Mac album *Tusk* in 1979. We find her using an oceanic metaphor when she sings, "Drowning in a sea of love," a location of death preferred by everyone in love. This is her true home to which she wants to go. By using such an oceanic metaphor, Nicks shares much in common with Christian, Jewish, Islamic, and Hindu mystics. Her oceanic metaphor suggests the complete dissolution of all boundaries and an all-embracing power that possesses the ability to engulf a lover, an image that also suggests that Nicks loves love.

Love is not merely an answer to personal and social problems, but it is also a religious experience. Mariah Carey sings "When I Saw You" in her album *Daydream*. In this song she describes love at first sight that is akin to a religious experience because it transcends space and time, and the experience leaves her speechless and absorbed in her loved one. Such lyrics describe something like an ecstatic experience in which one finds oneself transported beyond or outside of oneself with a keen sense of awareness and concentration.

From the perspective of Sting, there is a mystical quality to love at first sight, according to "Saint Augustine in Hell" from his album *Ten Summoner's Tales*. In the song, the subject asks to be delivered from evil, but like Augustine he is in no hurry and steals a line from the saint's own works about being made chaste. Kierkegaard perceives a great problem with spontaneous love because it can be changed into its opposite, which is hate.[22]

After the break up of the Beatles, George Harrison composed "The Lord Loves the One (That Loves the Lord)." According to the lyrics, there is a divine law that states that if you do not love the Lord you will not be loved in return. Therefore there is a mutual reciprocity built into the law. Since Harrison was a devotee of the Hindu deity

Krishna, we can find a foundation for his position in the classical Hindu religious text *The Bhagavad Gita* (11.54-55). Another of his compositions, "Maya Love" compares love to the day, rain, and a stream. This loves flows within and without a person and is analogous to the sea. Whether Harrison is clearly aware of it or not, the term refers to that which is unreal or illusory in Indian thought. It is not entirely clear whether or not he wants to include that kind of connotation with respect to love unless he intends to say love is unreal in a positive way.

Besides its imperative and legalistic connotations, love is a powerful force. We get a hint of its power in the Beatles' song "Within You Without You," which is partially about what keeps people apart. That which divides people can be space, illusions behind which one hides, and a lack of perception of the truth. By accepting the basic premise that love can save the world, it is necessary to realize it within oneself. Since there is an internal and external stream of life, you will see in time that we are all united in and by love, which represents its power. In a song that was a huge hit for them, the Beatles' song "All You Need Is Love" from their album *Magical Mystery Tour*, affirms also that love is a power that enables one to know, see, and achieve anything. This even extends to salvation: "There's no one you can save that can't be saved."

Love is more than a feeling for Huey Lewis and the News in their tune "The Power of Love." It is curious that love can make one person cry and another sing. It is strong and transforms a bad person into a good person. Love is available to everyone from all walks of life. It is the impetus force of the world and makes it go around. It also possesses the power to save your life, and Lewis asks his listener to feel its power. But love can be more than a power because it can also represent reality. Lewis' song conforms wonderfully with Paul Tillich's theological reflections on the topic of love and power.

For Tillich, love is not simply an emotion; it is rather the "moving power of life."[23] Love also possesses the power to unite that which is separated, self-centered and individual. Tillich wants to stress the inner dynamic nature of love that drives it toward "reunion with the other one and ultimately with the ground itself from which it is separated."[24] In Tillich's theology *eros* drives to union with the beloved, whereas *agape* drives to acceptance of the beloved, which also involves the transformation of the beloved into one's utmost potential, although some rock composers advocate a different kind of potential. Unlike French post-structuralist thinker Michel Foucault's notion that power is diffused, Tillich's conception of power envisions a unity with love, which functions as the foundation of power and not its negation.

The Beatles in their song "Tomorrow Never Knows" invite their listeners to relax, shut off the noise that comes from one's mind, and just go with the flow of consciousness, which should not be confused with death. You are invited to give yourself to emptiness and discover meaning within yourself. The Beatles identify love with the cosmic reality that ties you together with everything else in the universe. Not only is the eastern religious influence obvious in these lyrics, the song also reflects the group's turn to drugs, such as marijuana initially and later LSD, which compromised their agnosticism and enabled them to reach dimensions of reality beyond normal consciousness and a direct experience of God.

It is possible to find something similar from a Western perspective in the work of Crosby, Stills and Nash in "Too Much Love to Hide" from their album *Daylight Again*. Since love is abundant, it cannot be hidden or contained. Love, however, presupposes trust. Once this is granted, it is possible to sing "I believe in love/ I believe when I see the light." This is a perfectly orthodox position because in 1 John God is defined as love (4:16), whether the three artists are aware of it or not. The connection of love and light is also orthodox New Testament symbolism. Jesus, who is the paradigm of love, is also called the light of the world (Mt. 5:14).

The Highest Love

The vast majority of rock 'n' roll lyrics focus on some version of *eros* and to a lesser extent *philia*. We will, however, find some hints of a higher kind of love in some lyrics, if we dig deep enough and listen long enough. But what is this highest form of love called *agape* by the ancient Greeks? Why is it considered a higher form of love than *eros* and *philia*?

Agape is contrary to *eros* because acquiring or possessing something characterizes the latter. In Sarah MacLachlin's song "Possession" a subject wants to kiss her beloved so hard that it will take his breath away. Since breath is analogous to life, she intends to gain complete control of the beloved, which is completely contrary to the spirit of *agape*. The Protestant theologian Karl Barth expresses this distinction in the following way: "It does not have its origin in self-denial, but in a distinctively uncritical intensification and strengthening of natural self-assertion."[25] *Agape* is characterized by mutuality or equal regard of the other. Another normative feature of *agape* is self-giving to the extent of self-sacrificial actions. This is a type of giving that demands nothing in return. It can be called a pure gift because it is unmotivated, purposeless, and completely gratuitous. The event of the cross for Christians symbolizes this perfect kind of love. As Reinhold Niebuhr expresses it, "The Cross symbolizes the perfection of *agape* which transcends all particular norms of justice and mutuality in history."[26] Moreover, *agape* is not an instinct or impulse; it is rather a reciprocal act in which a person is prepared to respond to God's action. Because it is an activity of God and a reciprocal activity of response by human beings, *agape* is dynamic. According to Tillich, *agape* represents the depth of love, or love in relationship, to the ground of human life. With *agape*, ultimate reality manifests and transforms human life and love.[27] For some Christian theologians, *agape* is paradoxical in a twofold way, manifesting a divine descent that "stoops to conquer, and the human *agape*, which rises above history in a sacrificial act."[28]

In probably the most lucid attempt to find *agape*, Steve Winwood searches for it in his song "Higher Love" from his album *Back in the High Life*. It is clear that Winwood in this song is not looking for *eros* because he begins by assuming that there is a higher love to be discovered. Without this higher love, life is not worthwhile and a waste of our time. In order to find this higher love, we need to begin by looking inside ourselves to see if we can find it. Thus his song is akin to a quest for this higher love motivated by an internal yearning to find such a love. As the world revolves, we hardly survive on our own, and we have difficulty seeing the truth because we are blinded by fear. Normally, we walk around blind in an awful world. It is Winwood's conviction that a higher love will allow us to transcend our human situation and spread light due to the fire in the soul. Thus, he connects this higher love with his soul, promising to wait for it, and hoping that he will not arrive too late for this love. Winwood's lyrics strongly suggest that he is not waiting for *eros*, but he is rather searching for *agape*. Reinhold Niebuhr agrees with the spirit of Winwood's lyrics in the sense that *agape*, a sacrificial and uncalculating love, represents the norm of life that the composer is attempting to find, and it completes the inherent incompleteness of erotic love. At the same time, erotic love (*eros*) needs *agape* in order to keep itself from degenerating into calculated decisions designed to further the interests of the self.[29]

There are some other rock lyrics that approach Winwood's quest for *agape*. The lyrics of Neil Diamond's song "Holly Holy" points in the direction of a sacred love, which is especially evident when he says "Holy holy love." Another example is the request by George Harrison in "Give Me Love (Give Me Peace on Earth)" for God to grant the gift of love. During the song, Harrison recites the sacred *mantra* OM, a sacred utterance that is combined with a request for a sacred love, that is, *agape*, which is the most powerful and selfless form of love.

The subject of John Mellencamp's song "Danger List" from his album *American Fool* is an untamable young man who asks to be shown someone to love. Now, this appears to be a request for *eros*. Although Mellencamp's lyrics suggest a form of love higher than *eros*, he sings about prayer and hopes that God still cares about him. Even though the subject might not be very religious, he appears to have a confidence in what it can produce for a person, and then he pleads that his soul be caught in someone's religion. Assuming that the earth is not his true home like many devout Christians, he speaks to God, and asks God to take him home. Mellencamp finally finds someone to love, and it is his Lord; this is the highest and most perfect form of love.

Along similar lines, Lenny Kravitz, a Jewish convert to Christianity, seeks a higher love that is permanent in his song "Baptized." Wearing a cross and Star of David during live performances to acknowledge his conversion to Christianity and his father's religious heritage, Kravitz asks to be baptized by God with a higher love that will free him from his loneliness, fear, and sins, and take him on a path of righteousness and rebirth.

Concluding Remarks

If one can read between the lines of the musical compositions, it is safe to say composers of rock lyrics would nearly unanimously agree that to truly know about love one must have experienced it at some point in one's life. Kierkegaard agrees in the following statement: "Like is known only by like; only someone who abides in love can know love, and in the same way his love is to be known."[30] However, this agreement conceals many differences between the contents of rock lyrics about love and what religious thinkers have to say.

If we consider the numerous songs that we mentioned, we may assert that there are some features of love rock composers fail to incorporate into their compositions. This is not as much a criticism as an observation of a state of affairs. One such example is that love can be a test for a person. The fact that love can be a test for Kierkegaard reveals "love itself is unconsciously uncertain."[31] If testing is related to possibility as Kierkegaard claims, it is also possible that the person being tested will not pass the test.

Another feature of love that is not evident in rock lyrics, even though it might be in the mind of the composers, is its dialectical relationship with justice. However love and justice are to be distinguished because justice, which is historical, discriminating, and concerned with balancing interests and claims, is a relational phenomenon that is a relative embodiment of *agape*. In other words, justice is an approximation of *agape*, although love is both a fulfillment and a negation of justice, according to Reinhold Niebuhr.[32] On the one hand, love demands justice as it works its way out in the world. On the other hand, love negates justice because it always transcends it and its tendency for calculation and discrimination. At the same time, love fulfils justice because love is redemptive and is able to encounter the other in his/her uniqueness. It is only by means of love and in love that the uniqueness of the other is known, and we are able to transcend differences.[33]

If the element of justice in love is not in the forefront of the minds of rock composers, there is ample evidence that many of them understand love as a potentially ecstatic experience, which is an authentically self-transcending moment in our lives because it propels us beyond ourselves. Either erotic love (*eros*) or an unselfish, sacrificial love (*agape*) can transport us out of ourselves. When we have this type of experience the world seems unreal. This common type of human experience can function as a sign for something transcendent within the world, and it can transport us to the limit and highest potential of our human natures. The ability of love to convey us beyond ourselves represents its inherent dynamic nature that is also connected to the power of faith.

Endnotes

---

[1] Søren Kierkegaard, *Fear and Trembling; Repetition*, trans. Howard V. Hong and Edna H. Hong (Princeton: Princeton University Press, 1983), pp. 59-60.

[2] Idem, *Philosophical Fragments*, Second Edition. Translated by David Swenson and Howard V. Hong. Princeton: Princeton University Press, 1962, p. 48.

[3] Idem, *Works of Love*, ed. and trans. Howard V. Hong and Edna H. Hong, Kierkegaard's Writings, XVI (Princeton: Princeton University Press, 1995), p. 234.

[4] Ibid., p. 245.

[5] W. H. C. Frend, *The Rise of Christianity* (Philadelphia: Fortress Press, 1984), p. 566.

[6] Augustine, *The Confessions of St. Augustin*, trans. J. G. Pilkington, Nicene and Post-Nicene Fathers of the Christian Church Vol. 1 (Grand Rapids, MI: Eerdman's Publishing, 1956), 7.6.8.

[7] Idem, *Letters of St. Augustin*, trans. J. G Cunningham, Nicene and Post-Nicene Fathers of the Christian Church Vol. 1 (Grand Rapids, MI: Eerdman's Publishing, 1956), LCXLVI, p. 588.

[8] Paul Tillich, *The Courage to Be* (New Haven and London: Yale University Press 1952; 1965), p. 172.

[9] Kierkegaard, *Philosophical Fragments*, p. 81.

[10] Karl Barth, *Church Dogmatics* IV/1, trans. G. W. Bromiley (Edinburgh: T. & T. Clark, 1961), pp.. 102-103.

[11] Tillich, *Courage To Be*, p. 176.

[12] Robert Cummings Neville, *Symbols of Jesus: A Christology of Symbolic Engagement* (Cambridge: Cambridge University Press, 2001), p. 214.

[13] See Gene Outka, *Agape: An Ethical Analysis* (New Haven: Yale University Press, 1972).

[14] Carey Ellen Walsh, *Exquisite Desire: Religion, the Erotic, and the Song of Songs* (Minneapolis: Fortress Press, 2000), p. 81.

[15] Kierkegaard, *Works of Love*, p. 66.

[16] Ibid., p. 19.

[17] Walsh, p. 71.

[18] Kierkegaard, *Works of Love*, pp. 24, 99, 104.

[19] Ibid., p. 121.

[20] Reinhold Niebuhr, *Faith and History: A Comparison of Christian and Modern Views of History* (New York: Charles Scribner's Sons, 1949), p.

179.

[21] Ibid., p. 174.

[22] Kierkegaard, *Works of Love*, p. 34.

[23] Paul Tillich, *Love, Power, and Justice: Ontological Analyses and Ethical Applications* (New York: Oxford University Press, 1960), p. 25.

[24] Idem, *Dynamics of Faith* (New York: Harper & Row Publishers, 1957), p. 114.

[25] Bath, *Church Dogmatics*, IV/2, p. 788.

[26] Niebuhr, *Nature and Destiny of Man*, II, 74.

[27] Tillich *Love, Power, and Justice*, p. 30.

[28] Niebuhr, *Nature and Destiny of Man*, II, 71.

[29] Idem, *Faith and History*, p. 177.

[30] Kierkegaard, *Works of Love*, p. 16.

[31] Ibid., p. 33.

[32] Niebuhr, I: 295.

[33] Ibid., I: 292.

Chapter 5
Supernatural Beings

It is not impossible to find references to God, the Devil, and goddess figures in rock 'n' roll lyrics. It is also possible to discover paradigmatic biblical themes in these same lyrics. Normally, we do not tend to associate rock lyrics with major biblical themes because there is a tendency to associate rock music with drugs, sex, violence, and dancing. Nonetheless, such religious themes as God's commandment to the Hebrew patriarch Abraham to sacrifice his son, the creation story, and the flood narrative can be discovered in rock lyrics as evident in the previous chapter. Bob Dylan, for instance, begins his song "Highway 61 Revisited" from the album of the same title with God's command to Abraham to kill his beloved son. This same biblical narrative forms the foundation for Kierkegaard's classical work in Christian thought, *Fear and Trembling*, which the author transforms into a meditation about faith. According to Dylan's contemporary humorous twist to the story, Abraham is finally convinced that God is not kidding, and God informs Abraham that He wants the killing performed on Highway 61. But why did Dylan think that Highway 61 was an appropriate venue for a sacrifice? The collaborative scholarly team of Spargo and Ream make the following astute observation:

> Doubtless Dylan meant to evoke the lore of the open road and legendary deaths, including most famously that of Dylan's childhood hero James Dean. On such precedent,

> the American highway proves hospitable to biblical scenarios in which human beings are put to absurdist tasks, forced to rationalize hardships, misery, or their own confused violent actions as acts of providence.[1]

Other rock artists have devoted time to other biblical themes with unusual results.

In the introduction to their album *Aqualung*, Jethro Tull gives their provocative version of the biblical creative narrative. In this revised edition man creates God in his own image, and gives God many names in order for Him to have dominion over the earth, a reversal of the biblical narrative. Man rests on the seven millionth day, leans on God, and witnesses that it is good. Then, man creates Aqualung from dust and many others like him. These inferior beings are dispersed into the void to be consumed by fire or separated from their kin. It is discovered later that Aqualung is a filthy old child molester. Finally, man becomes the God that he creates and rules the earth. The spiritual essence used to create God continues to exist in all beings, but ordinary humans do not recognize this. It is, however, important for humans to begin searching for this spirit according to the narrator. There are those who will find Jethro Tull's rendition of the creation story blasphemous, although I do not think that this is their purpose. Their controversial version of the biblical creation story is intended to free humans from depending on a supernatural being and to stress the need to rely upon themselves.

There are some similarities between Jethro Tull's creation narrative and that of some Gnostic sects, which were early competitors of the Jesus movement. Among some Gnostics, a Demiurge, which is identified with the Hebrew God, mistakenly thinks that he is the sole creator, and he is boastful about his accomplishments and feels unique, but he is ignorant of the creative source of the Mother. When the Demiurge or humans achieve *gnosis* (knowledge), it is this realization that involves the recognition of the genuine source of divine power. Coming to know the source involves knowing oneself in a genuine way and discovering one's spiritual origin, according to the Gnostics.

As one might expect based on the name of the group, the rock band Genesis devotes two of their songs to the theme of creation. In "The Serpent," the cosmos is in place, and God gets prepared to create humans. It is declared that man is wonderful, like an icon of the gods in flesh and blood. God creates man from dust with a body and soul, and He creates a woman to be a vessel for the Devil. Even though man is wonderful, there is a warning about the future and the destiny of this newly created creature. The first man speaks towards the end of the song and admits his loneliness and being tempted by the serpent. There is a hopeful note because man is confident of guidance from God. Genesis' second treatment of creation appears in their song "In the Beginning." The emphasis in these lyrics is on the cosmic waters, light, sound, and uncontrolled power. The Father and Son look down upon the new emerging world and the life that is emerging and see that it is good.

The rock artist Sting gives his version of the flood story from the Hebrew Bible with a contemporary twist in "Rock Steady" from his album *Nothing Like the Sun*. He and his wife respond to an advertisement in a newspaper for volunteers to work on a large wooden ship, the couple agrees to help the captain and join him on his adventure. After taking a taxi ride to the harbor, they meet an old bearded man surrounded by every imaginable animal. The old man tells them that he received a message from God on the radio about a deluge in the near future, but that God would protect him and two representatives of each animal. The old man says that he needs assistants to care for the animals after it rains for forty days and nights. The work is arduous for the volunteers, and they become weary and disillusioned. They send out a dove to find land and to discover if God is in fact merciful, which the dove confirms. If one subtracts the modern accretions to the biblical narrative, Sting's version of the story is a rather orthodox retelling of the narrative. Moreover, the creation and flood stories, as well as the Dylan reference to the story of Abraham, point to a supernatural being active on earth. If we consider a wider variety of rock lyrics, it will be possible to witness a broader treatment of God, the Devil, and the feminine supernatural element. In this chapter, there will be then an examination of references to God both alive and dead, some critical perspectives on God in rock lyrics, examples of references to the Devil, and a look at goddess figures.

God Alive and Dead

Jethro Tull's song about man creating God in his own image that I cited previously is a good example of the human longing to become divine or divine-like. We find something similar in the lyrics to the Kinks song "(Wish I Could Fly Like) Superman." Feeling depressed over his body when he looks in the mirror, the subject of the song wants to reshape himself and become a better man. In fact, he aspires to be like the comic book hero Superman. Due to the difficulty of surviving in a world with a multitude of problems, there is an existential need to become like Superman, a god-like figure due to his superior powers, in order to cope with life. The subject wants to be able to fly like the comic book character, but he laments that he cannot even swim. To become God or god-like is an ancient longing for human beings. When discussing the miraculous powers attained by ascetics and yogis in Indian religion in his book on yoga, Mircea Eliade, a historian of religions, calls attention to nostalgia for a divine condition as an obsession of these figures. Eliade observes that "the way of Yoga leads to a mythological perfection, the very perfection enjoyed by the personages of the Indian pantheon."[2]

When God or the sacred manifests itself in the profane world, this is called a hierophany in the parlance of religious scholarship. A hierophany is literally an in-breaking of the sacred into the world. Depending on the disposition, pre-understanding, prejudices, and personal agents to those that it manifests itself, a hierophany is open to a variety of reactions, understandings, and interpretations by those to which it is revealed. A humorous song about how different people and groups react to a strange phenomenon that manifests itself in a farmer's field is the subject of the lyrics "It Came Out of the Sky" performed by Credence Clearwater Revival. A farmer named Jody is plowing his fields when he spies something coming from the sky. The farmer's reaction is religious in the sense that Jody sees what Rudolf

Otto, a renowned German scholar of religion, calls the *mysterium tremendum* in his classic study, *The Idea of the Holy*. The farmer is described lying on the ground, shaking, and fearing for his life, which is a typical response to a sudden manifestation of the sacred. While the encounter with the hierophany might have been religious for Jody, other people offer other interpretive reactions. A scientist concludes that it is marsh gas, while the disgraced former Vice-President of the United States Spiro Agnew thinks it is from the planet Mars, and he wants to raise the tax for such visitors. The Vatican thinks that it is the second coming, whereas former President Ronald Reagan humorously attributes it to a nefarious Communist plot, and Hollywood producers want to create an epic film based on the incident. Meanwhile, Jody becomes a national hero and appears on television, and he claims that the strange phenomenon is his possession, while the government and Vatican claim it as their property. The humorous lyrics of Credence's song point to the wide variety of possible responses. We will find the same variety in lyrics about God because there are lyrics that express traditional orthodox views about God, others that seek to determine his location, and other lyrics with a more critical edge.

After Dylan's religious turn in the 1970's, we find several songs about God. His number "Father of Night" is, for instance, akin to a hymn of praise to God as Father of creation and humankind from his album *New Morning*. His song entitled "Ring Them Bells" from his album *Oh Mercy* focuses on the ringing of church bells throughout the land for all living creatures. The ringing church bells are intended to call attention to the unity of God. On his album *Saved*, there is a song entitled "Solid Rock" that compares God to a rock that predates the creation of the world. There is ample precedence in the Hebrew Bible for Dylan's use of the image of the rock and its attribution to God. A reader must only refer to Deuteronomy (32:4; 32:15), 1 Samuel (2:2), 2 Samuel (22:2-3, 47) and the Psalms (18:2, 31; 28:1; 42:9; 89:26) for depictions of God as one's rock. Many of these passages make a connection between God as a metaphorical rock and personal salvation. In the New Testament the apostle Paul refers to Christ as a rock (1 Cor 10:4). A rock is something permanent, strong, enduring, and reliable. These examples form the background for an old hymn entitled "Rock of Ages." Since this image is part of the heritage of the Judeo-Christian tradition, it should come as no surprise to see an artist like Dylan making metaphorical use of the rock.

Beside Dylan's efforts, the rock group October Project refers to God in their song "Adam and Eve" from their album *Falling Farther In*. The group uses the biblical figures of Adam and Eve as archetypes to portray the relationship between a boy and a girl and the end of their personal and inter-relational paradise. God speaks in the lyrics about being helpless and lost like human beings. In other words, God is similar to his fallen and lost creatures. The final verse changes the Hebrew Bible definition of God from "I am that I am" (Ex. 3:14). The Jewish thinker Martin Buber interprets Yahweh here describing Himself as being singular, being present in the present moment, and being present in the future. This also implies that God will make Himself known to His people and will be in direct relation to them, but one cannot know His being or essence. It is only His will that can be known, since it occurs within history.[3] The neo-orthodox Protestant theologian Karl Barth agrees partially with Buber that God makes Himself known and that knowing must not be abstract, but he disagrees with Buber about the notion of a direct relationship between God and human beings because human knowledge is corrupted by human's temporal and sinful existence. Thus human knowledge of God is imperfect in comparison to that of God, who knows Himself perfectly in one moment and for eternity.[4] Barth also argues that because God allows Himself to be known in time and human knowledge is imperfect, the true knowledge of God achieved in time must be continually repeated, since it is knowledge that depends on God's action.

In their song "The Miracle" from an album of the same title, the rock group Queen finds God's miracles in aspects of nature, in human creations, scientific advances, and wonders associated with famous people. But the miracle really needed is peace on earth and a prohibition against war. Another miracle needed is sufficient clothing and food for the poor. Queen unites in their lyrics the immanence of God with their social conscience. In a message addressed to everyone, Queen sings "All God's People" in their album I*nnuendo*. The group's message is for everyone to get in touch with their feelings, let their heart rule their lives, be comfortable with their conscience, be free, and most importantly to love each other. Because we are all related to God and thus form his people, these lyrics define God in relational terms, which are very biblically based.

In a song that is like a prayer to God from their album *The Innocents* to be saved from the Devil, the rock group Erasure urge in their song "Yahoo!" for others to find their way to God. These lyrics represent a traditional form of prayer, a supplication or petitionary form of prayer that asks God for something. The overall message of the lyrics is to make it clear that it is not right to give in to temptation even when one is very depressed. They pray to God to be set free from the snares of the Devil. Again, these lyrics are very orthodox. In addition to lyrics that resemble petitionary types of prayer, it is also possible to encounter lyrics that exult God, like "Gloria" by U2 from their album *October*. The subject admits to an overwhelming religious experience that results in the inability to stand and to speak. Although the subject admits to having nothing, he would give whatever he had to God. Nonetheless, what he can give is praise to God, praise represented by the lyrics of the song.

Responding to questions about the whereabouts of God and why He does not always respond to the requests of his people, Stevie Wonder offers his song "Heaven is 10 Zillion Light Years Away." Since heaven is so far away, it takes God a long time to arrive on earth. But this is not literally what Wonder believes because for him God is within each person. It is this basic conviction of his, as well as his faith in the universal love of God, which makes it difficult for him to understand racial hatred. How can skin color make someone inferior? In order for the hateful to be saved, they need the love of God to shine upon their evil souls.

We find a very different ethos expressed by the 90's rock group Nirvana in "Lithium" from their album *Nevermind.* The lyrics make it clear that it is possible to find your friends and God in your mind, achieving this by means of the drug lithium. This kind of religiosity is not that unusual, if we consider, for example, the work of Carlos Castenada and his work with the Peyote cult among Native American Indians. Castenada allegedly learned about the cult from Don Juan, a Yaqui Indian from Sonora, Mexico. By chewing the peyote buttons, Castenada gains a vision of a dog drinking water.[5] The dog represents Mescalito, the powerful drug itself, and Castenada describes him as gentle and terrifying and as a protector and teacher. The peyote functions to protect one from danger, and is used to obtain spiritual knowledge. Native American Indian practitioners think the way of peyote is superior to the path of the religion of white people, because it represents direct experience instead of learning from books. A Comanche informant nicely summarizes the attitude of the Indians: "The white man talks about Jesus; we talk to Jesus."[6] A similar but less drug-induced experience is evident in the compositions of other artists.

After the Beatles split, George Harrison began to compose lyrics that reflected his religious convictions. His song "My Sweet Lord" is basically a petitionary prayer to God. Harrison uses a series of action verbs (e.g., to see, be with, know, go, show) to make his case and lament the amount of time that it takes for God to reveal Himself. The God that is the object of Harrison's devotion is the Hindu deity Krishna, which is especially evident in his song "It Is 'He' (Jai Sri Krishna)." These songs and others written by Harrison reflect a strong Hindu devotional influence centered on Krishna, who is famous as a deity of love and compassion. In works such as the *Bhagavata Purāna* and the devotional poetry by figures such as Jayadeva, Candīdāsa, and Vidyāpati, the praises of Krishna are recited for public consumption, participation, and enjoyment. In a sense, Harrison's rock lyrics are part of that ancient Indian devotional tradition, if viewed from an intercultural context.

In contrast to Harrison's eastern turn to Krishna, the Police refer to what could possibly be another eastern deity in "Invisible Sun" from their album *Ghost in the Machine.* The invisible sun is a metaphor for something divine and life-giving. According to the lyrics, this invisible sun is the answer to the meaninglessness, ignorance, and suffering of life. The lyrics suggest a theological proof for the existence of the invisible sun, which is based on an argument from design similar to the theological position of St. Thomas Aquinas, a medieval Dominican thinker.

In his theological works, Aquinas advances five proofs for God's existence. All of these proofs rest to a certain degree on the fact that God created the world, suggesting thereby a principle of analogy of being (*analogia entis*). Aquinas' use of analogy helps us to understand how God reveals Himself to us through scriptural images and analogies, and allows us to understand how God can transcend our world and at the same time be revealed in and through that world. Since there is continuity between God and the world due to the expression of the being of God within the being of the world, it is perfectly legitimate from Aquinas' viewpoint to use things within the created world as analogies for God. Even though there is a correspondence between God and the created world, this does not mean that a created entity must be identical to God in order to be like Him. As creator of the world, God left His mark upon it. Thus it is possible for us to observe in the world signs of the divine ordering process, which is the most convincing evidence for God's existence and wisdom, made by its first cause and designer. Aquinas' fifth argument for the existence of God is called the argument from design or the teleological argument, which is based on the obvious traces of intelligent design in the world. Not only do natural processes and objects have a purpose, but they also appear to have been designed by an intelligent being. And since things are caused or designed by something else, Aquinas identifies the designer with God in a fashion similar to the lyrics of the song by the Police.

In sharp contrast to the position of Aquinas stands the neo-orthodox theology of Karl Barth, who denies that analogy can make God intelligible to oneself. Barth attempts to construct a genuinely Reformation theology based on revelation alone, whereas Acquinas' position suggests that it is possible to receive knowledge of God apart from His revelation. Barth objects that such a position causes a cleavage in God's nature, and it is a fundamental perversion of the theological point of departure. Barth holds that analogy must be *analogia fidei* (analogy of faith), which suggests a similar or partial correspondence of realities designated by the same words. In the analogy of faith God knows human beings, but they do not know God.[7] Since the word of humans can only point to the Word of God, there is only a partial agreement.

As I mentioned in chapter three, God is sometimes depicted as silent, as with the lyrics of "Nothing" by Depeche Mode, or too distant to be much help, as in the lyrics of "Oh My God" by the Police. In fact, the Police's lyrics accuse God of keeping his distance, sleeping and not seeing the world's misery. And sometimes this silent and/or distant God is pushed to the next extreme and depicted as in fact dead, as with the song "Up From Your Life" by James Taylor. Randy Newman in his self-titled debut album released in 1968, reflects the death of God debate during that time in American culture. In his song "I Think He's Hiding," Newman refers to God as "Big Boy" who may come soon, and demands humans behave ethically and morally. Will God like what He sees when He arrives or will He punish us with fire? The composer hears that God is dead, but he thinks that God is merely in hiding. These lyrics suggest Newman's response to the entire death of God debate. If God is dead, humans must rely upon themselves, which can prove to be a frightening experience for many people.

Taking seriously the proclamation of the prophet Zarathustra in Freidrich Nietzsche's *Thus Spoke Zarathustra*, figures like Thomas J. J. Altizer, William Hamilton, and others declared in the 1960's that God is dead, even though these theologians embodied different perspectives on the exact meaning of this event. During this period of time, Hamilton writes about waiting for God: "Our waiting for God, our godlessness, is partly a search for a language and a style by which we might be enabled to stand before him once again, delighting in his presence."[8] Hamilton argues that we do more than simply wait because we should turn toward love and our neighbor. It is possible to find Jesus concealed in the world in the person of our neighbor, and it is the task of the Christian to find Jesus.

Altizer argues that Christians live in a godless world. He makes his position very clear: "We must realize that the death of God is an historical event that God has died in our cosmos, in our history, in our *Existenz*."[9] Altizer's position entails a criticism of classical theism which viewed true Being as something transcendent instead of immanent. Altizer thinks that the God present in the incarnation terminates the otherness stressed by classical theism. If the incarnation of Jesus means that divine transcendent presence is now located within historical time and space in the present moment, we need to reassess our theological position to account for such a presence and the implication that identity and difference are re-identified. Altizer's position finds its echo in the postmodern stance of Mark C. Taylor. This is evident in the following remarks: "To embrace the death of God is to affirm 'the deleterious absurdity of time' in which meaning is eternally sacrificed in a potlatch that is as pointless as the pyramid on which it is staged. The sacrifice of God is the death of the transcendental signified, which marks the closure of the classical regime of representation."[10] Thus Taylor shares Altizer's emphasis on immanence over transcendence. Other theologians have anticipated such a position or reacted against it.

From his Nazi prison cell during World War II, Dietrich Bonhoeffer, a Lutheran pastor, perceived events differently from Hamilton, Altizer, and Taylor. Instead of the death of God, Bonhoeffer witnessed God being "more and more edged out of life, losing more and more ground."[11] Bonhoeffer argued that we need God, the church, and pastors because there are ultimate questions about life focusing on death, meaning, and guilt that can only be answered by a higher power.

In contrast to Bonhoeffer's Protestant perspective, Buber offers a Jewish viewpoint about the death of God: "Actually, this proclamation means only that man has become incapable of apprehending a reality absolutely independent of himself and of having a relation with it . . ."[12] Buber perceives an eclipse of God rather than a death of God. Although this eclipse of God cannot be proven, it is possible for human beings to experience it. Moreover, the eclipse of the light of God does not mean that it has been completely extinguished, because it is possible for it to return at any time.

Agreeing in spirit with Buber's position, Protestant thinker Harvey Cox thinks that "The death of God cannot be repealed, but it can be transcended."[13] Cox is critical of the so-called death of God camp because it might free us from the past but it leads us into a prison of the present. Cox finds radical theology to be a form of "presentism" that ignores the past, over-emphasizes the present and tries to lure us with the future.

Critical Perspectives on God

Prior to Bob Dylan's religious conversion, it was possible to find lyrics he composed in which God is presented in a critical way in order to make social and political points. A good example of this is Dylan's song "With God on Our Side" from his album *The Times They Are A-Changin'*. Dylan sings about God being on the side of the winners and conquerors. He cites the whites over the Native American Indians, the Americans in the Spanish-American War, and allies during the First and Second World Wars. Since we forgave the Germans for exterminating six million people, they now have God on their side as well. If we have to fight the Russians or have a nuclear war, we will have God on our side. Dylan raises the question of whether Judas Iscariot had God on his side when he betrayed Jesus with a kiss. Dylan admits to a bit of confusion: "If God is on our side/ He'll stop the next war." These lyrics suggest that God will stop the next war only if He is on our side. What if he is not on our side? This is exactly the question that Dylan wants us to contemplate. These types of lyrics can also be viewed as ridiculing American Christianity for its apology for nationalistic myths such as "manifest destiny."[14]

A rather mean-spirited God appears in the lyrics of "God's Song: That's Why I Love Mankind," by Randy Newman from his album *Sail Away*, released in 1972. The song is structured around two episodes to which God is asked to respond. The initial episode involves a problem about the following question: Why did Cain kill Abel if the Hebrews were suppose to multiply? After Seth asks God for an answer, God gives a surprising response, saying humans mean nothing to Him, but he loves humankind because of its folly. Moreover, God finds humankind foul and is amused by their prayers for assistance. In another episode, Christians and Jews are enjoying a party together, and Buddhists and Hindus join them via satellite television. A leader for each group asks God why there are such serious problems on the earth. And if God does not intend to help people, please leave them alone. God responds that even though he perpetrates cruel actions against humankind, people still have faith in Him. Newman portrays a cynical and vindictive deity who takes a perverse delight in the sorry plight of humankind. In fact, this arbitrary God directly inflicts pain and suffering on people without any rationale or purpose.

Newman's lyrics take a presumptuous position by sitting in judgment on God. In a possible response to the *hubris* (pride) the lyrics of Newman's song, the French religious thinker Blaise Pascal (1623-62) comments powerfully and devastatingly on human beings:

> What a chimera then is man! How strange and monstrous! A chaos, a subject of contradictions, a prodigy. Judge of all things, yet a stupid earthworm; depository of truth, yet a cesspool of uncertainty and error; the glory and the refuse of the universe. Who will unravel this tangle?[15]

Although humans have a capacity for God according to Pascal, the basic human problem is centered on pride and despair. While pride results because humans know God without acknowledging their wretchedness, despair results because humans are aware of their own wretchedness without knowing God. Moreover, humans desire happiness, but this desire is a source of unhappiness because the gulf between humanity and happiness is too wide, and only God can fill it. The path to be followed by humans is the "wager" for Pascal, with each person wagering for or against the existence of God. If one remains indifferent, this involves choosing against God. Each person must decide where his/her interest lies. Pascal believes that it is reasonable to wager for God because by winning the wager one gains everything, and if one loses one loses nothing. So what is at stake is little in comparison to what one might win. A person must thus risk what is certain for what is uncertain. If one makes his wager for God, faith then becomes a real possibility, which clearly implies that wagering is to your advantage and happiness, according to Pascal.

Within a context that appears hopeless, two characters are in unspecified trouble in the song "Miracle" from the album *Blaze of Glory* by Jon Bon Jovi. The male character sings to a woman and asks what is on her mind because she seems to be carrying a heavy burden. The male figure concludes that it will take a miracle to save the two of them. Although the female figure is seeking salvation, the male character informs her that her savior left some time ago, angels have also left, and salvation itself took the last train out of town. In a prophetic vision, the male figure sees a coming flood, horror and catastrophe. It is presumably this coming flood that will wash away any hope of future miracles. The lyrics of Bon Jovi's song depict an apocalyptic deluge devoid of any future hope. Such apocalyptic expectations are an ancient part of the Christian religious tradition. We will devote more space to this topic in a later chapter.

Another kind of vision that can be discovered in rock 'n' roll lyrics is that of a *deus otitosus* (distant deity). Harry Chapin composed a song for his album *On the Road to Kingdom Come* where he not only depicts established religion in a state of decay, but God is simultaneously silent within heaven. A similar *deus otitosus* appears in the lyrics of "Praying for Time" by George Michael. Due to hunger and ignorance, there are many needy people, but this is a time of little charity. It is rather a period of greed, niggardliness, hate, and lack of hope. Unfortunately, God is not keeping score because He lets His children outside to play, turns His back on humankind, and creeps out the back door. It is difficult to hang on to hope when there is none to be discovered within a cosmic context in which God is distant and uncaring, and there is no opportunity to have a dialogical relationship, in Buber's sense of relation, with such a remote deity.

Religious practitioners of the Judeo-Christian-Islamic tradition would find it difficult to have a dialogical relationship with an idol. In a song entitled "Tiki God," the rock group called The Presidents of the United States of America sings about an idol found by a boy named Bobby Brady, who had no idea about what he had discovered. The Tiki God is a vicious and harmful deity that Bobby discovers in a bottle in the ocean. Bobby asks the deity to punish his girlfriend who had previously wronged him, and her body is later found in a river. It is implied that this is the handiwork of the divine idol, which reflects a strong iconoclastic tradition in the lyrics.

Presuming to know what God wants, Roger Waters of the rock group Pink Floyd composed two songs called "What God Wants, Part

I and Part II," depicting a benevolent and malevolent deity. According to Waters' satirical lyrics, God gets whatever He wants. More specifically, God wants sex, crack cocaine, and a good fight. He also wants law and organized crime, peace and war, voodoo, shrines, jihad, and crusades. This seems to be a God who cannot make up His mind. In the second part of the song, there is a not very subtle criticism of televanglists, who represent a church united by money, and the God of such a church wants all kinds of money. Although he does not make the equation explicitly in his lyrics, Waters seems to suggest that God is equivalent to money. The postmodern a/theologian Mark C. Taylor tends to agree with Waters that God becomes money within the context of consumer capitalism that "generates a sacrificial economy, which eventually becomes all-consuming."[16]

In contrast to the lyrics of Waters, the rock group the Crash Test Dummies with their song "God Shuffled His Feet" achieves a more humorous effect. After presumably creating the world, God becomes exhausted, and He says that people should enjoy a picnic. As people are sitting around drinking wine with God in their midst, they begin to ask him questions: Does one eat in heaven? Can one get a haircut in heaven? In response to these trivial questions, God shuffles his feet, and He tells a story about a boy with blue hair and his concern about the reaction of his friends to his unusual hair. Again, God shuffles his feet as the people sit staring at Him and waiting. Since God does not respond, someone asks for clarification about whether God's story is a parable or a "subtle joke." But God just shuffles His feet and looks at the people, and they "cleared their throats and stared right back at

Him." This depiction of God is less of a *deus otitosus* than of an indecisive deity with a problem communicating clearly with humans. The anthropomorphic language is interesting because it suggests a deity acting like and created in the image of human beings. The lyrics of the Crash Test Dummies support in spirit the position of Ludwig Feuerbach (1804-1872), who argued that the source of God is human beings, suggesting that behind every theological statement about God is a hidden claim about humans.[17] Moreover, God is placed above humans as an alien being. From another perspective, Feuerbach argues that God is the human understanding, conscious of its own perfection and freed from individuality and suffering. As human understanding, God appears as moral perfection that is personified as the perfection of the human will, which calls upon human beings to become God. By calling human beings to be what they might be, God informs beings what they are not, which results in depression, although this is not an agonizing type of depression because the idea of God represents the essential characteristics of the nature of human beings.

In the song "God," in his album *Plastic Ono Band*, John Lennon expresses another perspective on God, who he claims is a concept created by human beings to measure the intensity of their pain. In the following verses, Lennon informs the listener about what he does not believe, a list that includes magic, sacred scriptures, sacred sounds, historical political figures, religious figures, a rock star, such as Elvis and even the Beatles. Lennon summarizes his reality as a belief in himself and his wife. Therefore, Lennon believes in something concrete and immanent, and he refuses to recognize anything transcendent. Lennon's lyrics suggest a human-centered view of the world that involves the worship of human beings instead of God. Therefore, Lennon's religion celebrates human beings, but he does not do so by attributing the attributes of God to human beings.

From the perspective of a Protestant reformer like Martin Luther, Lennon's faith is misplaced and his knowledge of God is empty. From the perspective of his theocentric theology, Luther acknowledges two kinds of knowledge about God: a general knowledge that God is and a proper or particular knowledge of what God is. Luther argues that all human beings possess a conceptual notion of God, a rudimentary idea of God inscribed on the human heart that is given by God and cannot be eradicated. This general knowledge informs human beings that God exists, that he created the world, that He is omniscient, that He is the bestower of all good, that He is righteous, and that He judges. There are two limits to this general knowledge because human beings cannot be certain about what God thinks of us and if He will help us, and humans do not know who God is. The particular knowledge of God, which is beyond natural reason, is completed by general knowledge about God because it acts as a corrective. Knowledge of God is made complete only through Christ.[18] Luther's controlling principle is that God is the center of all existence, unlike the God of Lennon's lyrics. Moreover, Luther's theocentric theology lacks the egocentric spirit of Lennon's lyrics.

An even more critical view of God than Lennon's is evident in the lyrics of "My God" by Jethro Tull from their album *Aqualung*.

According to the lyrics, people have made God conform to their religion by resurrecting Him from the grave. This act has a dire effect: "He is the god of nothing." But human beings represent the God of everything, an interior deity. A major restriction is not being able to ask Him to save you from sins and social graces. Moreover, with his image and plastic crucifix, Jesus confuses the group because the latter cannot discern what makes Jesus tick. Jethro Tull also cannot make sense of the confession of sins. Jethro Tull appears to have problems with religious elements added by pious devotees that have nothing to do with the historical Jesus.

Such a critical perspective would horrify a Protestant reformer like Martin Luther because he thinks that knowledge of God is made complete only through Christ.[19] Luther contends that the incarnate Son of God is a veil in which Divine Majesty presents Himself to us.[20] This veil suggests concealment that points to the divinity of Christ hidden in his humanity. Since the divinity of Christ is not obvious to either physical sight or reason, it can only be apprehended by faith. What is disclosed is beyond human understanding. God is always hidden (*Deus Absconditus*) for Luther as He is, apart from Christ. Since God is hidden in His revelation in Christ, not everything is revealed in Christ. Luther argues that Christ is represented in two different ways: as a gift and as an example. A person cannot distinguish this twofold office of Christ.

These various examples of critical attitudes toward God suggest that the power of God is not simply hierarchical because the critic is not without power; otherwise he/she would be unable to respond to perceived inadequacies of the divine being. The French anti-structuralist Michel Foucault makes it clear that where there are relations of power there is also resistance.[21] In fact, resistance is only possible within a power complex.

Although Foucault does not do it, Tillich equates God with power, which is necessarily implied by the assertion that God is Being-itself.[22] Tillich does not mean to claim that power is an attribute of God, but it is rather to assert that God represents the power of being. A God without power is a contradiction in terms. Tillich and Foucault's notions of power do converge to a certain extent when the former calls attention to the power of God being in everything and above everything, which suggests the ubiquitous nature of power in the work of Foucault, although the ubiquity of power does not mean that everything is power.

The Dark Side of the Supernatural

The figure of the so-called Prince of Darkness or Satan seems to be especially popular with heavy metal rock bands. With such groups as AC/DC, Black Sabbath, Dio, Motley Crue, Judas Priest, Iron Maiden, and performers like Ozzy Ozborne in such songs as "Speak of the Devil" and "Sabbath Bloody Sabbath," it is possible to find lyrics that invoke the Devil's name and demonstrate respect for Satanic values like cruelty, drugs, ugliness, depression, violence, suicide, joylessness and general noise and confusion. In one of his books on the Devil, Jeffrey Burton Russell attributes such music to adolescent resentment of authority that uses "the terms and symbols of the occult to express cultural rebellion rather than personal belief."[23] But I want to ignore such groups in order to stay focused on classical rock music, even though the examples might not be as rich in comparison to heavy metal bands.

If we examine its origin, the name Satan derives from a verb meaning, "to oppose," "to obstruct," or 'to accuse" and it refers to an angelic messenger who does God's dirty work on earth.[24] There is also the Hebrew term *mal'ak* meaning voice of God or spirit of God. This ambivalent term gradually separated from Yahweh and began to stress something destructive until it came to signify the shadow of God. Finally, it became an evil angel.[25] In Zechariah (3:1-2), Satan is, for instance, a powerful angelic figure appointed as God's accuser against humankind. In the New Testament, Satan does not play a predominate role, but he does assume a major role in the divine drama because "the gospel writers realize that the story they have to tell would make little sense without Satan."[26] Popular Christianity has transformed the Devil into a frightening figure and into something ridiculous or impotent.[27] This evolution of Satan plays a prominent role in numerous rock compositions.

While dreaming of walking through a jungle, the subject hears voices telling him to run because of the presence of the Devil in the lyrics to "Run Through the Jungle" by Creedence Clearwater Revival. The subject of the song imagines a multitude of guns and Satan telling them to take aim with the Vietnam conflict forming the context for the lyrics. After the break up of the band, its lead singer and major composer John Fogerty recorded "Hoodoo Man," a song about a voodoo-man who controls the Devil and can also take various animal forms and fly like a bird.

In a somewhat less serious vein in the musical *Hair*, the subject compares his being expelled from high school heaven with the fall of Satan from heaven and his banishment to hell in the number "Going Down." The intention behind these lyrics is humorous. The comic aspect of Satan can be traced back to at least the later Middle Ages. Russell explains some of this scatological humor: "The Devil is funny, but he is also repulsive, and he is funny in a way that makes us despise and shun him rather than empathize with him."[28] The number from *Hair* resembles what Russell identifies as a level of Middle Age humor manifesting elevated irony.[29]

The Devil presents himself as a man of high class and culture in "Sympathy for the Devil" by the Rolling Stones. The Devil admits to destroying the faith of humans and stealing souls. He was present when Jesus experienced his "moment of doubt and faith." He was also present when Pilate washed his hands, and he was there working behind the scenes at other tragic historical occurrences. Finally, the Devil addresses the listener and asks him/her to guess what motivates the Devil's evil. From his perspective, honest people are criminals, and sinners are really saints, an example of his inverted perspective. In fact, the Devil's entire world is an inverted version of this world.

Bob Dylan depicts the Devil as "Man of Peace" in a song, which emphasizes that Satan appears under disguises, and we can never be sure about any person's identity. He might thus deceitfully appear under the guise of a humanitarian or a philanthropist. Whether Satan arrives as a man of peace or not his arrival will usher in the end time, and the conclusion of historical time is expected to arrive soon. Dylan is historically accurate when referring to the various forms of the Devil, although before the eleventh century he is usually human and afterward he is likely to be a human/animal monster or simply animal.[30] But he is often a figure associated with darkness.

The Indigo Girls use light symbolism to good effect in their song "Prince of Darkness." The subject finds herself between heaven and hell, she is almost pulled under to the place of darkness, but she does not want to be a pawn for the Devil. The Indigo Girls' use of the color black conforms to Christian tradition, although the second most used color associated with the Devil is red, a color of blood and fire.[31]

The subject of "Satan's Bed" admits that Satan still visits him, but he will not sleep in Satan's bed, according to the rock group Pearl Jam on their album *Vitalogy*. The composer Kurt Cobain confesses, "I'll never suck Satan's dick," which suggests that he will never succumb to the Devil. All lovers of rock 'n' roll music will find comfort in these lyrics. But if we consider the way that Cobain died from drugs and shotgun blast, this might actually be what he did, if we take into consideration the demonic aspect of drug addiction.

During 1995, Randy Newman released his musical *Faust*, which was inspired by the German poet Goethe's work. The musical begins with the song "Glory Train," a celebration in part of God's creation during which God says that He sees difficult times in the future. This number is also a song about salvation. God asks His creatures if they have been saved, and they answer affirmatively. God sees people united and waiting for the train of salvation, and He says to let faith be your sole guide. The lyrics make it clear that the train of salvation arrives at a moment of no hope. In turn, the Devil, who loses his place in heaven for a minor mistake, replies to God that he has never heard such "bullshit" even from God, a master of it. The Devil claims that what God says is all a lie, and the Devil also asserts that some fearful fools lost in the desert invented him and God, rendering religion, God, and the Devil all figments of human imagination.

As the centuries pass in Newman's musical, the Devil reigns in hell as an able and fair administrator, even though he can be vicious, ruthless, and sadistic. The Devil pines to return to heaven, and he conceives a plan to gain revenge and respect. With such a purpose, the Devil visits heaven to find God bored and irritable. With Buddhists at the gates of heaven waiting for admittance, God tells the angels to put them out with the trash in the number "How Great Our Lord." Sensing an opportunity, the Devil alleges that God made a mistake when He created humankind, a charge that God denies. Thereupon, the Devil proposes a wager that he can corrupt Henry Faust, a schizophrenic student from Notre Dame University, after rejecting a Canadian candidate in the number "Northern Boy." Henry Faust is from Gainesville, Florida, and he is the child of a tailor and mother who runs a café, and he has tried to practice the golden rule in his life. If the Devil wins and corrupts Faust, he will be allowed to return to heaven. And if God wins, He will receive Faust's very tiny soul.

With their wager agreed, the Devil offers Henry Faust a contract that he foolishly signs without reading. The Devil finds Henry a dull, poorly mannered, and uncultured person that he dislikes. The Devil becomes aware of an English angel, who is upset about God's cavalier treatment of his country during the two world wars of the twentieth century, and the angel expresses his disappointment in the number "Little Island."

At the beginning of the second act of the musical, God sends Cupid to shoot the narcissistic Faust to get him to fall in love. The shot is successful because he falls in love with a poor girl named Margaret, the loveliest girl in South Bend, Indiana, whereas the Devil falls in love with Martha, a friend of Margaret. Tricked and rejected by Martha, the Devil sings "Bleeding All Over the Place." Newman's Devil possesses very human characteristics and emotions, which is very different from Goethe's complex and manipulative figure. Goethe's devil is a fool because he cannot understand that the essence of the cosmos is the power of love.[32] Meanwhile, Margaret falls in love with Faust in Newman's musical; she poisons her mother in order to be alone with him and kills her brother with the aid of the Devil. With Margaret pregnant, Faust and the Devil skip town and live in a cabin near Lake Superior. Racked with grief and shame, Margaret gives birth to Faust's child only to commit infanticide, gets convicted, and is sentenced to death at the Indiana State Prison.

Due to her goodness during life, angels carry Margaret to heaven even before she dies. Henry is impressed by this event to the extent that he asks God for forgiveness, and he then commits suicide. The Devil is confident of victory and his return to heaven. Before dying without dignity or courage, Henry repeats his plea for divine forgiveness. In response, angels descend to save him, and Henry waves to the Devil as he ascends to heaven. The Devil is obviously cheated out of his honestly won victory, causing his emotions to move from anger to depression, and God is even moved to pity him. The Devil sings "Happy Ending" as he feels a hot wind blowing, he feels his confidence growing, and acknowledges that he will eventually be all right. He lost to a dishonest deity, but he still possesses corruption and destruction. He admits to having Las Vegas, a hell on earth in his mind. Just thinking about all the decadence of Las Vegas gives the Devil a religious experience, and he begins to humorously speak in tongues much like a Pentecostal Christian having an overwhelming spiritual experience. Overall, Newman's musical is sympathetic toward the Devil, a spirit of negation, and critical of a bored and dishonest high God.

A different view of the Devil is offered by Bruce Springsteen in the lyrics to "A Night with the Jersey Devil." Associated at birth with the unlucky number 13, Springsteen's subject relates a tragic narrative of attempted murder at the hands of his father as an infant, his survival, and vengeful return to kill his father and siblings. While he sleeps, his mother attempts to burn him to death, and he burns until his soul becomes black. This personified Devil uses human skin and a skull to construct his guitar. Assuming a bestial and horrific appearance, he proceeds to drink human blood and eat human flesh. Nonetheless, this Garden State devilish figure is lost on earth, just as God is lost in heaven.

Overall, the various examples of rock lyrics which refer to the Devil point to the non-hierarchical nature of power. If the Devil represents the opposite of God, his figure demonstrates that power can emerge from the lowest depths of society and religious culture. The symbolic and metaphorical role of the Devil with respect to power implies that power does not start from the top of the hierarchy and move downward, but power is exercised more diffusely and locally, as Michel Foucault demonstrates with his book on prisons.[33]

The Goddess

There is a plethora of songs devoted to women, as mentioned in the first chapter of this book. The lyrics focusing on female figures are vaguely suggestive, or sometimes very lucidly suggestive, about references to goddess characteristics. Despite over five decades of rock lyrics that have depicted women both positively and negatively, there have also been lyrics that connect women to the supernatural by connecting women to aspects of nature or to the earth itself.

James Taylor explicitly makes an association of women and the earth in his song "Gaia" from his album *Hourglass*. According to Taylor's lyrics, aspects of the world around him evoke Gaia, a Greek name for the earth goddess. The earth is not a mother figure that we can leave behind or neglect because we owe our existence to Gaia. In a strong ecological message, Taylor thinks that we must stop destroying and polluting Gaia. Finally, the singer urges us to pray for the forest, fish, humans, and even the unbeliever. We find a similar type of message in the number "The Rape of the World" by Tracy Chapman from her album *New Beginning.* The earth is our mother for Chapman and represents the place of our birth, but we have been committing a heinous crime against her. By means of strip mining, bombs, urbanization, clear-cutting forests, dumping waste and poisons on her, we are guilty of the rape of the earth. In his song "Holy Ground," Steve Winwood equates such a sacred place with the earth, protesting that we should care for the earth and not abuse it because this sacred ground is a gift from God to all people.

The reverence for the earth expressed by these rock composers is shared by a feminist religious scholar like Christine Downing, who views Gaia as the mother of the beginning before the advent of time. Gaia represents the earth as animate and divine. Because she is never personal or humanized, she reminds us that the divine is transhuman and pre-human due to its being present from the beginning. With her generative essence, Gaia is the living presence of the earth, and she reminds us of a period when matter was rebellious. We need to re-grasp the rebellious, living, and eruptive aspects of the earth. This represents the earth as it is; it is not the earth subdued by humankind. In fact, Gaia can never be subdued or predictable because she stands for life and is opposed to stifling order.[34]

Besides a direct association of the earth with the sacred and mother goddess, some rock lyrics make a direct connection between women and other aspects of nature. Sting associates his girlfriend with the four seasons in his song "All Four Seasons" from his album *Mercury Falling.* The rock group called The Association connects a woman with an aspect of nature in their hit song "Windy." She not only possesses a name from nature that is light, but she also embodies other natural attributes like stormy eyes, lightening flashes, and wings that enable her to fly. The direct connection between a woman and aspects of nature are also evident in the lyrics of "Rio" by the rock group Duran Duran from an album of the same title. Rio dances on the sandy beach that resembles a winding river. Along similar lines of rock poetry, Elton John sings about a vision of such a woman in his recording "The One" from an album of the same title. Instead of the beach, this woman, who is a product of earth and water, dances on the ocean, runs along the beach, and rises upwards like fire. According to the lyrics of John's song, this vision is the future of each person before which he was an incarnation of the biblical figure Cain.

The lyrics sung by Duran Duran and John reflect attributes of an African goddess figure named Oshun. The goddess Oshun is a deity of the Yoruba of Nigeria who took her with them as slaves to Cuba and later into the United States of America. Oshun is river born, and her identification with cool waters explains her vivacious character and her hips that sway like a slow rolling river. She is described as beautiful and sweet tempered; she also reveals pleasure, flirts with men, and delights in their seduction, which manifests her role as the great coquette. She loves jewelry, rich gifts of silk, perfume, and sweet foods. In short, Oshun was the "material girl" long before Madonna arrived on the pop cultural scene. Oshun is called La Puta Santa (the whore saint) in Cuba, a designation that partly describes Madonna, according to some of her critics. Nonetheless, Oshun plays the role of a mother by giving herself to her lovers much like a mother does to her children. Giving birth to many children herself, she possesses the power to bestow children on barren women who seek her aid, and she helps women with difficult pregnancies and child-birth.[35]

For some male rock stars, the female is manifested as a savior figure. Jimi Hendrix's song "Hey Baby (The Land of the New Rising Sun)" welcomes the arrival of a female offering universal salvation. This female figure offers shelter from the problems of the world and consolation for the weary. And in their song and video called "Mysterious Ways," from their album *Achtung Baby*, the group U2 becomes acolytes for a female deity associated with a cult of the earth. The video suggestively shows the singer kneeling to perform cunnilingus on the mysterious goddess of nature. Moreover, she also reveals herself as the moon, rain, sky, and light.

Although they do not really depict them as goddesses, rock lyrics do portray other women as embodiments of evil. The song "Lucretia MacEvil" by the rock group Blood, Sweat and Tears describes the central subject as an evil woman who openly flaunts her sexuality, which seems to suggest a direct connection between evil and the overt manifestation of her sexual nature. According to the rock group INXS in their tune "Suicide Blonde," the subject can strip off her clothing to the beat of the music, but her clothing stays on her body. Presumably, her sexually suggestive movement gives the illusion of undressing.

Besides being openly sexual, other women are depicted as extremely dangerous. The duo of Daryl Hall and John Oates make this clear in their song "Maneater." The female figure in Kim Carnes' number "Bette Davis Eyes" is ferocious and will roll you like a toy.

Other women are depicted as dangerous and mysterious. Some examples of this trend are the following: "Wild Thing" by the Troggs; "Gypsy Woman" by the Impressions; and "Black Magic Woman" and her attempt to turn her lover into a devil by Santana. These dangerous types of women embody some of the life- threatening attributes of the Hindu goddess Kālī in her dark and terrible form as a blood-thirsty shrew.

The Hindu goddess Kālī is called the black one because of her dark color. She is naked and immodest. She is often depicted in Indian art and texts surrounded by jackals, snakes, and ghosts, standing on a corpse in a cremation ground. When she is depicted with four arms, she holds a sword, a noose, a freshly severed head, and a cup made from a human skull filled with blood. Around her neck hangs a garland of human heads, newly cut human hands dangle from her waistband, and two dead infants form her earrings. She appears with a sunken belly, sagging breasts, sunken reddish eyes, and disheveled hair, with long fangs framing her mouth, a lolling tongue, and blood trickling out of the corners of her mouth. This horrid looking goddess delights in death and destruction, and she represents the mistress of time with her lolling tongue that consumes all things, while her dancing represents the pulsating of the universe. The sexually aggressive goddess is the mad mistress of a mad world that is self-intoxicated and moving inexorably towards its own destruction.[36]

In "Goddess in the Doorway," from a solo album of the same name, Mick Jagger expresses a much different kind of vision of a goddess than that given by the Hindu goddess of death. Jagger expresses his bizarre situation by juxtaposing dogs on the roof of a house with demons in the bedroom, while the subject looks for truth in the basement with his patience growing weaker. Then, he describes a goddess with smooth and supple flesh with eyes like diamonds. Inside the album, she is depicted with a golden color, not unlike the Greek goddess Aphrodite, and he admits that he is looking for her temple, shrine, or vision of her.

Metaphorical Goddess of Rock 'n' Roll

If Elvis Presley approaches the status of the male god of rock 'n' roll for some rock fans, the closest thing to a metaphorical goddess figure is Madonna, although there are younger pretenders to this mantle like Brittany Spears, Mariah Carey, Shakira, and Lady Gaga. This attribution of metaphorical divine status upon her is not connected to her popularity or her outrageous style. I interpret Madonna's antics as essentially playful in nature. The scholar Colleen McDannell misses the playful element in her analysis of Madonna's video "Like a Prayer." McDannell views this video as a recreation of the myth of Pygmalion, a sculptor from Cyprus who falls in love with the beauty-ful statue he created, which then comes to life. McDannell observes, "In the commercialized version of this myth, it is the body of the rock star that brings the saint to life. The role of the beauty has been reversed: Madonna is not aroused by the black statue, rather the black statue cannot remain inert after being confronted by the intensity of Madonna."[37] In an otherwise outstanding piece of scholarship, Mc-Dannell overemphasizes the commercialization of myth and profiteering from it. What McDannell misses in her analysis is that Madonna embodies playfulness in the same spirit expressed by Cindi Lauper's hit song, "Girls Just Want to Have Fun."

Fun represents the essence of play, which is a voluntary activity that is free and superfluous. Play represents an interlude in our lives, but it is still an integral part of life. And yet play is distinct from ordinary life and creates its own kind of order, a temporary and limited perfection. Play casts a spell over us because it is enchanting, captivating, rhythmic, and harmonious. The tension within it relates to its uncertainty, even though it possesses its own rules that are binding and cannot be transgressed without falling into a state of collapse. There is a certain secrecy associated with play that suggests that it is for us and not for others. It gives us an opportunity to "dress up" and be different as it utterly absorbs us.[38] By assuming the role of a rock star, Madonna possesses ample opportunity to play.

Madonna is continuously and playfully re-inventing herself by periodically assuming new masks. In a sense she is nothing but her masks, and yet there is no single mask that completely represents her. The psychologist Carl Jung might say that she is whatever her public persona happens to be at a given moment, but she also deserves, in a spirit of playfulness, the mantle or persona of rock goddess based on her lyrics and videos.

A public persona that she adopted in 1984 was that of the "Material Girl" based on her album *Like a Virgin*, a very playful use of words for a woman who publicly flaunts her lascivious sexual nature. She confesses that she is a material girl in order to conform to the material world in which she is living. In the video to this song, she imitates Marilyn Monroe doing her famous rendition of "Diamonds Are a Girl's Best Friend" in the movie *Gentlemen Prefer Blonds*. In the video to this song, she depicts herself as a material girl that is unattached to material things. Unlike Marilyn Monroe, Madonna redefines what it means to be a material girl in the video by accepting the simple love of an average guy who picks her up in a truck and not a guy dressed in a tuxedo and riding in a limousine. By using the video to redefine a material girl, Madonna is also symbolically and playfully dethroning the paradigm of the Hollywood sex goddess in the person of Monroe, or at least attempting to accomplish this dethroning.

The same kind of usage and transformation of symbols and playfulness is evident in the number "Like a Virgin." In the title song to the album "Like a Virgin," Madonna takes the notion of virginity and turns it around. In the lyrics she does not say that she is a virgin, but she feels like a virgin when she is paradoxically having sexual relations with the man of her dreams because he makes her feel whole. In the video of this song, Madonna is filmed in the Italian city of Venice dressed in the white dress symbolic of the purity of a virgin, whereas black is the color of the whore or the libido. From a historical and religious perspective, the patron saint of Venice is St. Mark, symbolized by a lion, whereas Matthew is depicted as a human figure, John the Evangelist is symbolized by the eagle, and the ox represents Luke, a complex of symbolism dating back to Saint Jerome's commentary on Ezekiel (beginning of the fifth century).[39] The video depicts Madonna encountering a man-lion and having a sexual relationship with this figure in a gondola as it floats through the waterways of Venice. This entire scenario suggests that Madonna is having a sexual encounter with a saint of the Catholic Church. In fact, the saint cannot resist her beauty and purity. On the one hand, the video also suggests that Madonna feels like a virgin when having sex with a saint. On the other hand, the saint is freed of his virginity by the new redefined Virgin of the Catholic Church and newly crowned Madonna, who replaces the Virgin Mary and mother of Jesus. In short, there is the strong suggestion that there is a new goddess named Madonna. Some pious Catholics will find these suggestions blasphemous. But this is exactly the type of reaction that a former Catholic, such as Madonna, wants to evoke with her playfulness. It is not coincidental that the song "Like a Virgin" is in an album entitled The *Immaculate Collection*, a playful reference to the Mother of God and Madonna herself.

Another mask assumed by Madonna on her videos is that of the slut in the tune "Open Your Heart." The video depicts a peep show that one might find in New York City, where a girl performs by dancing in a lewd manner after a screen rises because male voyeurs put money into coin slots. Among the voyeurs in the video for this song are a couple of gay sailors and a sexual researcher taking notes. Madonna appears at first to be at the mercy of the gaze of the voyeurs, but this is deceiving. Eventually, it becomes clear that Madonna, the lewd dancing slut, is not only in control of her situation, but she is also free, whereas the voyeurs are in bondage to their own lust. As the video ends, Madonna leaves the theater and dances with a boy outside to demonstrate her detachment, control and freedom. The slut goddess is free to play, while the male voyeurs are captive to their sexual instincts.

Playing the role of the slut, Madonna resembles the African-Cuban goddess Oshun, a great coquette, and the ancient Greek goddess Aphrodite, who is beautiful but unchaste. Her husband, the crippled metal worker Hephaestus, fashions a net to catch Aphrodite with her lover Ares, the impetuous, drunken, and quarrelsome god of war. Aphrodite also gets involved in a love affair with Hermes, which results in the child Hermaphroditus, a double-sexed being. From another love affair with Dionysus, she gives birth to Priapus, an ugly child with enormous genitals. Besides these love affairs and the deviant off-spring of these sexual encounters, Aphrodite is connected to the sea because she emerges from the salt waters, symbolic of potentiality and source of all possible existence, after being born from the genitals of her father Uranus. Moreover, Aphrodite is also a seducer of mortal men like Anchises, a king of the Dardanians. Since it is unhealthy to sleep with a goddess, the offspring of their sexual union is Aeneas, who is made lame by a lighting bolt of Zeus. All of this sexual activity results in her identification with prostitutes and doves that suggest love. Her heavenly chariot is drawn by sparrows, which are known for their wantonness and fecundity.[40] Aphrodite is famous for her golden color and gold ornaments that are bright and synonymous with her beauty. Like Aphrodite, Madonna is known to be generous with her sexual favors in a way similar to Janis Joplin. In fact, both Joplin and Madonna re-invent the whore to represent a sexual rebel.

Changing roles a bit, Madonna becomes a goddess of sadomasochism in her number "Express Yourself." Again, she is playing a role by donning a collar and chain and groveling like a cat or a dog. She is in bondage, but she still maintains control of the situation with her playfulness. A couple of years later in 1992 she released the song "Erotica" from the album of the same title, in which she plays the role of a mistress for an evening. The same sadomasochistic message is present as in the video for "Express Yourself," with the union of sexual satisfaction and pain. She explicitly invites her lover to explore her body with his hands, and to allow her mouth to wander wherever it wants on his body.

However, the most revealing role assumed by Madonna is that of a savior figure in the video of her song "Like a Prayer," composed by her and Patrick Leonard. The lyrics to this number are very different and less provocative than the video. In the lyrics, she hears a voice calling her name and feels like it transports her home. This call is akin to a prayer that puts her down on her knees; it is a power that she can feel. She further explains that the angelic voice transports her out of her body, and she gains a sensation of flight and ascent, an experience expressed by dancing in an endless dream with a voice whispering to her. This mysterious experience is similar to an ecstatic state in which one is transported outside of oneself, which suggest that the lyrics evoke an image of a powerful religious experience.

In contrast to the lyrics of her song, the video is much more provocative and controversial. The video plays with the opposition between black and white, sacred and profane, inside and outside of the church, female and male, peace and violence, love and hate, dream and reality, and female savior and whore. Even though a black chorus backs the white Madonna and she encounters a black messiah, she wants to call into question the entire structure of binary opposites. When does the dream state begin and end? What is reality? What kind of love is salvific?

As the plot of the video unfolds, Madonna falls asleep in a pew. When the black Christ figure comes to life the couple proceed to have a sexual encounter. Since the black messiah is a captive of the church, he needs to be saved. And it is Madonna, a new savior goddess, who will liberate the black Christ. If the *agape* form of love represents the savific type of love of the New Testament, it is *eros* (an erotic, passionate, sexual) love that will be the black messiah's vehicle of liberation from his captivity to the church.

The symbolism of the salvific act is very rich with a variety of hermeneutical possibilities. The *eros* from the modern-day Aphrodite frees the black messiah from a kind of slavery. The sexual love of the goddess supercedes *agape* as a vehicle of salvation, which opens up new religious possibilities. This passionate kind of love is both carnal and incarnate; it is seductive and dangerous. This erotic love is impure rather than pure, and it is not a selfless giving of one's self as with *agape* because there is a strong trace of selfish interest and satisfaction with this type of love. Moreover, it is a goddess figure that is the medium for salvation and not a male figure. Thus the old redeemer is himself redeemed by the new rock goddess. But if it is all a dream, as Madonna sings towards the conclusion of the song, she calls every event into question. There is no final conclusion because everything gets deferred until some future time.

The role of the redeeming goddess ironically saving the lamb of God is just another role played by Madonna, or another mask donned by the rock star. The burden of identifying her is left to the audience because she playfully wears many masks. Sometimes she wears more than one mask in a given song; because no single mask captures her true identity and fully represents her essence, she invites us to participate in the game and to enjoy it. In a spirit of play, we should never take the invitation or the game too seriously because that would spoil the fun.

Since Madonna enjoys playing so many different roles and wearing different masks, it is interesting that she does not to my knowledge assume the mask of a witch like the subject in the song "Rhiannon (Will You Ever Win)" by Fleetwood Mac, recorded in 1975. Rhiannon is a Welsh witch goddess of steeds and a maker of birds. This mysterious female can take flight at will. The lyrics are intended to serve as a warning to her male admirers because they will never be able to know her or control her. Being able to ride the winds, she continuously eludes the grasp of admiring and desirous males. This proto-feminist is a free spirit who taunts her male followers with the refrain "Will you ever win?"[41] There is no male who will conquer this free female spirit.

Similar to Madonna, another female singer reacting against her Catholic background is Sinead O'Connor. She imagines herself reacting to what she perceives as the anti-feminine and anti-sexual mores of Catholicism. Describing herself as a Christian who despises the church, she unites the Virgin Mary and Jesus in her person in order to re-invent a faith that is feminine, maternal, nurturing, and forgiving.[42] The freeing of female sexuality from the suppression of the church is evident in her album *Universal Mother*, released in 1994. On the album, O'Connor records a song composed by the feminist author Germaine Greer, "Charge of the Goddess." In this number, the goddess speaks to her devotees: Needy devotees meet during a full moon once a month in a secret place, where she will give them secret teachings that will free them. The goddess also instructs her devotees to strive for their highest idea and to not be deterred from reaching their goal. Identifying herself with the earth, stars, waters, and the desire within a woman's heart, the goddess pours her love on the earth. Moreover, she is defined as both without (as earth) and within a person (an internal spiritual presence).

Concluding Remarks

The rock scene and its artists are pervaded by narcissism and *hubris* (pride), which is often given expression by claiming or having bestowed upon one a kind of sovereignty. James Brown is the "King of Soul," Aretha Franklin is the "Queen of Soul," Michael Jackson is the "King of Pop," and Elvis is the "King of Rock." In his song entitled "Heroes," David Bowie imagines himself becoming king for just one day, whereas Mick Jagger impersonates the Devil, a rebel-monarch, who wants to depose the King of Heaven and usurp His reign in "Sympathy for the Devil." All of these titles of privilege bear witness to the power of fans and media to grant the titles, and so pointing to the diffuse nature of power.

Going beyond these kinds of attributions and wishful thinking, the Doors lead singer Jim Morrison staged-managed his own self-deification. His Dionysian message was to usurp the father figure and seduce the mother, according to his producer Paul Rothchild. This involved over-turning the old precepts and reconnecting with absolute reality by way of the mother.[43] Over the decades of rock history, many rock stars have been nearly deified by adorning fans, becoming simulated divine beings. Besides a simulation of divine status, this type of idolization represents an eclipse of the Judeo-Christian deity or a death of God for some composers. Within the vacuum created by the eclipse or death of the Judeo-Christian deity, there stand new pretenders to divine status—male and female rock stars—and old figures like the earth goddess, an ancient figure newly re-discovered and retrieved.

A fundamental problem for rock composers and theologians with respect to God is that God is ultimately a mystery, something that we cannot clearly grasp intellectually. Although the mysterious nature of God does not tell us anything about God, it does, however, tell us something about ourselves. It informs us that we have reached the pinnacle of our ability to comprehend. The symbol "God" plays a useful role "to designate that creativity, that mystery, which under girds our human existence in all its complexity and all its diversity."[44]

In retrospect, we can acknowledge a plurality of beliefs about supernatural beings. It is rare for lyrics to represent a defense or even a reinterpretation of traditional beliefs about God, the Devil, or goddess figures. The various composers often take a critical stance towards the inherited tradition. In a sense, composers bear witness to an older tradition about the nature of supernatural beings, and use their work to offer some new possibilities, criticisms, and suggestions. It is possible that what we witness with the lyrics reviewed in this chapter is an emerging secular faith characterized by a new polytheism of divine, semi-divine, and human deities. Again, by taking a critical perspective toward the presumably highest power in the universe, God, various rock artists manifest their own power.

Endnotes

[1] B. Clifton Spargo and Anne K. Ream, "Bob Dylan and Religion," in *The Cambridge Companion to Bob Dylan* ed. by Kevin J. H. Dettmar (Cambridge: Cambridge University Press, 2009), p. 92.

[2] Mircea Eliade, *Yoga: Immortality and Freedom*, trans. Willard R. Trask, Bollingen Series LVI, Second Edition (Princeton: Princeton University Press, 1969), p. 90.

[3] Martin Buber, *Moses: The Revelation and the Covenant* (New York: Harper & Row, Publishers, 1946; reprint 1958), p. 48.

[4] Barth, Church *Dogmatics*, II/1, p. 62.

[5] Carlos Castaneda, *The Teachings of Don Juan: A Yaqui Way of Knowledge* (Berkeley: University of California Press, 1972), p. 25.

[6] J. S. Slotkin, *The Peyote Religion* (Glencoe, IL: The Free Press, 1956), p. 46.

[7] Barth, Church *Dogmatics*, 1/1, p. 277.

[8] William Hamilton, "The Death of God Theologies Today," in *Radical Theology and the Death of God*, eds. Thomas J. J. Altizer and William Hamilton (Indianapolis: The Bobbs-Merrill Company, Inc., 1966), p. 48.

[9] Thomas J. J. Altizer, "America and the Future of Theology," in *Radical Theology and the Death of God*, eds. Thomas J. J. Altizer and William Hamilton (Indianapolis: The Bobbs-Merrill Company, Inc., 1966), p. 11.

[10] Mark C. Taylor, *Hiding* (Chicago: University of Chicago Press, 1997), p. 233.

[11] Bonhoeffer, *Letters and Papers from Prison*, p. 195.

[12] Martin Buber, *Eclipse of God: Studies in the Relation between Religion and Philosophy* (New York: Harper & Row, Publishers, 1952), p. 14.

[13] Cox, *Feast of Fools*, pp. 27-28.

[14] Spargo and Beam, p.89.

[15] Blaise Pascal, *Pensées*, trans. H. F. Stewart (New York: Pantheon Books, 1950; 1965), p. 150.

[16] Taylor, *About Religion*, p. 5.

[17] Ludwig Feuerbach, *The Essence of Christianity*, trans. George Eliot (New York: Harper, 1957), p. 213.

[18] Martin Luther, *Luther Works*, Vol. 1, p. 11.

[19] Idem, *Luther Works*, Vol. 31, p. 53.

[20] Idem, *Commentary on Galatians*, p. 44.

[21] Foucault, *Power/Knowledge*, p. 142.

[22] Paul Tillich, *Systematic Theology Volume I: Reason and Revelation Being and God* (Chicago: University of Chicago Press, 1951; 1966), I: 236.

[23] Jeffrey Burton Russell, *Mephistopheles: The Devil in the Modern World* (Ithaca: Cornell University Press, 1986), p. 257.

[24] Bernard McGinn, *Anti-Christ: Two Thousand Years of the Human Fascination with Evil* (New York: Harper Collins Publishers, 1994), p. 24; Jeffrey Burton Russell, *The Devil: Perceptions of Evil from Antiquity to Primitive Christianity* (Ithaca: Cornell University Press, 1977), p. 189.

[25] Russell, *The Devil*, pp. 197-203.

[26] Eliane Pagels, *The Origin of Satan* (New York: Random House, 1995), p. 12.

[27] Jeffrey Burton Russell, *Lucifer: The Devil in the Middle Ages* (Ithaca: Cornell University Press, 1984), pp. 62-63.

[28] Ibid., p. 243.

[29] Ibid., p. 261.

[30] Ibid., p. 210.

[31] Ibid., p. 69.

[32] Idem, *Mephistopheles*, p. 159.

[33] Foucault, *Discipline and Punish*, pp. 170-94.

[34] Christine Downing, *The Goddess: Mythological Images of the Feminine* (New York: Crossroad, 1981), pp. 135-150.

[35] Joseph Murphy, "Oshun," in *The Book of the Goddess Past and Present: An Introduction to Her Religion*, ed. Carl Olson (New York: Crossroads Publishing Company, 1983), pp. 190-201.

[36] David Kinsley, *Hindu Goddesses: Visions of the Divine Feminine in the Hindu Religious Tradition* (Berkeley: University of California Press, 1986), pp. 116-131.

[37] Colleen McDannell, *Material Christianity: Religion and Popular Culture in America* (New Haven: Yale University Press, 1995), p. 64.

[38] Johan Huizinga, *Homo Ludens: A Study of the Play Element in Culture* (New York: Roy Publishers, 1950), pp. 8-13.

[39] Gerhart B. Ladner, *Christian God, Cosmos, and Humankind: The World of Early Christian Symbolism*, trans. Thomas Dunlap (Berkeley: University of California Press, 1995), p. 28.

[40] David R. Kinsley, *The Goddesses' Mirror: Visions of the Divine from East and West* (Albany: State University of New York Press, 1989), pp. 207, 192.

[41] Reynolds and Press, p. 281.

[42] Ibid., p. 252.

[43] Ibid., p. 125.
[44] Kaufman, p. 109.

Chapter 6

Jesus, Superstar, Clown, and Antichrist

For a form of music that is supposed to be satanic and anti-religious according to some critics, it is curious that it is possible to find numerous references to Jesus in rock lyrics, even if we specifically exclude Christian rock groups. During the 1970's the rock group Ocean released a hit record "Put Your Hand In the Hand." Although not strictly speaking a rock group, the Edwin Hawkins Singers sang about when Jesus walked the earth in their rousing gospel/rock recording "Oh Happy Day." The Byrds and the Doobie Brothers both recorded "Jesus Is Just Alright," a misleading title because it is a song about personal acceptance of Jesus. Moreover, interest in Jesus inspired two rock musicals based on the events of his life: *Jesus Christ Superstar* and *Godspell*. These rock musicals will be examined later in this chapter for what they tell us about the treatment and understanding of Jesus. If there is a variety of opinion about the person of Jesus and what he represented during his lifetime, it is no wonder that the same ambiguity is reflected in some rock lyrics.

A good example of such a problem is the song "Jesus" written and performed by Cat Stevens for his album *Buddha and the Chocolate Box*, in which he depicts Jesus as misunderstood during his lifetime. According to the lyrics, Jesus left humankind his love to lead the blind to the light. Likewise, a long time ago, Gautama Buddha restored order to a chaotic world. By means of his wisdom, he knew in what direction humankind was moving. And like Jesus, the love of the Buddha will lead humankind toward the light. Stevens' lyrics mistakenly suggest similarities between the message of Jesus and the Buddha that focus on love. The path of liberation espoused by the Buddha was a way of liberating knowledge or intuitive insight into the nature of reality, although a Buddhist version of love (e.g., *karunā* or compassion; *mettā* or loving kindness) played a part in his message. The Buddha taught that it was necessary for each individual to work towards his/her own salvation, whereas Jesus' message of love presupposed the saving grace of God. In his rush to find similarities, Stevens distorts the differences between these two influential teachers. Stevens sings about a singer and the daughter of a gardener and how they conceive a child lying on the naked earth with the universe above them in "The Boy with the Moon and Star on His Head" from his album *Catch Bull at Four*. The child of this romantic union is born with a moon and a star on his head, and he preaches about love. The symbol of the star suggests height, light, and transcendence and/or a heavenly realm, whereas the moon possesses many symbolic connections that include the rhythms of life, birth and death, cosmic waters, vegetation, fertility, fate, and time. It is time that is governed and measured by the phases of the moon in some religious traditions.[1]

Lyrics similar to a hymn-like ode to Jesus appears in Bruce Springsteen's "Jesus Was an Only Son" from the album *Devils and Dust*. The song depicts Jesus walking to Calvary with his mother at his side. It also refers to his earthly life reading the Psalms, recalls the garden of Gethsemane, and requests a different destiny from his Heavenly Father. At the end, Jesus comforts his mother and reminds her of God's creative action.

A curious kind of tale is presented by the Dave Matthews Band with "Christmas Story" from their album *Remember Two Things*. The lyrics represent a strange summary of the life of Jesus. The song relates the tale of the three wise men who shower the child Jesus with love, but not much is known about his childhood except that he worried his mother. He later meets Mary Magdelene, a professional prostitute, and gives her a fee, presumably for a service that she rendered him, a possibility for which there is no biblical evidence. Nonetheless, this kind of encounter is evidence that Jesus associated with socially undesirable elements, an accusation supported by textual evidence (Lk 18:35; 7:37-50; Mk 10:46). Besides mention of the last supper with his disciples, Jesus' heart is described as overflowing with love. When he was crucified Jesus said to his Father that he could see what will be, although he feared that he shed the blood of innocent children. Jesus asks God the Father why He in His anger filled His son with so much love. The authors of these lyrics appear to have a problem with the sacrificial symbolism of the crucifixion. The lyrics also suggest that Jesus was cursed or doomed by His Father because he was filled with an excess of love. Reinhold Niebuhr clarifies the Christian position: "The grace of sacrificial love prevents mutual love from degenerating into a mere calculation of mutual advantages."[2] It is the self-sacrificial nature of the love that makes it the highest form of love and suggests its excessiveness.

Another curious use of Jesus is evident in the song "UB Jesus" by the group Talking Heads from their album *Look Into the Eyeball.* The song begins with the subject asking his girlfriend to be his personal savior. In a verse in which he seems to be addressing so-called Jesus Freaks, he sings, "You might know Jesus but you'll all join in hell." Then, the subject asks his girlfriend to become Jesus, a request in line with his initial one for her to become his savior. Next, there is a confession that his girlfriend's car is hell, presumably because of its use for sexual encounters and singing, although the subject confesses to feeling good when he is burning within the confines of her car. Finally, the subject presents his depiction of Jesus as a big, strong bully that will punish a person who does not get along with others. These kinds of lyrics are far from the usual portrait of Jesus as the caring, loving, and peaceful figure. These lyrics find an echo in the Middle Ages at which time Jesus was viewed as a stern, threatening, angry judge. Because ordinary people viewed Jesus in this way, they turned to his mother Mary to serve as an intercessor. Mary was viewed as gentle, loving, and forgiving, and common people believed she could not be refused by her son. In light of this type of historical development, the sphere of purgatory became her special sphere of influence during the Middle Ages.[3]

The narrative of Jesus is sometimes used for more political purposes. Phil Ochs unravels a tale, for instance, in his "Crucifixion" from his album *Pleasures of the Harbor* about various types of heroes and their eventual fall. The crux of his criticism is that we tend to take a morbid delight in the sagas of fallen heroes of whom Jesus is one example. In another of his songs called "The Ballad of the Carpenter," Ochs uses an outline of the life of Jesus to make a socio-political point about wealthy and poor people. Jesus was poor, worked among and cared for the impoverished, was protected by the poor, and betrayed for silver by the rich. It was thus the wealthy class that had him crucified and laughed as he died. But the dream of the impoverished carpenter endures about improving the lives of the poor, and it is up to us to make his dream a reality.

The types of lyrics surveyed thus far demonstrate that Jesus is a problematic figure for rock composers because they cannot fully accept the orthodox configuration of him with such notions as his bodily resurrection and ascension. It is possible, nonetheless, to find particular themes in rock lyrics associated with Jesus that one can also discover in Christian thought and history. Therefore, this chapter will examine the significance of a need to become contemporary with Jesus. Two major portraits of Jesus as a superstar and clown are comparatively different and informative rock depictions of Jesus. The exact opposite of Jesus also appears in rock lyrics with the figure of the Antichrist, which also serves as a provocative counter-example to the message of Jesus. Finally, a look at some lyrics about the path to salvation finds examples of both a faith-based path and a path of knowledge.

Becoming Contemporary with Jesus

The influential Danish religious thinker Søren Kierkegaard emphasizes the necessity of becoming contemporary with Jesus as part of his explanation about what it means to be a Christian.[4] Kierkegaard refines his answer by developing four themes. In order to lead a Christian life, one must be willing to suffer and be in conflict with the world by carrying a cross. Besides following a life of suffering, to be a Christian involves leading a life of discipleship in which Jesus is one's model, which means to accept the requirement of unconditional obedience. A third theme is becoming contemporary with Christ, which means to actually encounter the concrete figure of Jesus Christ and be confronted by the humble one. This is a wholly objective encounter with Christ in which He meets us, challenges us, invites us, and requires a decision from us. The importance of this decision is the fourth theme of what it means to become a Christian. Since it is a difficult task to become a Christian and simply thoughtless to remain a nominal Christian, it is necessary to make a decision to become a Christian in reality. The imperative to decide even requires courage to renounce Christianity: "In brief, it is easier to become a Christian when I am not a Christian than to become a Christian when I am one."[5] What Kierkegaard wants to accomplish is transforming those who are merely being-a-Christian into those who are Christians in reality. Thus, it is necessary to make a decision, and this involves a leap of choice.[6] Although most rock musical composers have probably never read or even heard of Kierkegaard, there are many songs that stress the importance of becoming contemporary with Jesus.

The song by Ocean called "Put Your Hand In the Hand" is a good example of this motif among composers of rock lyrics. The group instructs you to place your hand into the same hand as the person who calms the Sea of Galilee. The lyrics depict a subject who trembles when reading the Bible, but other people forget the message of the New Testament, which causes the subject shame to think that we have been unable to live according to the ideals expressed in the text. In order to recapture the spirit of the message of Jesus and to make it a reality in our present life, we must become contemporary with him by placing our hand metaphorically in his.

We find the Rolling Stones treating Jesus very differently in two distinct recordings. Their song "Blinded By Rainbows" from their *Voodoo Lounge* album echoes the emphasis on becoming contemporary with Christ advocated by Kierkegaard. This is accomplished by two powerful questions about feeling pain from the nails and lance cutting his flesh. The Stones composers—Jagger and Richards—view being contemporary with Jesus as a feeling, whereas it is a more a state of being for Kierkegaard. In one of their earlier hit recordings, Jagger and Richards collaborate on "Jumpin' Jack Flash" who is a Christ figure. The character Jack Flash, who is also an identity assumed by Mick Jagger jumping and strutting around a concert stage like a peacock, is miraculously born, crowned with a spike through his head instead of a garland of thorns, dies by drowning instead of crucifixion, and suffers bleeding feet, but it is implied that he is reborn to communicate his message just as Jesus appears to his disciples after his death. If Jumpin' Jack Flash is a contemporary version of a Christ figure, is he a rock star redefined to represent a new kind of Christ figure?

Falling into a dream state, the subject of "When Love Comes to Town" by the Irish rock group U2 from their album *Rattle and Hum* awakens on the street to the sensation that the world is dancing. He looks up to see the Devil looking down at him. The subject confesses to being at the crucifixion, holding the scabbard for the soldier's sword, throwing the dice, and seeing the conquering power of love.

Becoming contemporary with Jesus implies responding to his message. This forms the basis of "Jesus Children of America" by Stevie Wonder from his album *Innervisions*. We know that Jesus loves children. But are you hearing and responding to his message? Wonder calls into question the religion of the so-called holy-roller. In turn, he mentions Transcendental Meditation because it gives one an innervision and peace of mind. Finally, he admits that Jesus died on the cross for everyone, and confesses his need for the savior.

In contrast to her industrious friends, the subject in "Shame On You" by the Indigo Girls from their album *Shaming of the Sun* would rather go down to the river and wash away her sins. A friend tells her that she and Jesus share the same heart, the major difference that keeps her and Jesus apart "is that I keep fuckin up." Again, not being able to keep to the straight and narrow path does not destroy being able to be contemporary with Christ.

There are also rock lyrics that reflect some kind of encounter with Jesus. While on a walk near his home, a subject encounters a man walking on the water of the river in the lyrics of "Walk on the Water" by Creedence Clearwater Revival. When the Jesus-like stranger calls his name he runs away due to being frightened and overwhelmed by the sight of a miraculous event. In their song called "Jesus" from their first album, the rock group Queen describes seeing Jesus in a group of people and witnessing him cleansing a leaper. Christ is a refuge for a sailor adrift at sea in a storm in the lyrics of "Tremor Christ" by Pearl Jam from their album *Vitalogy*. The sailor places his faith in Christ and is saved from the danger of the storm.

The figure of Jesus appears in some rock lyrics as someone who is not accepted or is used to make a critical point. The principle subject of Bob Dylan's song "Property of Jesus" cannot accept the notion that he and everyone else are "property of Jesus." He resents this notion because Jesus rejects all the materialistic things that he cherishes. The subject's hardened heart makes it impossible for him to accept his condition as property because he would rather own property than be considered it. Instead of saving us according to "Hymn 43" composed by Jethro Tull from their album *Aqualung*, Jesus should save himself from those who use his name to perpetuate death. The target of the group's criticism is the industrial-military complex, but their critical message is made more powerful by their reference to Jesus. From another critical perspective, Depeche Mode sing about a personal Jesus who hears your prayers, cares about you, and comforts you in their song "Personal Jesus" from their album *Violator*. And yet those merchants of religion selling easy faith abuse the figure of Jesus. If you are lonely, you only have to pick up the telephone, and you will be transformed into a believer. Thus Depeche Mode uses the figure of Jesus to criticize the commercialization of religion.

John Mellencamp, using Jesus to good affect in his song "When Jesus Left Birmingham," offers another critical perspective. According to the lyrics, when Jesus leaves Birmingham, Alabama, a symbol for the Christianity of the Bible belt of the southern United States, his disciples and general populace go crazy by laughing and partying. The subject's girlfriend is not religious and would rather party, although she appears to be blessed in a profound way. The lyrics suggest that Jesus leaves Birmingham because of the type of Christianity practiced there that is characterized by lies and liars. The subject knows that he needs salvation now, and imagines himself with a rosary in a garden asking for forgiveness. The subject concludes the song by challenging the fundamentalist Christianity promoted and practiced in the deep South to save his soul.

The rock group Live finds Jesus irrelevant in "Operation Spirit (The Tyranny of Tradition)" from their album *Mental Jewelry*. The subject admits that he has heard a lot of talk about many things that mean nothing to him. He even heard talk about his spirit and soul, but he let them go because anxiety and pain are better companions. He concludes also that Jesus is irrelevant at the present moment. Even though Jesus might have represented something beautiful, the subject is more concerned about pain and suffering in the present moment. At best, Jesus lives inside one's prayer.

The miracles that Jesus performed in the New Testament narratives are irrelevant for the present, according to the lyrics of "It's a Miracle" composed by Roger Waters of Pink Floyd from his album *Amused to Death*. Now, miracles are economic in nature. Products produced by such corporations as Pepsi and McDonalds are found in remote, unlikely places. With some ironic humor, Waters sings that there is sex in Pennsylvania, a tree is planted in Brazil, and a Manhattan doctor does not charge a dying man for his services, all of which are modern-day miracles. It is also a miracle that the human race becomes civilized by means both of the grace of God and socio-economic pressures. The writer comically imagines an earthquake at a theatre where Andrew Lloyd Webber is playing piano for one of his musicals, and the shock causes the lid of the piano to come crashing down, breaking his fingers. From Waters' comic perspective, the termination of the musical would be a miracle or a welcome respite.

Jesus the Superstar

With lyrics by Tim Rice and music by Andrew Lloyd Webber, the musical *Jesus Christ Superstar* was a huge success, and it continues to be performed in theatres around the world and especially on college campuses. More conservative religious leaders took exception to aspects of the musical by calling it anti-Christian and even satanic.

If one compares the musical with the Synoptic Gospels and their portrayal of the ministry of Jesus, there are some striking differences that emerge. Judas plays a more significant role in the musical than any of the three Synoptic Gospels or the Gospel of John. Mary Magdalene also plays a more prominent part in the musical, although her role does not compare to the predominance of Judas. The larger role for Mary Magdalene is reminiscent of Gnostic texts like the Gospel of Philip where she functions as a symbol of divine wisdom and is described as an intimate companion of Jesus. And in the Gospel of Mary, she argues with the apostle Peter over the leadership of the community and the correct teachings of Jesus. The musical places greater emphasis on the betrayal, trial, and death of Jesus, which are events from the latter part of his life. This bias of the musical tends to give greater status to figures like the high priest Caiaphas, Pilate, and King Herod. Of all of these characters, Judas is probably the most interesting and complex figure.

At the beginning of the musical, Judas claims that he can see where events are heading. He claims that Jesus has begun to believe what people are saying about him, and refers to the problem of the messianic consciousness of Jesus, a topic of considerable scholarly debate for the past couple of centuries. The debate about whether or not Jesus considered himself the Messiah is rooted in the Synoptic Gospels where it is possible to find two answers given in these texts to the following question: Are you the Messiah? In the Gospel of Mark (14:62) an affirmative answer is given, Jesus evades the question in the Gospel of Luke (22.67) and in the Gospel of Matthew (26.64). Although the Messiah is a person anointed by God for some special task, it is not completely certain that Jesus used this term for himself.[7] Nonetheless, Jesus appears to be convinced that he possesses authority to speak and act on behalf of God, although there is no developed notion among the people of Israel at that historical time that the Messiah must suffer. It is possible that Jesus viewed his death as necessary in order for him to fulfill his divinely assigned role.[8]

The problem with Jesus from the viewpoint of Judas in the musical is that Jesus has begun to believe what people are saying about him. According to Judas, at the beginning of the ministry of Jesus, the carpenter from Galilee was just a man because there was no talk of God. In fact, Judas thinks that Jesus would have been better off remaining a carpenter because he would not have upset anyone. Due to the fact that Jesus, the Apostles, and others live under the hegemony of the Roman Empire, Judas astutely argues that they must confine themselves to their social station and not call attention to themselves. Judas claims to be the right hand man of Jesus and asks his Master to listen to him. He informs Jesus that people think that he is the Messiah, but he also ominously warns that they will turn against him when they discover that they are wrong. Thus far, Judas is portrayed as a commonsensical and practical individual without faith in the divinity of Jesus. Judas also plays a prophetic role when he warns Jesus that he is risking his life, his movement is going sour, and his followers are blind.

As events unfold for Judas, he is depicted as being concerned about his eternal damnation. He rationalizes his conspiracy with the high priest Caiaphas by saying that Jesus has lost control of himself and his situation. Judas also claims that Jesus would not care about his coming to the high priest. Despite Judas' protests about not wanting their blood money, the priests convince him to take the money and remind him about all that he could do with it.

The encounter between Judas and Jesus at the Last Supper is interesting because Judas admits to having once admired Jesus, but he now despises him. In turn, Jesus calls Judas a liar. Is Judas a liar about once admiring him or because he now claims to despise him? Judas asks Jesus in effect the following question: What if I just remained at this supper and ruined your ambition? Moreover, Judas criticizes Jesus for being a pathetic destroyer of the Apostles' ideals, and accuses him of letting things get out of hand. Basically, Judas turns the tables on Jesus and transforms him into the betrayer and not himself, an innocent and prophetic figure who must perform his duty for everyone's best interests. In comparison to the Gospels and Christian tradition, Rice and Lloyd Webber have engaged in a bit of revisionist history. By casting Judas in the original musical as a black man, Rice and Lloyd Webber connect Judas with a figure that has been persecuted by the institution of slavery, thought of as unworthy, and conceived by detractors as not fully human. The musical implies that just as the black man has been misunderstood and mistreated, a similar case can be made for the figure of Judas in the New Testament.

Mary Magdalene is the most interesting female figure, and plays a larger role in the musical than she did in the Gospel accounts of the life of Jesus. In one scene Mary Magdalene cools Jesus' face prompting Judas to object because her moral status is contrary to the teaching of Jesus. Judas also criticizes Mary Magdalene for using an expensive ointment to soothe Jesus when it could have been used to benefit the poor, but Jesus comes to her defense by telling Judas that there will always be poor people, and Jesus and the disciples do not have the resources to extricate them from poverty. Mary Magdalene confesses in one of the best numbers of the musical that she does not know how to love Jesus. She admits to being changed by her encounter with Jesus, and she struggles to make sense of his influence upon her. In addition to acknowledging Jesus' humanity, Mary admits she loves him and is attracted to him, but he also frightens her. This double movement of attraction and repulsion is typical of an experience of the holy, as we have noted previously in relation to the scholarly work of Rudolf Otto and his book *The Idea of the Holy*. Along with the other Apostles, Mary thinks that everything is fine with the course of unfolding events, and they do not foresee the ominous future troubles envisioned by Judas. When the Apostles ask what is happening, Jesus replies that it is best to concentrate on the present moment and not be concerned about the future. Becoming frightened at the thought of Jesus' death, Mary Magdalene and the Disciples want to begin anew. If we separate Mary from the Disciples for a moment, the lyrics depict them as self-centered and looking for posthumous fame by means of their writings.

In addition to the calculating high priest Caiaphas and a Pilate haunted by his own dreams, King Herod appears and offers a song that combines the attitudes of many of Jesus' persecutors. Herod asks Jesus for proof that he is the Christ in a mocking tone of voice. Herod challenges Jesus to transform the king's water into wine. Herod promises Jesus freedom, if he can walk across the king's swimming pool. By wanting visual proof of Jesus' status, Herod is symbolic of those who are clueless with respect to the nature of faith with its uncertainty and risk. When Jesus does not respond to Herod's questions the king calls him a joke and a fraud to His face. If this is Herod's opinion, it does not represent the overall portrait of Jesus in the musical.

There are those who would point to contradictions between the characterization of Jesus in the Synoptic Gospels and the way that he is portrayed in the musical. In a response to Judas' criticism of Mary Magdalene's use of an expensive ointment on Jesus, the response of Jesus makes it seem that he does not care for the plight of the poor. In contrast to this portrait of Jesus, the Gospel of John depicts Jesus rebuffing Judas (12:1-8). At a moment during the Last Supper, Jesus confesses that he does not think that he will be remembered. Within the Garden of Gethsemane, where Jesus asks his Father to take this cup from him, Jesus admits that he was inspired early in his ministry, but now he is simply sad and tired. During this scene, Jesus is also depicted as self-absorbed and selfish because he asks his Father what his reward will be if he should die. It is apparent that Rice and Lloyd Webber want to probe the darker side of the personality of Jesus. This is a difficult task because the Gospels give us an idealized portrait of Jesus, rendering Rice and Lloyd Webber's probing highly speculative and non-historical.[9]

From what has been just stated, it is difficult to understand why Jesus is a superstar. In the lyrics to "Jesus Christ Superstar," Judas admits that he does not understand Jesus and why he chose to be born in such a strange land. The choir asks Jesus to identify who he really is and to let them know if he is in fact the Messiah. The composers take Jesus out of his historical and cultural heritage when Judas asks if he is in the same place as the Buddha, and he asks questions about the validity of Muhammad's actions. Finally, Judas asks Jesus if he intended to die the way that he did on the cross. These kinds of questions and Jesus' silence calls into question his messianic consciousness. Did Jesus actually think that he was the Messiah during his life? The musical suggests that Jesus was uncertain about his identity and that Jesus thought that his ministry was a failure. This is, of course, rather disturbing to conservative Christian critics of the musical and its depiction of Jesus.

If we see Jesus through the eyes of Judas in the musical, Jesus is ambitious and wants to be accepted as divine by his followers. If we accept the assessment of Judas, Jesus is a sad pathetic figure and destroyer of the ideals of his disciples. Again, we can ask: Why is he a superstar? Or is he merely a superstar in hindsight? Or is the title "Superstar" intended to motivate us to reevaluate whether in fact Jesus ever was a religious Superstar?

Jesus the Clown

Another musical focusing on the life of Jesus is *Godspell*, based specifically on the Gospel of Matthew. It covers the ministry of Jesus from its beginning to the end with his death and resurrection, whereas *Jesus Christ Superstar* concentrates on the final days of his life. If *Jesus Christ Superstar* emphasizes the darker features of the life of Jesus and his betrayal by Judas, trial, and death, *Godspell* is more positive and up-beat with its music, lyrics and overall message. An especially unique feature is that Jesus and his disciples are depicted as clown figures, which represents the key to grasping the message of this wonderful musical.

If we look at the beginning of the musical and the lyrics of the various songs, we find the beginning of the musical evokes memories of the ministry of St. John the Baptist and his preparation for the advent of the Messiah. The second song, “Save the People,” carries the hopeful message of salvation for everyone in which nature testifies to the righteousness of God. The number “Day By Day” represents a prayer and dialogue between God and the self. The self prays for three things: sight, love, and ability to follow God more faithfully. The laws of God in the song “Learn Your Lessons Well” guide the self, although the singers see sinners daydreaming instead of adhering to God’s laws. These sinners are commanded to pay attention because there will be a quiz at the end of time. Although learning the law might not directly help with your eternal salvation, it cannot harm you. Thus for your own good, one should read and heed the laws of God. If the laws of God should be our guides, there is also an inherent justice because when you get to heaven you will be blessed to compensate for all the problems that you suffered during your life. Even though the rich have it all during life, they cannot take their wealth with them when they die. Thus the lyrics to “All For the Best” presuppose that death is the great equalizer of the socio-economic classes.

Throughout the musical, there are songs that directly reflect Christian religiosity. In “Bless the Lord,” God is depicted as more merciful and loving than wrathful. This song is typical of adoration in which the performers extol God's greatness, power, and majesty. As in Psalm 29 in the Hebrew Bible, there is no human self-interest involved and the reasons for praise are not included within the hymnic adoration.[10] The members of the cast offer a prayer of thanksgiving in "All Good Gifts" because God sends us many gifts necessary for life, which are all manifestations of God's love. This song represents a very elementary form of praise that can also be found in Psalm 30 of the Hebrew Bible, which takes the form of individual gratefulness for divine favors and benefits received by a person. Within the context of the songs of thanksgiving, it is common for one to publicly recount how God has helped during a period of crisis or distress. A song of confession is offered with "We Beseech Thee," a song about disobedience, sin, and lack of repentance. In respect to "Turn Back O Man," the cast sings a song about repentance. There is no song of praise or thanksgiving for the Legalist and Pharisees, whose selves and converts are fit for hell, even though they may have confidence that heaven awaits them. But they are nothing more than blind guides and fools. In summary, some of the songs represent in different ways the three major forms of Christian praise: celebratory recital, testimony giving and hymnic adoration. With respect to the first type, one publicly recounts how God helped during a period of hardship. The giving of testimony reflects the recounting of God's salvific acts for his people that constitute a sacred historical narrative, whereas hymns of adoration extol God's greatness, majesty, and power.[11] These types of praise evident in *Godspell* closely parallel the forms of praise in the Book of Psalms.

In contrast to *Jesus Christ Superstar*, the musical *Godspell* is not ambiguous or uncertain about its understanding of the nature of Jesus. In the number "Light of the World," it is the singers who inform Jesus that he is the light that illuminates the sinfulness and darkness of the world, and they entreat Jesus to let His light shine so that humans can know some kindness again. The symbolic experience of light transforms a person ontologically, and reveals the world of the spirit or "the world sanctified by the presence of God."[12] With the original creation of heaven and earth, God utters his initial creative words, "Let there be light" (Gen 1:1-5), and there is the separation of light and darkness. The primal light of the creative act of God becomes identified with Jesus in the New Testament. In the Gospel of John (1: 9-10), Jesus is, for instance, the light of humanity that dispels the primordial darkness and enlightens everyone, as the musical makes clear.

At the event of the crucifixion in the musical, Jesus states "Oh God, I'm dead," and the chorus responds, "Oh God, you're dead." This does not mean that God is dead in a way similar to the position of some postmodern thinkers because it is indicative of a position that Jesus is divine. This conclusion is confirmed by the end of the song with "Long live God, long live God" and the interspersed injunction to prepare the way of the Lord. This uplifting ending to the musical does not fully answer why Jesus and the disciples appear as clown figures. Are we supposed to laugh at them? Should we take Jesus and his message lightly? Is his ministry and message a joke? Is Jesus nothing more than a buffoon? If we examine the significance of the clown, we are led to a very different type of conclusion.

Significance of the Clown

The clown is the personification of the person of humor, who stands midway between faith and despair and is grounded in seriousness, a pre-condition of humor. Lying on the boundary between the sacred and profane, the rational and the irrational, cosmos and chaos, humor needs faith in order to avoid becoming superficial and empty, whereas cynicism is humor surrendering to despair.[13]

The most prominent feature of the clown is self-contradiction.[14] The clown is crude and mean and yet gentle and magnanimous, clumsy and inept but also agile, and he/she can be ugly and repulsive but not without elegance and charm. In short, the clown's behavior is undignified, unreasonable, and sometimes even idiotic. The enlightened Zen Buddhist monk Ikkyū of the fourteenth century, for instance, patronized the brothels and wine shops of the city of Kyoto. Ikkkyū composed poems critical of the lechery and beastly behavior of ordinary people, while at the same time he engaged in sexual relationships and wine drinking himself.[15] Among Native American Indian tribes, the *heyoka* of the Sioux is a person who has had a vision of a Thunder Being, and he rides backwards on his horse, wears his boots on the wrong feet, walks backwards, and wears heavy clothing in the summer and goes naked in the winter.[16] Some members of Jesus' family think that he is crazy, and they want him out of public view (Mk 3:31-35). The figure of Jesus embodies contradictory elements, such as king and commoner, or prince and pauper, which are not very different from the gentleman and tramp Charlie Chaplin portrayed in many motion pictures in the early decades of the twentieth century. With his humanity and incarnational status, Jesus represents the coincidence of opposites. According to social norms, the clown's behavior, appearance, dress, speech and logic are all wrong.

The second major feature of the clown is his/her contempt for status. It is not unusual to find a circus clown wearing, for example, a stiff top hat, carrying a useless and flexible cane, and attaché case in order to lampoon a businessman. By his/her contempt for status, the clown stands outside of rank and order and debunks both of them. Within the Zen Buddhist tradition, there is a vigorous iconoclastic spirit that is evident when a monk asked the Chinese Chan master Yun-men, "Who is the Buddha?" And the master replied, "A stick of dried dung." Or the Zen monk Ikkyū donned dung spattered cow blankets instead of appropriate clerical robes for an official function because the clown figure manifests total disregard for worldly status.[17] Among Native American Indians, the Pueblo clowns burlesque the Kachina dancers by dancing out of time and rhythm, stumbling about and grimacing, whereas Zuni clowns speak Spanish or English before the gods, which is a practice that is strictly taboo for ordinary people.[18] Another Pueblo clown venerates a doll on the ground as a saint, while a Zuni clown is seen lampooning a tribal shaman by wearing a bear paw on his left hand, a wolf snout on his nose, and acting wild.[19] Along a similar pattern of behavior, Jesus defies, for instance, social custom and directs scorn toward royalty.

The third major feature of a clown is assuming the role of an imposter by arrogating human dignity and status. In the case of the Zen monk Ikkyū, he carried a fake sword of a samurai warrior through the streets, and he performed a funeral for a dead cat for a bereaved, childless couple. At the age of seventy-seven, while serving as the abbot of a Zen monastery, Ikkyū entered an illicit love affair with a blind singer named Mori. Due to his violations of the Zen Buddhist monastic code, this behavior can be interpreted as him impersonating a monk. As an imposter, Ikkyū composed poems about enlightenment and fornication. From another cultural perspective, a Native American Hopi male clown dressed as a woman and went to the plaza with a wash basin and began to wash her legs, spreading them to reveal a huge, false vulva, whereas another Hopi clown donned a large false penis and approached a female clown, and both of them engaged in vigorous copulation.[20] Among the Tewa tribe, Alexander Stephen reports a clown snatching off the breach cloth of another clown and dragging him by his penis.[21] Among the Pueblo, witnesses saw two clowns simulate sexual intercourse with a woman with one clown behind and another against the woman's head, while a third clown masturbated in the center of the plaza.[22] From another perspective, Jesus satirizes the prevailing political and social authority by riding into Jerusalem on a donkey accompanied by regal pageantry. Of course, Jesus is a mere peasant in comparison to earthly kings, but his kingdom is spiritual rather than earthly.

The fourth feature of the clown is his/her role as taboo breaker and victim. The clown accepts being utterly grotesque in order for others to despise, insult and torment him/her.[23] Ikkyū was mocked and criticized for parading through the streets of Kyoto with a human skull that he secured to the end of a long bamboo pole.[24] Jesus frequents dinners and parties, and he associates with prostitutes, thieves, and social misfits. The clown must pay for his/her transgressions by assuming the role of victim. Zuni clowns eat, for example, bits of stick, refuse, live puppies, and stones.[25] A Hopi clown of the American southwest drank three gallons of well aged, foul-smelling urine, rubbing his stomach after each drink and shouting how sweet it tasted.[26] Toward the end of his life, Jesus is mocked by his enemies, dressed in mock royal paraphernalia with a robe and crown, crucified amidst taunts, and hangs from the cross with a sign over his head lampooning his role as king of the Jews (Mk 15:26). Even after the clown has been disgraced, mocked, and defeated, the clown raises from the dirt in order to face his/her despisers to let them know that their victory is short lived. In short, the clown returns repeatedly to lampoon the foolishness of society as he/she refuses to admit final defeat. This scenario suggests that becoming the victim of society and being victorious over the vengeance of society is an unending cycle. In the end, it is society that is the benefactor because it is renewed and reinvigorated by the antics of the clown.

Finally, the clown is a symbol of disorder because he/she wears ill-fitting rags, baggy, sagging pants, and battered hats, attire that marks him/her as a bum and a disorderly person. In a famous portrait of Ikkyū, he is depicted by the painter with a growth of beard and unshaven skull, which is considered unseemly and out of character for a Zen monk.[27] It is reported that one Pueblo clown wears a hide or cotton mask, dons feathers, is painted, wears shabby clothes and leg rattles along with a berry necklace; he often speaks in a high pitched or falsetto voice much like the entertainer in the 1970's called Tiny Tim.[28] During the Midwinter ceremony, Iroquois clowns wear false faces, rags, very short skirts, out-sized bras, and girdles.[29] The disorderliness of the clown indicates that he/she stands outside of order and censure, and it also represents an expression of contempt for and principle opposition to all order. By means of his enlightened state, Ikkyū transcended the ethical distinctions between good and evil, and he could thus justify his sexual and drinking habits. Ikkyū was convinced that the enlightened individual must go where people are located in order to save them, even if this location includes brothels. What the clown is doing is reducing to absurdity all presumptuous claims that any human order can ever be absolute. Ikkyū, who represents the chaos of absolute freedom, is an undignified, marginal, and contemptuous being because he is unwilling to fit into social order and unable to take the demands of society seriously. The comic element within the life of Jesus and the Christian tradition suggests that one should not take the world with ultimate seriousness. These five characteristics of the clown form the context for the musical *Godspell*, and they suggest something about the power of the clown.

The spirit of the musical *Godspell* is captured by the Christian thinker Harvey Cox from a chapter of his book "Christ the Harlequin." Cox writes, "Christ the clown signifies our playful appreciation of the past and our comic refusal to accept the specter of inevitability in the future. He is the incarnation of festivity and fantasy."[30] Cox's point is that we must learn to laugh at the hopelessness around us before we can become hopeful.

Long before Cox expressed his theological opinion, Kierkegaard emphasized the importance of becoming sensitive to the comic. According to Kierkegaard, a genuine form of the comic is moving within a person. Moreover, human existence is a striving that is equally both pathetic and comic. Because the striving of human existence is infinite, it involves ultimate pathos, whereas it is also comic because this striving includes self-contradiction.[31] The comic element encounters the absurdity and self-contradictory nature of the incarnational event of the god-man.

Jesus as Mother and Rebel

If we look at the Hebrew scriptures such as the book of Isaiah (49:1, 15), it is possible to find references to God as a mother figure bearing the Israelites within His bosom, conceiving them in His womb, or nursing, consoling them with His breasts (Isa 66:11-13). In the book of Ecclesiastes (24:24-26), the wisdom of God is depicted as feminine. The descriptions of God as a woman nursing, giving birth, and drying tears of His children are all feminine and domestic images that are intended to emphasize the approachability of God.[32]

During the Middle Ages of Europe, some male and female mystics of the church conceived of Jesus as a mother figure. During the twelfth century, the mystic and church leader St. Bernard of Clairvaux (1090-1153) used maternal images to describe Jesus in order to stress his nurturing features. St. Bernard makes it absolutely clear that the soul's bridegroom is Jesus Christ. Another example is the abbot of Igny named Guerric (died ca. 1157), who used motherhood to describe the relationship of Christ, Peter, and Paul. He also used maternal language to describe the relationship between Christ and the soul.[33] When Jesus is referred to as a mother figure, writers are trying to evoke symbols and metaphors of fertility, security, compassion, nurtureing, and union. During the later Middle Ages, Julian of Norwich had a series of revelatory visions. In a later vision, Julian saw Jesus as a mother figure, and she concludes "And so Jesus is our true Mother in nature by our first creation, and he is our true Mother in grace by his taking our created nature."[34] Hence, Julian's vision of her maternal Jesus embodies notions of nurturing, loving, caring, and generating.

Curiously enough, it is possible to find a couple of references to Jesus playing female roles in rock 'n' roll lyrics. In "Imitation of Christ" by the Psychedelic Furs from their album *All of This and Nothing*, Jesus is the person to whom the lyrics are directed. The group sings that words and lies are nails, making the individual the crucifier. The key passage relates that Jesus is a woman, but your friends will be amused at such an odd woman and laugh themselves silly at her pathetic breasts, although we need not take the reference about breasts too literally. These lyrics are an attempt to indicate how difficult it is to accept the possibility that Jesus could be conceived as female.

In "Thunder" from his album Prince and the *New Power Generation*, the artist Prince receives a promise that he will be able to see Jesus in the light of morning. Love or Jesus speaks and tells him that everything will be fine and to save his soul. Unaware of how it was born, Love jumps into his body with an attitude and kisses him on the mouth. Love's kiss runs through his veins and the bed starts to shake, which confuses the singer because he wonders if he is encountering his savior or the Devil. Love is feminine, and tells Prince that only off-spring of their union will remain. Does this mean that only some will be saved? Does this make Prince the father of a holy remnant that is destined to be saved? The lyrics are ambiguous. It is clear, however, the Jesus is the female lover or bride of Prince. This seems to be a rather provocative suggestion. But it is not so controversial when we place the possibility suggested by the lyrics of Prince in the context of bride symbolism associated with Christian mystics.

The inspiration for the symbolism for bridegroom mysticism was found by Christian mystics in the Song of Songs of the Hebrew Bible interpreted as a Christian allegory and combined with the influence and language of the Gospel of John (15:4) where Jesus says to his disciples "Abide in me, and I in you." By treating such texts and their symbolism in an allegorical way, Christian mystics like St. Bernard of Clairvaux in the twelfth century presented an account of Jesus as the bridegroom of the soul. In his work entitled "On Loving God," St. Bernard commented on a passage from the Song of Songs (1:15) that refers to a flower strewn bed. He writes, "By the mention of the bed she makes it plain enough what she desires; and when she says that it is strewn with flowers she indicates clearly why she hopes to be granted her desire . . . ."[35] St. Bernard makes it absolutely clear that the soul's bridegroom is Jesus Christ. The female mystic Mechtild of

Magdeburg of the thirteenth century received visions that she related to a male compiler of her visions that the soul was God's bride. In one poetic expression, she states:

> You are my lamb in your suffering;
> You are my turtledove in your sighing;
> You are my bride in your waiting.

She thus combines images of innocence, love, and union into her vision.[36] As a Benedictine abbess, Hildegard of Bingen shared Mechtild of Magdeburg's notion of Jesus as the bridegroom by actually dressing her nuns on feast days as brides in preparation to receive holy communion.[37] This vision of a female Christian mystic and other such figures does not exhaust the possible ways in which Jesus has been conceived throughout history.

Instead of assuming the role of a woman, superstar or clown, Jesus adopts a more political and critical role in the Jackson Browne song "The Rebel Jesus." The song opens at Christmas time. Jesus is called "Prince of Peace" and "Savior," traditional titles for him. People pray to him and fill the churches at this time of year. But these worshippers have transformed nature from a sacred temple into a den of thieves, which is all done in the name of Jesus. We guard our possessions and give to the poor once a year if the spirit of generosity moves us. If someone raises questions about the sources of poverty, they get persecuted like Jesus. By rebelling against the empty piety and hypocritical religiosity of his own time, Jesus serves for artists like Browne and many others as a source of inspiration for taking a critical stance against social, economic, and political injustices. Although it is not Browne's intention, there is always a danger of transforming Jesus into a political revolutionary. John P. Meier warns us that "Compared with the classical prophets of Israel, the historical Jesus is remarkably silent on many of the burning social and political issues of his day. He can be turned into a this-worldly political revolutionary only by contorted exegesis and special pleading."[38] Elaine Pagels agrees, "Jesus himself is unlikely to have been a revolutionary."[39]

A Rock Antichrist

In what appears to be an album that is intended to respond directly to *Jesus Christ Superstar*, Marilyn Manson released an album entitled *AntiChrist Superstar* in 1996. The performer's name takes the first name of Marilyn Monroe, a famous film star who committed suicide, and the surname of Charles Manson, convicted mass murderer. This represents a symbolic union of *eros* (love or desire) and *thanatos* (death). Beyond the mere intentionally provocative name, the performer actually wants to depict himself in his album as the Antichrist, or more precisely rock star as Antichrist. Marilyn Manson is, however, a different kind of Antichrist because he depicts himself as an androgynous figure on the cover of his album entitled *Mechanical Animals*. This is the Antichrist as sexual freak, which humorously confirms Reinhold Niebuhr's claim that the figure of the Antichrist is indicative that "history remains open to all possibilities of good and evil to the end."[40]

The Antichrist figure is deeply rooted in the Judeo-Christian historical tradition. It is possible to trace the beginnings of the legend in apocalyptic thought, a type of eschatology or belief about the nature of the end of history, and messianic beliefs of late Second Temple Judaism (from the third century B.C.E. to 70 C.E.). From this Jewish foundation, the early Christian church connects the Antichrist legend with its evolving views about the figure of Jesus as the Christ (Christos, "anointed one"). Church historian Bernard McGinn makes this connection absolutely lucid in his excellent book on the subject: "Identification of Jesus with the returning messiah was the basis for the creation of the Antichrist legend."[41] In short, the Antichrist is a false messiah, a pseudo-Christ, a great deceiver and arch-hypocrite. Throughout the course of Christian history, there have been some religious figures who have been identified as the false prophet with the figure mentioned in the book of Revelation (19:20; 20:10), who will be dispatched at the end of time into a sea of burning sulphur. Another influential idea appears in pseudonymous letters of Paul (2 Thess 2:3) and Peter (2 Pet 2:1) that warn the early Christian community about a seducer who performs false signs and wonders. John (1 John 4:3) was convinced that the Antichrist was in the world during his lifetime. In fact, 1John (2:18) anticipates many such figures, and he ties this expectation with the end time. He even broadens the notion when he equates this figure with anyone who denies that Jesus is the Christ (2.22).

From a later historical perspective, the Antichrist has been identified with historical figures like the Roman Emperor Nero on the basis of the speculative numerology associated with the number of the Beast, 666. In fact, the Armenian name of the Antichrist became Neren, and the mark of the Beast could be discovered on coins bearing the image of the emperor. During the course of European history, wild barbarian tribes like the Goths, Huns, and Tartars were identified as representing the Antichrist, or at least his acolytes, the hosts of Gog and Magog. During the Middle Ages, the general outline of a biography of the Antichrist was accepted, and it affirmed that he would be a Jew from the tribe of Dan, and would be born in Babylon. A common epithet of this figure was "Son of Perdition" (*filius perditionis*), which means that he is the off-spring of a sexual relationship between a prostitute and the devil.

Probably the most essential feature of the Antichrist is that he is defined, as his name implies, contrary to Christ. During the mid-tenth century, a monk named Adso, abbot of the monastery of Montier-ender, composed a treatise modeled on this notion for Gerberga, who was married to Louis IV, king of the Franks. Later European history connects the Turks, Saracens, and even the Emperor Frederick II Hohenstaufen (1194-1250) with the Antichrist. It would be wrong to assume that Protestants were the only people pointing accusing fingers at Catholic popes because the Franciscans were not hesitant about making such charges. In 1305, Ubertino of Casale, who identified both Pope Boniface VIII and his successor Pope Benedict XI with the Antichrist, composed the *Tree of the Crucified Life of Jesus*. Apparently, Ubertino was motivated by his conviction that these popes were obstacles to the full unfolding of the order's eschatological mission,

The courageous Ubertino identified both popes with the number of the beast 666 (Rev 13:18) because their names came to this numerical total by means of transliteration into Greek.[42]

From outside the Catholic establishment, the English theologian John Wycliffe was the first person to identify the papacy itself with the Antichrist. The Protestant reformers Luther and Calvin believed in a collective Antichrist, a single kingdom, whereas the Antichrist was often viewed as a heretic and leader of heretics on the eve of the Reformation. The view of Thomas Müntzer (ca. 1489-1525) was more inclusive because he did not think that the Pope was the final Antichrist. Müntzer was convinced that the Pope represented only the herald of the figure to appear in the near future. Müntzer's opinion did not stop later notable figures from identifying the Pope with the Antichrist, such as the Presbyterian John Milton (1608-74), the Quaker George Fox (1624-91), the Baptist John Bunyan (1622-88), and the scientist and churchman Issac Newton (1642-1727). Therefore, the Antichrist can represent complete evil in either an individual person or a human collectivity, although he must be distinguished from the devil because he is primarily conceived as a human agent rather than a divine or semi-divine figure. This brief historical picture does not include the commercialization of the Antichrist by a performer like Marilyn Manson.

The lyrics of Manson's song "Mister Superstar" depicts the rock star as a god in the eyes of his fans, who worship him and desire to be like him. The devoted fan is portrayed as either willing to commit suicide for the star or kill the star, if the fan cannot possess him. The

Antichrist Superstar album also contains two songs that are written in an intentionally autobiographical mode. Manson depicts himself in "Angel with the Scabbed Wings" as an angel with a drug habit, who will deflower all the young girls, an obvious grandiose undertaking of major proportions, although this scheme to deflower all young women is not what it appears. Admitting that he is an angel of death and not spirit or life, he says his sexual relations with young girls dries up their wombs. Thus he does not propagate life, but rather spreads sterility and death. By calling himself a savior in the song, he means to suggest a savior of eternal death and not eternal life, in sharp contrast to the message of Jesus.

If we view Manson from the viewpoint of Gregory the Great, bishop of Rome from 590 to 604, and his work entitled *Moralia* (32. 16.23), Marilyn Manson would represent the testicles of the Antichrist because he corrupts the innocent. Moreover, Manson's lyrics are reflected in the works of the aristocratic German abbess Hildegard of Bingen (1098-1179) in her *Book of Divine Works* (3.10.30). She imagines the Antichrist as a sexual criminal not unlike Manson, although her Antichrist figure sexually assaults the Virgin Ecclesia instead of innocent girls.

In another autobiographical song to his fans called "Defamography," Manson admits that he does not know how he became a rock star. But the important thing is that this rock star is trapped in a rut, and he wants to escape or tear down the image of the rock star. For the fans that have created the rock god, he says, "I will bury your god in my warm spit/You'll be deformed in your porn." Manson's iconoclastic message is grounded in his contention that stardom leaves a real person hurting, portraying a man divided against himself in the lyrics of this song. Apparently, he speaks with two voices because one voice wants to be a rock star and the other does not want to be a star.

Beneath these conflicted feelings, there is, nonetheless, a sense of Manson's triumph over God. From the *Antichrist* album and the lyrics of "Track 99" Manson suggests that he overthrows God because God grovels and crawls at his feet. Not only does Manson defeat God, but God also recognizes His defeat and acknowledges the superiority of the self-proclaimed Antichrist. Moreover, the reign of the Antichrist is a present reality. If this is true for the sake of argument, it suggests for Reinhold Niebuhr "the inconclusive character of human history."[43]

In "Cryptorchild" Manson gives the listener an image of the time to come in which the moon eclipses the sun, symbolizing darkness and the arrival of bitter events. But in the song "Antichrist Superstar," he announces the time of the Antichrist, which is repeated in "1996." In the former song, he also calls fans to repent for creating him willingly. Even if a fan cuts Manson's head off, it will grow back because he is a hydra monster. From his album *Smells Like Children* and in "Rock 'n' Roll Nigger," Manson admits again to being created by fans in an act in which the world spreads its legs to produce a rock star. He announces, "I AM the all-American Antichrist." But America hates him for what he is and represents, and he is thus a lowly figure that he calls "Your shit" or "Nigger." But then Jesus was also a lowly nigger from Manson's provocative perspective. Even though Manson was created by American fans, they hate him, and his response to such a scenario at the end of the record is a series of repetitive shouts of "Fuck you." In fact, in his song "Cake and Sodomy" from his album ironically entitled *Portrait of an American Family*, he sings, "I am the god of fuck." And in "Snake Eyes and Sissies" from the same album he admits to having the Devil's hand and being a "pedophile's dream/ A messianic Peter Pan." It is odd that this strange Antichrist cares enough to pause in order to criticize television and Bible-belt preachers. Provocatively, Manson wants to know something about these preachers: If they are so good, why are there "shit stains on your face?" What he is attempting to convey is that these preachers are ethically and morally stained and polluted. Manson concludes the song by comparing himself to the deity of television and offering himself as the Antichrist to the phony god of television.

Manson also offers a couple of visions of the world and himself in the album *Antichrist Superstar*. He presents a vision of himself in "The Minute of Decay" as dying within a world that is already dead, which suggests that there is thus no hope and no cure for his predicament. The lyrics of "The Reflecting God" depict him going to God to find the truth, but he sees himself instead, which is a beneficial vision because it enables him to learn that heaven and hell are untrue. He claims that when he becomes god everyone will die, a point that is less about some sense of justice than it is about a lack of salvation or forgiveness. In the lyrics to "Wormboy," Manson sings that you are already living in hell. Therefore, there is no hell to wait for or enter in the future.

If we are already living in hell, the message from the Antichrist is absolutely no comfort to us. In short, his gospel is not good news; it is rather the exact opposite of the message of love from Jesus. From the perspective of the history of the Antichrist, this makes consistent sense. Hippolytus, a disciple of Irenaeus and presbyter in Rome from about 200 to 234 until his martyrdom, in chapter six of his work *On the Antichrist* argued that the Antichrist would be a perverted imitation of Christ. This opinion from a Christian martyr fits the projected image of Manson. Likewise, Joachim of Fiore (c. 1135-1202) compares the Antichrist to Jesus and, he concludes that the former will be a blasphemous parody of the life and teachings of Jesus.[44] Joachim, a former Abbot of the Cistercian monastery of Corazzo and founder of the Ordo Florensis at San Giovanni in Fiore, suggests that the Antichrist is an incarnation of the devil, a demonic inversion of Jesus.[45] In "The Beautiful People" Manson sings that it is not time to discriminate; it is rather a time to "hate every mother-fucker," which is his basic manifesto. In fact, he instructs others in "Irresponsible Hate Anthem" not to respond to hate with love, as Jesus would teach, but with more hate. This is made easier because the lyrics tell us that everyone is a nigger or a piece of dirt. The lyrics of this song reflect Manson advocating suicide, abortions and murder: "Let's just kill everyone and let/your god sort them out." His message of violence is also contained in the lyrics of "Lunchbox" from his album *Portrait of an American Family* where he threatens to kill anyone who causes him trouble. From the same album, in "Get your Gun," Manson offers a call to violence, and he defines himself in a twisted Cartesian way by stating: "I hate therefore I am." Besides killing and hating other people, he wants to do away with guilt in "Wrapped in Plastic," because it saps our strength and presumably keeps us from performing more violent acts. Within the context of one's suffering, it is not possible to expect comfort because the Anti-Christ betrays those who suffer, according to "Track 99." How can one make sense of these sick, provocative, and twisted lyrics of a self-proclaimed Antichrist?

Manson intends to shock and amaze adults, appeal to impressionable young people who are seeking for something with which to horrify their parents, and to bond them with their equally impressionable friends. In addition, a key to comprehending Manson is his anti-religious message of Antichrist, anti-god, hate, and violence. Manson represents more than a perversion of American cultural values and Christian religious values because Manson's lyrics manifest an anti-social and anti-religious message. The world from his perspective is an anti-divine order and represents the complete reversal of the sacred order. Manson creates his own mirror world that is wild, chaotic, dark, and contrary to any sacred order. He presents himself as a destructive force that threatens social norms, cultural values, meaning, and truth. The dark, degenerate, deviancy that Manson advocates is similar to the mirror world of the witch in many indigenous religions, which suggests that he represents a negation of power.

If we turn to Michel Bakhtin's book on the French writer Rabelais, the author's notion of carnival can help us to make some sense of Manson. For the sake of argument, let us assume that Jesus represents the hierarchy of the church and a disciplined social order, whereas Manson stands for the repressed pleasures of the subordinated social class. By abiding within certain pattern of rules, carnival inverts those rules, and creates an upside down world, providing "a parody of the extracarnival life."[46] Carnival is characterized by bodily excessiveness, bad taste, offensiveness, and degradation, which are features that characterize what Manson is doing with his parody of Jesus. From Bakhtin's perspective, Manson represents the lower order of society and its carnivalesque power to insist on its rights to a place in the culture. It constructs "a second world and a second life outside officialdom."[47] This is a world without rank or social hierarchy, which functions to liberate. It enables a creative playful freedom, which implies that carnival life is subject to "the laws of its own freedom."[48] From this perspective, Manson creates his own carnivalesque, upside, inside out world where he reigns over a kingdom of hatred.

From another perspective, Manson simulates the Antichrist similar to gambling casinos in Las Vegas that simulate New York City or a castle during the Middle Ages. From the postmodern perspective of a thinker like Jean Baudrillard, the simulation of the Antichrist by Manson is representative of the postmodern era, an artificial, malleable time. This tendency toward equivalence represents faking that which one does not possess. This suggests an absence rather than a presence and threatens the distinction between true and false, real and imaginary.[49] Baudrillard sees a logic operating with the simulation that is devoid of logical facts or reason. What he means is that the logic of simulation does not have anything to do with meaning or the real because it terminates meaning, and renders the real and illusion impossible at the same time because the latter is no longer possible without the former.[50] We are left with the phantom of simulation, a manifestation of the hyper-real, a more real than real, within a context in which the real never did truly exist.

It is possible that Manson's identification of himself with the Antichrist actually represents the culmination of the banality of the Antichrist. In other words, it is finally when we reach carnival and simulation that we have the full-fledged banality of the figure. In fact, as the religious historian Roberto Rusconi makes absolutely lucid, the danger of the Antichrist falling into banality was always historically present "by its utilization in a purely polemical and instrumental way."[51]

Path of Salvation and Visions of Unity

The Gospel of Luke (2:32) depicts Jesus as the light of the Gentiles and the way to salvation, while the Gospel of John (9.5) refers to Jesus as the light of the world. From a historical perspective, it is possible to identify three ways in which Jesus symbolically represents light in the Christian tradition. Since Jesus represented for Christians the messianic hope, people looked to the prophecy of the Roman poet Vergil and his *Fourth Eclogue* to be a prophecy about Jesus and the Sibylline tradition as sources of verification concerning the coming of Christ to judge human beings at the end of the world. Another method of discerning Jesus as the light of the Gentiles was to find in Gentile thought anticipations of the Christian doctrines about him. Finally,

Christian thinkers examined classical history and literature for persons and events that could be interpreted as types or prefigurations of Jesus.[52]

A similar message is given by Prince with his song "The Cross" from his album *Sign ⊕ the Times*. Prince initially paints a dark portrait of a place without hope or love, and introduces a message of the coming of the Messiah. It is important that you do not die without knowing the message of the cross, a "sweet song of salvation," which will unburden us of all our problems. From the perspective of Christian history, the cross represents the cosmic victory of the power of God over the power of the Devil and death by means of the resurrection of Jesus. Due to its connection to the power of God, the cross serves as a talisman and protection against evil.[53] At the end of the eleventh century, it became the central symbol of the crusades to Palestine, functioning also as a symbol of wisdom and an example of patience and charity within the context of suffering (1 Pet. 2:21-23). Moreover, the wisdom of the cross reveals divine love (John 15:13), which originates with and is grounded in God. True love assumes a self-sacrificing form. John of Damascus (c. 675-c. 749) suggests a deeper meaning of the cross as wisdom: "The very shape of the cross symbolized its comprehension of all the ways of God, the vertical and the horizontal bars representing the height and the breath of the universe, and their point of convergence where the head of Christ was laid representing the unification and ultimate harmony of all in Christ crucified."[54] These kinds of notions form the back-drop for Prince's lyrics, even if he did not specifically have them in mind when he composed the song.

In another song entitled “Elephants and Flowers” from his album *Graffiti Bridge*, Prince sings about a lonely boy looking for a savior in a city full of fools. The savior is one who creates everything and everyone, who is alive, and who possesses power. For those who love the living God, there will be peace, no confusion, no fear, no tears, no sorrow and no pain. Of course in the New Testament, 1 John is famous for its equation of God and love (7.8), and its assertion that anyone devoid of love does not know God, which prefigures the lyrics and message of Prince.

After his religious conversion, Bob Dylan composed the song “Saved” for an album of the same title. Before being born, the subject of the tune is corrupted by the Devil, but he is saved by the grace of God and delivered by the blood of the sacrificial lamb. He is joyful and thankful to be saved from the pit of hell. If grace is central to Dylan’s understanding of salvation, the rock group INXS emphasize surrender in their song “Everything” from their album *Elegantly Wasted*: “Fall into the arms of God/Pray that your soul’s not sold.” In contrast, if God is truly merciful, Sheryl Crow in her song “Redemption Day” imagines that there is a metaphorical train going straight to the gate of heaven. In the meantime, people must watch and wait for its arrival.

These more orthodox and traditional religious sentiments are challenged by Jewel’s song, “Who Will Save Your Soul” from her album *Pieces of You*. She acknowledges in her lyrics that we move through life performing ordinary acts, but the chorus asks "Who will save your soul when it comes to the flower?" Jewel replies that it must be you. We tend to neglect this simple message: We forget to begin to turn to God. Basically, these lyrics are addressed to women to take control of their lives. Mariah Carey gives a theologically contradictory message in her song "Make It Happen," because she says that she both believes in herself and prays for divine help. In the song, a poor, hungry, abandoned young woman tells how she learned to cope. Relying on God and having confidence in oneself can reconcile the apparent contradictory message. Even though life can be difficult, suicide is not an answer to your problems, a course of action that can only lead to not finding the answers to life. This is why it is important to keep one's faith, to struggle, and pray for help. The song ends with a confession of being lost, joy at being found, and thanks to God.

Mariah Carey's lyrics are an example of a cult of faith, a faith in faith, identified by the Jewish theologian and sociologist of religion Will Herberg. This is not a faith in a particular deity. Herberg identifies this cult of faith as an especially American phenomenon in this way: "The American believes . . . that 'faith,' or what we may call religiosity, is a kind of 'miracle drug' that can cure all the ailments of the spirit. It is not faith in anything that is so powerful, just faith, the 'magic of believing.'"[55] Within this cult of faith, there are two forms: an introvert and an extrovert. The first type of faith is thought to bring peace of mind from such afflictions as anxiety and guilt and thereby mental health. The latter type of faith is commonly known as positive thinking, a kind of thinking process possessing faith that is characterized by a lack of negativity and skepticism because it is always positive.[56] By having faith in faith, religion becomes its own object, which is the danger expressed, probably unwittingly, by Carey.

Stevie Wonder and James Taylor refer to salvation using different modes of thought. In "Higher Ground" from his album *Innervisions*, Wonder states, for instance, that he is looking for higher ground, and at the end of the song he sings: "God is gonna show you higher ground/He's the only friend you have around." Even though the world keeps turning and good and bad things continue to occur, he admits to previously living in sin, but God gives him another chance. This scenario implies a spiritual rebirth with the symbolism of ascent. The significance of this type of symbolism is made lucid by the historian of religions Mircea Eliade: "The act of climbing or ascending symbolizes the way towards the absolute reality . . ."[57] James Taylor's song "Boatman" from his album *Hourglass* embodies a message of salvation by presenting two images. The first image is an old couple drifting along in a boat on a gray day in silence. They begin to come to life and dive into the water, even though it is very cold. Nonetheless, the water reinvigorates them. The second image is of a person who is like a message in a bottle drifting in the sea just waiting to be washed ashore. Casting away fear, the subject severs any connection to the sky, finds level ground, and is amazed that nothing happens in response. The people in each set of images become self-reliant on the earth by severing ties to a transcendent Being, and they live each moment to the fullest as it comes and therefore become sane.

The theme of redemption appears in two interesting compositions by John Mellencamp. "Mr. Bellows" appears on his album *Mr. Happy Go Lucky*. The lyrics move from doubt to an acknowledgment of help to an emphatic assertion about a lack of salvation. If there is no salvation for him in these lyrics, Mellencamp finds a different kind of redemption in "Wild Night" from his album *Dance Naked*, a dangerous night that beckons him to come out to dance and make love. A person receives the call from the wind that catches him and propels him forward into the night. There is a strong Dionysian wild abandon in these lyrics. When the women of ancient Greek mythology are driven mad by Dionysus, a deity of inebriation, wild abandon, marginality, and madness, they cannot control themselves, and perform violent acts like murdering King Pentheus with their bare hands in Euripides' *Bacchae*.

In contrast to the lyrics of the two songs by Mellencamp, Peter Cetera and Jackson Browne perceive the necessity for a person to turn within. Since an interior man is lost, confused, and searches for his pride in "Man In Me" by Cetera from his album *World Falling Down*, it is necessary to turn within oneself because there is also an interior person who wants to be free, saved, and have his dignity restored. In "The Barricades of Heaven" from his album *Looking East*, Browne sees the necessity of saving oneself because heaven is barricaded. Relying on one's own strength to achieve salvation is often a message of eastern spirituality, although there are forms of spirituality in the East that are closer to the devotional spirit of Christianity.

We can find an eastern influence in the song "The Inner Light" performed by the Beatles and written by George Harrison. By turning within oneself, one can know everything. It is possible to see without perceiving, if your mode of perception is intuitive; by journeying further we come to know less. This type of opinion is found in the *Dao De Ching* (48) of Daoism: "The pursuit of learning is to increase day after day/ The pursuit of Dao is to decrease day after day."[58] A strong eastern influence is also evident in an album by Rusted Root called *When I Woke*. The inside cover of the album contains a *mandala* (sacred diagram) with a figure in a meditation posture. A song on the album is entitled "Ecstasy" and refers to living in such a world. "Infinite Tamboura" from the same album begins with a eerie sound similar to a sound that I heard at the sacred hemisphere at Auroville dedicated to the memory of Sri Aurobindo, an Indian philosopher and mystic, outside the city of Pondichéry. This reverberating sound is an attempt to capture the sacred in sound.

Eastern religiosity is expressed by "Bodhisattva" by Steely Dan. The *bodhisattva* is a central religious figure in Mahāyāna Buddhism that vows to save all beings and performs acts of selflessness for the good of others. While not doing well, the subject of "I Go Sailing" by Stevie Wonder from his album *Jungle Fever* meets a wise man who suggests that he turn within himself to find happiness. Taking this sagacious advice, the subject goes "sailing through rivers" of his mind, and is surprised at what he finds. The act of introspection is a common eastern religious motif, although it can also be found in the Judeo-Christian tradition. Stevie Wonder expresses a more clearly eastern religious notion in his song "Come Back as a Flower." During the morning, the subject experiences a strange thought by imagining that he is in a cosmic unity with everything else. Then he wishes that he could be reborn as a flower in order to dispense love.

Seals and Croft express a different kind of eastern religiosity in "Year of Sunday" from an album of the same title. They acknowledge they are fortunate to live in the "Year of Sunday" because people are returning to unity, and answering their prayers. Why? Because God's covenant with Abraham entailed bringing his family home, it is important not to leave anyone alone. God gives Moses the Ten Commandments and allows him to establish his own tribe. Jesus comes to teach us to love, whereas God gives Muhammad nationhood. After a period of darkness, the Bahā'u'llāh comes to announce the promised messiah, which ushers in the final event, the gracious gift of a "Year of Sunday." We can here witness the singing duo giving expression to their Bahā'ī faith. In "East of Ginger Trees," Seals and Croft end with a quote from Baha'i scripture about meeting the prophet Baha'ullah in a garden, an invitation to try the Baha'i faith.

There are also lyrics that suggest the monism characteristic of the Advaita Vedānta type of Hindu religiosity and philosophy. Bryan Adams' song "(Everything I Do) I Do It for You" expresses, for instance, a monism between two lovers with an invitation to search one's soul. By turning within oneself and examining one's soul, one person will discover the other. In a similar vein, the lyrics to the song "One" by U2 from their album *Achtung Baby* refers to two lovers breaking up. The singer wants to know what happened in their relationship, and expresses an impure monism because, although the lovers are unified, they are not the same, which might be called a qualified monism. Nonetheless, the song emphasizes dialogue between two people ending their relationship. And yet ironically, unity is stressed throughout the song that ends with the word "One."

An Indian type of religiosity is more clearly evident in some of the compositions of George Harrison like "Living in the Material World," which forms an interesting contrast with "Material Girl" by Madonna. Harrison grants that he lives in the material world into which he was born, and he confesses to meeting friends in such a world and getting lost in it, although he prays to find his way out of it. In order to escape this material world, he admits that he will need the grace of Krishna. In "Awaiting on You All," Harrison sings about opening up your heart to find what you need to become free of pollution and gain salvation. Once your heart is open, the solution is to chant the names of Krishna. The importance of chanting the names of God is contrasted with a church, temple, books, or rosary beads in order to stress the superiority of chanting.

Rather than embodying an eastern form of spirituality, other artists seem to find inspiration among western mystics. In "Into the Fire" from her album *Solace*, Sarah McLachlan sings in the chorus about being united as a spark in a fire. These lyrics reflect a primary notion in the thought of the great German mystic Meister Eckhart, who argues that the human soul possesses an immortal spark of intellect that is an imprint of divinity that makes us kin of God.[59] Eckhardt goes on to say that the spark of the soul enables the soul to become God by being absorbed into God: "My soul becomes more one with God than food does with my soul."[60]

The group October Project's "Paths of Desire" is reminiscent of a mystical experience: "I'm drawn to you/I'm caught in you." They sing of leaving reason behind them much like western mystics and religious thinkers crossing over sorrow. Within the context of reacting to the philosophy of the German thinker Hegel, Kierkegaard indicates the limits of reason when it encounters the "Unknown," which exists but is unknownable.[61] Meister Eckhart refers to the importance of unknowing, a process of knowing that is very different from ordinary knowing. Eckhart writes about coming to know God: "God is to be sought in opposites; in unknowing knowing shall we know God; in forgetfulness of ourselves and all things even to the naked essence of the Godhead."[62]

The intuitive visions common to mystical experience can also be discerned in certain rock 'n' roll lyrics. A good example is "Synchronicity" by the Police. According to their lyrics, synchronicity is a unity; it is the link that unites acting and thinking. It is also an extrasensory perception, and it is further defined as a connecting principle associated with the invisible, imperceptible, and inexpressible. Queen expresses another kind of unity in "On Vision" from their album *A Kind of Magic*. Recalling a dream that he had as a young man, the subject expresses a vision of unity under a single God and religion. Within this vision of unity, there is no good or evil, no right or wrong. But this vision of unity is unfortunately an illusion; it endures, however, as a wish and as a goal for which to work. According to "A Kind of Magic" what is magical is the vision of unity: "One dream, one soul, one prize, one goal." It is impossible for an embodied person to attain this, but the lyrics look forward to a period of sanity and end of conflict. The visions of the unity expressed by the Police and Queen do not address the plurality within the world. Such an attempt is made by Styx and their song "Come Sail Away," which begins with a vision of an apparent band of angels that beckon the singer to sail away with them. A later vision reveals that what one thought were angels is really a starship that beckons the singer.

A more secular type of salvation is evident in the musical *Tommy* by the Who. The central subject of this musical is a child witnessing his father's murder by his mother's lover, but his mother tells him that he did not really witness a murder. In response to witnessing such a horrific event, Tommy withdraws into a kind of catatonic condition and communicates with no one. This personal withdrawal from others liberates him initially into a magical world of his own thoughts and emotions. His stepfather is concerned about him at Christmas because all he does is pick his nose, smile and play pinball. Tommy's pleas to be seen, felt, and healed fall on deaf ears. His retreat into himself is reinforced by the mistreatment that he receives from others around him, such as his cousin Kevin, the Acid Queen, and perverse uncle Ernie. Tommy finds salvation in playing pinball because the machines do not mistreat him. Moreover, his withdrawal like a Hindu yogi or Buddhist monk in meditation enables him to develop a single-minded concentration and a deft touch not found in normal children. By attaining the status of a "Pinball Wizard," Tommy gains a kind of extrasensory perception or messianic power by becoming a machine himself, one that is able to master the mechanical manipulation of bumpers and digital counters. This kind of secular religion is a kind of postmodern religion that simply simulates religion in a mechanical way, which offers no solution to the basic human condition, or message of loving others. At best, this kind of postmodern religion offers only self-love. The machine offers lights, sounds, and action, but there is nothing permanent here, nothing truly alive, and nothing meaningful or significant. The basis of this kind of religion is a huge vacuum of meaning. Instead of meaning one gets simulation and meaninglessness that turns a being of flesh and blood into a narcissistic machine.

Concluding Remarks

If we take the lyrics in this chapter seriously and ponder them, it is possible to conclude that contemporary westerners have problems with the notion of transfiguration, resurrection, and ascension of the body of Christ or the possibility of a bodily resurrection for all people because of the absence of such references in rock compositions. There are many references to the death of Jesus, but a glaring absence to references about his bodily resurrection. Of course, the absence of such references in rock musical compositions could be completely innocent. But I think there is something more involved in this lack of attention to these kinds of details. It seems to me the fading of the significance of the bodily resurrection tells us something about the current acceptability or plausibility of certain beliefs of the Christian tradition. Nonetheless, composers use the main outlines of the life and ministry of Jesus to make a variety of points.

We have seen that numerous rock composers suggest becoming contemporary with Jesus in a fashion reminiscent of Kierkegaard. In two very different musicals, Jesus is depicted as a superstar and as a clown figure. We also called attention to Jesus assuming the role of mother and rebel. We discovered that there is support for the former in the Christian tradition, but there is little scriptural support for the revolutionary role for Jesus in a political sense. And we called attention to the figure of the Antichrist in the Christian tradition and its adoption and simulation by Marilyn Manson as a counter to the fundamental message of Jesus. If there is one thing that these various portraits of Jesus make clear, it is that he means different things to different people. There are also instances when rock composers take a certain poetic license with the narrative of Jesus for their own theological purposes or socio-political agenda, but this is a practice with a long history. Moreover, if Jesus is a personification of power for Christians, the anti-Christ, or his impersonators such as Manson, represents a negation of power.

The discussion about the path to salvation finds rock composers emphasizing love, grace, turning within one's self, or saving one's self. We noted references to intuitive visions, an eastern religious influence, and a Dionysian spirit. And we called attention to a secular form of salvation in the musical *Tommy*. What this means is that there is as rich a plurality of opinions about the quest for salvation as there are with portraits and interpretations of Jesus, a plurality that reflects the larger world in which we live.

Endnotes

[1] Mircea Eliade, *Patterns in Comparative Religion*, trans. Rosemary Sheed (Cleveland: World Publishing Company, 1958), pp. 154-183.

[2] Niebuhr, *Faith and History*, p. 185.

[3] For references to these points, see Marina Warner, *Alone of All Her Sex: The Myth and the Cult of the Virgin Mary* (New York: Knopf, 1976), p. 318; Jacques Le Goff, *The Birth of Purgatory*, trans. Arthur Goldhammer (Chicago: University of Chicago Press, 1974), p. 178; Jaroslav Pelikin, *Mary Through the Centuries: Her Place in the History of Culture* (New Haven: Yale University Press, 1996), p. 143.

[4] Kierkegaard, *Philosophical Fragments*, p. 85.

[5] Idem, *Concluding Unscientific Postscript*, p. 327.

[6] Ibid., p. 91.

[7] E. P. Sanders, *The Historical Figure of Jesus* (London: Penguin Books, 1993), p. 242.

[8] Howard Clark Kee, *What Can We Know about Jesus?* (Cambridge: Cambridge University Press, 1990), p. 78.

[9] John Dominic Crossan, *Jesus: A Revolutionary Biography* (New York: Harper Collins Publishers, 1994), p. x.

[10] Bernard Lang, *Sacred Games: A History of Christian Worship* (New Haven: Yale University Press, 1997), p. 28.

[11] Ibid.

[12] Mircea Eliade, *Mephistopheles and the Androgyne: Studies in Religious Myth and Symbol*, trans. J. M.. Cohen (New York: Sheed and Ward, 1965), p. 77.

[13] M. Conrad Hyers, "The Comic Profanation of the Sacred," in *Holy Laughter: Essays on Religion in the Comic Perspective*, ed. M. Conrad Hyers (New York: Seabury Press, 1969), pp. 24, 27.

[14] I have followed the features of the clown identified by Wolfgang Zucker, "The Clown as the Lord of Disorder," *Theology Today*, 24/3 (1967): 308.

[15] James H. Sanford, *Zen-Man Ikkyū*, Studies in World Religions (Chico, CA: Scholars Press, 1981), p. 132.

[16] John G. Neihart, *Black Elk Speaks* (New York: Washington Square Press, 1972), pp. 159-163.

[17] Sanford, p. 28.

[18] Mischa Titiev, *The Hopi Indians of Old Oraibi: Change and Continuity* (Ann Arbor: University of Michigan Press, 1972), p. 255.

[19] Elsie Clews Parsons and Ralph L. Beals, "The Sacred Clowns of the Pueblo and Mayo-Yaqui Indians," *American Anthropologist*, 36/4 (1934): 491; Barbara Tedlock, "The Clown's Way," in *Teachings from the American Earth: Indian Religion and Philosophy*, eds. Denis Tedlock and Barbara Tedlock (New York: Liveright, 1975), p. 108.

[20] Alexander Stephen, *Hopi Journal*, ed. Elsie Clews Parsons, Columbia University Contributions to Anthropology 25, 1: 386.

[21] Ibid., p. 491.

[22] Charles Lange, *Cochiti* (Carbondale: Southern Illinois University Press, 1968), p. 304.

[23] Zucker, p. 310.

[24] Sanford, p. 39.

[25] Frank Hamilton Cushing, *Zuñi Breadstuff*, Indian Notes and Monographs, Heye Foundation 8, 1920, p. 621.

[26] Stephen, p. 328.

[27] Donald Keene, "The Portrait of Ikkyū," *Archives of Asian Art*, 20 (1966-67): 58.

[28] Parsons and Beals, p. 496.

[29] Elizabeth Tooker, *The Iroquois Ceremonial of Midwinter* (Syracuse, N. Y: Syracuse University Press, 1970), p. 53.

[30] Cox, *Feast of Fools*, p. 142.

[31] Kierkegaard, *Concluding Unscientific Postscript.*, p. 84.

[32] Caroline Walker Bynum, *Jesus as Mother: Studies in the Spirituality of the High Middle Ages* (Berkeley: University of California Press, 1982), p. 129.

[33] Ibid., p. 120.

[34] Julian of Norwich, *Showings*, trans. Edmund Colledge, O.S.A. and James Walsh, S.J. (New York: Paulist Press, 1978), p. 296.

[35] Bernard of Clairvaux, *Selected Works*, trans. G. R. Evans (New York: Paulist Press, 1987), p. 180.

[36] Mechthild of Magdeburg, *The Flowing Light of the Godhead*, trans. Frank Tobin (New York: Paulist Press, 1998), p. 55.

[37] Lang, 344.

[38] John P. Meier, *A Marginal Jew: Rethinking the Historical Jesus*, Vol. 1 (New York: Doubleday, 1991), p. 199.

[39] Pagels, p. 7; See also Raymond E. Brown, *The Death of the Messiah* (New York: Doubleday, 1994).

[40] Niebuhr, *Faith and History*, p. 235.

[41] McGinn, *Antichrist*, p.33.

[42] Roberto Rusconi, "Antichrist and Antichrists," in *The Encyclopedia of Apocalypticism, Volume 2 Apocalypticism in Western History and*

Culture, ed. Bernard McGinn (New York: Continuum Publishing Company, 1998), pp. 304-305.

[43] Niebuhr, *Faith and History*, p. 126.

[44] See figura 2, XIV, Bernard McGinn, ed. *Apocalyptic Spirituality, Classics of Western Spirituality* (New York: Paulist Press, 1979), p. 141.

[45] Richard K. Emmerson and Ronald B. Herzman, *The Apocalyptic Imagination in Medieval Literature* (Philadelphia: University of Pennsylvania Press, 1992), p. 13.

[46] Michel Bakhtin, *Rabelais and His World* (Cambridge: Massachusetts Institute of Technology, 1968), p. 7.

[47] Ibid., p. 6.

[48] Ibid., p. 7.

[49] Jean Baudrillard, *Simulacra and Simulation*, trans. Sheila Faria Glaser (Ann Arbor: University of Michigan Press, 1994), p. 3.

[50] Idem, *Forget Foucault*, (New York: Semiotext(e), 1987), p. 82; *Simulacra and Simulation*, p. 82.

[51] Rusconi, p. 318.

[52] Jaroslav Pelikan, *Jesus Through the Centuries: His Place in the History of Culture* (New Haven: Yale University Press, 1985), pp. 34-45.

[53] Ibid., p. 97.

[54] Ibid., p. 105.

[55] Will Herberg, *Protestant-Catholic-Jew: An Essay in American Religious Sociology* (Garden City, N. Y: Doubleday & Company, Inc., 1955), p. 89.

[56] Ibid., pp. 89-90.

[57] Mircea Eliade, *Images and Symbols: Studies in Religious Symbolism*, trans. Philip Mairet (New York: Sheed & Ward, 1961), p. 51.

[58] Wing-tsit Chan, trans. *The Way of Lao Tzu (Tao-te ching)* (Indianapolis: The Bobbs-Merrill Company, Inc., 1963), p. 184.

[59] *Meister Eckhart*, 2 Vols. Ed. Franz Pfeiffer and trans. C. De B. Evans (London: John M. Watkins, 1956), I: 32, 84.

[60] Ibid., I: 88.

[61] Kierkegaard, *Philosophical Fragments*, p. 63.

[62] Eckhart, I: 55.

Chapter 7

Time and Death

Based on a wide variety of rock 'n' roll lyrics, it's clear their composers are fascinated by time. The rock group Chicago suggests, for instance, the mysterious nature of time in their hit "Does Anybody Really Know What Time It Is?" The lyrics raise some profound questions: Does anyone truly grasp the nature of time? Do I have time enough to die? Before this, the Byrds' song "Turn! Turn! Turn!" found its inspiration in Ecclesiastes (3) where there is a season for everything: a time for war, a time for peace, a time to be born, a time to die, a time to mourn, and a time to dance. The biblical spirit of Ecclesiastes can also be discovered in the song "Take It As It Comes" by the Doors in which there is a time to live, lie, laugh, die, walk, run, and shoot one's arrows at the sun. The message of the song is not to get ahead of oneself because it is better to slow down and accept things as they come. A similar message is evoked by the Indigo Girls with "Everything In Its Own Time" from *Shaming the Sun*: "A lesson learned a loving God and things in their own time/In nothing more do I trust/We own nothing." Playing with images from Pslams (23) instead of Ecclesiastes, the rock group U2 rewrites their own biblical message in "Love Rescue Me" from *Rattle and Hum*. The subject walks through a shadowy valley, fears no evil, curses his rod and staff, does not find comfort, and asks for love to rescue him. If the rod and staff represent the past, the subject stands at the entrance to a new world that will be characterized by love.

Besides finding ways to sing about time by using biblical images and ideas, rock composers have also used images associated with motion to refer to time. U2 uses the metaphor of a train to emphasize the movement of time that can leave you behind it in "Zoo Station" from *Achtung Baby*. Here time is like a train that transforms the future into the past and leaves you stranded at the station, suggesting the relentless nature of the movement of time. In contrast to U2, Harry Chapin imagines time flying away in "Dreams Go By" from *Portrait Gallery*. Time not only flies away for Chapin, it takes our vocational dreams with it, but it is impossible to know where these dreams go. In "The Best Was Yet to Come" by Bryan Adams from *Cuts Like a Knife*, he ponders how strange it is that time flies away when the best events have not yet arrived. According to Simon and Garfunkel in "Leaves That Are Green" from *Sounds of Silence*, times passes swiftly, like green leaves that eventually turn brown and wither. A different kind of problem concerns the group Styx in "Too Much Time On My Hands" where time is ticking away with the subject's sanity. Styx's lyrics combine the loss of time with boredom, lack of hope, lack of direction, and lack of activity. In another number by Styx "Crystal Ball," the lyrics depict a person trapped alone in time and wondering what the future holds. The subject seeks a crystal ball to peer into the future because there are so many things he would like to know. A very different attitude toward time is expressed by James Taylor's "Secret of Life" from *JT*. He equates the passing of time with the secret of life. Taylor is suggesting that we not fight the flow of time, but that we should go with its flow and enjoy ourselves in the process.

Even though Taylor's message may be sagacious advice, other lyrics lament time or emphasize its brevity. Jackson Browne's album *Late for the Sky* includes "Farther On," a lament about time. Lonely, filling his loneliness with illusion and fantasy, and holding on to cherished memories, the subject of the lyrics loses his way, laments that heaven seems further away, and the angels have grown older; he grasps that his life is coming to an end. In his song "The Real Life," John Mellencamp emphasizes the brevity of life and considers what we do with our lives. The subject of the lyrics begins to work at twenty-one after graduating college, but he quits suddenly at age forty-three to live his life the way he wants. Mellencamp wants his listeners to realize that life is too short to feel captured and constricted by a job. Like Mellencamp, the Police express the brevity of time in "No Time This Time" from *Regatta de blanc*. Since time is short, there is no opportunity for conversation, knowing, explanation, sharing, and demonstration. They imply it is preferable to slow the world down and even stop it from rotating. Any attempt to do this is like trying to scale a prodigious wall. These types of lyrics concerning the brevity of time are linked to the shortness of human life, which amounts to a means of measuring time from a human viewpoint.

It is this human perspective applied to time that leads some composers to refer to time as a robber, a punisher, or something that we can capture like a trophy of war. In his song "Time" from *Mona Bone Jakon*, Cat Stevens stresses the rise and fall of time that eventually strips a person of everything. From another perspective, Hootie and the Blowfish sing that time punishes you, destroys your dreams, and is no friend. The subject of the lyrics claims that he does not believe in time, but he actually does believe in it because he is well aware of its dangers. In fact, he is being driven crazy thinking about time. Steely Dan's lyrics express a much different attitude to time than Stevens and Hootie or the Blowfish. Their song "Reeling In the Years" gives the impression that one can stow away time. In contrast to Steely Dan's lyrics, there is "Time" by INXS from their album *Full Moon, Dirty Hearts*, which depicts time as both shaping you and breaking you. These lyrics suggest that we are shaped by our past and broken by the present and possibly the future.

The Protestant theologian Reinhold Niebuhr agrees with the spirit of these lyrics because he thinks historical time always remains morally ambiguous to the end because the perfect love of Jesus is defeated and not victorious in the genuine course of history.[1] There are other examples of lyrics that emphasize particular aspects of time, such as procrastination, punctuality, seizing the moment, and taking immediate action. These kinds of lyrics reflect a tendency of rock music to stop time, or to expand the time that we are able to live in the present moment.[2]

Another perspective is provided by Fleetwood Mac, who stress the future in "Don't Stop" from their album *Rumours*, the theme song for the 1992 Democratic Convention and Bill Clinton's campaign for the Presidency. The essence of the lyrics is always to think about the future that will soon be here, whereas the past is gone, and the future will be better. The subject of "Peace of Mind" by Boston feels trapped in the daily competition of life in which people cannot decide who they should be; he wants to find some respite from all the confusion, and thinks the future is coming too slow as he eagerly anticipates the future. The orientation towards the future embodies an optimistic expectation, suggesting that we must not become captive to the past. Early Christians expected an early end of time, and they also learned about the right or proper time (*kairos*) that represents the present moment in which God brings about a new dimension of reality, a fulfilled time that ushers in the Kingdom of God (Mk 1:15).

Rather than emphasizing the present or the future, other rock lyrics view time in a nostalgic manner. In "Bookends" Simon and Garfunkel look back to a time of innocence that is now lost. All that is left is an old photograph that preserves the memories of that special time. In *A Saucerful of Secrets* and "Remember a Day," Pink Floyd expresses nostalgia for their youth when they were free to play, a moment when time appeared to stand still. Certain philosophical kinds of questions are raised about time: Why can't we remain the same and continue to play? Why does time bring about changes? Why are we a captive to the flow of time? These kinds of questions are timeless and cross-cultural.

A strong nostalgia for the past is evident in "Glory Days" by Bruce Springsteen from his best selling album *Born in the U. S. A.* The lyrics recount an encounter between two former schoolmates who have a few drinks and talk about the old days. The song tells about the subject's visits to a comely female friend who is divorced, and they talk about the old times. The song is about the passage of time and nostalgia for lost innocence, simplicity, and glory. But time passes quickly and "leaves you with nothing mister but boring stories of glory days."

Styx expresses a different type of nostalgia in their song "The Best of Times." The present represents the end of paradise due to a broken romantic relationship. Instead of a world dominated by fear, the composer images a paradise for two lovers that will form their personal paradise. These kinds of lyrics offer the listener a vision of an ideal time, an integrated time of normally separate aspects of life—"the individual and the social, the mind and the body, change and stillness, the different and the same, the already past and the still to come, desire and fulfillment."[3]

In an interesting song simply entitled "Old" from *You're the One*, Paul Simon's subject reminisces about his youth and the first time that he heard songs by Buddy Holly that recall the cold war. It is curious to him that wars and genocide continue just like Buddy Holly's songs. The subject also recalls the first time he smoked pot and ties that event with hearing the Rolling Stones song "Satisfaction" when he was young and unemployed. This motivates him to reflect that Jesus, Buddha, Muhammad, wisdom, the Koran, and the Bible are all old. The song concludes with a recollection of the ages of the human race, the universe, and the observation that God preceded these by billions of years. With considerable justification, it can be said, "God is old" in a metaphorical sense.

In addition to a nostalgia for times past, some rock lyrics invert and mock time. For instance, Bill Haley's tune "Rock Around the Clock" and Chuck Berry's "Reelin' and Rockin'" use the image of the clock. Both numbers invert time measured by a clock for work into something more pleasurable and fun. By representing a glorification of pleasure and play, these songs function to implicitly or explicitly criticize society for its overemphasis on the necessity of labor to the detriment of play.[4] Nonetheless, these various examples enable us to recognize that time and music are intrinsically related.[5] The lyrics used thus far simply reflect the temporality of music that is prior to the lyrics.

From these types of examples, it is clear that many rock composers are fascinated by time just like philosophers and scientists. For rock composers, this can be explained in part by the close association between music and time. Rock composers also show concern for the events that occur within history. Immersed in the flux of time, rock composers reflect concerns with death, various types of death, and human responses to death that are connected to fond memories, sadness, and profound love. The remainder of this chapter will deal with these types of time-related issues.

The Terror of History

There is probably no scholar who calls our attention to the terror of history as much as Mircea Eliade, who argues that modern individuals have fallen into history—a living hell—where they are threatened by the terror of history. Falling into the dark hole of history suggests that human beings have lost the center of their being. In contrast to the endless present experienced by religious individuals in archaic societies, who live in the security provided by the myths of their culture, history represents a different mode of existing in the face of risk and danger. Eliade sees the irrational lurking within history.[6] Within the terror of history of the current time, there are no transcendent values, and without such values human existence is meaningless. With a demonic element reigning and decreeing crimes, cruelty, and absurdity, historical sufferings are devoid of any trans-historical significance. Unable to find ultimate meaning in the drama of history, contemporary beings are condemned to hopelessness. The meaningless flux of time confronts us as the terror of history, and we are paralyzed before the overwhelming onslaught of this demonic force, which is often represented as the awesome specter of death.[7]

Billy Joel acknowledges the terror of history in his song "We Didn't Start the Fire" from *Storm Front*. He mentions a litany of people, places, things, and events of history from 1949 to 1989. The chorus captures the sense of the terror of history by using the metaphor of a world on fire. This is not something for which the current generation is responsible because the fire was always burning, and they are trying to put it out. In other words, these lyrics suggest that there have always been problems in history, and human beings tried to oppose them as best they could. Hence, the lyrics of the chorus suggest those human beings are victims of the terror of history. Joel ends his song by basically raising the question: Will problems ever cease after we are dead?

Billy Joel strikes a more hopeful note with "Two Thousand Years" from *River of Dreams*. According to the lyrics, in the begining of history, angels and prophets gave light. Endowed with faith and will, humans overcame obstacles and were victorious. In retrospect, time is relentless in its destructive abilities and we only need to look at the many kingdoms that have risen and fallen during the course of history to know this. Because we are currently at the crossroads of time, we need to grasp the moment for our children and not repeat the mistakes of the past in order to end sorrow, hate, and fear. In a new world, there will be no war. There will instead be miracles along with science and poetry, and people will be granted the ability to see truly by prophets and angels.

If Joel suggests that we can learn lessons from historical mistakes, Sting disagrees in his song "History Will Teach Us Nothing" from *Nothing Like the Sun*. Sting advocates reason as a guide and freedom from the past. In fact, he wants to discard the past because it embodies no lessons for us and thus will teach us nothing. But why is this true? He answers that history is a "catalogue of crime" characterized by power, oppression, scarcity, and aggression. Therefore, we can only learn more evil from the historical past. Since reason can go astray and we can never be totally free of the past, are we not condemned to repeat the mistakes of the past? Sting's lyrics neglect to mention progress in areas like medicine and technology that improve the quality of life for many people.

If Sting's lyrics reflect a nostalgia for a more enlightened, aware, and free human being within the flux of time, we may at best be stuck with nostalgia for no-time, which is expressed nicely by the song "Overs" by Simon and Garfunkel from their album *Bookends*. They sing about the lack of good times, only bad times, and humorously, the *New York Times* on the windowsill. The sly humor embodied in these lines may be our best hope with coping with the terror of history. If in the face of hopelessness we can respond with humor we can be free to shape our destinies to some degree in the face of the terror of history.

Sting uses a more lucid call for the abolition of time in the title song of his album "Brand New Day," about people getting hurt in love affairs. The lyrics acknowledge that love can be a painful experience. The lyrics call all lovers to begin anew by setting their clocks to zero in order to restart them. Of course, this is impossible, but there is nothing wrong with wishing that you had such an opportunity.

Sting's wish to abolish time and Simon and Garfunkel's nostalgia for no-time corresponds with one of two reactions to time in the work of Eliade: an abolition of time and a more traditional answer to the terror of history in the form of a re-evaluation of Christianity. If the growth of history increases alienation from any transhistorical model, Eliade stresses the need to abolish time. From Eliade's perspective, this proposal is not as romantic as it appears, because he gives various precedents from history that include ancient alchemists, dreams, and poetic and literary creations that imply an abolition of time.[8] On the other hand, Eliade also calls for a re-evaluation of Christianity that includes a creative freedom grounded in God and supported by the highest being that is engendered by faith, which forms one's defense against the onslaught of the terror of history. By revolting against the irreversibility of time, one can recreate one's world and free oneself from the threat of time.[9] If one can abolish time, one can always start one's life anew.

The Encounter with Death

A primary characteristic of death is its certainty for all living creatures. The German philosopher Martin Heidegger cites an old piece of German folk wisdom that affirms that as soon as you are born you are old enough to die. Probably, no rock group is more associated with death than the Grateful Dead, who embodied the belief in the certainty of death, as evident by their album covers adorned with skeletons and other reminders of death. Initially called the Warlocks, the group discovered a new name from an old Irish and Scottish phrase based on folk ballads that referred to departed souls who were required to return to earth and perform good deeds, which were necessary before the soul was allowed to rest in peace. Once peaceful repose became possible these deceased persons could than rest eternally and become the grateful dead.[10] But the Grateful Dead was not the only rock group to address the topic of death.

Pink Floyd captures the spirit of German folk wisdom about death with "Childhood's End" from *Obscured by Clouds* with the following lines: "But everything one day will cease/All the iron turned to rust/All the proud men turned to dust." The universal and inescapable nature of death is stressed by Randy Newman's song "Old Man" from *Sail Away*. The picture that he paints with his lyrics is bleak because no one helps because no one needs the dying person, and there is no God to provide comfort to the dying. The certainty of death is stressed by Prince with "Sign ⊕ of the Times." People are dying from disease, committing suicide, killing themselves by gang violence, and doing drugs. A hurricane kills people in a church, and a woman murders her infant because she could not afford to feed it. Prince combines this scenario of death with political priorities when he notes the government ignores these social ills to send men to the moon or explore space.

Death is connected to nothingness. Again, Martin Heidegger makes this perfectly clear: "The 'nothing' with which anxiety brings us face to face, unveils the nullity by which Dasein, in its very basis, is defined; and this basis itself is as throwness into death."[11] The two best expressions of nothingness in rock lyrics that I have discovered are "Paint It Black" by the Rolling Stones and "Dust in the Wind" by Kansas. The Stones' subject wants to paint everything black: a red door, girls in colorful summer clothing, cars, flowers, and even the sun. Turning introspective, he sees that his heart is black. This emphasis on blackness suggests the nothingness of death, even though death is not mentioned in the Stones' lyrics, whereas Kansas equates dust in the wind with the nothingness that we really are.

Besides the uncertainty about the exact moment of death and the brevity of human life, other lyrics concentrate on the process of death. An old, long haired, lover of rock music is married with three kids in Jethro Tull's song "Too Old to Rock 'N' Roll: Too Young to Die." The subject decides to take his motorcycle for a ride on the highway, and he hits something while going 120 miles per hour: "And he was too old to Rock 'n' Roll but he was too young to die/ No, you're never too old to Rock 'n' Roll if you're too young to die." The lyrics compare the mature lover of rock music with his children, and it concludes that he is not too old for rock music and certainly too young to die just as his children are too young to die. But is there such a thing as being too young to die? What the group wants to object to is the injustice of dying young.

Although the New Testament recognizes this kind of injustice, its emphasis is upon death as a punishment for sins (Rom 6.23), and the sinner pays a debt by his/her death (Rom 6.7). The apostle Paul strongly suggests that this scenario is fair, but he quickly adds there is a victory over death because God gives Christ as a free gift on the cross for eternal life. If our primordial ancestor Adam caused all humans to die by means of his original sin, it is Christ who brings resurrection of the dead (1 Cor 15:21-22). For Paul, the death and resurrection of Christ forms a single unitary salvation-event and a propitiatory sacrifice from which the forgiveness of sins results. The guilt contracted by sins is canceled. The notion of a propitiatory sacrifice is combined with the notion of a vicarious sacrifice, which means that he died "for us" (2 Cor 5.14). Such a union of sacrificial notions means that Christ died for everyone, and those who live do so not for themselves "but for him who died and was raised for them" (2 Cor 5:15). This type of New Testament understanding of death is difficult to find among rock lyrics, although it is possible to find references to the process of dying.

The Rolling Stones in "Sister Morphine" from *Sticky Fingers* stress the process of dying. Lying in a hospital bed, a patient awakes and asks for morphine to kill the pain, although he does not know what happened or how he got in the hospital. He feels that he is dying, and he is convinced that in the morning he will be dead. In a similar type of setting, a young boy is on a life-support machine because of an accident in a canoe, in "Adrian" from *Pieces of You* by Jewel. While on the life-support apparatus, the boy is no longer able to go outside and play. All the residents of the town are sorry for little Adrian, and many think he should be taken off the machine because the doctor has said that his condition is hopeless. It is a short distant from the hospital to the streets of the city. In the lyrics to Bruce Springsteen's emotionally moving and powerful song for the hit motion picture *Philadelphia* "Streets of Philadelphia," he imagines himself suffering from AIDS to the drum beat of a funeral march. The disease renders him a shadow of his former self. His feelings of complete hopelessness and abandonment are captured by the following lines: "Ain't no angel gonna greet me/It's just you and I my friend." As he feels his life ebbing away, he wants to know whether others will receive him, or whether he will be abandoned on the streets of the city.

In a song with some similarities to so-called "near-death" experiences, Meat Loaf sings about a man who imagines his own death from a motorcycle accident in "Bat Out of Hell." His body is mangled at the bottom of a pit, and he hears a tolling bell, presumably tolling for the accident victim. He sees his heart beating, breaking out of his body, and flying away like a "bat out of hell." Somewhat similar to the lyrics of Meat Loaf's song is "American Tune" by Paul Simon from his album *There Goes Rhymin' Simon*. He dreams his soul rises above his body, and it smiles reassuringly back at him. He finally dreams about flying. Simon's lyrics are remarkably similar to "near-death" experiences.

In his best selling book entitled *Life After Life*, Raymond Moody describes the experiences of people declared clinically dead and later restored to life. They are remarkably similar. Such people report out of body experiences that are confusing and frightening. They find themselves in another body inaudible and invisible to others, describe-ing these bodies as devoid of solidity or weight, making it possible for them to pass through physical objects but unable to grasp them. Their movement is rapid; within this timeless state, their vision and hearing are intact, although they cannot communicate with others. They feel isolated and lonely. After going through a long tunnel, they meet a being of light and are able to communicate with this being by means of the direct transfer of thoughts, using one's native language. People tend to identify this being of light with a religious figure from their own religious tradition.

There are other songs that connect death with some kind of biological immortality. In Blood, Sweat and Tears' hit "And When I Die," the subject says that he does not fear death, and he accepts that he will be at peace. He only asks that his coffin be bundled because it is cold in the earth. He wants to die naturally and not violently. He does not believe in heaven, and prays that there is no hell. When he dies, however, he will know for sure if there is a heaven or hell. In short, he will know what the dead know, a knowledge that represents genuine wisdom. The lyrics make it clear that, even if there is no afterlife, the subject looks forward to a biological immortality, because when he is gone a child will take his place. In other words, an individual person may die but the species survives. That the dead know the secrets of life and death is also evident in the lyrics to "Daniel" by Elton John. Daniel's airplane crashes on a flight to Spain. The singer recalls his brother waving goodbye and the red taillights of the plane in the sky. Then, he sees visions of his brother, laments his death, acknowledges missing him, and asks his brother if he still feels the pain. Although Daniel has died, his eyes see and know more than the living. In the final stanza to the song, Daniel becomes a star. Does this represent his after-life? The lyrics seem to suggest an astronomical form of immortality.

The religious message of the Indigo Girls' song "Secure Yourself" is evident first in the vision of a person bleeding, a raging warrior telling us to have no fear, and a scream and thunder. The song's answer to the apparent chaos and violence is: "Secure yourself to heaven," which is just the beginning. The lyrics acknowledge that the deceased needs no burial space because they can travel through and beyond the sun. By securing oneself to heaven, anyone can join the chosen or elect.

The doctrine of election is definitely different in the theology of the reformer John Calvin since he teaches a doctrine of "double predestination" that he defines in the following way: "We call predestination God's decree, by which he determined with himself what he willed to become of each man. For all are not created in equal condition; rather, eternal life is foreordained for some, eternal damnation for others. Therefore, as any man has been created to one or the other of these ends, we speak of him as predestined to life or death."[12] In a further distinction, Calvin calls election predestination to life, while reprobation is predestination to death. And Calvin denies that God's decision is based on His foreknowledge of a person's merits; it is simply that God wills to do so. Calvin's doctrine is meant to convince a person that salvation comes exclusively from God. Another distinction Calvin makes in his doctrine is between general and particular, a distinction that means that the proclamation of God's word is directed to all humankind, although God's election is not general because it is particular in the sense that it is given to only some.[13] Moreover, reprobation is a necessary correlate of election in the sense that God does not leave the damned to their personal devices. By passing over some people, God condemns them to death in what Calvin refers to as "the dreadful decree," a negative side of his doctrine.[14] For those who might object to such an apparently harsh doctrine, Calvin justifies it by stating that all human beings are odious to God because of their sinful nature. A person would be hard pressed to find rock lyrics reflecting Calvin's doctrine.

According to Bob Dylan's song "Death Is Not the End" from *Down In the Groove*, if you become sad, lonely, and your world falls apart, or if life becomes incomprehensible, or if your dreams have been destroyed, death is never the end of human existence. The spirit does not die where the tree of life grows and the light of salvation shines forth hope. The religious message of Dylan's song is absent in the lyrics to "Flowers Never Bend with the Rainfall" by Simon and

Garfunkel from *Parsley, Sage, Rosemary and Thyme* and its denial of death. Unable to know what is real, touch what he feels, or hides behind his illusion, the subject of the song pretends that he will not die. He wanders within a reality that is really a fantasy, and he continues to pretend that his life will never end.

The Beatles' "Blackbird" is closer in spirit to Dylan's song. The Beatles play off paradoxes like death is birth, blindness is sight, and night is day. Resembling the mythological phoenix that dies and is reborn, the blackbird sings, flies, and sees at the moment of his death that he is reborn. This kind of symbolism plays an intrinsic role within initiatory contexts in many religions, and it is certainly germane to the Christian context and its belief in ultimate victory over death established by Jesus' resurrection (Mk 9:9).

Another popular song that strongly reflects a Christian influence is "Spirit in the Sky" by Norman Greenbaum. He sings about going to a celestial spirit after death. He also refers to his friendship with Jesus and his lack of sin. In contrast to Greenbaum's heavenly spirit in a place that he calls "the best," Peter Lombard (c. 1100-60), a former bishop of Paris and author of the *Sentences* that became a standard textbook of theology during the Middle Ages, provided structure for the scholastic notion of heaven as an empyrean, a place beyond all the celestial spheres. This is a place that is a no place, a place of boundaries, a place that spreads out to infinity.[15]

Suicide, War and Murder

There are many reasons a person might commit suicide, and several of these are found in rock lyrics. On their album *Sounds of Silence*, Simon and Garfunkel included two songs about suicide. In "Richard Cory," they sing about a rich industrialist who had everything a person could desire in a material sense. In contrast, a person working in Cory's factory was miserable and envious of the industrialist's wealth and fame until one day the newspaper announced Cory's suicide. In "A Most Peculiar Man," a lonely, peculiar man lives in a room by himself, friendless and uncommunicative. One night he turned on the gas oven and lay down in his bed to die.

There are other lyrics that focus specifically on younger people committing suicide. On their album *Maybe You Should Drive*, the Barenaked Ladies sing about a young couple that reunites in "Everything Old Is New Again." The young man spends time bandaging his young lover's wrists after an attempted suicide. The lyrics combine themes of madness in the world with wasted youth, anorexia, fear, and the belief that an after life might be better than one's current life. The Counting Crows' "Round Here" on *August and Everything After* examines an odd, dying, liminal figure named Maria. She comes to Nashville hoping to meet someone who looks like Elvis. She takes off her clothing, claims to be close to Jesus, knows she is misunderstood, and cannot behave normally when she is nervous. She thinks about committing suicide by jumping from the top of a tall building because she is tired of living. In "Blasphemous Rumours" by Depeche Mode from *Some Great Reward*, a sixteenth-year-old girl attempts suicide by cutting her wrists because she is bored with life, but she fails. Her mother accepts the blame for her daughter's failed suicide. The mother gets on her knees and prays, saying God has a sick sense of humor: "And when I die/I expect to find Him laughing." At eighteen, after finding a new life in Jesus, the girl is hit by a car and ends up on life-support. She dies on a beautiful sunny day. This song expresses indignant outrage about the unfairness and injustice of this young girl's predicament, because her conversion to Jesus is of little use to her after her earlier failed attempt at suicide.

Critics have accused rock composers of encouraging suicide. Although there may be some evidence of this, many composers try to discourage teenagers or anyone else from thinking that suicide is an answer to the problems of life. An excellent example of this trend is "Don't Try Suicide" by Queen from *The Game*. The message of the song is very clear: It is not worth it. Besides, if you do commit suicide, no one will care. R. E. M. makes a similar pitch to young people in "Everyone Hurts" from *Automatic for the People*. Since everyone experiences pain during his/her life, one must endure the pain and not contemplate suicide. Earlier Sly and the Family Stone espoused an anti-suicide message with "Life" and their emphasis on getting high on life. Everyone experiences some sadness in life. But if you love another person, it is impossible to be sad anymore. Finally, the Dave Mathews Band say they cannot believe someone would not want to live in "Lie in Our Graves." They cannot fathom why someone would want to lie in their graves and wonder if their lives had been a success or wondering about what they might have become instead of themselves.

Besides suicide, another area of focus for rock composers is war. The Band and Joan Baez recorded "The Night They Drove Old Dixie Down." The song is about a southerner whose brother is killed by a Yankee solider during the Civil War, which serves as a surrogate for the war in Vietnam. We can skip from the Civil War to the Vietnam conflict for "Goodnight Saigon" by Billy Joel, who sings about training for and the actual experience of combat. The well-trained GI's are ready to give their lives after basic training. Their attitudes change when they see those killed leaving in numbered, plastic bags. In the jungle they are afraid and pray for help and protection. The men bond closely together as brothers, but in the face of death the pledge of togetherness proves tenuous.

Rock composers have not neglected World War II. The 10,000 Maniacs' "Grey Victory" from *The Wishing Chair* is about the flight of the Enola Gay and the dropping of the atomic bomb on Japan. In another song by the group, "My Mother the War" from *Secrets of the I Ching*, they sing about the global nature of war, and waiting for news of another conflict. War spits out human bodies, which makes war sound like the Hindu goddess Kālī. On the same album, 10,000 Maniacs include songs about infanticide in lesser-developed countries in "National Education Week" and a depiction of the horrors of gas warfare in "The Latin One," contrasting this horror with the imagined glory of war.

Besides war and suicide, the subject of death also appears in songs about murder. Bob Dylan's "Ballad of Donald White" is an autobiographical tale. As he is about to be executed for murder, White tells his life-story, a tale of woe that begins when he left home. In his travels he did not make any friends because he could never get along with anyone he met. Due to a lack of education, he turned to stealing and did time in various jails and discovers that the other prisoners were like him. He also finds serenity in jail. Due to overcrowding, he is released into society, even though he begged the prison authorities not to release him into the dangers of society. He kills a man on Christmas Eve, is found guilty, and sentenced to die. He gives thanks for not having parents to grieve over him, and no friends to witness his disgrace. After bidding farewell to the woods he roamed, crowded bars, and people who hate him, he raises a question about men like him: "Are they enemies or victims/Of your society?"

In the "Ballad of Hollis Brown" from *The Times Are A-Changin'*, Dylan turns again to the theme of murder. Here poverty and desperation drives a poor farmer in South Dakota to kill his wife, five children, and himself with the seven shotgun shells he bought with the last of his money. This sad tale of murder and suicide is intended to highlight the extremes that poverty can drive some people to.

Another ordinary figure is the focus of "Tucson Arizona (Gazette)" by Dan Fogelberg from *Windows and Walls*. A lonely young man named Tony lives at home with his mother and siblings and works at a lousy job. His father died of alcoholism and his brother was killed in Vietnam. Tony's only real friend is an old Chevy automobile, and his soul is similar to vacant space. The other person in this musical drama is Mary Estelle Hanna from Louisiana, who dreams of getting to Los Angeles and becoming a movie star. While working in a lower class bar, she meets Tony, and he asks her for a date. In order to convince her to go out with him, he tells her that he has some cocaine. When neither of them come home the sheriff is called, and Mary's body is discovered later that night, whereas Tony's body is discovered two weeks later with a gun in his hand. The local newspapers and neighbors speculate about what could have driven a good person to such actions.

A personal favorite of mine is a song about a condemned man by Queen's "Bohemian Rhapsody" from *A Night at the Opera*. As a young man is awaiting his execution, he raises some significant religious and philosophical questions about the nature of reality, even though he paradoxically admits to being an unconcerned and tolerant person. He laments to his mother that he has thrown his life away by killing another man when it seemed that his life had just begun. He confesses his feelings about facing death, experiences bodily aches and shivering, laments that he does not want to die, and he wishes that he had not been born. The chorus breaks into the song at this point to plead for his life and to protest the death penalty. The lyrics return to the condemned man, who now says paradoxically that nothing matters to him any more after having stated that he does not want to die, which seems to be a final resignation to his fate.

Death of the Famous and not so Famous

Even though this part of the chapter overlaps a bit with the previous section with respect to its topic, I want to give special attention to songs about famous persons who have died and contrast their deaths with people who were common mortals. An excellent example of a famous person's death captured in rock lyrics is Elton John's "Candle in the Wind" from *Goodbye Yellow Brick Road.* In his farewell to Marilyn Monroe, John depicts her as a person with grace surrounded by people that he describes as crawling insects. As the title of the song implies, Monroe lived a precarious existence and was uncertain whom to trust when she needed help. The most difficult role that she ever played was her own life of loneliness and mental anguish, which was the price that she paid for being a Hollywood superstar. She was even persecuted after her death by the press who had to report that she was discovered nude after her suicide. Her life burned out like a candle but her legend lives on. John later altered the song for Princess Diana of Great Britain after her tragic death in an automobile accident in Paris that John entitled "England's Rose."

In a song reminiscent of Elton John's tune about Marilyn Monroe, Natalie Merchant composed "River" for *Tigerlily*, about a young Hollywood star that dies tragically and the reaction of the public. The lyrics claim that the public distorts and destroys his memory because his death was connected to false rumors and his life was exposed to public scrutiny. As a member of 10,000 Maniacs, Merchant also sings about the matador Manolete in "Death of Manolete" from *Hope Chest*. The matador is killed in the arena by a bull. This cultural idol dies to the consternation of women, teenage girls, and young boys who challenge the bizarre traditions of old men.

Changing perspectives from Hollywood and the bullring to rock 'n' roll stars, a good example of the deaths of the famous can be found in the Righteous Brothers hit song "Rock and Roll Heaven." The lyrics make it clear that if there is such a place, the band must be terrific. The lyrics eulogize dead rock stars like Jim Croce, Bobby Darin, Otis Redding, Jimi Hendrix, Janis Joplin, and Jim Morrison. Besides the tribute to the dead rock artists, the lyrics embody two fundamental messages. The first message is that life is not simply a single performance because there is something eternal about life. In other words, some mode of existence continues after we die, with the artist imagining a special kind of heaven for a particular type of people. The second message is also universal in its intention: Everyone is a star.

Even though some famous people died when it sank, it was the ocean liner Titanic that was ultimately most famous and impressed upon our psyche as one of the single most dramatic calamities of the twentieth-century. Harry Chapin tries to capture the spirit of the tragedy in "Dance Band on the Titanic." Chapin mentions the false sense of invincibility about the ship, and he describes the members of the dance band, the party in first-class, lack of sufficient lifeboats, and a startled and frightened radio operator sending out an S.O.S. as the ship sinks. Meanwhile, the band plays the hymn "Nearer My God to Thee," which proves to be prophetic for those who die. In part, Chapin's song portrays the victims of the tragedy performing a dance of death, with his emphasis on the hymn and the band playing and inviting people to dance. The dance of death is an old motif in Western culture that can be traced back to the medieval period.

Beginning in the thirteenth century, the dance of death owed its origin to a French poem that was performed sometimes as a masque. During these performances, men dressed as skeletons and danced with figures representing the various strata of society. The dancing person did not represent death itself as much as a corpse in a dance of the dead. In a vivid sense, the dancer, impersonating a corpse, represented living beings in their future condition. The dance served to symbolize social equality because death was a phenomenon that leveled the various ranks and professions of society.[16] Jackson Browne embodies the spirit of the medieval dance of death in "For a Dancer" from *Late for the Sky*. Browne reflects on his inability to fully understand death, and thinks that we must all perform our own dances and die our own deaths.

Human Response to Death

Mention has already been made about anxiety caused by the advent of imminent death, visions received just before death, and the dance of death on the Titanic. Crosby, Stills, and Nash express the wide range of human reactions to death in "Wooden Ships," which arrive in a foreign land as one of the passengers or sailors dies. The reaction of his friends to death moves from the shock of horror, to disbelief, to acceptance, and finally to numbness.

Some artists have been motivated to compose songs in direct response to tragedies in their own lives. After losing a girlfriend in an airplane crash, James Taylor wrote "Fire and Rain." His song represents an anguished response to his loss. He confesses that he always assumed that he would see her again. His pain is so intense that he asks Jesus for help in coping with his loss. Since there will be no future for them, he is left grieving with his memories of her. From another perspective, Eric Clapton wrote "Tears In Heaven" after the tragic death of his young son. Clapton's song is a series of questions for his son concerning whether or not his son would recognize him or hold his hand if they meet in heaven, and he generally attempts to imagine what a reunion with his dead son would be like. The lyrics contain a confession by the artist that heaven is not a place he belongs or could stay for long, even if he did get there. Clapton takes a certain amount of solace from knowing that there is peace and no more tears in heaven, which suggests that he imagines that his son is content and happy there.

The death of a close loved one is also the theme of the "The Living Years" by Mike and the Mechanics. Due to frustration the younger generation blames the older one. The subject admits that he is a prisoner to his father's heritage, and wishes that he could have told his father that he loved him while he was still alive. The father and son did not communicate very much while the father was alive because they did not speak the same language, but it is too late to admit these problems after death. The quarrel between the present and the past destroys any future attempts at a dialogical encounter. But the message of the lyrics is: Do not yield to fate or give up. The subject admits regretfully that he was not present when his father died and he did not get to tell his father everything that he had to say. And yet, the spirit of his father is captured later when his baby is born. He movingly laments: "I just wish I could have told him/In the living years." This is a song about love, generational differences, and lack of effective communication.

A strange attempt at communication with the dead is evident in the tune "Lady D'arbanville" by Cat Stevens from *Mona Bone Jakon*. The singer asks a series of questions of his beloved who lies in her grave. He cannot accept her death: "This rose will never die." The inability to accept the death of a loved one is also evident in "Beloved Wife" by Natalie Merchant from *Tigerlily*. A husband sings about his departed wife, the love of his life. Not only can he not believe his loss, but he also feels that he has lost the very best of himself, and does not know how he will continue to live. The man's wife died a lingering death after fifty years of marriage. The husband knows that he will not be able to marry again, and he wonders if he should commit suicide in order to join his wife.

If coming to grips with the death of a parent or other family member is difficult, the death of a friend is equally hard to comprehend. In "Objects in the Rear View Mirror May Appear Closer Than They Are" from his album *Bat Out of Hell II: Back Into Hell*, Meat Loaf sings about his friend Kenny who dies in an accident. Even though their close relationship and the death of his friend seem very far away now, he draws a lesson from his experience in an attempt to cope with his loss: "And if life is just a highway—then the soul is just a car." Presumably, a soul can crash on the highway of life and be extinguished.

By connecting the lyrics of the song to Alice's fall into Wonderland from the classic Lewis Carroll story, the group October Project juxtaposes interior and exterior in "Bury My Lovely" from *Falling Farther In*. On the outside, the sun is brightly shining, but inside the subject of the song is dark. The apparent reason for the darkness within him is the death of a loved one who appears before him in the image of an angel. He wants to join his beloved, but his body imprisons him. He calls for help but his call goes unheard by anyone. In another number on a similar theme "Funeral in the Heart" from the same album, October Project sings about a man who is slowly dying inside after the loss of a loved one, as his world falls apart. Alone as he grows older, he cannot hold onto his dreams, a song, or the person he was in the past.

Death in rock lyrics is not always the death of a loved one. "Allentown" by Billy Joel reveals a threefold theme of death. Allentown is a Pennsylvania city that is dying economically because the steel mills are closing and unemployment is widespread. The subject is depressed and tired of waiting for the economic situation to improve, a desperate situation that drives him to consider suicide. The lyrics also reflect on the death of the American dream. The subject's father was a veteran of World War II. After the war, there was a general expectation that if you graduated high school, worked hard, and were patriotic, you had a good chance of doing as well economically as your parents. But the economic hard times in Allentown prove that the American dream is dead.

A common human reaction to the possibility of death is fear, a topic for "Don't Fear the Reaper" by the Blue Oyster Cult. The subject is a person who has died and is attempting to be reunited with his beloved. The subject speaks to his beloved and tries to dissipate her fears of death, which is personified by the figure of the reaper. The subject reasons that the seasons do not fear the reaper because they return to life after dying. And just as the sun, wind, and rain are elements of nature, death is likewise an element of nature. Like the Shakespearean characters Romeo and Juliet they will be reunited in the afterlife. Finally, the two lovers run to each other and they begin to fly away, only looking back to bid farewell as they enter the afterlife and eternal happiness together.

Another response to death is courage, as in "Let Me Die in My Footsteps" by Bob Dylan. The image here is a person not cowering before death, but rather meeting death standing tall. The song contains a criticism of apocalyptic believers who think that the end of the world is near. The problem with such doomsday thinkers is that while they are learning how to die they have neglected to learn how to live. The lyrics compare dying above ground in a heroic fashion to dying underground like a coward, because the subject would rather die above ground before being buried in contrast to being buried by his own cowardice.

The subject of cowardice and courage in the face of death is the theme for the Protestant theologian Paul Tillich. According to Tillich, if a person is estranged from the ultimate power of being (God), this demonstrates the extent to which one is determined by one's finitude. In such a situation one experiences time as mere transitoriness devoid of actual presence and space as simply spatial contingency. A person's finitude also suggests that they are under the domination of death and its absolute threat against them, and are driven by the anxiety associated with having to die. Within the context of his method of correlation, Tillich argues, "Faith accepts 'in spite of'; and out of the 'in spite of' of faith the 'in spite of' of courage is born."[17] It is this courage nurtured by faith that enables us to cope with death by means of self-affirmation "in spite" of the absolute threat of death.

If courage is one possible response to death, humor is another. "Forest Lawn" by Tom Paxton is a humorous look at a famous cemetery in California, which was also the focus of a satirical novel by Evelyn Waugh named *The Loved One.* The subject of Paxton's song wants a simple funeral and knows that he can get it at Forest Lawn, although he can also have an expensive and elaborate affair. He can be assured of a "casket lined in fleece" and fireworks spelling out "rest in peace." A customer can also be assured of music at one's funeral because they have both a "heavenly choir" and a "military band." Airplanes will salute you and drop a "cross in a parachute." Or you can have "topless dancers in golden wings." A mortician can put a smiling face on your cadaver, and a bust of you can be rigged to tip its hat when mourners pass. After you are buried, you can have tapes of Billy Graham piped into your casket. In fact, you can have virtually anything, if you have the financial resources.

Another example of death and humor is "Only the Good Die Young" by Billy Joel. The subject is trying to convince his Catholic girlfriend to have sex with him. He tries to demonstrate the contradictions in her religious upbringing, but she apparently continues to hide behind her religion. By being good, she risks dying young, according to her would-be lover, whereas sinners live longer and enjoy life more. Basically, the subject states that sinners have more fun. Joel's lyrics indicate humor helps mortal human beings to cope with the stresses of life, and it also suggests that where there is humor there is hope.

Memory, Love, and Death

There is often an intimate connection in life between death, love and memory. We tend to remember those that we loved throughout our lives even more fondly after they have departed. Items like lockets of hair, engraved tombstones, charitable gifts, endowments to cultural organizations, or having a building or street named for a departed person are all associated with the cultivation of memory. A typical university library is, for instance, analogous to a tomb of memory because books bear inscriptions, study carrels have plaques, and reading rooms are dedicated to deceased people. Their names are there to evoke memories from those who see and read the inscriptions or plaques.

What one might refer to as a cult of memory is also evident in rock 'n' roll lyrics. Simon and Garfunkel's "So Long, Frank Lloyd Wright" from *Bridge Over Troubled Water* is a farewell tribute to a great architect, someone with the ability to alter one's viewpoint. In a song about the assassination of Martin Luther King Jr., the black civil rights leader, by U2 "Pride (In The Name of Love)" from *Rattle and Hum*, they call King a man of love. The lyrics closely connect King with Jesus, claiming King not only came in love to justify us, but he was also betrayed with a kiss like Jesus. Their overall message is that those who come in the name of peace pay a heavy price. In "The Late Great Johnny Ace" from *Hearts and Bones*, Paul Simon tells an intriguing story about a black artist and former Beatle. After a radio announcement about the death of a black artist, the subject writes for a signed photograph, even though he is not a big fan of the deceased. Many years later a stranger tells him about the death of John Lennon. The two men visit a bar where they play songs by the black performer, Johnny Ace. Ironically, the death of someone who really touched them is mourned using the music of someone they hardly knew.

In a song reminiscent of the "The Living Years" by Mike and the Mechanics, Dan Folgelberg reminisces about his father in "Leader of the Band." He tells us that his father was a quiet man of music whose inner feelings were kept to himself. As his father's eyes grow older and he becomes more tired, the son realizes how his father gently sculpted his soul and those of others, although it took the son a long time to understand this. He confesses that his own life has probably been a poor attempt to imitate his father. And yet, he feels a kind of mystical bond with his father because he imagines his father's blood is within his instrument, and the father's song plays within the soul of his son. Folgelberg's song is an attempt to thank his father for all that he gave him, and it is an acknowledgment that he represents a living legacy to his father. Folgelberg's lyrics function as a testimony to what his father meant to him, an example of thankfulness and a creative way to perpetuate his memory.

The close connection between love and death was legendary in Romantic literature and poetry during the eighteenth century. Many Romantic poets wrote about death as something beautiful, an illusion of art, by concealing itself beneath the mask of beauty. It also became desirable as a consoling power, a hope, and even something longed for. Death was often depicted as an absorption into the whole. In his poem "Adonais," Shelley responded to the death of Keats by asserting that his departed friend was now one with Nature, and his voice could be heard in its sounds. If we look closely enough, we can find the same connection in some rock lyrics. In her song "Oh Father" from *The Immaculate Collection*, Madonna sings in an autobiographical way about the death of her mother and her conflicts with her father. In the lyrics, she confesses, "I have sinned." In the video, there is a scene where she dances on her mother's grave as a little girl, a scene that vividly depicts the union of love and death.

Love, death and thoughts of suicide are combined in "Love is Blindness" by U2 from *Achtung Baby*. Although love is directly associated with blindness in the minds of many people, the subject does not really want to see because he would rather be obscured by darkness and contemplate suicide. Upon further consideration, the subject realizes that suicide is a dangerous idea that does not make sense.

Stevie Wonder combines love and death in "These Three Words" from *Jungle Fever*, whose lyrics recall a church sermon. Wonder asks: When was the last time you told your parents you loved them? Since those you care about can be taken away suddenly, you should not hesitate to say you love them. The same question is raised about a relative or a friend, and the same advice is given. Since life is precarious, there is comfort in knowing that you've told loved ones often how much you loved them before they die.

But what can be said about a person apparently incapable of love? Such a person seems to have a death wish. This is evident in "Blaze of Glory" by Jon Bon Jovi. The outlaw figure of the song lives an austere lifestyle and does not have a clue about where he is going and has forgotten where he has been. He confesses to being "a devil on the run" and "a candle in the wind." During his life, the only thing that he did not have to steal or win was being born sinful. He admits to being a killer like Cain of Genesis. He prays to die like a man, and asks God to keep his soul, in his own rendition of a child's bedtime prayer. When the outlaw asks God to let him die like a man by allowing him to take a bullet, these lyrics give the impression the subject is in love with death.

In order to perpetuate the memory of the heroic 343 dead New York City firefighters after the terrorist attack on the twin towers at the World Trade Center on September 11, 2001, Bruce Springsteen composed "Into the Fire" for his album *The Rising*. The album symbolizes the refusal of the country to be defeated by hateful fanatics. This tribute to the dead firefighters is intentionally religious, beginning with the blues, which signifies the feelings of survivors, and concluding with gospel music signifying hope. The religious aura of the song is reinforced when Springsteen asks that the faith and hope of the firefighters bestow upon the survivors the same Christian virtues.

Concluding Remarks

Rock composers' fascination with time can be partly explained by the simple fact that music exists in time and possesses duration, making time an integral aspect of music since time determines rhythm. Moreover, music enables us to stop time as we ponder its passing.[18] This does not mean that time is devoid of any religious significance in rock music. Like sacred church music, rock music can be viewed as an attempt to redeem time. As the contemporary theologian David Ford writes, "Music obliges us to rethink time."[19] We can view just such a situation in the number "We Didn't Start the Fire" by Billy Joel, because it obligates us to rethink time and what has occurred in time. Moreover, rock music redeems time in the sense that it makes the past present, and the presence of the music anticipates the future, as in the Fleetwood Mac song "Don't Stop."

This close association between music and time does not completely dissipate the terror that one experiences when one encounters history and the events that occur within the flux of time. Within historical time and place, rock composers are well aware that we encounter death by means of old age, illness, suicide, war, or murder. In a sense, composers seem to agree that death is a great equalizer because it affects rich and poor, famous and obscure, and old and young alike. If it is a guaranteed fact that everyone will eventually die at some point, the responses to death are more uncertain.

Three typical responses among rock composers are anxiety, grief, and courage. But these three responses do not reflect the importance of memories of loved ones, sadness at our loss, or the deep love we often have for the deceased. It is music that gives us an experience of the passing nature of time that shapes our memory. Simon Frith expresses this feature of time in the following way: "In most general terms music shapes memory, defines nostalgia, programs the way we age (changing and staying the same)."[20] Frith's statement does not mention the deep void death creates in the social lives of the survivors. If this chapter demonstrates anything, it is that rock composers have often written insightfully and movingly on the topic of time and death, which are phenomena inextricably connected to each other, since both are grounded in socio-historical existence as ubiquitous and interwoven networks.

Endnotes

[1] Niebuhr, *Faith and History*, p. 135.

[2] Simon Frith, *Performing Rites: On the Value of Popular Music* (Cambridge: Harvard University Press, 1996), p. 157.

[3] Ibid., p. 157.

[4] George Lipsitz, *Time Passages: Collective Memory and American Popular Culture* (Minneapolis: University of Minnesota Press, 1990), p. 112.

[5] Begbie, p. 26.

[6] Mircea Eliade, *Ordeal by Labyrinth: Conversations with Claude-Henri Rocquet*, trans. Derek Coltman (Chicago: University of Chicago Press, 1982), p. 121.

[7] Mircea Eliade, *The Myth of the Eternal Return*, trans. Willard R. Trask (New York: Pantheon Books, 1954).

[8] Mircea Eliade, *A History of Religious Ideas, Volume 1: From the Stone Age to the Eleusinian Mysteries*, trans. Willard R. Trask (Chicago: University of Chicago Press, 1978), p. 55; *Shamanism: Archaic Techniques of Ecstasy*, trans. Willard R. Trask, Bollingen Series LXXVI (New York: Pantheon Books, 1964), p. 103; *Myths, Dreams and Mysteries: The Encounter between Contemporary Faiths and Archaic Realities*, trans. Philip Mairet (New York: Harper & Row, 1967), p. 36.

[9] Idem, *Myth of the Eternal Return*, p. 162.

[10] Friedlander, p. 192.

[11] Martin Heidegger, *Being and Time*, trans. John Macquarrie and Edward Robinson (New York: Harper & Row, 1962), p. 356.

[12] Calvin, *Institutes of the Christian Religion*, 3.21.5.

[13] Ibid., 3.22.10.

[14] Ibid., 3.23.7.

[15] Jeffrey Burton Russell, *A History of Heaven: The Singing Silence* (Princeton: Princeton University Press, 1997), p. 120.

[16] See Phillippe Ariès, *The Hour of Our Death*, trans. Helen Weaver (New York: Knopf, 1981); *Western Attitudes Toward Death*, trans. Patricia M. Ranum (Baltimore: Johns Hopkins University Press, 1974).

[17] Tillich, *Courage to Be*, p. 172.

[18] Gary Giddins, *Rhythm-A-Ning* (New York: Oxford University Press, 1985), p. 246.

[19] Ford, p. 123.

[20] Frith, *Performing Rites*, p. 149.

Chapter 8
Eschatological Themes

If the focus of the previous chapter concentrated on time in general and the three moments of time, this chapter is concerned with the future moment of time, more precisely the eschatological moment or end time. It will be, however, possible to see an emphasis on the present in some cases. Unlike some religions of India and China, in Western religion the golden age does not reside in the past; if there is a golden age or paradise to be attained, it lies in the future. Besides eschatological themes, this chapter will also examine three types of notions about paradise in rock lyrics: earthly, interior, and transcendent. Finally, we will attempt to discern possible reasons for the scarcity of references to hell and the last judgment in comparison to references to the end time and paradise.

The End of Time

The themes of this chapter are concerned generally with events at the end of time and more specifically with notions of paradise. We can find a song about the end of time, for instance, in "When the Ship Comes In" by Bob Dylan on *The Times Are A-Changin'*. The subject of the song imagines the end of time as the arrival of a ship, which will be preceded by natural disasters, although animals will happily greet the end time. The lyrics juxtapose the awakened (responsive and saved) with the sleepers (non-responsive and condemned). The subject sees the arrival of the ship as liberation from bondage, during which time foes will be condemned and drowned. *The Freewheelin' Bob Dylan* features a song about a person who finds himself at the gates of heaven, standing before Saint Peter in "I'd Hate to Be You on that Dreadful Day." If you ask the saint what time it is, his reply is that it is too late, a response that causes you to begin perspiring and have nightmares. There will be no cure for your headache. You will stand exposed for everyone to see, and will find yourself short of change for a quart of wine. In response to your yelling and screaming, a voice will say you should have heeded the word of God when you lived on earth. Dylan is describing the period just before judgment is passed on a hapless soul. It may seem strange to critics of rock 'n' roll music for rock composers to create songs dealing with a rather overt religious theme. The two examples from the corpus of Dylan's compositions do not exhaust his contribution to the subject.

The topic of eschatology includes apocalyptic literary speculations that are characterized by bizarre visions, strange symbolism and supernatural happenings. The term "apocalyptic" comes from a Greek term meaning "to uncover, reveal." The central topic of Jewish apocalyptic literature is God's revelation concerning the end-time. Isaiah 24-27 is often called a "little apocalypse" in which the writer portrays the final judgment of God upon all nations as a cosmic catastrophe.

Apocalyptic literature tends to be composed during times of persecution; it uses a spiritual code language that makes it a sealed book (Dan 12:4) to others outside the inner circle of faith. The best example of this type of literature is the book of Daniel from the Hebrew Bible composed shortly after the outbreak of the Maccabean wars around 165 B.C.E. The author was a pious Jew whose religious faith demanded total loyalty to the Torah (law) no matter the consequences. The writer of Daniel believed that he was living in the last days, and he related a series of visions in which Daniel saw four beasts, representing political forces opposing God arising from a watery chaos. Finally the last and worst beast with ten horns appeared to him. Another excellent example of this type of literature is the New Testament book of Revelation, whose similar kinds of visions are echoed in some rock lyrics.

Jackson Browne's song "Before the Deluge" and Barry McGuire's "Eve of Destruction" are good examples of apocalyptic visions. Because of its biblical references, "A Hard Rain's A-Gonna Fall" by Bob Dylan is an even better example. Dylan's song dates to the Cuban Missile Crisis of October 1962. The lyrics warn of impending doom using images from the Hebrew Bible and New Testament, although Dylan also uses the metaphor of rain to suggest the comforting presence of God, which reminds one of passages from Psalms (72:6) and Hosea (6:3): "He will come to us like the showers, like the spring rains that water the earth." In the book of Revelation, after the seven seals are broken (6-8), the writer reports seeing and hearing different things that suggest the cataclysmic end of the world. Likewise, Dylan's "blue eyed son" reports seeing other kinds of wonders like a baby surrounded by wild wolves, instruments of death held by young children, a warning given by a clap of thunder, and the sound of a cosmically destructive wave. Dylan's lyrics need to be understood within the context of the Cold War between the United States and the Soviet Union. The American religious historian Martin Marty observes that "the shadow of the bomb colored religious and cultural language and was often credited with having helped produce 'the Age of Anxiety.'"[1] Other rock composers used dualistic imagery to convey their apocalyptic visions.

According to "The Battle of Evermore" by Led Zeppelin for instance, the forces of light are pitied against the forces of darkness and will ultimately prevail. This song embodies ancient eschatological themes about what will happen at the end of time that remind one of Manichaeism with its radical separation of matter and spirit and its sharp opposition between light and darkness, along with its concomitant devaluation of the created world.

The roots of eschatology can be traced to Hebrew prophets, such as Amos (8.2), who was the first prophetic figure to proclaim the end was close for the northern kingdom of Israel.[2] Later prophets referred to a day of final judgment. The eschatology of the Hebrew texts is characterized by its basically corporate nature, which implies that Israel is the people—an elected community—of God, which is destined to be restored at the end of time, a period both of judgment and salvation. Judgment focuses on historical action, while salvation represents a fulfillment or transfiguration of historical existence. Because the ancient Hebrews did not want to escape from the world, time, and history, there is an anticipation of a new world, a new time, and a new history in their texts (Is 65:17; 66:22). This new age represents a period in which people will live in unity with God under his rule, a Kingdom of God. In addition to this hope of a coming

Kingdom of God, there evolved the notion of a Messiah, one anointed by God, who would act as a divine agent to accomplish renewal on earth. Ancient Hebrews conceived of the Messiah in a variety of ways that included a person emerging from within the Jewish community, a figure of mysterious origin, or a divine being who would descend from heaven. There will also be a gathering together of the dispersed Jews (Jer 31:10), and the world will return to the peace of Paradise (Jer 31: 12-14; Hos 14:5-7; Zech 8:12-13). With the book of Daniel, Hebrew eschatology becomes individualized when the text (Dan 12.2) refers to the resurrection of the dead at the end time. As the ancient Jewish faith develops, this notion is extended to a general resurrection at the end of time at which the wicked receive final judgment and the righteous receive a reward for their faithfulness. The uniqueness of Hebrew eschatology is connected to salvation history because of the close connection between God's management of history by means of his providence and his election of the Jewish community as his chosen instrument by means of his covenant with them.

Influenced by Hebrew texts and Jewish ideas about the end of time, New Testament texts reflect an expectation of the imminent end of time and the arrival of the Messiah. Beginning with John the Baptist announcing the impending arrival of the Messiah in the Synoptic Gospels (Mk 1:4-8; Mt 3:1-6; Lk 3:7-9), many parables of Jesus also reflect an eschatological crisis (Lk 12:16-20; 13:6-9). According to Matthew (25:1-13), people will not be ready for judgment unless they repent now, much like the members of a wedding party must be prepared for the bridegroom when he arrives at a late hour. Matthew

(7:24-27) depicts Jesus exhorting his listeners to prepare themselves like the wise man who builds his house on a secure foundation for the impending eschatological crisis. Due to his crucifixion, resurrection, and ascension, the early Christian community understands Jesus as the long-anticipated Messiah of God, a person ushering in the new age with Jesus designated as the Alpha and Omega (Rev 1:8), the first and last. Christians are urged to wait for his return (*parousia*) when the forces of evil dominating the world will be annihilated, the dead resurrected, and the entire creation judged and renewed. Therefore, the *parousia* of Christ brings not only the end of this world, but it also ushers in a new earth and a new heaven (2Pet 3:13). This kind of scenario suggests that the *parousia* happens both in time and to time in the sense that it terminates the process of historical time while also transforming it.[3]

The imminent return of the Messiah to the Christian community becomes a problem when the return is delayed, which facilitates a reinterpretation of the original Hebrew messianic eschatology. The apostle Paul, for instance, changes his views of the end time from an earlier expectation of the impending arrival of Christ during Paul's own lifetime (1 Thess 4:14-17) to the possibility that he might not live to see the return of Christ (Phil 1:19-25). Paul's writings reflect a tension between what has already happened and what is to come in the future (1Cor 15:24-28; 1Thess 4:13-17). In contrast to the letters of Paul, the Gospel of Matthew (24:4-25) modifies the eschatological message in order to differentiate between the kingdom of the Son of Man (a present, morally mixed form of the church) and the kingdom of the Father that will purge all evil elements. The Gospel of Luke (21:9) and Acts (2:33; 3:20-21) alleviates the sense of urgency about the end of time by depicting Christ as already ruling at the right hand of God, whereas the Gospel of John shifts emphasis from a future fulfillment to the present availability of the age to come, emphasizing the eschatological time as a "now" moment.

Manifesting the influence of Jewish apocalyptic notions around the end of the first century CE, the book of Revelation (21) depicts the coming of a new heaven and earth at the end of time. Probably composed by a Jewish man whose real identity is unknown, this book was organized according to the numerical principle seven (e.g., seven messages, seven, seals, seven trumpets, seven bowls, and seven visions) because it was a number of cosmic significance and represented reality.[4]

Many of these Jewish and Christian eschatological notions can be discovered in rock lyrics. It is possible to find, for instance, further evidence in the lyrics of Dylan. During a period of despair, people are building boats, ships, or monuments in expectation of dire events in Dylan's song "Quinn the Eskimo." But with the arrival of Quinn, there will be joy. Thus the people and creatures of nature eagerly anticipate the return of this messianic figure. The messianic motif is also evident in Dylan's song "When He Returns" from *Slow Train Coming*, that relates the following scenario: When God returns at the end of time righteousness will be restored. Because God knows your deeds and needs, there is no reason for duplicity. God will establish His throne upon His return, unconcerned with human plans.

The restoration of righteousness or fairness at the end of time is a theme of "Junior" by John Mellencamp. Junior is a frightened, homeless little man, who does not really know what he is missing because he never had much of anything. He feels that he is living a personal hell, and imagines that the hell at the end of time must be really awful. If he had any part in the design of judgment day, homeless people would all be wearing crowns in heaven for all the suffering that they experienced on earth. These lyrics recall Jesus' words that the last shall be first in the kingdom of God (Mt 19.30).

The subject of Steve Winwood's "Wake Me Up on Judgment Day" is disappointed with life. Because ordinary life is like to a bad dream, he wants to sleep through life until the judgment day. He wants to be awakened by the sound of golden trumpets at the end of time, and he asks for eternal life. These lyrics suggest both ancient Jewish ideas and the book of Revelation (8.6-13) in which seven angels are given seven trumpets that announce a series of catastrophic events at the end of time. In the ancient Jewish conception, the Messiah will come in glory to the earth when the trumpet sounds that will raise the dead to be judged according to their deeds during life.

Before the end of time, certain ominous signs will appear as a warning to the living that the end of time is approaching. An excellent depiction of this phenomenon is "Bad Moon Rising" by Creedence Clearwater Revival. The bad moon is a metaphor associated with trouble such as natural disasters. The song tells people to play it safe and hide because a bad moon can mean death, and a voice of "rage and ruin" can be heard. The fundamental message is that the end time is coming and one should be prepared to die. Nonetheless, the metaphor of the moon also embodies the potential for spiritual rebirth and renewal. The moon is a rich symbol in early Christianity that represents connections to water (high and low tide), human reproduction, fertility, and the church that dies in Christ only to be reborn and to give new birth itself.[5]

Besides natural disasters functioning as a prelude to the end of time, sometimes a prophetic figure is presented as a harbinger of the end time. This is evident in "Dark Time" by October Project from *Falling Farther In*. The subject imagines a dark, gloomy time arriving. As this time dawns, a tried old prophet arrives and summons the people to a feast and invites them to wait for liberation. Even though there is no religion practiced in the "hollow and cold" temple, the prophet falls to his knees and asks a higher power to take his body and soul and to make him whole, but this and other prayers are no help. The gloom of the scene is emphasized; fear is pervasive and the churches are empty of both parishioners and priests. In Queen's "The Prophet's Song" from *A Night at the Opera*, a mad prophetic figure warns people about a coming storm, cold, and earthquake that will usher in widespread death. People need to flee for their lives because death is a prelude to the fires of hell. These types of lyrics are typical of apocalyptic prophecies that warn of a coming judgment, accounting, and end. Queen suggests the solution to the coming cosmic catastrophe is love.

Jethro Tull also plays a prophetic role in "Cold Wind to Valhalla" from *Minstrel in the Gallery*, inviting young women to join them on a trip to the heaven of Norse mythology. These types of songs recall ancient Hebrew prophets like Isaiah, Hosea, and Jeremiah who called their people to return to righteousness and to repent for their transgressions; otherwise, the people face a severe punishment. Like Hebrew prophets, apocalyptic prophecies attempt "to interpret their times, to console and guide, to suggest the meaning of the present and future. Typically, they relate fear to hope: tribulation and horror will usher in public and private bliss, free of pain or evil."[6]

Some rock lyrics assume a critical stance in response to prophets of doom. According to John Mellencamp's ironically "Another Sunny Day" from *Dance Naked*, there are many doomsday prophets spreading a message of despair. The singer admits the planet is dying and we have plenty of other bad news to feed our fears, but the talk of doom and gloom keeps us benighted. He does not want more prophets of doom and gloom planting seeds of despair. Those seeking signs of the end of time are involved in a vain quest; their time can be better spent in more fruitful pursuits. In fact, the worst things we do are those things we do to each other.

Huey Lewis and the News in "When the Time Has Come" strike a more hopeful note. Although walls will crumble into the sea, a drought will prevail over the land, and other disasters will occur, everything will eventually clear up and the sun will shine. Then everyone will be cheerful and wiser because judgment day has dawned. At redemption time, we will not have to worry about a thing because we will be transported to the kingdom of God.

In the New Testament, the kingdom of God is not a territory ruled by a kingly figure, but rather the final state of creation when all inhabitants and everything on the earth will be subject to the will of God. In the gospel of Matthew (5:3), the kingdom of God is a gift for the poor in spirit. The New Testament reflects two versions of the kingdom of God; it is a present reality embodied in the mission and message of Jesus (Mt 12:28; Lk 11:20), and it is also something that will arrive in the near future (Mk 1:14; Mt 4:17). In fact, the prayer that Jesus gives to his disciples embodies a petition for the imminent coming of the kingdom (Mt 6:10; Lk 11:2), a totally new situation in which the apocalyptic promise will be fulfilled and history will be consummated according to the plan of God. Taking the New Testament's notion of the Kingdom of God as a Christian symbol, a theologian like Tillich views it as a dynamic power that functions to respond to the ambiguities associated with human life.[7]

In sharp contrast to the New Testament message with respect to the end of time, some rock artists have responded with a hedonistic message or humor. We can find the former response in the song "1999" by Prince from his album *Sign ⊕ the Times*. The subject awakes from a dream and thinks that it is judgment day because he sees a purple sky in his dream and people running everywhere from the destruction. He thinks that if the end time is coming in 2000, he might as well party like it is 1999. If he must die, he reasons that he might as well party until the very end of time. Similarly, in "It's the End of the World as We Know It (And I Feel Fine)" by R.E.M., the world is impersonal and takes care of its own needs. So people should act selfishly and save themselves. The world is such a negative place that its end should not be lamented.

Earthly Paradise

Some rock composers view paradise as a place on earth. The Moody Blues' "In My World" from *Long Distance Voyager* finds a heaven on earth in the close relationship with a beloved person. Bryan Adams recorded "Heaven," whose title serves as a metaphor for a relationship between a man and a woman. In this case heaven is both this-worldly and interpersonal. Love between couples is depicted as paradise, although it is not quite a true paradise, in "Almost Paradise" written by Eric Carmen and Dean Pitchford and performed by Mike Reno and Ann Wilson for the motion picture *Footloose*. Examples of this idea of paradise on earth could be endlessly multiplied.

Just to cite a further example of this type, we can consider U2's "Peace on Earth (All That You Can't Leave Behind)." The subject says peace is what we need now because he is sick of all the pain and suffering. As the song unfolds, the subject asks Jesus for help. He turns angry because no one brings peace on earth, and he wonders what use it is to ask for assistance. These kinds of lyrics represent millennium hopes, which traditionally refer to a thousand years in which the world would be at peace and its inhabitants perfectly good and happy. This scenario implies that millenarianism can be distinguished from eschatology (doctrine of last things) because eschatology places its hopes for a better future in a hereafter, while millenarianism expects a future social and spiritual bliss on earth that will arrive in the foreseeable future. There is a further distinction between pre-millenarianism and post-millenarianism. Eugen Weber elucidates this distinction:

> Pre-millenarians expected Christ to return to earth and then set up his millennial rule; post-millenarians believed he would return after the church had established the millennium. In pre-millenarian scenarios, the kingdom of God comes abruptly, violently, with little human input. For post-millenarians, human effort affects the world's progression toward the messianic kingdom. Christ would return after his church had won many converts and reformed the world.[8]

The pre-millenarians are not as optimistic about reforming the world, and they foresee the world getting worse until the return of Christ, whereas the post-millenarians find hope in the possibility of political and social change.

In the musical *Hair*, the age of peace is called the "Age of Aquarius," which was also a big hit song for the 5th Dimension. The signs of this age of peace are: the moon is in the seventh house, Jupiter is in line with the planet Mars, peace guides the planets, and love directs the stars. Not only will love characterize this age, but so will harmony and understanding, sympathy and trust, and liberation. Following closely upon the Age of Pisces, the Age of Aquarius (a bearer of water) is suppose to dominate human affairs during the two thousand and hundred years of its existence of a time of peace, love, harmony, satisfaction, and happiness. During this time of peace, spiritual perfection will be the most important human goal along with spiritual harmony with others and the world.[9] This type of song also reflects the ethos of the flower children of the Sixties and anti-war protestors, and the influence of New Age religions.

Along similar lines of nostalgia for an Age of Aquarius, there is the dream of Caledonia, an ancient homeland. Caledonia appears in the albums of Van Morrison during the mid-1970s. Morrison sings about a land where his ancestors begin life anew. Within this gilded kingdom, all people live in harmony with each other as an extended family. From the perspective of the historian of religions Mircea Eliade, Van Morrison's nostalgia for Caledonia represents an attempt by modern individuals to recapture and relive the paradisiacal state of original plenitude, freedom, beatitude, and harmony in contrast to the meaninglessness of profane existence. This return to the beginning to find one's roots demonstrates a desire to begin anew and to regain a lost paradise.[10] It is also possible to find this nostalgia for paradise among other artists.

The theme of an earthly paradise appears on at least three of the albums of Cat Stevens. In "Land O' Free Love and Goodbye" from *Numbers*, Stevens sings of natural beauty and abundant water, but the most important characteristic of this earthly paradise is that it is a land of free love governed by a God of love. On *Buddha and the Chocolate Box*, there is a song with the innocent-sounding title "Music," in which music functions as the central metaphor for paradise. The subject admits to his own marginality, although he is a good person and lover of life, trying to do God's work. Since the world will soon end in war, it is only music that will save us because if everyone joins the band, there will be unity and harmony instead of war. The presence of music in heaven can be traced historically to a Greek harmonic view that was adapted by Christians through the writings of Boethius (c. 480-c.524), a Roman Christian philosopher and states-man killed by the Arian emperor Theodoric and considered a martyr by Christians.[11] Another composition by Cat Stevens "Peace Train" from *Tea for the Tillerman*, expresses nostalgia for a paradise on earth whose major characteristic is peace and unity. This will be a paradise of the living and not the dead, an imminent achievement.

Besides Stevens, other rock composers have been fascinated by the notion of an earthly paradise. Sometimes, the paradise is conceived in general or vague terms. Don Henley, for instance, locates paradise in the days of his youth in "The End of the Innocence." He knows a natural place where innocence can be recaptured. However, true innocence is gone because of the threat of war, although he tries to defend himself and his girl friend from the loss of an earthly paradise. Seals and Crofts imagine an earthly paradise in their song "Ruby Jean and Billie Lee," a paradise that will be born again into an overpowering light that will unite black and white and usher one in a kingdom of non-violence, love and justice. It is destiny that brings the couple together on earth to enable them to build the promised-land. From another perspective, Meat Loaf presents a vision of angels connected to his heart in "Heaven Can Wait" from *Bat Out of Hell*. In this vision, all the gods come to earth to sing for him, and the melody enables him to fly without pain or fear. He feels released, although he does not know to where. But it does not matter because he can feel paradise. Due to his foretaste of paradise on earth, he does not want to leave, implying that heaven can wait. Canned Heat depicts a more unspecified paradise in the song "Going Up the Country" that is an open invitation for anyone who wants to go to a place that is new, and where the water tastes like wine, and one can just jump into the water and remain drunk all the time. As an undergraduate at a large university, I knew many students who thought this would indeed be an earthly paradise.

Tracy Chapman sings about "Heavens Here on Earth" on *New Beginning*. We can look for answers to life's questions in the stars, God, or life on other planets. But heaven can be discovered here on earth. Why? We carry within our spirit the way to find the path out of the labyrinth because "We create the pain and the suffering and the beauty in this world." We can have heaven on earth if we have faith in humankind; and respect for the earth; believe in peace, love and understanding; have faith in the truth; and fill ourselves with love, compassion, forgiveness and a spirit of sacrifice. She confesses to having encountered spirits and angels within a world that must be our temple or church. Chapman's lyrics reflect an anthropocentric faith because truth is divine, and there is no sense of transcendence in the lyrics.

Other composers depict heaven on earth as a more specific place. An excellent example of this trend by rock composers is Joni Mitchell's "Woodstock" recorded by Crosby, Stills, Nash and Young on their album *Deja Vu*. In the lyrics, Woodstock, a rock celebration and concert on a farm in up-state New York, is compared to a paradisiacal garden. The subject meets what she calls a "child of God," and asks him where he is going. He admits that he does not really know who he is, but he is convinced that life is a learning process. Once they get to their destination, see the throng of people, hear the music, and see the celebration, she imagines seeing jet fighters in the sky turning into butterflies. Mitchell seems to suggest that a garden like this, where people can come together to celebrate, is not only desirable, but it should be permanent. Likewise, Bruce Springsteen's "Thunder Road" is equated with an earthly heaven, a promised land where there will be freedom. He confesses to the girl who he wants to run away with him that he is no savior. The redemption he can offer is beneath the hood of his automobile.

An earthly paradise is deeply rooted within the human imagination. In Greco-Roman antiquity, we find, for instance, the theme of a garden conjoined with that of a golden age and happy isles of bliss, a place of adventure outside of prevailing social and legal orders. The earthly paradise is described as a landscape resembling a garden, usually located in the East near the equator, a wild and divinely blessed state of nature, a pastoral setting evoking notions of love.[12]

The song "Fire Lake" by Bob Seger and the Silver Bullet Band begins with a question: Who wants to take a risk that paradise exists? Even Uncle Joe runs off to Fire Lake, and he's someone afraid to do anything. Fire Lake is full of bronzed beauties, evoking images of a sexual and sensual paradise similar to the Muslim paradise with its *hurs*, virgin wives reserved for faithful males in paradise. According to the Qur'ān, these beautiful maidens have beautiful dark (44:54) or big eyes (56:22), and have only clean thoughts (52:20). These virgins

(55: 74; 56; 36) are cloistered in pavilions. In contrast to the Muslim paradise, there is no marriage in the resurrected life of Christian paradise at least during the formative period of Christianity, a situation that also implies no sexual relationships.[13]

With respect to specific locations, it is not unusual to discover any paradise depicted in rock lyrics as an actual warm location—real or imagined. A good example of a real place appears in "California Dream-in'" by The Mamas and the Papas. The song begins with a description of a typical winter's day with a gray sky and brown leaves on the trees. In the song winter symbolizes death, while sunny California represents life. A pause at a local church to pray proves fruitless, although sunny California remains alive in dreams.

Jimmy Buffett offers the most long-lasting image of an earthly paradise in "Margaritaville". This imaginary place is a tropical paradise where one can pass time by playing guitar, eating sponge cake, and drinking margaritas, which are always in plentiful supply in the blender. The relaxed and laid-back atmosphere of the place is emphasized by the tattoo the subject cannot recall getting or under what circumstances.

It is easy to imagine lying on the beach in a place like Margaritaville and watching sailboats glide over the water. There is, however, another form of paradise for Christopher Cross in his song "Sailing." This paradise is not far away because it manifests itself in sailing. A person can find tranquility, joy, innocence, freedom, reverie, fantasy, sanity, and serenity while sailing. When your sailing, your dreams and the wind can transport you to paradise, and the canvas of the sails provides the miracles. This might not be an overtly religious song, but the words used to describe sailing evoke a spiritual experience.

Sting creates a poetically romantic portrait in "Fields of Gold" from *Ten Summoner's Tales*. He reminisces about walking in fields of golden barley with his beloved, her falling into his arms, and her hair falling among the golden grain. Although this happened long ago, the subject is confident his loved one remembers him. The important point is that the two lovers shared a moment together of earthly paradise. With the symbolic and metaphorical use of the sun and fields of golden barley and the importance of remembrance in the lyrics, Sting suggests it is possible to approach an immortal love on earth.

On their album *Naked*, Talking Heads include two songs about paradise. The first song is "Totally Nude," and its subject demonstrates his freedom through his nudity and living in the trees with insects, and calls himself "nature boy." Rather than being confined to the indoors, he wants to discover life, and he asks nature to take him away. He comes to realize that the trappings of civilization like clothes and money are unnecessary. In the other song from that album, "(Nothing But) Flowers," two people in love stand in a Garden of Eden like Adam and Eve. The accoutrements of a prior civilization have disappeared: cars have been replaced by flowers, a factory has been replaced by mountains and rivers, a shopping mall has been replaced by flowers, a highway has become a field with trees, a town has become flowers, and parking lots have been replaced by a peaceful oasis. By returning to the original paradise, the subject finds that he is unhappy and uncomfortable in a pristine state of nature. Longing for former convenience stores and fast food establishments, the subject feels stranded and confesses that he cannot adjust to this type of lifestyle, without cherry pie, candy bars, chocolate chip cookies, and microwave ovens.

If some rock composers want to depict an earthly paradise, there are others that warn us against such folly. This earth is no heaven because the hungry and destitute stumble and stagger on its streets, according to "City of Angels" by 10,000 Maniacs from *In My Tribe*. These people are lacking angel wings and halos. There is nothing sacred in Los Angeles, a fallen city at best. This same group makes a similar point in "Eden" from *Our Time in Eden*. In this song, it is time that destroys any earthly paradise. For those who might be dreaming of California, Natalie Merchant answers with "San Andreas Fault" from her album *Tigerlily*. The song is specifically directed at those who believe the image of Hollywood as a place where one can become a star in films or magazines; this is an illusion. California is not a land of milk and honey since an earthquake can make the walls of paradise come tumbling down in a vast wave of destruction. Hence, Merchant wants to make lucid the tenuous nature of all earthly paradises.

Interior Paradise

In contrast to rock composers who conceive of an earthly paradise in either vague or more specific terms, there are other artists that view paradise as an interior state. In "Heaven" from *All of This and Nothing*, the Psychedelic Furs locate paradise, for instance, in the heart. In a similar vain, James Taylor sings that we are living in paradise and are unaware of it in "Up Er Mei" from *Hourglass*. Since we have been taught about a transcendent place beyond the suffering of this world, we are unaware that we are already living in paradise. Besides describing it poetically as being "Blind in the Buddhaland," Taylor reminisces about climbing up Er Mei and visiting temples, although these lyrics suggest that paradise is within oneself. This interior kind of paradise reflects either an eastern religious influence on the rock composers or a western mystical influence.

Among some rock composers, the interior paradise is a direct creation of one's fertile imagination or dream state. Expressing nostalgia for a simpler lifestyle, Elton John imagines sailing away from the complexity of modern city life to a more innocent place in "Simple Life" from *The One*. The Beatles' song "Strawberry Fields Forever" depicts a vision in one's imagination of a place of beauty, peace, and serenity. In another example, a homeless man dreams of living in a large home in heaven and walking with God in "Mansions in Heaven" by John Mellencamp. The homeless man senses the end of his life coming, and imagines angels descending to take him to heaven. In "Immortality" by Pearl Jam from *Vitalogy*, a truant thinks that there is a trapdoor in the sun that equates with immortality and thinking of immortality absorbs him. Eliade calls attention to the connection between the sun and immortality in his cross-cultural religious scholarship.[14]

Light symbolism plays an important role in conceptions of heaven where it is connected to the empyrean, a place of luminosity and splendor where God dwells with the blessed and angels.[15] Dionysius the pseudo-Areopagite (c. 500) says in heaven the light of God will cover the blessed, or they will receive a conceptual gift of light from God.[16] In Dante's *Divine Comedy*, light symbolism also plays an important role in conjunction with Beatrice's eyes shining with the light of love in the *Paradiso*.

Besides the role of the imagination in identifying heaven, some rock composers refer to the mind of visions. The title of "Heaven Is in Your Mind" summarizes Steven Winwood's message in his recording. The album *Innervisions* by Stevie Wonder includes "Visions," which relates a series of visions: a place of no hatred where love reigns supreme; everyone being free; and a beautiful place. Can we find these visions in life? Wonder claims that he is a realist because he knows everything comes to an end. A radically different vision is given by Counting Crows in "Rain King" from *August and Everything After*, where attaining heaven is like flying into a sea of bird pens and feathers along with "instruments of faith and sex and God." This occurs within the belly of a black-winged bird. According to the lyrics, thinking of heaven evokes thoughts of death.

An especially fascinating dream vision is offered by "Island of Souls" and "The Soul Cages" by Sting from his album of the same name. Since the lyrics to these songs are intimately related in a narrative fashion, they will be treated together at this point. Beginning with "Island of Souls," a son dreams that he and his hard-working father escape from their desolate and dreary lives, aboard a ship that carries them to an island of souls. In this strictly spiritual paradise, there are no corporeal bodies with which to toil because the souls are completely free from their bodies. In "Soul Cages," these devices are any physical or mental entity that binds a person. According to the narrative, a boy is captured in a fisherman's net, but he makes a wager with the fisherman that he can beat the fisherman in a wine drinking competition. If the boy wins, he will be set free. But if the fisherman wins, the boy will remain captive forever in a cage. The fisherman utters a curse as he lies in a drunken stupor and watches the soul of the boy leap free. Sting ends "Island of Souls" by saying the boy and his father travel to an island of souls. Sting's lyrics strongly suggest the sort of spiritual paradise devoid of materialism and sensuality that is often evident in visions of paradise.

Dream visions are common in many religious traditions where they function as sources of prophecy and a recognized form of cognition. Within the Hindu, Buddhist, and Christian cultural contexts, dreams are a form of interior perception. It is possible for dreams to bestow charismatic or religious authority upon the dreamer, but this possibility usually involves proving one's dream in real life by some kind of authentic action. This scenario suggests that dreams and their interpretations can be subjected to some kind of empirical verification. It is also often possible to gain insight in a dream state because it acts like a memory regained.[17] Moreover, dreams offer a certain kind of continuity in the sense that they enable humans to look simultaneously in two directions: backward toward a beginning and also forward toward an end.[18]

The Search for a Transcendent Paradise

Wandering and walking in a variety of places and situations, the subject's goal is to get to heaven before its doors are closed in "Tryin' To Get to Heaven" by Bob Dylan from *Out of Mind.* All situations and places are devoid of meaning, but heaven apparently has some meaning. In a reflective and quizzical song entitled "Eternity Road" by The Moody Blues from *To Our Children's Childrens' Children*, the group sings about traveling on the road of eternity carrying a heavy load, a journey that will culminate with the discovery of peace of mind. In sharp contrast is the road to "Shambala" by 3 Dog Night, populated with kind and helpful people. Upon entering Shambala, one's light will shine, and the revivifying waters of this paradisiacal place will wash away one's troubles, pain, sorrow, and shame.

References to a transcendent paradise are often used to compare the joys and beauty of paradise with life on earth. Bob Dylan and Prince use this comparison to good effect in their songs "Gates of Eden" from *Bringing It All Back Home* and "Let's Go Crazy" from *Purple Rain.* According to Dylan's lyrics, within Eden there is no twisted truth concerning war and peace and no sound is emitted from Eden, although there is laughter inside the gates. Since there are no kings in Eden, there is no hierarchy of authority and no one has dominion over another person. Eden is a sinless place where there is no distinction between real and unreal. There is total freedom within

Eden to do whatever you want but die, and no trials take place here. Furthermore, there is no truth exterior to Eden because it embodies all truth. By describing Eden in such terms, Dylan is offering a critical perspective on life on earth. Prince also compares the present life to an after world and stresses the difference between them. We have to get through life, and we are basically on our own. If you become depressed you can go crazy and "punch a higher floor" of the elevator of life. If you don't enjoy this life, you should count your blessings and you will find that you at least have friends. If others reject you, there is no need to get depressed because you can just go crazy by looking "for the purple banana." It is true that we are all going to die, and wonder about the purpose of life. Prince urges others to live now before they die. Even though we must be strong in the face of death, there is still an after world of unending happiness where the sun is always shining.

In the lyrics of some artists, heaven assumes attributes similar to structures on earth. As a cloud comes over a lawman and he senses his imminent death in "Knockin' On Heaven's Door" by Bob Dylan, he tells his mother to take his officer's badge off and bury his guns because he will not need them anymore. His dying puts him at the gates of heaven. If the plural term "gates" is the operative designation in Dylan's song, "stairway" is the essential attribute in the lyrics to "Stairway to Heaven" by Led Zeppelin. In this song, a woman is trying to buy her way into heaven, a mistaken notion because a materialistic path does not lead anywhere. For those who are patient, wait, and persevere, a new era is dawning, and we will be led to reason and happiness. Moreover, if you listen, you will hear the message about a spiritual unity. Thus, it is not possible to build a materialistic "stairway" to a transcendent heaven. If heaven resembles to some degree earthly features, it is possible to trace such a notion to Irenaeus (c. 140-200), bishop of Lyons, who thinks that the next life is a continuation and completion of this life. Moreover, if someone suffered in this life, such a person would be compensated in the next life because this is exactly what God promised.[19]

Different ideas about the Christian vision of heaven arose over the course of history. The New Testament did not have a single view of heaven and little is said about the celestial paradise, in part because the earliest Christian writers expected the imminent return of Christ and the end of the world. With the thought of the apostle Paul, there is an emphasis on the present nature of heaven because Christ's salvific action is eternal.[20] During the fourth century, heaven is depicted as an ecclesiastical community. The early Augustine conceived of heaven in an ascetic manner as a "world of immaterial, fleshless souls finding rest and pleasure in God."[21] Around 408, Augustine altered his view from souls linked to God in ecstatic unions to the expectation of reuniting with friends and family in a new social milieu.[22] Thus, the notion of a social reunion in heaven that can be discovered in rock lyrics and the attitudes of ordinary people can be dated back to Augustine.

The theme of reunion is also evident in the numbers recorded by Mariah Carey and the Righteous Brothers. In their hit entitled "Rock and Roll Heaven," the Righteous Brothers conceive of heaven as a big reunion of deceased rock stars, who will presumably have an eternity to play their music together. According to "One Sweet Day" by Mariah Carey from *Daydream*, the lyrics tell the story of the death of a loved one. The deceased is now shining down from heaven on the singer, who envisions a reunion in heaven someday. These notions of reunion stand in sharp contrast to the medieval view of St. Thomas Aquinas with his more static view of heaven in which there is no active life. Aquinas thinks that there will only be a contemplative life of bliss as the soul enjoys the beatific vision of God.[23]

A different type of spin is given to heaven by the Talking Heads in "Heaven" from *Fear of Music*. This group equates heaven to a bar in which a band plays one's favorite tunes all night long. The same party occurs each night with the same people leaving at the same time. Basically, heaven is depicted as a boring place at which nothing happens. This view of heaven stands in direct contrast to the Victorian conception of heaven as a place of activity, service and work instead of a place of idleness.

A less material type of vision of heaven is offered by Norman Greenbaum's "Spirit in the Sky." The singer hopes to go there when he dies because it is "the best." The lyrics suggest a person having a beatific vision reminiscent of the idea of such a vision in the work of Thomas Aquinas of the thirteenth century. The enjoyment of such a vision depends on one's will that follows from an act of the intellect. Greenbaum's lyrics, like the theology of Aquinas, imagine a heaven without boundaries. Within this type of boundless heaven, those who are saved will enjoy themselves in the company of angels, the eternal celestial glory that is associated with the direct vision of God.

Concluding Remarks

If we reflect upon and reconsider this survey of eschatological themes in rock 'n' roll lyrics, the single most glaring omission from rock lyrics is the mention of hell, or some other place of punishment. It is possible to find exceptions like Phil Ochs' number "Crucifixion" from *Pleasures of the Harbor*. It is as if rock composers have banished hell from their consciousness. This is a curious development because, for the ardent critics of rock music who represent various kinds of conservative Christianity, hell is a real possibility, depending on the judgment of God.

The Eagles "Hotel California" does imply the notion of hell, but it is a curious hell because it is a place one can freely enter and never leave, akin to a kind of living hell. It is this lack of freedom and the absurdity of one's situation that constitutes a patron's hell. In his album *River of Dreams*, Billy Joel echoes the Eagles when he identifies a big hotel as hell in "Blonde Over Blue." This hotel is an absurd place with windows that cannot open, a bar that has just closed, no phone to call home, and a working television set with an inoperative channel changer. Even in these examples, there is no mention of the devil or harsh punishment for one's sins committed during life. Any acknowledgment of predestination or eternal damnation also seems to be missing from the religious sensibilities of rock composers. This implies that the eschatological themes reviewed in this chapter are without eternal risk or danger to the individual soul.

Another important aspect of traditional Judeo-Christian eschatology neglected by rock composers is the last judgment. We find nothing of Ezekiel's (37) vision of the dry bones that God will clothe with flesh and raise, nor do we witness anything akin to Daniel's vision of a trial for the righteous and the wicked (12:3). We also cannot find reference to the so-called "Little Apocalypse" in the three Synoptic Gospels (Mt 24:1-25; 46; Mk 13:10-37; Lk 21:5-38) that reflects the influence of the book of Daniel. In the first event, there will be an arrival of a series of false prophets and the mysterious "Abomination of Desolation" previously mentioned by Daniel. This is traditionally associated with the preaching and persecution of the Antichrist figure. The second coming (*parousia*) introduces the Son of Man on the clouds of heaven when angels will gather the elect. The last judgment is rendered with the Son of Man sitting on a throne of glory. When all the nations are gathered before him, he will separate the saved from the damned based on their actions. Finally, the end of this present world comes. According to the letters of the Paul, those persons alive when Christ returns will not suffer physical death, and those previously deceased will be bodily resurrected (1Thess 4:13-18). These dramatic types of scenarios makes one wonder why rock composers did not make fuller use of such vivid images.

Based on what we have witnessed in this chapter and chapter 5, rock composers appear to have a vision of a benign deity, who is likely to forgive one's mistakes and transgressions during life. The image of God as a stern judge seems to be far removed from the minds of rock composers. The divine harsh judge is even absent from a rock musical like *Jesus Christ Superstar*, with its examination of the darker side of the personality of Jesus. If it is missing in this musical, it is most certainly absent from *Godspell* with its joyous message of love and celebration. There is something religiously interesting occurring here. I think that this trend manifests a redefining of the nature of God, and a conviction that a loving God could not condemn people, who are by nature weak and vulnerable to all kinds of temptations, to hell and eternal punishment. Rock lyrics seem to suggest that the overpowering, terrible, frightening, legalistic, demanding, and harsh judge of Calvinistic religiosity has been eclipsed by a more benign figure of love, forgiveness, and understanding. It is also very possible that rock composers agree —unknown to themselves—with Reinhold Niebuhr that the Last Judgment stresses the moral ambiguity associated with the whole of history, and it negates all utopian visions.[24] In probably an unconscious way, rock composers are making a contribution to constructing the religious sensibilities of their listeners, which suggests that rock lyrics have the ability to shape theological and religious ideas.

We have also seen that rock lyrics continue themes from the prevailing Judeo-Christian religious tradition while also introducing influences from eastern religious cultures. The eschatological themes associated with the end of the world, judgment, and either an earthly or transcendent paradise represents examples of the traditional Judeo-Christian tradition. At the same time, the influence and influx of representatives of eastern religious traditions is also evident in rock lyrics that stress the need for turning within oneself and finding an internal heaven. This trend of eastern religious influence reflects the immigration of peoples from Asian cultures in significant numbers. And it also reflects cross-cultural fertilization of religious ideas, practices, and attitudes that began in the 1950s. As this trend of cross-fertilization continues in western nations, these eastern notions will continue to appear in rock lyrics in the future with unforeseeable results.

Endnotes

---

[1] Martin E. Marty, *Modern American Religion Volume 3: Under God Indivisible, 1941-1960* (Chicago: University of Chicago Press, 1996), p. 117.

[2] John J. Collins, "From Prophecy to Apocalypticism: The Expectation of the End," in *The Continuum History of Apocalypticism*, edited by Bernard J. McGinn, John J. Collins, and Steven J. Stein (New York, London: Continuum, 2003), p. 64.

[3] Jürgen Moltmann, *The Way of Jesus Christ: Christology in Messianic Dimensions* (London: SCM, 1990), p. 317f; *The Coming of God* (London: SCM, 1996), pp. 13-22.

[4] Adela Yarbro Collins, "The Book of Revelation," in *The Continuum History of Apocalypticism,* edited by Bernard J. McGinn, John J. Collins, and Stephen J. Stein (New York, London: Continuum, 2003), pp. 196, 198.

[5] Ladner, pp. 135, 213.

[6] Eugen Weber, *Apocalypses: Prophesies, Cults, and Millennial Beliefs through the Ages* (Cambridge: Harvard University Press, 1999), p. 31.

[7] Paul Tillich, *Systematic Theology Volume III* (Chicago: University of Chicago Press, 1963; 1964) p. 356-57.

[8] Ibid., p. 172.

[9] James F. Harris, *Philosophy at 331/3 rpm: Themes of Classic Rock Music* (LaSalle, IL: Open Court, 1993), p. p. 193.

[10] Eliade, *Patterns in Comparative Religion*, pp. 434, 383.

[11] Russell, *A History of Heaven*, p. 24.

[12] Jean Delumeau, *History of Paradise: The Garden of Eden in Myth and Tradition,* trans. Matthew O'Connell (New York: Continuum, 1995), pp. 9-10, 98, 150.

[13] Colleen McDannell and Bernhard Lang, *Heaven: A History* (New Haven: Yale University Press, 1988), p. 26.

[14] Eliade, *Patterns in Comparative Religion*, pp. 136-137.

[15] McDannell and Lang, p. 82.

[16] Dionysius, *The Divine Names*, trans. Colm Luibheid, in *Pseudo-Dionysius* (Mahwah, N. J: Paulist Press, 1987), pp. 52-53.

[17] David Shulman, "Dreaming the Self in South India," in *Dream Cultures: Explorations in the Comparative History of Dreaming*, eds. David Shulman and Guy G. Stroumsa (Oxford: Oxford University Press, 1999), p. 559

[18] Ibid., p. 60.

[19] McDannell and Lang, p. 53.

[20] Russell, *A History of Heaven*, pp. 41-42.

[21] McDannell and Lang, p. 59.

[22] Ibid., p. 60.

[23] McDannell and Lang, p. 89.

[24] Niebuhr, *Faith and History*, p. 237.

Chapter 9
The Prophetic Thread

The Judeo-Christian-Islamic tradition attests to the importance of the prophetic element in religion. Islam claims that Muhammad is the seal of the prophets, which implies that the historical revelation that he received from Allah and delivered to humans represents the final and most perfect message of God. Long before Muhammad appeared on the historical stage, prophets played a pivotal role within Judaism. The Hebrew word for prophet is *nabi'*, a term that refers to a person who communicates the divine will by being called to be God's spokesperson. The Greek term (*prophētēs*) that gives rise to the English term "prophet" literally means a person who speaks for another. The prophet receives a promise from God that words will be put into the prophet's mouth (Jer 1:9). Besides being the vehicle for divine communication, Hebrew prophets conceive of themselves as sent by God to be God's messenger to the people. This means their authority rests with God and not with themselves. This is evident in the prophetic message, which often begins with the formula, "Thus says Yahweh" and concludes with a similar type of utterance (Jer 2:1-3; Is 45:11-13; Amos 1:3-5). The usual purpose behind God's speaking is to accentuate the urgency of the present. Therefore, the prophet is primarily concerned about some present situation, and the prophet feels an urgent need to communicate God's will to the people in order to get them to respond immediately.

A fundamental characteristic of the prophet is the personal call he receives from God, which forms the basis of the prophet's authority, a secondary or derived authority. Beyond the call, the prophet possesses personal *charisma* (a gift of leadership). Prophets receive no monetary rewards for their work because they propagate ideas for their own sake and not for some kind of reward. For some of his contemporaries, Jesus was a charismatic and prophetic figure. In the Gospel of Matthew (21.11) the crowds say, "This is the prophet Jesus from Nazareth of Galilee." In the same gospel (Matt 5:17), Jesus proclaims, "Do not think that I have come to abolish the law or the prophets; I have come not to abolish but to fulfill." The identification of Jesus as a prophetic figure has important consequences for the Christian movement: "The identification of Jesus as prophet was a means both of affirming his continuity with the prophets of Israel and of asserting his superiority to them as the prophet whose coming they had predicted and to whose authority they had been prepared to yield."[1] This prophetic tradition of the major monotheistic faiths can also be discovered in the compositions of rock artists, assuming that one makes an effort to look at the lyrics.

Rock performers are not prophets in the sense of being messengers of God. There are, however, some superficial and some more pronounced common points that connect rock performers with prophetic figures, even though the differences are dramatic enough to caution us about confusing the two types. Nonetheless, although rock composers are speaking for themselves, they do call our attention to problems in the present moment, they protest these conditions much like a prophetic figure would, many of them are charismatic on stage, and they often communicate an important message to their audience. It is obvious that many rock artists feel a religious, moral, and ethical duty to call attention to social problems. For these kinds of reasons, some rock stars play a prophetic role in a way reminiscent of what David Chidester calls "authentic fakes," but who fulfill a religious role by performing "authentic religious work in and through the play of American popular culture."[2]

The lyrics of rock 'n' roll composers have protested socio-economic injustices, air pollution, overcrowding, guns, war, governmental abuses, business practices, and even child abuse. These are all issues that reflect the historical times of the composers and their response to the problems around them. In the 1960s, Bob Dylan led the way with other composers following his lead.

Dylan stresses that the evils of slavery, war, hunger, and death are not so far removed from us at the present moment in "Long Ago, Far Away." A long time ago, there was a man preaching about peace and brotherhood, and he was nailed to a cross. Dylan's point is that such terrible and unjust events also occur today. In one of his most famous compositions, "Blowin' in the Wind" from his album *The Freewheelin' Bob Dylan* also recorded by Peter, Paul and Mary, Dylan raises an effective series of questions about being a human being, war, responses to suffering and death, freedom, and bondage. The response to all of these questions is: "The answer, my friend, is blowin' in the wind." In other words, there is no definitive answer.

However, it is urgent that people think about the questions and what their own responses should be.

Dylan also plays the prophet with his song "The Times They Are A-Changin.'" Here he warns about coming change like an apocalyptic prophet. The signs of change are ominous because the water is rising, and one must swim or drown. The song is also an invitation for all kinds of people to respond. Dylan purposely and effectively uses language that echoes that found in the New Testament: "For the loser now/Will be later to win." In other words, the old is giving way to the new, and the last or those at the bottom of the social ladder will ascend to the top. Another message is for politicians and parents to get out of the way and cease obstructing the inevitable future changes. Not only has Dylan continued to protest various issues in his songs throughout his career and carry on the legacy of folk singers like Woody Gutherie and Pete Seeger, he has been an inspiration to rock composers who followed him, including Jackson Browne, John Mellencamp, Bruce Springsteen, Billy Joel, and many others.

These composers and others protested the Vietnam war, called for peace, verbally attacked the military-industrial complex, called attention to poverty and hunger, wrote lyrics about the issue of abortion, criticized the death penalty, and protested political injustice, violence, and racism. Rock composers have examined religion critically, and they have called attention to manipulative preachers and certain nefarious religious practices. Others have criticized both organized religion and cults. By composing lyrics about these types of issues, rock composers function to reflect the important and controversial events of their era in America. The civil rights movement, the fight against discrimination and racism, the Vietnam War, social injustice, social violence, and environmental pollution are all issues that shaped the compositions of socially aware composers.

Issues of War and Peace

During the 1960s, issues of war and peace were given the most attention, with the Vietnam conflict and anti-war movement shaping and inspiring the lyrics of many rock composers. In fact, the rock musical *Hair* can be grasped, for instance, as one long anti-war protest with such numbers as "Three-Five-Zero-Zero." The pervasive influence of the Vietnam War is also very evident in the album *Lives in the Balance* by Jackson Browne; the album contains four anti-war songs. Browne's composition "Lawless Avenues" is about a Hispanic son who is killed in Vietnam, and his mother's struggle to understand his death. The title song "Lives in the Balance" is critical of government lies as the country drifts into greater involvement in the conflict in Vietnam. According to the lyrics, government officials sell the war to the public like a company might sell any product that it manufactures. "For America" is about those families that send their sons to Vietnam and whether or not they will think that their way of life is safer when the next war comes. In another album entitled *Lawyers in Love*, Browne protests war in "Say It Isn't True" by saying that war is not a good way to use the human mind, which can be better used in more productive ways. Browne protests violence in general in "It is One" from *Looking East* and in "Rock Me on the Water" from *Saturate*

Before Using, where he sings about signs of strife everywhere and roads congested with the homeless. The answer to these problems is essentially religious because one is instructed to use Jesus as a guide and the gospel as a plow to grow something positive. In *World in Motion*, Browne not only protests war with "Anything Can Happen," but also protests defense spending to build weapons of mass destruction with his song "How Long."

An earlier version of an attack on the military-industrial complex is offered by Dylan in "Masters of War" from *The Free-wheelin' Bob Dylan*. Dylan protests the politicians, generals, and owners of the military-industrial complex who make war and the various instruments of destruction. But these makers of war safely hide, while others are exposed to danger. They are akin to Judas, and they lie and deceive like him. Dylan says that he sees through the deception and lies of these masters of war that make parents fearful of bringing children into the world. Although the promoters of war might think the protester is young and uneducated, he knows that even Jesus could never forgive them for their heinous sins. The profits made from creating war can never purchase forgiveness or retrieve the lost souls of the masters of war. The song concludes with a wish for their death.

Besides Dylan and Browne, other artists like Neil Young, Billy Joel, Marvin Gaye, and Sting have added their voices to the anti-war message. In "War of Man" from *Harvest Moon*, Neil Young juxtaposes small animals in a warm and safe nest with their mothers with the horrible sounds and sights of battle. He compares dreams of a little girl with war. His overall message is that war disrupts the tranquility of nature and human society, so there are no winners. In "Leningrad" from *Storm Front*, Billy Joel sings about a boy growing up in the former Soviet Union and another in the United States. The political and military tensions seem insignificant when the two meet as men, and the Russian makes the daughter of the American laugh at his antics as a circus clown. Marvin Gaye argues that war is not a viable answer to settling differences in "What's Going On" because only love can conquer hate.

In addition to the single voice raised against war, rock groups have also made important contributions to war protest. In "Night Time for the Generals" from *American Dream*, Crosby, Stills, Nash and Young protest military figures and those in the intelligence profession for being mad with power. They like to play the role of God by giving but mostly taking away, and they destroy liberty. The group Buffalo Springfield recalls the era of the Vietnam War protests with people carrying signs in the streets and singing songs in "For What It's Worth." In one of the hardest hitting anti-war songs, Creedence Clearwater Revival makes it clear in "Fortunate Son" that rich and influential people do not send their sons to war because they would rather send the sons of ordinary citizens without political, economic, or social connections. The rich are lying frauds who live lavishly and then plead poverty when the taxman arrives. The singer protests that he is not among the fortunate sons of those who are wealthy. Using stronger language in their anti-war recording "War Pigs," Black Sabbath condemns the generals that make war and equate them with witches, sorcerers of death, and evil-minded operators of the war machine that brings death and destruction. While the generals wage war, the politicians who start the war hide and send the poor to fight. The lyrics imagine a day of judgment for the generals, but it is not God they encounter at the end of time. As the generals come crawling on their knees to beg for mercy, they encounter Satan with his wings spread wide open. Finally, 10,000 Maniacs' "Anthem for Doomed Youth" in *Hope Chest* sings that it is wrong to conscript the youth of the country against their will because there are others who really enjoy killing more than unfortunate conscripts, the "doomed youth" of the title.

The personal price of warfare is presented by Bruce Springsteen in a few of his songs, such as "Lost in the Flood" on *Greetings from Asbury Park*, where he draws a connection between the external Vietnam War and the interior mental and emotional conflict that continues after a solider returns home without expressions of gratitude from a public tried of the conflict. Springsteen finds a Vietnam hero in Ron Kovic, a paraplegic veteran and leader of the antiwar movement, to serve as the central focus of "Born on the Fourth of July," a song inspired by Kovic's autobiography that became the theme song of the motion picture adaptation of the book. In a third example, Springsteen sings in "Devils and Dust" about an American solider captive in a distant war (Iraq), who envisions a valley of dry bones in a dream. This vision is similar to that of the Hebrew prophet Ezikiel (37:5-6), but in the solider's dream the dry bones remain dead and cannot be resurrected.

In a strong prophetic mode, Jim Hendrix's song "1983. . .(A Merman I Should Turn to Be)" imagines a world torn apart by war. In order to save his life and escape the devastation, the subject takes his lover Catherina to escape to the sea, where they will live underwater and presumably survive. The lovers leave unbelieving friends behind, although they pause one last time to have sex on the beach before the sea and its inhabitants welcome them.

The urgency of the portrait painted by Hendrix's imaginative lyrics is also evident in "Peace on Earth" by U2 from *All That You Can't Leave Behind.* They sing about the need for immediate peace and their frustration waiting for it. They end by invoking the help of Jesus: "Jesus can you take the time/To throw a drowning man a line." Obviously, U2 is not shy or reluctant to ask for divine assistance.

Writing about the divine assistance afforded by the good news in the letter to the Ephesians, the Protestant theologian David Ford thinks this work testifies to Jesus as the peace of the Christian community, a community also empowered to realize this peace. He states: "Yet the politics of faith and hope in this peace is one that not only patiently modifies the way society works but also generates institutions which can risk trusting that that reality is the truth before God."[3] This is a point that none of the rock composers appears to consider.

Socio-Economic Issues

Sometimes war is one issue in conjunction with such problems as disease and famine in songs like "10,000 Years (Peace Now)" from

Mental Jewelry by Live. Cultural, religious, and political leaders have had their say with no positive result because they have failed to realize that we need peace now. Despite separation and selfishness, the lyrics conclude the world is not simply one concerned person's problem, but a problem for everyone. Mariah Carey expresses a similar spirit in "There's Got to Be a Way" as she laments racism, homelessness, and other social evils, such as war, destitution, sorrow and hunger. The lyrics presuppose that the world is fragmented, and she wonders if there is not a way to bring the world together to alleviate pain. We should help isolated, homeless people because there is enough to share. Acceptance and love will help alleviate the problems of racism and other social ills.

Socio-economic problems get attention from John Mellencamp in "Rain and the Scarecrow" which tells the story of a man who loses his farm due to a bank foreclosure on the property. With the scarecrow on a wooden cross, Mellencamp creates a cruciform image that is religiously suggestive. While sitting on the front porch holding a Bible, his grandmother asks to be taken to heaven. "Down and Out in Paradise" consists of three letters written to the President of the United States. The first letter is from a suburban man who lost his job when his company moved, and he wonders how he is going to feed his kids. The second letter is from a former dancer from Las Vegas whose husband has left her with their children. The final letter is from a young boy with family problems and worries about a nuclear war. All three people wonder how this could happen in an earthly paradise like the United States.

Other social issues such as hunger attract the attention of some artists. For instance, Jackson Browne protests hunger in "Looking East." "Tell Me Why" by Genesis from *We Can't Dance* paints a portrait of grieving mothers, children dying of hunger, homeless, and starving people. The subject wonders if God is watching this grim situation. Within the context of this suffering, he also wonders if God can provide some hope. But there does not appear to be anyone—divine or human—listening.

Socio-economic issues are important to Bruce Springsteen in "The Ghost of Tom Joad," a song about jobless people living on the streets. This is the new world order: poor people living under a bridge, living in temporary housing shelters, families living in their cars or a cardboard box, sleeping on a rock, and bathing at the city waterworks. The singer is sitting by the light of a campfire waiting for the ghost of Tom Joad, a character in John Steinbeck's *Grapes of Wrath*. A preacher sits smoking a cigarette waiting "for when the last shall be first and the first shall be last." Finally, the ghost of Tom Joad appears saying he is present wherever people are being abused by the police, wherever there is hunger, wherever there is strife and hatred, wherever someone is trying to get on their feet or trying to find a decent job, or wherever someone is trying to gain freedom.

The theologian David Ford calls attention to the fact that Jesus was not only immersed in the religion of his time, but he was also engaged in the economics and politics of his historical period. If we want to learn something from Jesus at the present time, Ford writes "The challenge to those who want to learn from him today is to be involved in our situations with comparable perception and sharpness, in ways that testify to the abundant generosity of God, our acceptance of it, and our imitation of it."[4] In this way, the spirit of Jesus can stand with the ghost of Tom Joad.

The issue of abortion concerns Madonna in "Papa Don't Preach" from *True Blue*, a song that received considerable criticism from pro-abortion feminists. The lyrics tell the story of a pregnant teenage girl who anticipates her father will be upset about the news, but she wants to remind him that she is not a little girl anymore. Based on the ethical lessons taught to her by her father and church, she decides to keep her baby, rejecting the options of abortion or adoption. Meanwhile, her friends tell her to give up the baby because of her youth, but she is afraid to ask her father for advice. However, she thinks that her father would see things differently if he could see how much in love she is with her boyfriend. The irony in these lyrics is in the tension between Madonna's normally critical stance regarding her Catholic nurturing and her very Catholic decision not to abort her illegitimate child. Another anti-abortion song is "Peace Frog" by the Doors, based on a poem by Jim Morrison, "Abortion Stories." The "blood in the streets" is a metaphor for the death of unborn fetuses around the world, reflecting the social turmoil that the abortion controversy causes in society and how it deeply affects women.

A clever way to get your point across about the injustice of the death penalty is to use metaphors like Paul Simon in "Pigs, Sheep and Wolves" from *You're the One*. The wolves live on the hill and never do any harm, whereas the pigs are barnyard thugs and the sheep are followers. After a sheep wanders from the flock and is discovered dead, the police arrest a wolf. The court-appointed lawyer is income-petent, which results in the wolf being convicted and sentenced to death. When the time for the execution arrives the governor is running for re-election and decides that it would be politically unwise for him to be lenient with the convicted murderer. While the media runs around asking everyone for their opinion and other countries protest the impending execution, the pig admits to committing the perfect crime. The listener is invited by the songwriter to draw his/her own inference about the justice of the death penalty.

Sinead O'Connor protests a different kind of injustice in "Famine" on *Universal Mother*, as she criticizes British policy in Ireland. While the Irish are allowed to eat potatoes, the armed British army takes meat, fish, and vegetables back to England, leaving the Irish to starve and without money to educate their children about Irish history. This scenario leads to a loss of Irish identity and a loss of hope, leading to alcoholism, drug addiction, and child abuse. Recalling a time when the Irish worshipped God as a mother figure, O'Connor offers a solution that includes recalling lost history, grieving, forgiving, knowing, and understanding.

These socio-economic issues relate to social and political justice in the final analysis. The issue of justice forms the background of the lyrics of many of these songs. But the rock composers do not link love and justice in an unambiguous way. For Reinhold Niebuhr, justice does not have an autonomous basis of its own and is not definable by itself. Justice is best comprehended as a relational term with *agape* (sacrificial love), which is to be distinguished from justice, although they should not be sharply separated. In fact, justice needs love to be itself, love without justice is no longer love.[5] Niebuhr conceives of their relationship as a dialectical tension. It is possible to witness this relationship within the world by grasping justice as love in the world. What Niebuhr means is that in the complex of human and worldly relations, justice is the manifestation of agape: "Love is both the fulfillment and negation of all achievements of justice in history."[6] In this manner justice can only be an approximation of love in the sense of a relative social embodiment of love.

In contrast to the more idealistic notions of the rock composers, Niebuhr warns us from his realist position of the following:

> There is no justice, even in a sinful world, which can be regarded as finally normative. The higher possibilities of love, which is at once the fulfillment and the negation of justice, always hover over every system of justice.[7]

What Niebuhr means is that love negates justice by transcending it, implying that justice is not its own norm because it stands under the judgment of love. Since justice is historical, it must be concerned and discriminate in conflicts to achieve a balance among interests and claims. Although love transcends justice, it is able to meet justice in freedom and fulfill it. The primary reason for this is that justice is redemptive, whereas love grants justice that is lacking in this sinful, contingent world. These types of distinctions are completely absent in the lyrics mentioned thus far, and might be too much to expect from a product of popular culture.

Nonetheless, the community attempts to practice justice and love in its rules and laws, according to Niebuhr's position. These principles of justice have a positive and a negative relation to love: "The positive relation of principles of justice to the ideal of brotherhood makes an indeterminate approximation of love in the realm of justice possible."[8] In a positive sense, the laws are instruments of brotherhood by extending the feeling of obligation towards another. However, any historic conception of justice will embody some aspects that contradict the law of love.[9] Because the principles of justice are the product of social evolution and process, the laws and rules of a community are always contingent upon the stability of that society at any particular time. If the society is in decay, newer and more comprehensive laws will challenge the old laws. Niebuhr wants to call our attention to the fact that principles of justice will always be limited by the historical situation and the taint of self-interest.

In contrast to Niebuhr, Sinead O'Connor's song sees only injustice and her call for a kind of gnosticism, forgiveness, and return to goddess devotion does not share the relational vision of love and justice advocated by Niebuhr. And in contrast to Mariah Carey's idealistic call for acceptance and love to alleviate social problems, she seems to neglect a place for justice and an acknowledgement of its limitations.

Issues of Violence

"Hand to Mouth" opens with stories about a man who kills people and a prostitute who dies leaving an infant because she could not bear living at a mere subsistence level. In this song from his album *Faith*, George Michael says the nation tends to forget about those in need. He talks about believing in the gods of America and the land of the free. But no one warned him that the gods do not believe in anything, and they have no concern for the individual. Michael's lyrics are a wonderful example of America's "civil religion," a term coined by Robert N. Bellah in an essay in *Daedalus* in 1967. Bellah defines it this way: "This public religious dimension is expressed in a set of beliefs, symbols, and rituals that I am calling the American civil religion."[10] The gods of this civil religion are historical figures like George Washington, Thomas Jefferson, and Abraham Lincoln. A person can visit their shrines and temples in Washington, D. C. There is an Egyptian obelisk dedicated to Washington, and there are two temples, one Greek, one Roman, housing large statues of the other two deities of the American civil religion, Jefferson and Lincoln. Michael's lyrics testify that he has lost faith in the ability of these deified men to help the needy.

With the proliferation of guns and violence in American society, it is no surprise that some rock composers would address these issues. For example, the rock group INXS protests the proliferation of guns in "Guns in the Sky" from *Kick*, released in 1987. They imagine that it would be nice to stop the world in order to let off all the fools enamored of guns. From a different perspective, Stevie Wonder in "Each

Other's Throat" from *Jungle Fever* protests family violence by saying the ideal of treating each other as kin does not reflect the reality of contentious interpersonal relations. Wonder laments fatalities caused by family violence.

Among feminist theologians, Mary Daly is a consistent critic of violence, especially violence against women. In *Gyn/Ecology*, she looks at what she calls the misogynistic roots of androcentric aggression. This type of violence originates on a merely biological level, but it also involves the symbolic world of thought, language, and behavior.[11] Daly grants that violence is a pervasive feature of human existence, but she urges everyone to work to eradicate it. Daly's work also reminds us of the violent and hateful messages of rap composers and hip-hop's roots in a violent, urban environment. In contrast to rap and heavy metal performers, Daly appears to view herself as a spokeswoman for a radical movement to make women more aware of their situation and to expose the violence committed against them.

If most imagined revolutions entail violence to a lesser or greater degree, it might not be what we bargained for. This sentiment is expressed by Talking-Heads in their aptly titled "The Revolution" from *Look Into the Eyeball.* Once the revolution begins to unfold, the band confesses, it's "Not like I expected it would be." Thus unleashing of violence becomes dangerous for everyone, including the revolutionaries.

A much different type of spirit is expressed by the pacifist theologian John Howard Yoder, who uses Jesus as his model. The way of Jesus emphasized by Yoder involves sharing the divine nature, being forgiving as God is forgiving, and loving indiscriminately. The participant must also grasp oneself as being "in Christ" as the fundamental understanding of Christian existence, which means dying with Christ and sharing his resurrected life, loving, giving and subordinating oneself, and serving others. Besides participating in the life of Christ, a disciple must also share in his death, which means suffering with him, being willing to give one's life as Jesus did, embodying a suffering servanthood, accepting suffering without complaint, suffering hostility, and essentially suffering to the point of death if necessary. From Yoder's perspective, death represents victory and freedom from the bondage to sin.[12] What Yoder is suggesting is that our actions should conform to the actions of Jesus, who must be our model of behavior.

It is not simply a matter of renouncing violence, because Jesus, Yoder argues, condemned "the compulsiveness of purpose that leads to the strong to violate the dignity of others."[13] The Christian pacifism that Yoder calls for does not aim to accomplish certain ends similar to war; it aims to find a way to denounce violent means and be free of violence and its destructiveness. Yoder argues his position is based in the character of God and the work of Jesus.[14] Moreover, the Christian pacifism advocated by Yoder involves taking responsibility for one's actions by perhaps refusing to choose sides in a dispute. By one's lack of collaboration, one favors the victims being oppressed. It is difficult to find such a strong pacifism being advocated by rock composers, although many of them claim to abhor violence in its many forms.

The French religious thinker Jacques Ellul responds to pacifists such as Yoder by saying they are unrealistic. He provides a different type of approach to violence. Ellul summarizes his position by stating "Christian realism demands that a man understand exactly what he is doing, why he is doing it, and what the results of his doing it will be."[15] Ellul views violence as necessary in the sense that one finds it spatially and temporally ubiquitous. States are founded and maintain their existence by means of violence. Basically, Ellul agrees with Thomas Hobbes, a seventeenth century English political theorist, that violence is the natural condition of society. Moreover, Ellul thinks that it is unjustified to make a distinction between violence and force.

Ellul identifies five laws of violence. Continuity is the first law: Once violence is started it is very difficult to stop it because it is an easy and practical method. The second law is reciprocity, and he cites the Gospel of Matthew (26:52) about taking up the sword and perishing by it. The third law is sameness, because a person cannot distinguish between what is just and unjust violence due to the fact that all violence is identical. That violence gives rise to more violence is the fourth law, and the fifth law is that whosoever uses violence attempts to justify it and oneself.[16] Ellul wants to counter violence with the violence of love, which is a demand that the other be allowed to live. Although he is using provocative language, what Ellul is referring to is a spiritual love that does not seek personal advantage, possession, or domination. For spiritual violence to be viable, three conditions are necessary: (1) rejection of victory, (2) exclusion of physical or psychological violence, and (3) being grounded in faith in the Christian promises.[17] Ellul's spiritual violence should not be confused with moving in the direction of Yoder's pacifism. As we witnessed in chapter 4, there are some rock composers seeking a higher form of love that is similar to Ellul's spiritual love, although the prevalent type of love is that seeking possession and domination.

Issues of Racism and Ecology

The composers of rock lyrics have not hesitated to address the issue of racism. In their song "Black and White," 3 Dog Night make it clear that the world is populated by black and white people much like the world turns light by day and dark by night, juxtaposing the daily cycle of the world with radical distinctions. For 3 Dog Night, radical harmony is a beautiful sight, just as it is for Paul McCartney in "Ebony and Ivory." If black and white can co-exist in harmony on a piano keyboard, there is no reason why humans of different races cannot live together, since people are basically the same everywhere.

A less harmonious note is struck by Bob Dylan's "Oxford Town" about racism in the southern town of Oxford, Mississippi, a grim, unhappy place where the sun does not metaphorically shine. Dylan makes clear that the response there to dark skin is violence, discrimination, and even death. Dylan's song "The Death of Emmett Till" protests the killing of a black man from Chicago by whites in Mississippi. The lyrics emphasizes the cruelty of the crime by comparing the screams of pain in the barn where the black man is being tortured with the sounds of laughter on the street. There is no rationale for the killing except the perverse pleasure of watching a hated black man slowly die. The killing of this innocent man is followed by a hypocritical trial of two confessed white killers by a jury of men who are accomplices to the crime. The unjust nature of the crime and trial is evident as the two confessed killers emerge from the courthouse free men, suggesting that such a crime demonstrates the degradation of the human race. Those who cannot protest such an injustice must be already dead.

Another artist critical of racism is Phil Ochs, who often uses historical events to make his point. In "Days of Decision," Ochs recalls the deaths of three young civil rights workers in the south, challenging everyone to make a decision about whether or not they want to put an end to racism with the time for decision now. Ochs' "Too Many Martyrs," is about the slaying of civil rights leader Medgar Evers. But Evers is not the only martyr to be killed by those wanting to enforce racial segregation. In a final example of Ochs' concern about the evils of racism, he directs his ire at the state of Mississippi and its history of murdering blacks, focusing his criticism at the people of the state, its schools for fostering racial hate, its police for violence, its judges for not dispensing justice, its government for its corruption, its laws for being unfair, and finally its churches with crosses covered with rust. The pastors pander to the racism of their members, while "The fallen face of Jesus is choking in the dust/ Heaven only knows in which God they can trust." Ochs' ardent feelings about the state are evident when he suggests that it find another country to belong to.

The problems associated with racism during the 1940s and 1950s in America concerned the Protestant theologian Reinhold Niebuhr, writing prolifically on a wide range of social issues from his teaching position at Union Theological Seminary in New York City located in close proximity to Harlem. Towards the end of World War II, Niebuhr could see the growing resentment of black soldiers having to fight for freedoms that they did not enjoy at home. Niebuhr put it this way in an essay in 1944: "The reason for the increasing resentment undoubtedly lies in the fact that a much larger number of Negroes have by education and other advances achieved the ability to resent and resist injustice than in the past."[18] Besides the growing resentment among blacks, Niebuhr could see an increase in tension between blacks and white supremacists that he traced to the latter's fear that their privileged position in society would be imperiled. Rightly, Niebuhr could see that this tension would continue to grow as blacks attempt to claim the democratic justice for which they had been fighting in Europe and the Pacific. Moreover, Niebuhr perceives the race issue as a universal human ailment.[19]

Niebuhr traces racism to racial pride that he argues is rooted in idolatry, an attempt by one group to make its race and culture God. In addition, racial bigotry is strongest, as in the case of the white southerner, when a sub-group is widely, ethnically, and culturally divergent from the dominant type. The accusations of inferiority by the dominant group are actually expressions of feelings of insecurity related to their ambiguous social position. Besides its connection to idolatry, racial bigotry represents a form of original sin.[20] This form of original sin can not be eradicated by scientific enlightenment alone, because it does not go deep enough to reach the root of the problem: "Race bigotry, in other words, must be broken by repentance and not merely by enlightenment."[21] The act of repentance must not be limited to individuals, but it must necessarily encompass the entire community.

Niebhur demonstrates confidence that the law possesses considerable power in raising democratic standards of a society, although it is not omnipotent. If a law transgresses the moral or social mores of a social majority, the people will defy, evade, or nullify a law passed by a national majority. Niebhur makes an interesting observation: "The majority of the community must accept a law without enforcement if it is to be enforceable."[22] If we consider the issue of racial equality, we are dealing with something at the apex of the ideal of justice that point towards love as its final norm. However, equal justice is only an approximation of brotherhood under the conditions of sin: "A higher justice always means a more equal justice."[23] According to Niebuhr, equality is always an essential ingredient of justice. As people strive towards justice, they are also able to envision something grander. With these kinds of thoughts, it is possible to see the prophetic role that Niebuhr played during his career with respect to important social issues.

In an especially prophetic song, the group Me Phi Me's "Revival" from the motion picture *Reality Bites* imagines a man sitting in pain, then wading through water trying to find his soul. The lyrics use water, cleansing, and a baptismal to suggest spiritual and cultural rebirth. Towards the end of the song, there is a prophetic vision of an

African revival that no power can stop. The song reflects the influence of a black thinker like Marcus Garvey and his notion of a black rebirth in Africa. But if this is not possible, the rebirth of black identity will occur in Mississippi and other southern states.

Me Phi Me's optimistic vision stands in stark contrast to the observation and concerns of the black scholar Cornel West, who perceives nihilism as a danger to the black community in America that threatens its existence. West explains what he means: "Nihilism is to be understood here not as a philosophical doctrine that there are no national lived experience of coping with a life of horrifying meaninglessness, hopelessness, and (most important) lovelessness."[24] If there is no hope, meaning, or love, people tend to engage in anti-social behavior or self-destructive behavior that can include crime, drugs, or self-inflicted pain.

In addition to protesting racial problems, rock 'n' roll lyrics since the time of the rock musical *Hair* and its tune "Air" have addressed various ecological issues. Marvin Gaye protests sea and air pollution from mercury poisoning and radiation in his song "Mercy Mercy Me (The Ecology)." From another perspective, Dan Fogelberg describes a world out of control and life being like a game of dice in which the odds diminish with each consecutive roll in "Gone Too Far" from *Windows and Walls*. Fogelberg thinks that the earth is a dying star due primarily to over population and pollution. Finally, Billy Joel's "No Man's Land" from *River of Dreams* makes it clear that such a piece of land is governed by the economic law of supply and demand. The lyrics are critical of the lumber business, banks, and other kinds of big businesses. Due to a lack of manufacturing jobs, people are prone to boredom. Joel depicts people as zombies given TV, the top 40, a sports franchise, and major theatrical attractions to keep them occupied. Joel's portrait of life is similar to that described by T. S. Eliot's "The Wasteland."

The issue of ecology attracts the attention of the Protestant feminist theologian Rosemary Radford Ruether, who does not want to indulge herself in romantic musings about the environment or fall into an anthropomorphic animism. She rather thinks that we must assume "responsibility to become the caretaker and cultivator of the welfare of the whole ecological community upon which our own existence depends."[25] Moreover, we must use our native intelligence to create a new kind of ecological thinking that depends on a different kind of rationality, which will integrate the linear left-brain kind of thought with the spatial and relational type of right-brain thought. She thinks that we only have two viable options: "either to learn to use our intelligence to become servants of the survival and cultivation of nature or to lose our own life-support system in an increasingly poisoned earth."[26] Ruether subsequently calls for an "ecofeminist theocosmology."[27]

In a song that takes a critical stance toward hate crimes, war, ecological terrorism, and religious righteousness, the Dave Matthews Band uses the title of "The Last Stop" from their album *Before These Crowded Streets* to very good effect as a metaphor for their criticism. Playing a symphony of death, the band uses the "last stop" to shed light on false assumptions. Hate culminates in tears, war is not a way to peace, and hammering nails into trees is not a good way to save them. The lyrics critically attack a false righteousness of a person who thinks that he/she is a messianic figure. The overall message of the song is that answers to social, political, and ecological problems are not as simple as a matter of black and white.

The B-52s, Bush, and Natalie Merchant give somewhat less ambiguous critical messages. In "Channel 2" from Cosmic Thing, The B-52s sing about a television channel that gives nothing but static, a metaphor for the problems in the world with space junk, ozone holes, air pollution, drugs, environmental pollution, climate change, and war. Despite all these problems, they envision that something positive is about to occur, and see the coming of an Age of Aquarius. Bush's "The Disease of the Dancing Cats" protests mercury pollution specifically and its devastating environmental impact on the land, animals and people. With a somewhat broader vision, Natalie Merchant, in the title song of *Motherland*, sees a wasteland of sprawling concrete that continuously expands. She sees the earth disappearing due to lust and greed. With this bleak vision framing her lyrics, Merchant asks the earth, a mother figure, to cradle her and comfort her. These kinds of sentiments elicit notions of an earth mother goddess as Merchant certainly intends to do. In another song from the same album "This House Is on Fire," Merchant's subject admits she is aware of all the warnings and danger signs, but also admits she doesn't have the gift of prophecy. If we confuse right and wrong for too long, something dreadful will happen, like this tinderbox of a world blowing up in your face. Although she denies having the gift of prophecy, her music seems prophetic.

In a way similar to these rock artists, Rosemary Radford Ruether uses apocalyptic images to make her point more emphatic, referring to the population explosion, environmental damage, growing poverty, and global militarization as the four horsemen of he Apocalypse.[28] But she singles out global militarization as the ultimate polluter of the earth.

Issues of Religion

In a generally positive assessment of a common American religious phenomenon, Neil Diamond looks at the revival meeting in "Brother Love's Traveling Salvation Show." On a warm summer night in a small American town, Brother Love preaches the gospel in a tent, an eagerly anticipated event. Diamond describes how Brother Love holds the audience spellbound and moves them emotionally with his words as everyone sings God's praises. Other composers do not share Diamond's rather benign portrayal of a tent preacher.

Paul Simon's "Duncan" focuses on a false preacher. In a cheap motel room, Duncan tells his story. He was born into the family of a fisherman and left home for New England. A poor young man with little confidence, he meets a young girl who is preaching to a crowd in a parking lot. He tells her that he is lost; she tells him about Pentecost. Later that evening they have a sexual encounter. The young man did not realize before that the coming of the Holy Spirit could be so physiccally enjoyable. Is the female figure a false preacher? Or is she just another lonely person looking for some companionship? Whatever the answer her religiosity seems shallow and hypocritical.

"MMM MMM MMM MMM" from *God Shuffled His Feet* by the Crash Test Dummies is critical of holy rollers. The main subject of the song is a boy who was in an accident and whose hair turned white as a result. His parents instruct him to come home directly after school. When his parents go to church they "shook and lurched all over the church floor." It is something that they had always done, suggesting that their strange actions defy rational comprehension.

Some rock composers are very critical of televangelists. Don Henley, for example, in "Little Tin God" from *The End of Innocence*, makes the critical point that it is not necessary "to pray to a little tin god" even if you fear death and punishment. There is no need to prostrate yourself before a resurrected modern savior. Henley is not referring to a figure such as Jesus here because his focus is televangelists who assume the position of God.

U2 in "If God Will Send His Angels" from *Pop* make a more sweeping condemnation of the commercialization of religion. They ask, Will everything be all right, if God does send his angels? If the angels arrive, what do we do then? It appears more likely that God's phone is off the hook since God doesn't seem to have time for people and their problems. Jesus used to be someone one could depend on, but something disastrous occurred when he was forced into show business. Now, it's difficult to get his attention because he is too busy with his new job of entertaining.

Jethro Tull is critical of organized religion from a different perspective in their song "Wind Up," the story of a boy in Sunday school. The headmaster and other adults "groomed him for success" and taught him the so-called "book of rules." They told him what not to do, and they set limits on him and his imagination. He confesses that an artificial and impersonal God is forced on him each Sunday to such an extent that you have to wind this God up. But God intervenes in his life and instructs him otherwise, and he realizes that his instruction has been false. He returns to the headmaster to tell him that he has been wrong "as you lick the boots of death born out of fear." The headmaster is a good example of someone who has never questioned or examined his own beliefs. Instead, he accepted what he had inherited without genuine spiritual reflection, and blindly led others in the same uncritical way.

Alanis Morissette takes a more specifically anti-Catholic stance in "Forgiven" from her album *Jagged Little Pill.* She sings about Catholic girls confused by the moral instruction that they receive, which results in a life without fun but full of guilt. This implies that later in life they have to play catch up to compensate for the fun they missed earlier. The subject admits to singing in the church choir and confessing her sins, but her brothers never went blind from masturbating, although she may as well have gone blind. She reminisces about people who went to church on Sunday because they needed to cling to something, and having their minds passively made up for them. But she loses her faith along the way: "What I learned I rejected but I believe again." This is a narrative of faith lost and recovered, but she still wants to know if she will be forgiven.

A Catholic context frames a more iconoclastic recording by Frank Zappa's "Father O'Blivion" from *Apostrophe (')*. According to Zappa, Father Vivian O'Blivion is making pancakes and loses track of time. Why? Because a leprechaun masturbated him the previous night, causing father to sing "Lock Around the Crock" "as he stumbled on his cock." He is delighted when his erection "ripped right through his sock." The song ends with Father O'Blivion singing the praises of his pancakes. Zappa is poking fun at a Catholic priest's vow of celibacy and his difficulty controlling his desires. Zappa uses sexual humor to cut through the pretensions of the office of the priest and any claim to moral authority.

Another humorous look at religion appears in Meat Loaf's "Everything Louder Than Everything Else" from *Bat Out of Hell II: Back Into Hell* album. In a direct response to a line in Don McLean's "American Pie," Meat Loaf says "The three men I admire most are Curly, Larry and Moe." Meat Loaf substitutes the Three Stooges for the Trinity of the Father, Son, and the Holy Ghost to make a humorous point about the absence Christianity or other religions. There is no sense worrying about the future because it eventually becomes the past, so one should live for the present without religion.

Sting takes a more serious and critical look at Christianity in "All This Time" from *The Soul Cages*. Two priests arrive at his house to conduct the last rites for a dying man. While they do so, the subject notices the river flowing ceaselessly to the sea. If it were up to him, he would bury the man at sea. The priests recite the Beatitudes (Matt 5: 3-12). The young man thinks he hears the dying man question the usefulness of saving the world. The subject recalls the flowing river, and then remembers how his teacher related the history of the place he lives and how the Romans prayed to their stone gods that never made a sound. Eventually, the stone images and walls crumbled, while the river flowed to the sea. Sting sings, "Men go crazy in congregations," but can be healed individually. These lyrics suggest the flowing river is a stream of consciousness that does not end like an ordinary life, and the silent Roman gods are comparable to the silent Christian God.

Many rock composers are critical of organized religion, a position similar to that of the Jewish thinker Martin Buber. Buber's polemic against religion is directed at the structures of belief and ritual. These kinds of structures make it impossible for a person to have a direct relationship with God. Buber's inclusivistic type of thinking is opposed to freezing faiths into systems because they always subvert relationship, which is always primary and essential for him.

Instead of a critical view of Christianity or any other faith, Sarah McLachlan takes a critical perspective on cults in "Building a Mystery" from *Surfacing*. She sings about a person involved in a syncretistic cult. The subject writes suicide poetry, wears a cross, uses voodoo dolls, searches for ghosts, wears sandals in the midst of winter, and constructs a shrine. The subject may be mixed up, but he is able to build a mystery around his secret god. The lyrics pose a question for all listeners: Why would anyone follow such a cult leader?

Some rock composers raise the larger question: Why would anyone practice religion in the first place? A primary example is John Lennon, who offers critiques of religion in two songs from *Plastic Ono Band*. The first, "Working Class Hero," equates religion with things, like sex and television that do nothing more than keep a person drugged. In "I Found Out," Lennon asserts that God is nothing but a concept that enables humans to measure their pain.

Lennon also criticized Christianity in his private life, for example, by drawing a caricature of a deceased Pope Pius XII begging to enter heaven. Another cartoon depicted an electric guitar nailed to a cross, while another portrayed God looking down at Jesus with the caption "God larfing, thinking 'Oh Christ!'" These kinds of satirical depictions of Christianity are forms of self-exorcism for Lennon.[29] He claims that there is no Jesus, and the Hindu deity Krishna is not much better because he "Just keep you crazy with nothing to do/Keep you occupied with pie in the sky." The lyrics of these two songs are reminiscent of Karl Marx's claim that "religion is the opium of the people." Lennon claims to have verified Marx's assertion.

In contrast to the Marxist position of Lennon, the 10,000 Maniacs depict religion as something obsolete in "Planned Obsolescence" from *Hope Chest*. Their basic lyrical argument is that religion since it is incomparable to science, which represents the standard of truth. If the truth of religion is not equivalent to the truth of science, this necessarily means that aspects of religion like piety, ritual, martyrdom, prophetic vision, mysticism, sacraments, and revelation are all obsolete. These lyrics recall the argument of Sigmund Freud in his *The Future of an Illusion* that religious claims to validity cannot measure up to the truths of rigorous science, which in the final analysis assumes the place of God for Freud. In contrast to the 10,000 Maniacs and Lennon, Jethro Tull provides a different and more positive view of religion in "Wind Up" from *Aqualung* by making the point that God is not a once a week deity, which is something the subject knows directly because God told him so in response to a question.

Some people may take personal offense at criticism of Christianity, and they will be angry with outsiders attacking their faith. The criticism offered by rock composers needs to be kept in a historical context, since such attacks have occurred throughout the course of history. It is only necessary to recall Protestant reformers like Martin Luther and John Calvin. In the nineteenth century Søren Kierkegaard attacks what he calls Christendom, which forgets the essential core of the Christian message and devalues individual existence and Christian faith and life. Kierkegaard views Christendom as tied to Hegelian philosophical speculation, whereas Christianity is absurd because it recognizes that the eternal truth comes into existence and time; it is also paradoxical and requires an inwardness of faith where truth abides.

Concluding Remarks

At the very least, lyrics about issues of war and peace, socio-economic problems, violence, racism, ecology, and criticism of religion demonstrate a social and political conscience among rock performers. In addition to the kinds of lyrics examined in this chapter, this social and political awareness is confirmed by concerts to raise money for the needy: Live Aid, War Child Rock Against Racism, AIDS awareness benefits, Farm Aid, Rock the Vote, and free concerts given to raise money for other social and political causes. There are examples of an occasional prophetic voice calling upon others to become aware of injustices and to act to redress them. Along with this prophetic voice, there is a strong streak of charity towards others less fortunate and an effort to make a contribution to improving the world in which we live. These kinds of actions and sentiments do not imply that rock music simply reflects its times but it meaningfully attempts to shape the times by calling for corrective action. Therefore, it is misleading to posit a simplistic cause and effect type of relation between the historical period and rock music.[30]

The call for justice to address the many socio-political problems mentioned in this chapter suggests, as Paul Tillich asserts, that justice is always immanent within power because they are intrinsic to the power of being. It is the creative power of being that supports concrete justice within the world. Nonetheless, the ontological unity between love, power, and justice remain divided within history, although it is possible for them to be partially reunited in time. Love and justice help to overcome any strife in their relations.

The kinds of socio-political issues raised in this chapter tend to counter-balance charges that rock music is decadent, immoral, sinful, and a threat to civilization. If rock music is the product of the devil, it is a devil with a social conscience, or even a social gospel. Of course, even if critics could acknowledge its social conscience, this does not mean that these same people will be content with the politics of rock composers, who tend to be more liberal and left-wing than the voices their conservative critics. This socio-political voice of rock music is another way in which rock is subversive and challenges listeners to re-examine their convictions, presuppositions, and accepted biases and prejudices.

Endnotes

[1] Jaroslav Pelikan, *Jesus Through the Centuries: His Place in the History of Culture* (New Haven: Yale University Press, 1985), p. 16.
[2] David Chidester, *Authentic Fakes: Religion and American Popular Culture* (Berkeley: University of California Press, 2005), p. vii.
[3] Ford, p. 136.
[4] Ibid., pp. 268-269.
[5] Reinhold Niebuhr, *Moral Man Immoral Society* (New York: Charles Scribner's Sons, 1960), p. 258.
[6] Idem, *Nature and Destiny of Man*, II: 246.
[7] Ibid., I: 285
[8] Ibid., II: 256.
[9] Ibid.
[10] Robert N.Bellah, "Civil Religion in American," in *American Civil Religion*, eds. Russell E. Richey and Donald G. Jones (New York: Harper & Row, Publishers, 1974), p. 24.
[11] Mary Daly, *GynEcology: The Metaethics of Radical Feminism* (London: The Women's Press, 1979), p. 357.
[12] John Howard Yoder, *The Politics of Jesus: Vicit Agnus Noster*, Second Edition (Grand Rapids, MI: William B. Eerdmans Publishing Company, 1972, 1994), pp. 115-127.
[13] Ibid., p. 237.
[14] Ibid., p. 239.
[15] Jacques Ellul, *Violence: Reflections from a Christian Perspective*, trans. Ceclia Gaul Kings (London: Mowbrays, 1969; reprint 1978), p. 82.
[16] Ibid., pp. 94-103.
[17] Ibid., pp. 168-171.
[18] Reinhold Niebuhr, "The Negro Issue in America," *Christianity and Society*, Vol. 9 (1944): 5.
[19] Idem, "The Intractability of Race Prejudice," *Christianity and Crisis*, Vol. 22 (October 29, 1962), p. 186.
[20] Idem, "Christian Faith and the Race Problem," *Christianity and Society*, Vol. 10 (Spring 1945), p.23.
[21] Ibid., p. 23.
[22] Idem, "Fair Employment Practices Act," *Christianity and Society*, Vol. 15 (Summer 1950), p. 3.
[23] Idem, *Nature and Destiny of Man*, II: 254.
[24] Cornell West, *Race Matters* (Boston: Beacon Press, 1993), p. 14.
[25] Rosemary Radford Ruether, *Sexism and God-Talk: Towards a Feminist Theology* (London: SCM Press Ltd., 1983), p. 88.

[26] Ibid., p. 89.

[27] Idem, *Gaia and God: An Ecofeminist Theology of Earth Healing* (London: SCM Press Ltd., 1993), p. 247.

[28] Ibid., p. 111.

[29] Steve Turner, *The Gospel According to the Beatles* (Louisville: Westminster John Knox Press, 2006), p. 91.

[30] John Street, "Rock, Pop and Politics." in *The Cambridge Companion to Pop and Rock*, eds. Simon Frith, Will Straw, and John Street (Cambridge: Cambridge University Press, 2001), p. 246.

Chapter 10
Is Rock Music a Religion?

We have seen that many rock lyrics explore essential issues connected to human existence, such as loneliness, boredom, angst, fear, and despair. In addition we examined evidence in rock lyrics for issues such as evil, sin, temptation, guilt, hopelessness, and impermanence. We have surveyed the problem of the self in relation to others, and to God. Chapter 4 surveyed love in rock lyrics, and chapter 5 discussed supernatural beings and the rock star as a divine figure. Certainly rock composers have been interested in the figure of Jesus, and one rock artist even simulates the Antichrist. Rock composers, however, demonstrate an even greater fascination with time and death. It may have surprised some readers to find eschatological themes identified with rock music in chapter eight, although many would not have been surprised to find prophetic themes in rock lyrics in chapter nine. It was demonstrated throughout these chapters that subjects and issues of concern to rock composers were also evident in the work of religious thinkers and sacred texts.

Throughout this book, I have presupposed that "religion" is a difficult term to define precisely in a way that is totally adequate in a cross-cultural context. Although many scholars have tried to define it, there is no single definition of religion that is universally accepted. Therefore, it seems wise to follow John Hick's notion of family resemblance, which he borrowed from Ludwig Wittgenstein (1889-1951), an Austrian philosopher of language. A major advantage of

Hick's approach is that it avoids seeking the essence of religious phenomena. By family resemblance, Hick claims that elements of religion are like members of a family because they share many resemblances and differences, but there are sufficient commonalities among religions and elements of a particular religion to discern that they share a concern with the real, however a specific religion might define it.[1] What Hick intends to assert is that religions are not connected by strict identity but by a web of interconnected similarities. This allows him to identity four major dimensions of religion: (1) theoretical (beliefs and doctrines); (2) practical (rites and moral codes); (3) social (institutions and roles of followers); (4) experiential (emotions, visions, attitudes).

The plethora of religious themes covered in this book does not necessarily imply that rock music represents a new form of religion per se. At the very least it suggests, however, that rock music shares a number of religious concerns, and is not as obscene, vulgar, lewd, immoral, sinful, and threatening to American culture as critics would claim. In addition to the religious themes covered thus far, rock music exhibits other religious features that give rise to the question this chapter addresses. It is a question posed by David Chidester in an essay in 1996.

In Chidester's essay, he argues that rock 'n' roll is a religion. He specifically argues against the position that rock is a religion without beliefs. Various religious themes addressed in previous chapters clearly support Chidester. In his essay, Chidester alludes to the difficulty of defining the nature of religion. Then he uses the model of the potlatch to refocus the definition of religion: ". . . religion is a repertoire of cultural practices and performances, of human relations and exchanges, in which people conduct symbolic negotiations over material objects and material negotiations over sacred symbols."[2] Another important point that Chidester makes is that religion is present in American popular culture in a rather complex way. This final chapter proposes to begin to unravel some of this complexity by examining certain religious phenomena associated with rock music instead of the ideas covered in previous chapters. This process of unraveling other religious dimensions of rock music will tend to focus on ritual types of actions and on the performative aspects of rock music.

Ritual Activity

Ritual activities involve a wide variety of physical actions, styles, and cognitive sensibilities. Ronald Grimes catalogs many ritual components, enumerating, for instance, action (e.g., movement, dance, performance, mime, music, rhythm, gesture, and play), space (e.g., geography, cosmology, shrines, and sacred places), time (e.g., season, holiday, or repetition), objects (e.g., masks, customs, icons, and art), symbol and metaphor, divine beings (e.g., gods, demons, and ancestors), and language (e.g., sound, song, poetry, story, and myth). Grimes also catalogs types of ritual that can include any of the following: rites of passage; festivals; pilgrimage; purification; exchange; sacrifice; worship; magic; healing; interaction rites; meditation rites; rites of inversion; and ritual drama.[3] I propose to examine types of ritual activity connected to rock music such as action, space, time, objects, and divine beings. The previous chapters have been an exercise in examining language and ideas, so there is no point in revisiting those aspects of ritual components. I also intend to focus on types of ritual such as rites of passage (e.g., initiation), festivals, pilgrimage, and rituals of exchange.

The action associated with rock music takes place, among other locations, at a concert venue, a high school gym, a fraternity party room, an automobile, or the privacy of a person's home. Common elements associated with the action are music, dancing, singing along, or just listening. Whatever the venue, music entertains us and provides a respite from life. It enables us to escape from the routine of everyday existence and refreshes us. Music also gives us an opportunity to express our feelings, to think about the lyrics, to feel the rhythm, and to experience harmony. Sometimes, music helps to recall past personal events and to get in touch with a deeper level of our feelings. These features of music appear in the origins of Christian worship. The Gospel of Mathew (26:30) reports a hymn was sung at Jesus' last meal with his disciples. Leaders urged Christians to sing psalms, hymns, and spiritual songs (Eph 5:18-20; Col 3:16-17). Other religions testify to the importance of music and the place it is performed.

Similar to early Christians, the Irish rock band U2 and solo artist Shakira synthesize music and prayer in their compositions. In Shakira's "How Do You Do?," the lyrics begin with lines borrowed from the "Lord's Prayer" asking for forgiveness. Shakira's lyrics also ask for forgiveness in Hebrew and Arabic, addressing all of the three major monotheistic faiths. A bit less ecumenical than Shakira's composition and more specifically Christian, U2's song "Gloria" is a prayer of petition for God's presence. In contrast to Shakira's use of Hebrew and Arabic, U2 uses Latin phrases "*In te Domine*" ("in you Lord"), a direct reference to Psalm 31 "*In te Domine spervai*" ("In you, O Lord, I take refuge"). The other Latin reference, "*excultate,*" appears in Psalm 33 with the injunction "*Exultate iusti Domino*" ("Exult, you just, in the Lord"). The term "Gloria" stresses the singer's gratitude towards God and his attempt to glorify God through his music. Another part of the lyrics acknowledges his music is a gift from God, and he profusely thanks God for this gift acknowledging he would be nothing without God.

Rock music is sometimes performed within the sacred space of a church or another type of religious edifice. But for the most part, the space associated with rock music is the profane space of the concert hall, outdoor stadium, or gym, performance venues where a person can listen, sing, and dance. Just as worship requires some kind of space, so does rock music. And just as liturgical dance forms an important part of worship in the church from a very early historical period, dance is synonymous with rock music. James F. White makes the connection between music and dance within the context of Christian worship lucidly when he observes "Music is a body art. Our inhibitions may keep us from acknowledging it, but music calls our whole body into motion."[4]

By means of dance, we celebrate with our bodies and give expression to our feelings. It is not unusual to witness people dancing at rock concerts. The music invites a response expressed by dancing, an action associated with the spontaneity of a rock concert. Spontaneity was also part of the apostle Paul's ministry (1 Cor. 14: 26-33). Sometimes, activity at a rock concert develops into an ecstatic kind of worship not unlike that attested by the early Christian community (1 Cor. 12:4-31). In fact, Paul himself excelled at such forms of worship (1 Cor. 14:18).

If rock music is not performed in a sacred space, a place set aside and consecrated, it is also not performed at a sacred time. Even though rock composers demonstrate a keen interest in time as evident in chapter 7, this fascination does not evolve into performing during a sacred time associated with a religious calendar, holiday, or holy days or seasons. Rock concerts do have a tangential connection with the repetitive nature of sacred time because rock bands take to the concert trail periodically, performing the same songs over and over, and that favorite recording can be played over and over as well.

Although rock music is not performed within a sacred space or time, it does manifest sacred objects. Madonna is famous or infamous depending on one's viewpoint, for consistently using Christian sacred objects in her act. In her video of "La Isla Bonita," she prays before a home shrine decorated with sacred Catholic objects and candles ablaze. Collen McDannell observes:

> Madonna used Catholic objects to assert the meanings that she gave them; mocking, rejecting, or modifying the meanings given by the institutional church. For her, the objects were beautiful and sexy ornaments that did not need to be connected to an established religious tradition.[5]

However, it can be added that the sacred objects' connection to an established religious tradition is what makes them significant. It is their pre-established symbolic meaning that motivates believers to become offended when a performer such as Madonna, who often associates them with overt sexual connotations, uses them, and gives them an additional meaning that might stand in total contradiction to their traditional connotation.

A case can be made that the rock star is a sacred object, in the sense that he/she becomes an icon for his/her fans. In fact, faithful fans have deified some rock stars; a good example of this is Eric Clapton's fans during the later part of the 1960s. As Clapton's reputation as a guitarist grew, it reached a point where graffiti in the London Underground stations proclaimed "Clapton is God," and it was not unusual at a live performance for some member of the audience to shout, "Give god a solo!"[6] In order to view the sacred icon, a fan must purchase a ticket to the concert where the rock icon will be on display. This is an ancient kind of religious practice in Hinduism and Catholicism. Within the context of Hinduism, a devotee travels to a temple to receive a view (*darshan*) of the image of the god or goddess enshrined within the confines of the temple. Not only does the devotee see the god or goddess, but the deity also sees the devotee. Something similar occurs at a rock concert where fans get an opportunity to see the rock icon live and hopefully to be seen in turn. Just as a Hindu deity enshrined in an ancient stone temple rules like a king or queen, rock stars often dress like royalty when they make themselves available for viewing by their devotees. It is not unusual for fans to attempt to touch the rock icon and at times attempt to rip off pieces of his/her clothing. These items worn by the icon become sacred objects to be cherished by the fan (a term etymologically associated with fanatic). A different form of iconography is made available to visitors to Graceland who can view Elvis' many gold records on the walls.

Just as Christian worship is characterized by a duality between revelation and response empowered by the Holy Spirit, we have rock performers giving the revelation in the form of their music and the audience responding often with enthusiasm and joy. Nonetheless, church worship is very different than rock music because the ultimate purpose of the former is union with God.[7] But just as some Christian services involve procession, it is also possible to find this type of phenomenon at a rock concert with a figure, such as Bruce Springsteen, leading some of his audience in a riotous parade around a concert venue. And no matter how repetitious rock music tends to be, the audience never seems to get tired of it, and it is this repetitive nature that rock music shares in common with ritual.

Repetition is an integral part of all music because "Music depends on repetition—in some form—to highlight the endlessly different hierarchy of metrical waves."[8] Repetition is not opposed to novelty. In fact, it can promote new features by highlighting "the ever-different metrical network, and insofar as at least one parameter of the music draws attention to its ever-different character."[9] The repetitive nature of music can be tied to a ritual performance like the Christian Eucharist celebration. A repetitive feature both stabilizes and destabilizes it, can cause it to go flat, but does not efface its temporal integrity, provides for improvisation, and is dependent on the interpenetration of the three moments of time.[10] Repetition gives coherence to music, although too much repetition can result in monotony; it provides in a fashion similar to a ritual action, such as the Eucharist, an integration of sameness and difference.

Rock music along with worship music and preaching are forms of communication, even though the rock artist is not speaking with the authority of God, the sacred scriptures, or a church. Moreover, rock concerts do not share with Christian worship any recollection of salvation history, although rock music offers its own kind of secular salvation, in the sense of helping a person find their identity, as evident by lyrics discussed in the second chapter of this work.

There is a similarity between the performance of a rock star on stage and a preacher in a pulpit because it is important for both of them to make eye contact with his/her audience in order to communicate more effectively. The Gospel of Mark (10:21) draws an association between Jesus looking at someone and loving him. This connection between looking and love is evident at rock concerts, even though it usually takes the form of love from audience members towards the performers. It is not usual for a performer to receive an ecstatic or hysterical reaction from fans when he or she looks directly at them or when one makes physical contact with them.

During a concert with the E Street Band at Madison Square Garden in New York City I witnessed, Bruce Springsteen blurred the distinction between rock performer and preacher when he transformed his concert into a revivalist meeting about mid-way through the concert, even though this was done with a considerable amount of levity and humor. In a spirit of play, Springsteen recalled the River Jordan of biblical times when he began to sing "take me to the river" and "wash me in the water." Once he had the audience existentially and rhythmatically in tune with him, he began to preach about wanting to find that river of life, that river of love, that river of faith, that river of hope. He said he wanted to find that place where one can be transformed in a river of sanctification and a river of resurrection. He told his audience, "You have to work at it." Even though everyone gets an opportunity for a second chance, you have to seek it out because you cannot find it by accident. After acknowledging that one needs help, he invited the audience to join him, and he would take them to a rock 'n' roll exorcism, a rock 'n' roll baptism, and a rock 'n' roll barmitzvah.

Springsteen continued by giving his parishioners a view of his version of paradise. There will be a river of cool beer at reasonable prices, "no fucking cell phones" (greeted by thunderous applause and cheers), and pizza for everyone. Then he took the occasion to introduce the members of the E Street Band. He introduced his pianist as "dean of the universe," another member as the "minister of faith," and still another as the "minister of the big beat drums." He called his back-up vocalist Patti Scalpa the "first lady of love," while his saxophone player was the "minister of soul." Springsteen, sweating profusely, concluded this part of the concert by getting the audience to wave their hands above their heads in unison. He shouted, "Let's have a new freedom." As shouts of approval rang throughout Madison

Square Garden, Springsteen began the repetitive chorus of "It's all right." The rhythm of the number and response of the audience connected them to a ritual performance.[11] Soon everyone was singing along to the hypnotic, repetitive chorus of "It's all right" as the revival meeting came to an end, and all present were saved by the power of the music. After watching this energetic and inspiring performance, it is difficult to imagine any genuine revival meeting being as successful. And Springsteen accomplished this without dispensing any sacramental food or beverage.

Authorities attempt to suppress its usage, but drugs of various kinds serve as the unofficial and unsanctioned holy sacrament at rock concerts. The participants take the sacrament of drugs much like Christian worshipers partake of the Eucharist in memory of Jesus establishing the Lord's Supper (Mk 14: 22-25; Mt 26: 26-29). The Christian Eucharist can be understood from a variety of viewpoints. It is a sacrifice, and it represents the presence of Christ, an act of thanksgiving (Acts 2:46), which is a form of commemoration of Jesus, and a communion or fellowship (I Cor 10: 16-17). Taking drugs (a rock version of a eucharistic substance) at a concert lacks the religious symbolism and meaning of the Christian rite, but it does share with it a sense of communion and fellowship when taken with or shared with others. The two ritualistic activities also share in the phenomenon of a physical substance becoming a vehicle for the spiritual. Drug usage and Eucharistic celebration also share an experiential commonality, although taking drugs is closer in spirit to something like the peyote cult among Native Americans.

If rock musical performances lack a sacred time and place, they share certain actions like movement, dance, mime, music, rhythm, gesture, and play with religious forms of ritual. Rock possesses its own kinds of sacred objects that tend to become consecrated by contact with the performers and are revered by faithful fans. And the most revered object is the rock star, who can assume a divine status bestowed by fans. Therefore, the rock star is a divine figure created by the fans, although not necessarily in the precise image of the fans. Of course, any divine status is enhanced by the personal charisma of the artist.

Rites of Passage

In many religious societies around the world, rites of passage mark important moments in the course of a person's life. Although Roman Catholics still observe various rites of passage, the use and recognition of rites of initiation is absent from America life at the present time, which means there is a ritual vacuum in the teenage years for many adolescents. With the exception of confirmation among Catholics and others, one can even argue confirmation is not a true rite of initiation because it does not transform one into a full responsible adult, although it does make you an adult member of the church in a sacramental sense. There is basically no rite of passage in America for making the transition from adolescence to adulthood. Probably, the event in American society that approximates most closely an initiation rite is the high school graduation ceremony. With many students extending their education and entering college for four years or more of study, high school graduation, which is a secular rite, tends to lose its significance. It is my contention that rock musical culture unwittingly fills the ritual void.

Listening to rock music, attending concerts, buying the newest releases, down-loading music on one's computer, learning to play an instrument, or actually participating in a band are activities that are suggestive of ritual activity during the teenage years. Being a teen in America will necessarily expose you to rock music. It is as if you are born into it or have fallen into it. You do not know how you got there, but it is within the midst of rock music that the average teen finds him or herself. This is what it means to discover oneself within the world of rock music. The pervasiveness of rock music in teen culture suggests that rock serves as a rite of passage for teenagers without a formal ceremony marking the occasion. As a member of this group due to your age, you share an immediate bond with other teens, even though not all teens like the same type of rock music. Nonetheless, being part of the rock scene marks your transition into adulthood. Of course, once you graduate from high school or college you always have the option of continuing your listening habits. You may remember certain events from your teenage years when you hear a song many years later, in part because the music has shaped your sensibilities and life. Bruce Springsteen does a terrific job of capturing this idea in "Glory Days" and the Little River Band does also with "Reminiscing." If you define adulthood with your highest level of educational achievement, getting your first job, marriage, or a combination of these personal events, you reach it after listening to countless hours of rock music. So it is the music that assists and marks your transition into adulthood.

A rite of passage marks a transition in a person's life when one is separated from childhood, makes a transition to a more responsible stage of life, and is finally incorporated into society as an adult. To conceive of rock music as a rite of passage for American teens is not as far-fetched as it might appear, since like ritual, rock music is a product of the human imagination. If both ritual and rock music need inventors, they both also need to be continually renewed. Just as ritual is profoundly a product of culture, so is rock music. And both are maintained by tradition and cultivated in a deliberate fashion.[12] Rock music and ritual also structure a way of being in the world that is both ideological and sensual.[13] In addition, rock music and ritual are both guardians of the status quo. Unlike ceremony that tends to conserve and guard what already exists, ritual and rock music are both deeply creative and subversive features of culture. They can both be transformative for the individual. Grimes puts it nicely when he states, "To enact any kind of rite is to perform, but to enact a rite of passage is also to transform."[14]

The informal rite of passage represented by rock music takes place at stadium and concert halls, college campuses, high school gyms, in automobiles, in private homes, on television, and now on the Internet. Television came, for example, into widespread use in America in the 1950s and eventually became wedded to rock music by variety shows and now MTV. The universality of television in American homes is truly remarkable because it unites the entire country electronically. Writing about the 1950s, Martin Marty, a distinguished American religious historian, observes, "For some, television virtually became a substitute religion, and the set served as a familiar altar and icon-bearer."[15] Religious programs have been a presence on television since its inception, never more so than now. A viewer can watch religious programming on one channel and rock videos on another. Therefore, television plays a role in this rite of passage just as downloading music or clicking on a web site for some rock artist does. Rock music fills the void left by a lack of a formal rite of passage for young people in a complex and subtle process, and television and the Internet are a small part of it.

Rituals of Exchange

Among many religious traditions, ritual exchange plays an important role. Hinduism, Buddhism and Native American tribes come readily to mind. The Native Americans of the northwest coast region are famous for their practice of the potlatch, an extravagant type of giving. Of course, the exchange of a life for the redemption of humankind from its sins plays a central role in Christianity. The theologian John Millbank argues that authentic gratuity can characterize a gift if there is a delay of return that is unpredictable and embodies an indeterminate duration, and the counter gift must not be identical to the original gift.[16] The figure of Christ with his delay and non-identical repetition fits the definition of a gift and counter-gift. For our purposes, the ritual of exchange plays a vital role in the rite of passage associated with rock music.

When a teenager buys rock music he/she pays the purchase price. This transaction represents a ritual exchange that is not unlike a sacrificial offering to the rock god (specifically defined as the artist or group, although the recording company gets its share). This exchange is like the ancient sacrificial motif of "I give that I may receive." This is not to claim that there are not other modes of exchange that do not involve the transfer of money. Moreover, the consumption of rock music is not only a public event, since it can also be private and secretive.[17] Once the music is purchased the teenager can sing along with the performers, listen to it, dance to it, or do all three simultaneously. Some teens spend a lot of their money on music, and they will even have part-time jobs to earn money to support their buying habits. The size and extent of one's collection is often a matter of pride and prestige among their envious peers whose collections do not measure up to the object of their envy. It is as if the teen rich in music rises in status in comparison to his/her peers and experiences a richer and more rewarding rite of passage because the ritual has been more excessive.

This entire process is captured by the Kingsmen's song "Louie, Louie." In one of the few intelligible parts of the song, the group sings "Let's give it to 'em, right now!" This magical incantation has drawn the attention of David Marsh, who argues that the song is a paradigm of the sacred gift that is at the center of the potlatch of rock music. Moreover, Marsh interprets this gift incantation as manifesting the religious secret of the gift that is similar to acts of conspicuous destruction among Native Americans of the Pacific Northwest.[18] It is a bit curious to note that the process of the exchange never exhausts the swap because the exchange of money for rock recordings is not simply an economic transaction. The exchange takes the teen to the limit because the purchase is a sacrificial offering that is more aneconomic than it is economic, placing the teenager at the limit where he/she gets an opportunity to be gratuitous and excessive.

Rock and the Ritual Process

If rock music embodies in part a rite of passage when none exists in a formal and organized religious sense and part of this ritual manifests a dynamic ritual of exchange, what we have is a peculiar kind of ritual process, a social drama. What is being enacted is an ambiguous script that always remains in a state of flux until the teenager stumbles into adulthood. There is no tradition on which a teen can depend for knowing exactly what to do, say, or think. However, there is a peer group that helps to shape the individual teen. The teenager just flows with the process, reacts to it, and interacts with others experiencing the process. This suggests that teens and others in the music business are constantly creating popular musical culture, molding new attitudes, tastes, and perceptions. The actors in this ritual process are active creators of popular culture. Moreover, they establish whatever continuity they can within the flux of change. Teenagers are not passive inheritors of a popular cultural system that they have been simply preprogrammed to passively accept and not challenge. When writing about performance in ritual, the scholar of ritual behavior Catherine Bell observes, "From this perspective, change is a dynamic process integral to how persons live and reproduce to how persons live and reproduce culture and not the disruption of some intrinsically static sate of affairs."[19]

This process and drama is sometimes captured by the theme of journey or searching. The metaphor of journey is evident in such songs as "Take It Easy" by the Eagles, "Born to be Wild" by Steppenwolf popularized by the 1969 cult movie Easy Rider, "Trucking" by the Grateful Dead, "Keep on Trucking" by Eddie Kendricks, "Like a Rolling Stone" by Bob Dylan, "Born to Run" by Bruce Springsteen, "Midnight Rambler" by the Rolling Stones, "Rambling Man" by the Allman Brothers Band, and "Running on Empty" by Jackson Browne with its vision of running into the sun and yet paradoxically running behind.

The subject of "The Wanderer Starring Johnny Cash" by U2 from *Zooropa* sees signs as he is searching. The subject sees a city without a soul, and encounters citizens sitting outside of a church who tell him that they want the kingdom of God without God in it. He continues to search for sensual experiences and he persists to search for a single good man. The song ends strangely with the subject going for a walk with a Bible and a gun, and he laments that he thought that he was the chosen instrument of God, ending with a suggestion of suicide.

In her album *Ray of Light* and "Sky Fits Heaven," Madonna is traveling down a road, looking for instructive signs to guide her life and inform her decisions. She mentions, for instance, holding onto the light of love and the fit between fate and karma that one should presumably use to one's advantage. These types of songs suggest undertaking a search or pilgrimage to find one's true identity.

From another perspective, this ritual process is a contest. The anthropologist Victor Turner proposes that rock music is engaged in a contest over what it means to be a human being in a modern society. If one considers rock as a rite of passage, a dynamic form of exchange, as a concert carnival, its sacrament of any kind of drugs (including alcoholic beverages of various sorts), and an invitation to lose one's inhibitions in a celebration of life and music, rock represents an anti-social structure. As many teenagers know from attending concerts, and as an event like Woodstock confirmed for many people, Turner is correct that rock music is a vivid cultural expression of what he calls *communitas*, a spontaneously created feeling of community among friends or total strangers that stands as an antithesis to the predominant social organization, and so representing an anti-structure.[20]

During a typical rock concert, there is an overflow of music experienced externally and internally by the audience members that possesses a transforming affect on them. What is created in part is a new and brief community of song that represents a spontaneously created new vocal and social community. The overflowing nature of the music affects a person's body by pulling it into the rhythms of the music and encouraging it to flow with these rhythms. The human body gains energy from the music and bestows energy on the communal experience. Clapping hands, waving hands and arms in communal unison, dancing in place by oneself or with others, a person experiences an existential and communal integration that ideally has a transforming effect on the individual and group. This overflowing of music is what the early rock musical impresario Phil Specter attempted to do by crowding as many musicians as possible into a recording studio to create his famous "wall of sound" with the objective of creating an overflow of musical sound that is both excessive and overwhelming.

This is a vivid example of the excessive nature of rock music, which often leads to laughter, raucous behavior, socially offensive vocal and bodily actions, bad taste, and degradation. This is what Michel Bakhtin calls carnival, based on a suggestion from his scholarly work on the French writer Rabelais, to make sense of the disparities between social order and the repressed pleasures of those subject to a society controlled by the forces in power. To represent the power of those who are subordinate and to insist on their rights to a meaningful cultural voice, Bakhtin uses the related term *carnivalesque* to refer to a realm outside the official social order devoid of rank and social hierarchy.[21] Carnival functions as a liberating mechanism by allowing for creative and playful freedom. Are there any legal restrictions upon carnival? Bakhtin thinks that it is subject to the laws of its own freedom, although there are rules that give it a pattern.[22] But it works by inverting those self-made rules and constructs an inverted world. Within the context of this inverted world, the carnival parodies the socially structured, outside realm. Because carnival is related to flesh and elevation etymologically, it can be understood as the elevation of the body.[23] Therefore, it empowers the body.

When the body—singing and dancing—breaks free from social and cultural constraints a person experiences joy (*jouissance* in French). Joy is a moment of pleasure that occurs at the point where prevailing culture becomes fractured, and a person stands in a liminal situation that by definition is indefinite, ambiguous, and indefinable. From a teen's position on the margin of society, a youth is able to grasp him-or herself as an outsider in contrast to the mass culture of the adult world. The teen can view him-or herself in opposition to the mass culture represented by adult taste, and so also recognize the social subgroup that teens represent on the margins of the prevailing adult culture.[24]

Dance and Ritual

Unlike ballroom dancing in which it is necessary for a woman to be invited to dance, respond to her partner, and follow the lead of the male dancer, rock dances tend to give the female partner more autonomy and represent less of the male dominance and female surrender typical of ballroom dancing. In rock dances women dancers are not led, which embodies a feminine resistance and a subversive kind of dancing in comparison to older forms of dance. Each dancer alone performed the Twist of the 1960s, for example. This freer and more autonomous type of dancing is revelatory in both a personal and social manner because it allows dancers to reveal themselves to themselves, and it reveals much about American society, reflecting such values as individualism, vitality, strength, speed, passion, energy, and repetitiveness.

Dance is a complex phenomenon that can assume the form of art, social interaction, entertainment, worship, and play. Some anthropologists find a connection between dancing, singing, and playing. In fact, among the Samburu tribe of northern Kenya who live as pastoral nomads, they use the term play as a metaphor for dancing and singing.[25] Another anthropologist characterizes communal dancing as a form of play among the Venda of southern Africa.[26] Not only does dance express a vital energy and life force, it can celebrate joy and sorrow. Moreover, it can produce power as well as empower the person dancing, which is evident in various examples of warrior dances among tribal peoples.

Similar to dancing among numerous tribal cultures, dancing to rock music is closely associated with sexual activity, which offends the Puritan streak in many American critics. From the perspective of its critics, dancing to rock music expresses basic animal instincts. As a form of body language and thus action that communicates behavior, dance often conveys covert and more explicit sexual messages between dancing partners, which is certainly true also of certain tribal cultures. John Middleton calls attention to the dances of courtship called *walanga* among younger people of the Lugbara tribe of Uganda.[27] Among other features of their dances, the performances of dances of the Temiar, a tribe located on the Malay peninsula, allows an opportunity for flirtation between young people during either the serious or playful types of dances.[28] In contrast, the Azande beer dance serves to channel the forces of sex into socially more harmless ways.[29] Among the Melpa of the highlands of Papua, New Guinea, the tribe's *mørli* dances are boisterous affairs that manifest high sexual tension, and they are very sexually explicit performances.[30] These various examples of dance behavior from tribal cultures are not merely a way to express a sexual message non-verbally, but it is also a way to deal with underlying social tensions and feelings of aggression towards others. It is possible to notice here a synthesis of body, thought, and feelings being given expression in a non-verbal way for more than just the conveyance of sexual messages. Moreover, dance is a way of arranging and categorizing human experience and intending some purpose that can reveal simple movement, something more aesthetic, a process, or a means of conceptualization.[31]

By its ability to take a person from the ordinary world and put him or her in a more highly sensitive realm, dance manifests the ability to transform that person. This is certainly true within the context of initiation. Among some indigenous cultures, a young person dances his/her initiation, although this is not the sole feature of the rite. Among the Venda of southern Africa, part of the initiation process for young girls of the tribe involves a circle dance called the *domba* that creates an enclosed space that symbolizes a womb. The individual initiate becomes a womb in which a fetus, which is symbolized by the bass drum, is nourished by the vigorous dancing that signifies sexual intercourse while the semen is represented by the ashes of the fire.[32] The female initiation ceremony among the Bemba of Zambia enables each initiate to dance from one status and social role to another in the sense of moving from child to adult, immaturity to maturity, and disorder to order.[33] Something similar occurs with the circumcision dance for adolescent boys among the Samburu of northern Kenya.[34]

A prominent feature incorporated into rites of initiation in many religions is learning the secrets and fundamental knowledge of the initiate's religious culture. This is also true of dance, a form of nonverbal bodily movement, which serves as a way to learn about one's culture. The importance of knowledge and learning in rites of initiation and dance inextricably connects them together in many religious cultures. The close association between dance and initiation within these tribal cultures is also evident in a much less formal way in dancing to rock music among American teenagers. In other words, dancing is an important part of the initiatory scenario of rock music, even though this feature is not explicit. In a real sense, American teenagers listen and dance to rock music as they evolve into their new adult status, which represents a genuine transformation characterized by more formal and explicit rites of passage because, in a way similar to formal rites of initiation, dance enables us to hear and understand the music. By dancing, a performer expresses the music, enters into it, and dances in such a way as to unfold with the music.[35]

In indigenous cultures around the world and a major religion like devotional Hinduism, dance represents a form of communication between humans and deities. The dance scholar Hanna provides a rationale for this: "That dance is enjoyable for participants and spectators make it therefore appropriate as entertainment for the deities and ancestors . . ."[36] In the case of a rock concert, the deities are ironically also performing on stage. Of course, there is great pleasure in belonging to a group of like-minded teenagers who are also enjoying the music.

Whether the music is played by a live band at a concert venue or over loudspeakers at a high school gym, dance patterns, which represent movement of organized energy, have the ability to function as boundary markers.[37] This makes the dance floor the sacred territory of the dancers, which is made sacred by dancing itself and not by any formal act of consecration. This manifests the power of dance and music to not only transform people but to also transform what is profane space into a short-lived sacred space. This is also true with respect to time because rock music and its accompanying dancing possess the power to suspend the flow of time, and it can transform the present moment into a sacred and special time. By arresting ordinary clock time or duration, dance offers "to those with relevant predispositions and in an appropriate mood an opportunity to be in a particular time frame."[38] This is not without a certain aesthetic value because dance possesses the ability to create an illusion.[39]

It is not, however, an illusion that rites of initiation often include violence in the form of such actions as circumcision, scarring, knocking out teeth, and other kinds of violence inflicted upon the human body. In his insightful book on music, the French scholar Jacques Attali argues that music channelizes childhood and represents a substitute for violence.[40] If we add dance to this observation, it is possible to find verification in east Africa among the Swahili with their dance called *beni-ngoma*, a caricature of a military parade, with its idiom of masculine display and competition between rival dance associations that can over-flow into outbreaks of violence.[41] It is not, however, necessary to follow Attali when he claims that music, a form of noise, is violent because it disturbs, disconnects, and kills. By agreeing with him that music is a simulacrum of a sacrifice because it channels noise (violence) and possesses a monopolizing power to destroy by ritual murder, it is not necessary to adhere to the myth of the origin of violence created by René Girard that Attali accepts in his book. It is possible to agree, however, that music and dance (an activity that Attali does not consider) embody violent features. If one compares its violent features with rites of passage in religious cultures, the connection of rock music and dance with rites of initiation becomes even more evident.

The violence associated with dance helps to make it frequently marginal and anomalous. Its energy and violence can be contrasted with ordinary life, which transports people out of their structured environment and into a timeless realm. By means of the ecstatic nature of dance, the dancers literally stand outside of normal society and its social interaction.[42] These types of features cause outsiders to be apprehensive about rock music and dance. Of course, these same critical outsiders can rightly point to incidences of violence associated with rock concerts. But what they see is only the violence because they fail to see rock's function as a rite of initiation for American teens.

Cultic Nature of Rock Music

The term "cult" possesses various kinds of negative connotations in America today because of young people being induced to join groups with questionable intentions.[43] However, a cult is a small group of people that follow a leader, who is often a charismatic figure for the followers, because something in them resonates with the leader's message and persona. There is no rock figure who surpasses Elvis Presley as a cult figure, although there have been many pretenders over the decades. His status is so engrained into popular culture that one need only say "Elvis," and another person knows immediately to whom one is referring. This cannot be said about many performers of any artistic genre except the "King of Rock 'n' Roll." In fact, Elvis's persona for some fans reaches messianic dimensions in the sense that his life is historically significant. Similar to the narrative of Jesus in the Synoptic Gospels, John Fogerty relates the story of Elvis in the lyrics of "Big Train (from Memphis)" in which Presley represents a harbinger of cultural transformation.

The foundations for the Elvis cult were constructed during his life-time, although the cult has blossomed after his premature death from drugs. After his death, it was not unusual to be standing in a check-out line of a grocery-store and see the headlines of tabloid newspapers announcing Elvis' latest appearance. These appearances are akin to divine epiphanies. In fact, Elvis is an even more ubiquitous figure today because of his many impersonators. Elvis is everywhere. His well-known love of gospel music and his practice of singing sacred songs for hours before he recorded a secular tune contribute to the religious aura of these appearances for the faithful. The depth of the feelings that fans have for their "King" is made evident in a profound way by the many handmade shrines one can find on roadsides, porches, and yards throughout the rural southern United States.[44] People in the rural South are convinced that Elvis was one of them, a kinsman who beat the odds against folks from humble origins becoming successful and beating a cultural and social system stacked against them.

These types of people and other fans make pilgrimages to Elvis' birthplace in Tupelo, Mississippi on US Route 78 and to his mansion Graceland in Memphis, Tennessee. These two locations function in different ways: the former is associated with his humble origins much like the narrative of the historical Jesus, and Graceland is intertwined with his success, his love for his mother, and his tragic death. The sites of his birth and death enable fans to sanctify Elvis' memory and to perpetuate it. These sites also allow pilgrims to participate in a spiritual experience. Much like the significance of Rome and Jerusalem for Christians and Jews, Benares for Hindus, and Mecca for Muslims, these sites are places of sacred pilgrimage for Elvis' fans.

Paul Simon's song "Graceland" confirms that it is a holy place that possesses spiritual power because it offers comfort and reconciliation to everyone regardless of one's socio-economic status. Traveling with a child from his first marriage and feeling like a pilgrim on a journey to a sacred place, Simon cannot explain his rationale for going to Presley's home in Memphis, Tennessee, but he expects to be welcomed. Due to his distress over the breakup of his marriage, the subject appears to be looking for something that will comfort or cure him of his malaise. The lyrics suggest Graceland is a sacred place that possesses the power to cure you of your ills, much like Lourdes in France and its association with the healing power of the Virgin Mary. Of course, the places associated with the birth and death of Elvis re-inforces the religious aura of his public persona.

The deification of the man began during his lifetime as he assumed superhuman and mythic proportions. This can be illustrated by the following anecdote when Elvis performed in Las Vegas:

> As a tribute to the moon landing of 1969, when Elvis appeared the band blared out "Also Spake Zarathustra," the theme song of the movie 2001: A Space Odyssey. It made Elvis seem cosmic, otherworldly, like an angel from outer space. An epiphany from the thrones of heaven.[45]

If we return to the mid-1950s, Elvis was the Greek god Dionysius, a virile super-stud who drove women insane with his irresistible sexuality. Elvis was the divine symbol urging others to celebrate their raw, uninhibited, animal sexuality. His pelvic thrusts were an open invitation to let go of one's sexual inhibitions.[46] And his later flashy jumpsuit, akin to liturgical clothing, set him apart just as priestly vestments or ochre colored robes distinguish many religious figures. Elvis' divine status is made stable at Graceland, a place close to heaven, a heaven on earth, or a place representing the Elysian Fields of Greek religion.

The religious aura of Graceland forms an extension of Elvis' physical person. During Tribute Week, there are all-night candlelight vigils held by the faithful on the night before the anniversary of his death in the "Meditation Gardens" where Elvis is buried. In the predawn period on August 16, the pilgrims to Graceland circle his grave with lighted candles only to extinguish the flames with the rising of the sun, a powerful symbol that is associated with light in many religious traditions across the globe. The faithful often leave votive offerings that reflect their faith and devotion to the "King." There is, for instance, a stone wall on the western side of Graceland that the pilgrims cover with spiritual graffiti that reflects their spiritual thoughts, prayers, and fondest wishes.[47]

Elvis' birthplace gives the visitor a different experience that may for some people prove to be more religious because along with the modest home there is a small museum and chapel. The chapel contains a stained glass window of the Crucifixion depicting Christ with extended arms and no facial features. Behind the pulpit, the visitor is given a view of Elvis' house and birthplace through a large window.[48] What is especially interesting is the way the window frames the humble nature of Elvis' origins symbolized by the house, and the faceless figure of the stained glass window invites a visitor to suggestively supply the face of Elvis for the crucified figure. Thus both his birthplace and mansion contribute to Elvis' religious aura.

His religious persona is enhanced by supposed sightings of Elvis, by the multiplicity of his many impersonators, and by personal appearances and communications with the faithful. It is reported that

Julian Campo, an Elvis impersonator, experienced strange voices instructing him to proceed to the Meditation Garden of Graceland and to pray at the grave. It is at this location that Elvis spoke to Campo about the importance of being more humble and encouraged him to continue to impersonate him in a caring and grateful way.[49]

For all the Christian symbolism associated with Elvis, he was a seeker during his own life who dabbled into mysticism and eastern religions while he was on the west coast. He is reported to have been a frequent visitor to an organization called the Lake Shrine of the Self-Realization Fellowship in Pacific Palisades, California.[50] For those faithful making pilgrimages to Graceland, it is his connection to southern Christianity that matters most to them and speaks with greater authenticity to them in part because it is a religiosity that they share in common.

In summary, there are remarkable parallels in the lives of Elvis and Jesus. Besides their humble origins, faithful devotees make pilgrimages to sacred sites connected to their lives. After the death of Jesus and Elvis, perfectly rational people testify to seeing appearances of them. From a cult centered on Jesus that develops into a Jewish sect and finally into a church with a priesthood that spreads the good news, the impersonators of Elvis function to spread the good news of Elvis via his music. After examining ways in which Elvis is depicted in film and books, an author concludes that Elvis functions as an apocalyptic messenger and as what he calls the "Memphis Messiah" and the "Jumpsuit Jesus" in film. He defines the latter as "a drug-addled rock star convinced of his own messianic destiny, an impersonator in a post-colonial setting offering salvation to the lost."[51] Associated with both Jesus and Elvis, there is also a cult of holy relics, which in the case of the latter includes items such as toenails, warts, hair, records, and used paper cups. Both Jesus and Elvis inspired impersonators with Jesus inspiring such figures as Jim Jones of Jonestown infamy and David Koresh of the Waco, Texas tragedy.

A rock music fan possesses other types of options with respect to places of pilgrimage other than Graceland. For some time, rock pilgrims known as "deadheads" have followed the Grateful Dead from one concert venue to another, subsisting on substances equivalent in function to sacred religious substances but assuming the form of drugs and alcohol. Moreover, with the opening of the Rock 'N' Roll Hall of Fame in Cleveland, which is the alleged birth place of rock music because it is where Alan Freed christened the new music with a name, faithful fans can come to see the sacred relics connected to rock gods and goddesses. In this respect, the place is akin to a Buddhist *stūpa* (burial mound) or Christian tomb used to hold sacred relics.

In addition to the cultic behavior surrounding the Grateful Dead and Elvis, what the press labeled Beatlemania exhibits similar characteristics. Beatle fans accepted them as savior figures with the ability to transform lives with their gospel of love. The early Beatle lyrics did not boldly embody religious themes because of their personal agnostic proclivities, but this changed after they began to experiment with drugs, which opened their consciousness and made them more introspective.[52] From a starting point around 1964, their lyrics reflected existential problems and a message of love, peace, social unity, and harmony. The group also experimented with Transcendental Meditation (TM) of Maharishi Mahesh Yogi, founder of the Spiritual Regeneration Movement Foundation, in 1967. Although the encounter ended scandalously with the yogi being accused of making sexual advances toward a young woman, the religious part of the experience is reflected in the Beatles' use of the *mantra* (a repetitive sacred formula) in songs such as "Hey Jude," "Let It Be," and "All Together Now."

If enthusiastic fans thought that the Beatles were saviors preaching a gospel of love, this conviction was confirmed in the animated film, *Yellow Submarine*, which represented a colorful, psychedelic retelling of creation, fall and redemption narratives. In the film, the Blue Meanies, representing the forces of darkness, seek to destroy the paradisal atmosphere of Pepperland, an idyllic place of beauty, music, happiness, and rich colors captured in rainbows, and manifested by birds and flowers. The victory of the forces of darkness is short-lived once the Beatles set off from Liverpool in a yellow submarine after being gathered together by Old Fred. Similar to legendary heroes of the past, the Beatles prove themselves by descending into the underworld to battle monsters. They overcome optical illusions, get caught in a time warp, and are dazzled by a multitude of colors. After successfully passing these initiatory trials, the Beatles are victorious over the Blue Meanies, and they restore harmony to Pepperland and save its inhabitants with their musical gospel of love.

Use of Sacred Symbols

During an interview concerning political and social awareness, Bono, lead singer of U2, stressed spiritual nature of rock music. Not only can rock music change things in the world and the lives of those who play it, sing it, and listen to it, but it also possesses a spiritually transforming ability. Said Bono:

> Rock is really about the transcendent feeling. There's life in the form. I still think that rock music is the only music that can still get you to that eternal place where you want to start a revolution, call your mother, change your job or change your mind.[53]

It addition to its general spiritual nature, rock composers sometimes borrow religious symbolism to make their point. A young man gains power from a chest wound in "The Lazarus Heart" from *Nothing Like the Sun* by Sting. The lyrics of the song suggest a rite of passage where an inflicted wound symbolically suggests death and eventual rebirth. Several religious symbols are combined by Sting in "When Angels Fall" from *The Soul Cages*. The subject imagines angels watching us as we sleep from above the stars. Then he wonders if the dream he is dreaming might be dreaming him. What is real? What is unreal? He imagines angels falling from their elevated positions and becoming mere shadows on the wall. When this occurs a period with no religion begins, and we should remove crosses from our walls and watch the churches fall. The ruins of the churches are visited by "ragged souls" seeking "their lost homes." The lyrics move from imagining the fall of angels to a demand that they be brought down and banished from sight, which represents complete freedom because there are no longer any controlling, divine forces.

Angels also play an important role in "Help Me Angel" by Steve Winwood. The subject appeals to an angel to direct him away from a path of evil to something more positive and brighter. The subject acknowledges he needs the superior angel's knowledge. Moreover, the subject puts his trust in a higher religious power. In "Now I Lay Me Down," another song where light symbolism plays a central role and is intertwined with a sacrificial scenario, by October Project relates a vision of a dream state in which the human body unites with the smoke of the sacrificial fire into a communion of human and sacred.

A different kind of religious symbolism is evident in "Green Children" from *Love Among the Ruins* by 10,000 Maniacs. The song spins a tale about two children born in a cave in Spain, who emerge from the cave colored green and speaking a strange, previously unheard language. The young girl is taught to speak by her new mother, and tells a tale of a dying sun and the children's origins on a distant star. Scientific men try to explain the weird phenomenon in terms of either "parallel worlds or a twist of time" in order to account for the sensation of falling from the sky. The lyrics are indicative of the problems that science encounters when attempting to explain empirically unusual experiences. Although the tale is strange and there is no mention of the mother of Jesus, this tale bears some remarkable similarities to children who have had encounters with the Virgin May in Europe and Mexico.

In addition, rock artists have resorted to religious symbolism in order to respond to their critics. John Mellencamp, for instance, responds to those who criticize the prevalence of sex and violence in rock lyrics in his composition "Serious Business." Mellencamp transforms himself into a Christ figure, a paradigm of the persecuted and innocent person: "Put me on the cross for all to see."

The Answer to the Question

Some scholars have argued rock music gives birth to a religion without beliefs.[54] Ardent critics view it as something sinister, and they would never classify it as a religion. Nonetheless, Chidester sees an ambivalent relationship between rock music and religion.[55] Because the precise nature of religion is hotly debated and ambiguous, it is possible to label rock music a religion in some sense. Frankly, this is all very vague. I want to argue that it is possible to be a bit more precise, although not absolutely certain, because rock is after all a product of popular culture, which makes it necessarily evanescent and ephemeral. Like other products of popular culture, rock music is constantly searching for what is new or different to appeal to the ever-changing attitudes and tastes of its audience.[56] Thus it needs a concomitant changing resource bank from which to draw ever-new resources to satisfy the nearly insatiable appetites of its audience. The constantly changing nature of rock music is part of the reason that it seems to be a religion without ideas. Although the ideas are present, the basic problem is that these ideas are not unified even within a single person or group of artists. We have seen that there are a plethora of religious ideas that parallel similar notions among professional religious thinkers.

Nonetheless, rock music contains more than just religious ideas, even though these ideas are not systematically or adequately developed. Rock lyrics do not offer the high culture of the theologian—not that one should expect it to provide such a sophisticated sort of reflection. Moreover, the rock music scene of teenagers manifests evidence of ritual activity like an initiatory rite of passage, rituals of exchange, engaging in an ever-unfolding ritual process, and possessing a cultic nature, demonstrated by the cult surrounding Elvis and the Grateful Dead and its so-called "Dead-Heads." With this type of scenario, it might be possible to label rock culture a form of folk religion, if we define it as a religious belief and behavior that is not incorporated into an ecclesiastical structure. Folk religion originates with the common people and remains unofficial and unstructured.[57] However, the major problem with this designation for rock music is that folk culture tends to endure, whereas products of popular culture such as rock music are constantly changing. Moreover, rock music also tends to be marginal to culture, whereas folk culture is not necessarily marginal within a society, even though it can stand outside prevailing social and religious structures. Rock stars may be deified, or nearly so, by their fans, but they are a non-elite social group regardless of the large sums of money that they may earn. Has there ever been a rock star that was a renowned scientist, doctor, or thinker? Although rock stars might be unsophisticated thinkers, they are creative and stand outside formal social structures and respond to a variety of needs by many people for whom such structures have proven to be inadequate.[58] If rock music cannot be classified as a form of folk religion within popular religion, can we still call it a religion?

Rock music is not a world religion, such as Christianity, Islam, or Buddhism, but it is still sensible to refer to it as a religion because it possesses a family resemblance to what we normally term religion. As we have witnessed, rock music manifests various types of religious thought and themes, possesses ritual elements associated with initiation, pilgrimage, dance, rituals of exchange and process, cultic nature, and use of sacred symbols. This makes it at least a peculiar type of religion because it shares so many features with many recognized religions, and in this sense bears a family resemblance. Moreover, we have witnessed the ways that rock music adopts religious thought and phenomena to create a sense of community, even if the community has a short lifespan. But what kind of religion is it? Where can it be placed within American culture?

The way that rock music tends to be very public and social for a variety of reasons connects it more accurately with the civil religion of America. It is not, strictly speaking, an integral part of the civil religion, which is a set of beliefs, symbols, and rituals that appeals to a broad spectrum of people, because it lacks the commonality of civil religion, a "structure of ideas and ideals, of aspirations and values, of beliefs and standards [which] synthesizes all that commands itself to the American as the right, the good, and the true in actual life."[59] The critics of rock music testify that from their perspective rock music does not qualify as a substitute for any of the major faiths or as part of the value system of the civil religion. The god of the civil religion tends to be understood as Unitarian, austere, and concerned for law and order.[60] This does not mean that civil religion is antithetical to Christianity or rock music because all three share much in common, and they all agree about a common faith to some extent. But its unsystematic, disorganized, liminal nature, and lack of doctrinal consensus all suggest that rock music is paradoxically a religion of no religion. Its texts demonstrate a strong Judeo-Christian influence that its creators inherited from the prevailing religious culture, but it would be expecting too much to find a unified message because there are too many voices and too many texts for this to happen.

Representing a religion of no religion, rock music functions in part as an expression of liberal democratic values, as was especially evident in chapter 9. Rock music lacks its own authentic theological voice, although it does give us a plurality of voices. These different voices often agree as much as they disagree. As a small part of the civil religion, rock music opens itself to criticism leveled against American civil religion as an "incoherent and alienating" entity.[61] For some religious thinkers, rock music is a travesty of true faith because it cannot offer a whole vision of life. This kind of civil religion relegates religious belief to a zone of personal preferences and matters of private conscience.[62] This is so despite its expression in texts or lyrics.

Civil religion and rock music generally have in common a mutual optimism, pragmatism, emphasis on individualism, egalitarianism, and pluralism. Both tend to disparage high culture in an aesthetic sense, and both tend to stress unity.[63] With these common features and the role that rock music plays in the lives of American teenagers, I would classify it as a sub-species of the American civil religion for its shared features with civil religion and because it influences and shapes a vast multitude of American youth. In a sense, rock music provides an initiatory passage into the national civil religion, which is as important a role as that played by our national school system. Rock music is part of the process of being a teenager in America and part of the process of becoming an adult member of the civil religion.

There is a dialogic process operating between rock music, which represents popular culture, and higher culture, culture with a capital C. The same process is simultaneously taking place between rock music and the civil religion of America. This is "an ongoing historical conversation in which no one has the first or the last word."[64] Everyone enters this conversation as a dialogue that is already under way. In part, this unfolding process implies that we cannot encounter the wholeness of culture, although this does not mean that we cannot find meaning as a skeptical scholar such as Masuzawa would assert. Masuzawa claims, "The culture idea is therefore less a conceptual tool than a bundle of arguments, moral persuasions, in brief, an icon of a certain epistemological position we are persuaded to assume."[65] When Masuzawa questions the need to be historical we can call into question her own Marxist position. What Masuzama misses is the fact that we are thrown into culture, we find ourselves already in culture, or we find ourselves in overlapping and competing cultures. Like Marx and Foucault, Masuzama tends to see hegemonic domination everywhere when in fact it is difficult to determine if the upper-case-c Culture or lower-case-c culture is attempting to suppress, contain, devalue, or dominate the other.[66] The dialogue between rock music and high culture and between rock music as a religious sub-species and the civil religion of America will continue to unfold in the foreseeable future. It will be interesting to see if rock music ever becomes a more established part of the civil religion. Its inherent marginal and excessive features would appear to rule out this possibility. But to the disappointment to its critics, rock music will continue to be a part of the initiatory process of passing from being a teen into becoming an adult in America for many years to come.

Endnotes

[1] John Hick, *An Interpretation of Religion: Human Response to the Transcendent* (New Haven: Yale University Press, 1989), p. 4.

[2] Chidester, "The Church of Baseball," p. 756.

[3] Ronald Grimes, *Beginnings of Ritual Studies* (Lanham, MD: University Press of America, 1982), pp. 1-2

[4] James F. White, *Introduction to Christian Worship*, Third Edition (Nashville: Abingdon Press, 2000), p. 115.

[5] McDannell, p. 63.

[6] Friendlander, pp. 210-11.

[7] White, p. 23.

[8] Begbie, p. 166.

[9] Ibid., pp. 164-165.

[10] Ibid., pp. 165-171.

[11] A number of authors have noted a connection between rhythm and ritual: Jon Michael Spencer, *Protest and Praise: Sacred Music of Black Religion* (Minneapolis: Fortress Press, 1990), p. 141; Angel M. S. Nelson, "Text, Texture, and Context in Theological Perspective," in *Theomusicology*, pp. 70-71; Cornell West, "On Afro-American Popular Music: From Bebop to Rap," in *Prophetic Fragments* (Grand Rapids, MI: Eerdmans, 1988), p. 186.

[12] Ronald L. Grimes, *Deeply Into the Bone: Re-Inventing Rites of Passage* (Berkeley: University of California Press, 2000), p. 344.

[13] Ibid., p. 334.

[14] Ibid., p. 7.

[15] Marty, p. 324.

[16] John Millbank, "Can a Gift be Given? Prolegomena to a Future Trinitarian Metaphysic," *Modern Theology* 11/1 (1995): 129-135.

[17] Will Straw, "Consumption," in *The Cambridge Companion to Pop and Rock*, eds. Simon Frith, Will Straw and John Street (Cambridge: Cambridge University Press, 2001), p. 55.

[18] David Marsh, *Louie, Louie* (New York: Hyperion, 1993), pp. 73-74.

[19] Catherine Bell, "Performance," in *Critical Terms for Religious Studies*, ed. Mark C. Taylor (Chicago: University of Chicago Press, 1998), p. 209.

[20] Victor Turner, *Dramas, Fields, and Metaphors: Symbolic Action in Human Society* (Ithaca, N. Y: Cornell University Press, 1974), p. 262.

[21] Michel Bakhtin, *Rabelais and His World* (Cambridge: Massachusetts Institute of Technology Press, 1968), p. 6.

[22] Ibid., p. 7.

[23] Taylor, *Erring*, p. 167.

[24] Keightley, p. 125.

[25] Paul Spencer, "Dance as Antithesis in the Samburu Discourse," in *Society and the Dance: The Social Anthropology of Process and Performance*, ed. Paul Spencer (Cambridge: Cambridge University Press, 1985), p. 140.

[26] John Blacking, "Movement, Dance, Music, and the Venda Girl's Initiation Cycle," in *Society and Dance: The Social Anthropology of Process and Performance*, ed. Paul Spencer (Cambridge: Cambridge University Press, 1985), p. 69.

[27] John Midddleton, "The Dance Among the Lugbara of Uganda," in *Society and the Dance: The Social Anthropology of Process and Performance* (Cambridge: Cambridge University Press, 1985), pp. 171-172.

[28] Sue Jennings, "Temiar Dance and the Maintenance of Order," in *Society and the Dance: The Social Anthropology of Process and Performance*, ed. Paul Spencer (Cambridge: Cambridge University Press, 1985), p. 49.

[29] E. E. Evans-Pritchard, "The Dance," 1 *Africa* (1928): 446-462.

[30] Andrew Strathern, 'A Line of Boys': Melpa Dance as a Symbol of Maturation," in *Society and Dance: The Social Anthropology of Process and Performance*, ed. Paul Spencer (Cambridge: Cambridge University Press, 1985), p. 124.

[31] Judith Lynne Hanna, *To Dance is Human: A Theory of Nonverbal Communication* (Chicago: University of Chicago Press, 1979), pp. 24-25.

[32] Blacking, p. 75.

[33] Audrey Richards, *Chisungu: A Girl's Initiation Ceremony among the Bemba of Northern Rhodesia* (New York: Grove Press, 1956), p. 125.

[34] Spencer, p.140-141.

[35] Frith, *Performing Rites*, p. 142.

[36] Hanna, p. 109.

[37] Ibid., p. 67.

[38] Ibid., p. 29.

[39] Ibid., p. 39.

[40] Jacques Attali, *Noise: The Political Economy of Music*, trans. Brian Massumi, Theory and History of Literature, Volume 16 (Minneapolis: University of Minnesota Press, 1985; reprint 1999), p. 110.

[41] See Terrence C. Ranger, *Dance and Society in Eastern Africa 1890-1970* (London: Heinemann, 1975).

[42] Turner, *The Ritual Process*, p. 126.

[43] Rupert Till argues for the cultic nature of rock music that he calls "implicit religion," possessing all the features of religion, even though

some aspects can be regarded as belonging within the secular realm in *Pop Cult: Religion and Popular Music* (London: Continuum, 2010).

[44] Gilbert B. Rodman, *Elvis After Elvis: The Posthumous Career of a Living Legend* (London: Routledge, 1996), p. 175.

[45] Karal Ann Marling, *Graceland: Going Home with Elvis* (Cambridge: Harvard University Press, 1996), p. 81.

[46] Rodman, p. 59.

[47] Ibid., p. 17.

[48] Ibid., pp. 121-122.

[49] Marling, p. 205.

[50] Ibid., p. 201.

[51] Gregory L. Reece, *Elvis Religion: The Cult of the King* (London, New York: I. B. Tauris, 2006), p. 88.

[52] Turner, p. 11. I disagree with Turner's shamanistic model for the group because I think that a preaching model is more accurate.

[53] Lisa McLaughin, "Can Rock 'n' Roll Save the World? *Time*, Vol. 158, No. 14 (Fall 2001): 53.

[54] David Shenk and Steve Silberman, *Skeleton Key: A Dictionary for Deadheads* (New York: Doubleday, 1994), p. ix.

[55] Chidester, p. 753.

[56] John Fiske, *Understanding Popular Culture* (Boston: Unwin Hyman, 1989), p. 170.

[57] Don Yoder, "Toward a Definition of Folk Religion," *Western Folklore* 33 (1974): 1-15.

[58] Peter W. Williams, *Popular Religion in America: Symbolic Change and the Modernization Process in Historical Perspective* (Englewood Cliffs, N. J: Prentice-Hall, 1980), p. 228.

[59] Herberg, pp. 74-75.

[60] Bellah, p. 28.

[61] Jeffrey Stout, *Democracy and Tradition* (Princeton: Princeton University Press, 2004), p. 1

[62] Stanley Hauerwas, *In Good Company: The Church as Polis* (Notre Dame: Notre Dame University Press, 1995), p. 199.

[63] These parallels are suggested by Will Herberg, "America's Civil Religion: What It Is and Whence It Comes," in *American Civil Religion*, eds. Russell E. Richey and Donald G. Jones (New York: Harper & Row, Publishers, 1974), p. 79.

[64] George Lipsitz, *Time Passages: Collective Memory and American Popular Culture* (Minneapolis: University of Minnesota Press, 1990), p. 99.

[65] Tomoko Masuzawa, "Culture," in *Critical Terms for Religious Studies*,

ed. Mark C. Taylor (Chicago: University of Chicago Press, 1998), p. 90.

[66] Bruce Lincoln, "Culture," in *Guide to the Study of Religion*, eds. Willi Braun and Russell T. McCutcheon (London: Cassell, 2000), p. 413.

Bibliography

Adorno, Theodor W. "On Popular Music." In *Cultural Theory and Popular Culture: A Reader*. Edited by John Storey. Englewood Cliffs, N.J: Prentice Hall, 1997, pp. 197-208.

Alschuler, Glenn C. *All Shook Up: How Rock 'N' Roll Changed America*. Oxford: Oxford University Press, 2003.

Altizer, Thomas J. J. "America and the Future of Theology." In *Radical Theology and the Death of God*. Edited by Thomas J. J. Altizer and William Hamilton. Indianapolis: The Bobbs-Merrill Company, Inc., 1966, pp. 9-21.

Ariès, Phillippe. *The Hour of Our Death*. Translated by Helen Weaver. New York: Knopf, 1981.

_____. *Western Attitudes Toward Death*. Translated by Patricia M. Ranum. Baltimore: Johns Hopkins University Press, 1974.

Attali, Jacques. *Noise: The Political Economy of Music*. Translated by Brian Massumi. Theory and History of Literature. Volume 16. Minneapolis: University of Minnesota Press, 1985; reprint 1999.

Augustine, *The Confession of St. Augustin*. Translated y J. G. Pilkington. Nicene and Post-Nicene Fathers of the Christian Church Vol.1 Grand Rapids, MI: Eerdman's Publishing, 1956.

_____. *Letters of St. Augustin*. Translated by J. G. Cunningham. Nicene and Post-Nicene Fathers of the Christian Church Vol. 1. Grand Rapids, MI: Eerdman's Publishing, 1956.

Bakhtin, Michel. *Rabelais and His World*. Cambridge: Massachusetts Institute of Technology, 1968.

Barth, Karl. *Church Dogmatics* I/1. Translated by G. T. Thompson. Edinburgh: T & T. Clark, 1949.

______. *Church Dogmatics* II/1. Translated by G. T. Thompson et. al. Edinburgh: T. & T. Clark, 1949.

_____. *Church Dogmatics* IV/1. Translated by G. W. Bromiley. Edinburgh: T. & T. Clark, 1961.

Bartholomew, C. and Mortiz, T. eds. *Christ and Consumerism: Critical Reflections on the Spirit of our Age*. Carlisle: Paternoster Press, 2000.

Baudrillard, Jean. *Forget Foucault*. New York: Semiotext(e), 1987.

_____. *Simulacra and Simulation*. Translated by Sheila Faria Glaser. Ann Arbor: University of Michigan Press, 1994.

Bell, Catherine. "Performance." In *Critical Terms for Religious Studies*. Edited by Mark C. Taylor. Chicago: University of Chicago Press, 1998,

pp. 205-224.
Bellah, Robert N. "Civil Religion in America." In *American Civil Religion*. Edited by Russell E. Richey and Donald G. Jones. New York: Harper & Row Publishers, 1974, pp. 21-44.
Berger, Peter L. *A Rumor of Angels: Modern Society and the Rediscovery of the Supernatural*. Garden City, N. Y: Doubleday & Company, Inc., 1970.
Bernard of Clairvaux. *Selected Works*. Translated by G. R. Evans. New York: Paulist Press, 1987.
Blacking, John. "Movement, Dance, Music, and the Venda Girl's Initiation Cycle." In *Society and Dance: The Social Anthropology of Process and Performance*. Edited by Paul Spencer. Cambridge: Cambridge University Press, 1985, pp. 64-91.
Bonhoeffer, Dietrich. *Letters and Papers from Prison*. Translated by Reginald H. Fuller. New York: Macmillan Company, 1962.
Brown, Raymond E. *The Death of the Messiah*. New York: Doubleday, 1991.
Buber, Martin. *Eclipse of God: Studies in the Relation between Religion and Philosophy*. New York: Harper & Row, Publishers, 1952.
_____. *I-Thou*. Translated by Ronald Gregor Smith. New York: Scribner, 1958.
_____. *Moses: The Revelation and the Covenant*. New York: Harper & Row, Publishers, 1946.
Bynum, Caroline Walker. *Jesus as Mother: Studies in the Spirituality of the High Middle Ages*. Berkeley: University of California Press, 1982
Calvin, John. *Institutes of the Christian Religion*. 2 Volumes. Translated by John Allen. Philadelphia: Fortress Press, 1965.
Campbell, C. *The Romantic Ethic and the Spirit of Modern Consumerism*. Oxford: Blackwell, 1987.
Castanda, Carlos. *The Teachings of Don Juan: A Yaqui Way of Knowledge*. Berkeley: University of California Press, 1972.
Chan, Wing-tsit. Translated *The Way of Lao Tzu (Tao-te ching)*. Indianapolis: The Bobbs-Merrill Company, Inc., 1963.
Chidester, David. *Authentic Fakes: Religion and American Popular Culture*. Berkeley: University of California Press, 2005.
_____. "The Church of Baseball, the Fetish of Coca-Cola, and the Potlatch of Rock 'n' Roll: Theoretical Models for the Study of Religion in American Popular Culture." *Journal of the American Academy of Religion*, Vo. LIX, 4 (1996): 743-765.
Cohen, Sara. "Popular Music, Gender and Sexuality." In *The Cambridge Companion to Pop and Rock*. Edited by Simon Firth, Will Straw, and

John Street. Cambridge: Cambridge University Press, 2001, pp. 226-242.
Collins, Adela Yarbo. "The Book of Revelation." In *The Continuum History of Apocalypticism*. Edited by Bernard J. McGinn, John J. Collins, and Stephen J. Stein. New York, London: Continuum, 2003, pp. 195-217.
Collins, John J. "From Prophecy to Apocalypticism: The Expectation of the End." In *The Continuum History of Apocalypticism*. Edited by Bernard J. McGinn, John J. Collins, and Steven J. Stein. New York, London: Continuum, 2003, pp. 64-88.
Cox, Harvey. *The Feast of Fools: A Theological Essay on Festivity and Fantasy*. Cambridge: Harvard University Press, 1969.
Coyle, Michael and Cohen, Debra Rae. "Blonde on Blonde (1966)" In *The Cambridge Companion to Bob Dylan*. Edited by Kevin J. H. Detmar. Cambridge: Cambridge University Press, 2009, pp. 143-149.
Crossan, John Dominic. *Jesus: A Revolutionary Biography*. New York: Harper Collins Publishers, 1994.
Cummings, Robert. *Symbols of Jesus: A Christology of Symbolic Engagement*. Cambridge: Cambridge University Press, 2001.
Cushing, Frank Hamilton. *Zuñi Breadstuff*. Indian Notes and Monographs. Heye Foundation 8, 1920.
Daly, Mary. *GynEcology: The Metaethics of Radical Feminism*. London: The Women's Press, 1979.
Delumeau, Jean. *History of Paradise: The Garden of Eden in Myth and Tradition*. Translated Matthew O'Connell. New York: Continuum, 1995.
DiMaggio, D. "Cultural Entrepreneurship in Nineteenth-Century Boston: The Creation of an Organizational Base for High Culture in America." In *Cultural Theory and Popular Culture: A Reader*. Edited by J. Storey. Harlow: Prentice-Hall, 1998.
Douglas, Mary. *Purity and Danger: An Analysis of Pollution and Taboo*. New York: Praeger Publishers, 1966.
Downing, Christine. *The Goddess: Mythological Images of the Feminine*. New York: Crossroad, 1981.
Eckhart, Meister. *Meister Eckhart* 2 Volumes. Edited by Franz Pfeiffer and Translated by C. De B. Evans. London: John M. Watkins, 1956.
Eliade, Mircea. *A History of Religious Ideas, Volume 1: From the Stone Age to the Eleusinian Mysteries*. Translated by Willard R. Trask. Chicago: University of Chicago Press, 1978.
_____. *Images and Symbols Studies in Religious Symbolism*. Translated by Philip Mairet. New York Sheed & Ward, 1961.

_____. *Mephistopheles and the Androgyne: Studies in Religious Myth and Symbol*. Translated by J. M. Cohen. New York: Sheed and Ward, 1965.
_____. *The Myth of the Eternal Return*. Translated by Willard R. Trask. New York: Pantheon Books, 1954.
_____. *Myths, Dreams and Mysteries: The Encounter between Contemporary Faiths and Archaic Realities*. Translated by Philip Mairet. New York: Harper & Row, 1967.
_____. *Ordeal by Labyrinth: Conversations with Claude-Henri Rocquet*. Translated by Derek Coltman. Chicago: University of Chicago Press, 1982.
_____. *Patterns in Comparative Religion*. Translated by Rosemary Sheed. Cleveland: World Publishing Company, 1958.
_____. *Yoga: Immortality and Freedom*. Translated by Willard R. Trask. Bollingen Series LVI, Second Edition. Princeton: Princeton University Press, 1969.
Ellul, Jacques. *Violence: Reflections form a Christian Perspective*. Translated by Ceclia Gaul Kings. London: Mowbrays, 1969; reprint 1978.
Emmerson, Richard K. and Herzman, Ronald B. *The Apocalyptic Imagination in Medieval Literature*. Philadelphia: University of Pennsylvania Press, 1992.
Ennis, Philip H. *The Seventh Stream: The Emergence of Rocknroll in American Popular Music*. Hanover, N.H: Wesleyan University Press, 1992.
Evans-Pritchard, E. E. "The Dance." *Africa* 1. 1928, pp. 446-462.
Fetherstone, M. *Consumer Culture and Postmodernism*. London: Sage, 1991.
Feuerbach, Ludwig. *The Essence of Christianity*. Translated by George Eliot. New York: Harper, 1957.
Filoramo, Giovanni. *A History of Gnosticism*. Translated by Anthony Alcock. Oxford: Basil Blackwell, *1990.*
Fisk, John. *Understanding Popular Culture*. London: Unwin Hyman, 1989.
Focault, Michel. *Discipline and Punish: The Birth of the Prison*. Translated by Alan Sheridan. New York: Pantheon Books, 1977.
_____. *The History of Sexuality. Volume I: An Introduction*. Translated by Robert Hurley. New York: Vintage/Random House, 1980.
_____. *Power/Knowledge: Selected Interviews and Other Writings 1972-1977*. Edited by Colin Gordon, Translated by Colin Gordon, Leo Marshall, John Mepham, Kate Soper. New York: Pantheon Books, 1980.
Frend, W. H. C. *The Rise of Christianity*. Philadelphia: Fortress Press, 1984.
Friedlander, Paul. *Rock & Roll: A Social History* 2nd Edition. Boulder, CO:

Westview Press, 2006.
Frith, Simon. *Performing Rites: On the Value of Popular Music*. Cambridge: Harvard University Press, 1996.
Frith, Simon and McRobbie. A. "Rock and Society." In *On Record: Rock, Pop and the Written Word*. Edited by Simon Firth and A. Goodwin. New York: Pantheon, 1990, pp. 371-389.
Giddins, Gary. *Rhythm-A-Ning*. New York: Oxford University Press, 1985.
Grimes, Ronald. *Beginnings of Ritual Studies*. Landham, MD: University Press of America, 1982.
_____. *Deeply Into the Bone: Re-Inventing Rites of Passage*. Berkeley: University of California Press, 2000.
Hall, Stuart. "Notes on Deconstructing the 'Popular.'" In *People's History and Socialist Theory*. Edited by R. Samuel. London: RKP, 1981, pp. 227-240.
Hamilton, William. "The Death of God Theologies Today." In *Radical Theology and the Death of God*. Edited by Thomas J. J. Altizer and William Hamilton. Indianapolis: The Bobbs-Merrill Company, Inc., 1966, pp. 23-50.
Hanna, Judith Lynne. *To Dance is Human: A Theory of Nonverbal Communication*. Chicago: University of Chicago Press, 1979.
Harris, James F. *Philosophy at 331/3 rpm: Themes of Classic Rock Music*. LaSalle, IL: Open Court, 1993.
Hauerwas, Stanley. In *Good Company: The Church as Polis*. Notre Dame: Notre Dame University Press, 1995.
Heidegger, Martin. *Being and Time*. Translated by John Macquarrie and Edward Robinson. New York: Harper & Row, 1962.
Herberg, Will. "America's Civil Religion: What It Is and Whence It Comes." In *American Civil Religion*. Edited by Russell E. Richey and Donald G. Jones. New York: Harper & Row, Publishers, 1974, pp. 76-88.
_____. *Protestant-Catholic-Jew: An Essay in American Religious Sociology*. Garden City, N. Y: Doubleday & Company, Inc., 1955.
Hick, John. *An Interpretation of Religion: Human Response to the Transcendent*. New Haven: Yale University Press, 1989.
Hill, Trent. "The Enemy Within: Censorship in Rock Music in the 1950s." In *Present Tense: Rock & Roll and Culture*. Edited by Anthony De Curtis. Durham: Duke University Press, 1992, pp. 39-71.
Huizinga, Johan. *Homo Ludens: A Study of the Play Element in Culture*. New York: Roy Publishers, 1950.
Hyers, M. Conrad. "The Comic Profanation of the Sacred." In *Holy Laughter: Essays on Religion in the Comic Perspective*. Edited by M. Conrad

Hyers. New York: Seabury Press, 1969, pp. 9-27.

Jameson, Fredric. "Reification and Utopia in Mass Culture." *Social Text*, Vol. 1 (1979): 130-148.

Jaspers, Karl. *The Perennial Scope of Philosophy*. New York: Philosophical Library, 1949.

Jennings, Sue. "Temiar Dance and the Maintenance of Order." In *Society and the Dance: The Social Anthropology of Process and Performance*. Edited by Paul Spencer. Cambridge: Cambridge University Press, 1985, pp. 47-63.

Julian of Norwich. *Showings*. Translated by Edmund Colledge, O.S.A. and James Walsh, S. J. New York: Paulist Press, 1978.

Kee, Howard Clark. *What Can We Know about Jesus?* Cambridge: Cambridge University Press, 1990.

Keene, Donald. "The Portrait of Ikkyu." *Archives of Asian Art*, 20 (1966-67): 55-68.

Kierkegaard, Søren. *Concept of Anxiety*. Princeton: Princeton University Press, 1980.

_____. *Concluding Unscientific Postscript to Philosophical Fragments*. Edited and translated by Howard V. Hong and Edna H. Hong. Princeton: Princeton University Press, 1992.

_____. *Fear and Trembling; Repetition*. Translated by Howard V. Hong and Edna H. Hong. Princeton: Princeton University Press, 1983.

_____. *Philosophical Fragments*. Second Edition. Translated by David Swenson and Howard V. Hong. Princeton: Princeton University Press, 1962.

_____. *Repetition: An Essay in Experimental Psychology*. New York: Harper & Row Publishers, 1964.

_____. *Sickness Unto Death: A Christian Psychological Exposition for Upbuilding and Awakening*. Edited and translated by Howard V. Hong and Edna H. Hong. Princeton: Princeton University Press, 1980.

_____. *Works of Love*. Edited and translated by Howard V. Hong and Edna H. Hong. Princeton: Princeton University Press, 1995.

Kinsley, David. *The Goddesses' Mirror: Visions of the Divine from East and West*. Albany: State University of New York Press, 1989.

_____. *Hindu Goddesses: Visions of the Divine Feminine in the Hindu Religious Tradition*. Berkeley: University of California Press, 1986.

Ladner, Gerhart B. *God, Cosmos, and Humankind: The World of Early Christian Symbolism*. Translated by Thomas Dunlap. Berkeley: University of California Press,1995.

Lang, Bernard. *Sacred Games: A History of Christian Worship*. New Haven: Yale University Press, 1997.

Lange, Charles. *Cochiti*. Carbondale: Southern Illinois University Press, 1968.

Lasch, Christopher. *The Culture of Narcissism: American Life in an Age of Diminishing Expectations*. New York: W. W. Norton Company, Inc., 1978

Le Goff, Jacques. *The Birth of Purgatory*. Translated by Arthur Goldhammer. Chicago: University of Chicago Press, 1974.

Levine, I. *The Opening of the American Mind: Canons, Culture and History*. Boston: Beacon Press, 1996.

Lincoln, Bruce. "Culture." In *Guide to the Study of Religion*. Edited by Willi Braun and Russell McCutcheon. London: Cassell, 2000, pp. 409-422.

Lipsitz, George. *Time Passage: Collective Memory and American Popular Culture*. Minneapolis: University of Minnesota Press, 1990.

Luther, Martin. *Commentary on the Epistle to the Galatians*. Translated by Theodore Graebner. Grand Rapid, MI: Zondervan Publishing House, 1949; reprint 1968.

_____. *Luther Works*. Volume 31. Career of the Reformer: I. Edited by Harold J. Grimm. Philadelphia: Muhlenberg Press, 1957.

Lyden, J. *Film as Religion: Myths, Morals and Rituals*. New York: New York University Press, 2003.

Lynch, Gordon. *Understanding Theology and Popular Culture*. Oxford: Blackwell, 2005.

Lyon, D. *Jesus in Disneyland: Religion in Postmodern Times*. Cambridge: Polity, 2000.

McDannell, Collen. *Material Christianity: Religion and Popular Culture in America*. New Haven: Yale University Press, 1995.

McDannell, Collen and Lang, Bernhard. *Heaven: A History*. New Haven: Yale University Press, 1988.

McGinn, Bernard. *Anti-Christ: Two Thousand Years of the Human Fascination with Evil*. New York: Harper Collins Publishers, 1994.

_____. Ed. *Apocalyptic Spirituality. Classics of Western Spirituality*. New York: Paulist Press, 1979.

McLaughin, Lisa. "Can Rock 'n' Roll Save the World? *Time*. 158/14 (Fall 2001): 53-55.

Marling, Karal Ann. *Graceland: Going Home with Elvis*. Cambridge: Harvard University Press, 1996.

Marsh, David. *Elvis*. New York: Thunder Mouth Press, 1982; reprint 1992.

_____. *Louie, Louie*. New York: Hyperion, 1993.

Martin, Linda and Seagrave, Kerry. *Anti-rock: The Opposition to Rock 'n' Roll*. Hamden, CT: Archon Books, 1988.

Marty, Martin E. *Modern American Religion Volume 3: Under God Indivisible, 1941-1960*. Chicago: University of Chicago Press, 1996.

Masuzawa, Tomoko. "Culture." In Critical Terms for Religious Studies. Edited by Mark C. Taylor. Chicago: University of Chicago Press, 1998, pp. 70-93.

Mechthild of Magdeburg. The Flowing Light of the Godhead. Translated by Frank Tobin. New York: Paulist Press, 1988.

Meier, John P. *A Marginal Jew: Rethinking the Historical Jesus, Volume 1*. New York: Doubleday, 1991.

Middleton, John. "The Dance Among the Lugbara of Uganda." In *Society and the Dance: The Social Anthropology of Process and Performance*. Cambridge: Cambridge University Press, 1985, pp. 165-182.

Millbank, John. "Can a Gift be Given? Prolegomena to a Future Trinitarian Metaphysic." *Modern Theology* 11/1 (1995): 129-135.

Moltman, Jürgen. *The Coming of God*. London: SCM, 1996.

_____. *The Way of Jesus Christ: Christology in Messianic Dimensions*. London: SCM, 1990.

Murphy, Joseph. "Oshun." In *The Book of the Goddess Past and Present: An Introduction to Her Religion*. Edited by Carl Olson. New York: Crossroads Publishing Company, 1983, pp. 190-201.

Neihart, John G. *Black Elk Speaks*. New York: Washington Square Press, 1972.

Nelson, Angel M. S. "Text, Texture, and Context in Theological Perspective." In *Theomusicology*. Edited by Jon Michael Spencer. 8/1 (Spring 1994): 64-77.

Niebuhr, Reinhold. "Christian Faith and the Race Problem." *Christianity and Society*.17/2 (Spring 1945): 21-23.

_____. "Fair Employment Practices Act." *Christianity and Society*. 15/3 (Summer 1950): 3-4.

_____. *Faith and History: A Comparison of Christian and Modern Views of History*. New York: Charles Scribner's Sons, 1949.

_____. "The Intractability of Race Prejudice." *Christianity and Crisis*, 22/18 (October 29, 1962): 181-82.

_____. *Moral Man Immoral Society*. New York: Scribner's Sons, 1960.

_____. *The Nature and Destiny of Man: A Christian Interpretation*, 2 Vols. New York: Scribner's Sons, 1955.

_____. "The Negro Issue in America." *Christianity and Society*, 9/3 (1944): 5-6.

_____. *Pious Secular America*. New York: Scribner's Sons, 1958.

Ochs, Peter. *Pierce, Pragmatism and the Logic of Scripture*. Cambridge University Press, 1998.

Outka, Gene. *Agape: An Ethical Analysis*. New Haven: Yale University Press, 1972.
Pagels, Eliane. *The Origin of Satan*. New York: Random House, 1995.
Parsons, Elsie Clews and Beals, Ralph L. "The Sacred Clowns of the Pueblo and Mayo-Yaqui Indians." *American Anthropologist* 36/4 (1934): 491-514.
Pascal, Blaise. *Pensées*. Translated by H. F. Stewart. New York: Pantheon Books, 1950; 1965.
Pavitt, J. *Brand New*. London: V & A, 2000.
Pelikin, Jaroslav. *Jesus Through the Centuries: His Place in the History of Culture*. New Haven: Yale University Press, 1985.
_____. *Mary Through the Centuries: Her Place in the History of Culture*. New Haven: Yale University Press, 1996.
Pichaske, David. *The Poetry of Rock: The Golden Years*. Peroria, IL: The Ellis Press, 1981.
Ranger, Terrence C. *Dance and Society in Eastern Africa 1890-1970*. London: Heinemann, 1975
Reece, Gregory L. *Elvis Religion: The Cult of the King*. London, New York: I. B. Tauris, 2006.
Reynolds, Simon and Press, Joy. *The Sex Revolt: Gender, Rebellion, and Rock 'N' Roll*. Cambridge: Harvard University Press, 1996.
Richards, Audrey. *Chisungu: A Girl's Initiation Ceremony among the Bemba of Northern Rhodesia*. New York: Grove Press, 1956.
Ricoeur, Paul. *The Symbolism of Evil*. Translated by Emerson Buchanan. New York: Harper & Row, 1967.
Rodman, Gilbert B. *Elvis After Elvis: The Posthumous Career of a Living Legend*. London: Routledge, 1996.
Romanowski, William. "Evangelicals and Popular Music: The Contemporary Christian Music Industry." In *Religion and Popular Culture in America*. Edited by B. Fordes and J. Mahan. Berkeley: University of California Press, 2000, pp. 105-124.
Roof, Wade Clark. "Blood in the Barbecue? Food and Faith in the American South." In *God in the Details: American Religion in Popular Culture*. Edited by E. Mazur and Karen McCarthy. New York: Routledge, 2001, pp. 109-122.
Roszak, Theodore. *The Making of a Counter Culture: Reflections on the Technocratic Society and Its Youthful Opposition*. Berkeley: University of California Press, 1968; reprint 1995.
Ruether, Rosemary Radford. *Gaia and God: An Ecofeminist Theology of Earth Healing*. London: SCM Press, Ltd., 1993.
_____. *Sexism and God Talk: Towards a Feminist Theology*. London: SCM

Press, Ltd., 1983.
Rusconi, Roberto. "Antichrist and Antichrists." In *The Encyclopedia of Apocalypticism, Volume 2 Apocalypticism in Western History and Culture*. Edited by Bernard McGinn. New York: Continuum Publishing Company, 1998, pp. 76-89.
Russell, Jeffrey Burton. *The Devil: Perceptions of Evil from Antiquity to Primitive Christianity*. Ithaca: Cornell University Press, 1977.
_____. *A History of Heaven: The Singing Silence*. Princeton: Princeton University Press, 1997.
_____. *Lucifer: The Devil in the Middle Ages*. Ithaca: Cornell University Press, 1984.
_____. *Methistopheles: The Devil in the Modern World*. Ithaca: Cornell University Press, 1986.
Sanders, E. P. *The Historical Figure of Jesus*. London: Penguin Books, 1993.
Sanford, James H. *Zen-Man Ikkyu. Studies in World Religions*. Chico, CA: Scholars Press, 1981.
Shenk, David and Silberman, Steve. *Skelton Key: A Dictionary for Deadheads*. New York: Doubleday, 1994.
Shulman, David. "Dreaming the Self in South India." In *Dream Cultures: Explorations in the Comparative History of Dreaming*. Edited by David Shulman and Guy G. Stroumsa. Oxford University Press, 1999, pp. 43-73.
Slotkin, J. S. *The Peyote Religion*. Glencoe, IL: The Free Press, 1956.
Spargo, B. Clifton and Ream, Anne K. "Bob Dylan and Religion." In *The Cambridge Companion to Bob Dylan*. Edited by Kevin J. H. Dettmar. Cambridge: Cambridge University Press, 2009, pp. 87-99.
Spencer, Michael. *Protest and Praise: Sacred Music of Black Religion*. Minneapolis: Fortress Press, 1990.
_____. *Sacred Symphony: The Chanted Sermon of the Black Preacher*. New York: Greenwood Press, 1987.
_____. Theological Music: Introduction to Theomusicology. New York: Greenwood Press, 1991.
_____. Theomusicology. Durham, N.C: Duke University Press, 1994.
Spencer, Paul. "Dance as Antithesis in the Samburu Discourse." In *Society and the Dance: The Social Anthropology of Process and Performance*. Edited by Paul Spencer. Cambridge: Cambridge University Press, 1985, pp. 140-164.
Stephen, Alexander. *Hopi Journal*. Edited by Elsie Clews Parsons. Columbia University Contributions to Anthropology 25, Volume 1, 1936.

Stout, Jeffrey. *Democracy and Tradition*. Princeton: Princeton University Press, 2004.
Strathern, Andrew. "'A Line of Boys': Melpa Dance as a Symbol of Maturation." In *Society and Dance: The Social Anthropology of Process and Performance*. Edited by Paul Spencer. Cambridge: Cambridge University Press, 1985, pp. 119-139.
Straw, Will. "Consumption." In *The Cambridge Companion to Pop and Rock*. Edited by Simon Frith, Will Straw, and John Street. Cambridge: Cambridge University Press, 2001, pp. 53-73.
_____. "Dance Music." In *The Cambridge Companion to Pop and Rock*. Edited by Simon Frith, Will Straw, and John Street. Cambridge: Cambridge University Press, 2001, pp. 158-175.
Street, John. "Rock, Pop and Politics." In *The Cambridge Companion to Pop and Rock*. Edited by Simon Frith, Will Straw, and John Street. Cambridge: Cambridge University Press, 2001, pp. 243-255.
Suchocki, Majorie Hewitt. *God Christ Church: A Practical Guide to Process Theology*. Revised Edition. New York: Crossroad Publishing Company, 1989.
Sutcliffe, Steven J. "The Dynamics of Alternative Spiritual: Seekers, Networks, and 'New Age.'" In *The Oxford Handbook of New Religious Movements*. Edited by James R. Lewis. Oxford: Oxford University Press, 2004, pp. 466-498.
Symykywicz, Jeffrey B. *The Gospel According to Bruce Springsteen: Rock and Redemption, from Asbury Park to Magic*. Louisville: Westminster: John Knox Press, 2008.
Taylor Mark C. *About Religion: Economies in Virtual Culture*. Chicago: University of Chicago Press, 1999.
_____. *Hiding*. Chicago: University of Chicago Press, 1997.
Tedlock, Barbara. "The Clown's Way." In *Teachings from the American Earth: Indian Religion and Philosophy*. Edited by Denis Tedlock and Barbara Tedlock. New York: Liveright, 1975, pp. 105-118.
Till, Rupert. *Pop Cult: Religion and Popular Music*. London: Continuum, 2010.
Tillich, Paul. *Courage To Be*. New Haven, CT: Yale University Press, 1952.
_____. *Dynamics of Faith*. New York: Harper & Row, Publishers, 1957.
_____. *Love, Power, and Justice: Ontological Analyses and Ethical Applications*. New York: Oxford University Press, 1960.
_____. *Systematic Theology* Vol. 1. Chicago: University of Chicago Press, 1951.
_____. *Systematic Theology* Volume III. Chicago: University of Chicago

Press, 1963; 1964.
Titiev, Mischa. *The Hopi Indians of Old Oraibi: Change and Continuity*. Ann Arbor: University of Michigan Press, 1972.
Tooker, Elizabeth. *The Iroquois Ceremonial of Midwinter*. Syracuse, N. Y: Syracuse University Press, 1970.
Turner, Steve. *The Gospel According to the Beatles*. Louisville: Westminster John Knox Press, 2006.
Turner, Victor. *Dramas, Fields, and Metaphors: Symbolic Action in Human Society*. Ithaca, N. Y: Cornell University Press, 1974.
_____. *The Ritual Process: Structure and Anti-Structure*. Chicago: Aldine Publishing Company, 1969.
Walsh, Carey Ellen. *Exquisite Desire: Religion, the Erotic, and the Song of Songs*. Minneapolis: Fortress Press, 2000.
Warner, Marina. *Alone of All Her Sex: The Myth and the Cult of the Virgin Mary*. New York: Knopf, 1976.
Weber, Eugen. *Apocalypses: Prophesies, Cults, Millennial Beliefs through the Ages*. Cambridge: Harvard University Press, 1999.
West, Cornell. *Prophetic Fragments*. Grand Rapids, MI: Eerdmans, 1988.
_____. *Race Matters*. Boston: Beacon Press, 1993.
White, James F. *Introduction to Christian Worship*. Third Edition. Nashville: Abingdon Press, 2000.
Williams, Peter W. *Popular Religion in America: Symbolic Change and the Modernization Process in Historical Perspective*. Englewood Cliffs, N. J: Prentice-Hall, 1980.
Williams, Raymond. *Culture and Society 1780-1950*. New York: Columbia University Press, 1983.
_____. "Culture is Ordinary." In *The Raymond Williams Reader*. Edited by J. Higgins. Oxford: Blackwell, 2001, pp. 10-24.
Yoder, Don. "Toward a Definition of Folk Religion." *Western Folklore* 33 (1974): 1-15.
Yoder, John Howard. *The Politics of Jesus: Vicit Agnus Noster*. Second Edition. Grand Rapids, MI: William B. Eerdmans Publishing Company, 1972; 1994.
Zucker, Wolfgang. "The Clown as the Lord of Disorder." *Theology Today*, 24/3 (1967): 306-317.

Index

Carl Olson

Dr. Carl Olson received his Ph.D. from Drew University. He teaches Religious Studies at Allegheny College.